Y0-AFS-637

GUIDE TO FINANCE FOR LAWYERS

By

JOHN D. AYER

2001

LEXIS®-NEXIS® • MARTINDALE-HUBBELL®
MATTHEW BENDER® • MICHIE™ • SHEPARD'S®

QUESTIONS ABOUT THIS PUBLICATION?

For questions about the **Editorial Content** appearing in these volumes or reprint permission, please call:

Gegenschatz, Cristina, J.D. .... 1–800–833–9844 (ext. 2113)
Outside the United States and Canada please call .... (212) 448-2000

For assistance with replacement pages, shipments, billing or other customer service matters, please call:

Customer Services Department at .... (800) 833-9844
Outside the United States and Canada, please call .... (518) 487-3000
Fax number .... (518) 487-3584

For information on other Matthew Bender publications, please call
Your account manager or .... (800) 223-1940
Outside the United States and Canada, please call .... (518) 487-3000

Library of Congress Cataloging-in-Publication Data

Ayer, John D.
Guide to Finance for Lawyers / John D. Ayer.
p. cm.
Includes bibliographical references and index.
ISBN 0–8205–5017–5
1. Corporations—Finance. 2. Finance. I. Title: Finance for lawyers. II. Title.
HG4026 .A97 2001
658.15'024'344—dc21

2001029195

Editorial Offices
2 Park Avenue, New York, NY 10016-5675 (212) 448-2000
201 Mission St., San Francisco, CA 94105-1831 (415) 908-3200
701 East Water Street, Charlottesville, VA 22902-7587 (804) 972-7600
www.lexis.com

(Pub.3139)

Statement on Fair Use

Matthew Bender recognizes the balance that must be achieved between the operation of the fair use doctrine, whose basis is to avoid the rigid application of the copyright statute, and the protection of the creative rights and economic interests of authors, publishers and other copyright holders.

We are also aware of the countervailing forces that exist between the ever greater technological advances for making both print and electronic copies and the reduction in the value of copyrighted works that must result from a consistent and pervasive reliance on these new copying technologies. It is Matthew Bender's position that if the ''progress of science and useful arts'' is promoted by granting copyright protection to authors, such progress may well be impeded if copyright protection is diminished in the name of fair use. (See *Nimmer on Copyright* §13.05[E][1].) This holds true whether the parameters of the fair use doctrine are considered in either the print or the electronic environment as it is the integrity of the copyright that is at issue, not the media under which the protected work may become available. Therefore, the fair use guidelines we propose apply equally to our print and electronic information, and apply, within §§107 and 108 of the Copyright Act, regardless of the professional status of the user.

Our draft guidelines would allow for the copying of limited materials, which would include synopses and tables of contents, primary source and government materials that may have a minimal amount of editorial enhancements, individual forms to aid in the drafting of applications and pleadings, and miscellaneous pages from any of our newsletters, treatises and practice guides. This copying would be permitted provided it is performed for internal use and solely for the purpose of facilitating individual research or for creating documents produced in the course of the user's professional practice, and the original from which the copy is made has been purchased or licensed as part of the user's existing in-house collection.

Matthew Bender fully supports educational awareness programs designed to increase the public's recognition of its fair use rights. We also support the operation of collective licensing organizations with regard to our print and electronic information.

Dedication

For Ginni and Sara Stone
and for Daniel and Zachary Beadle

Preface

I study war
so my children can study politics
so my grandchildren can study music and art.

—John Adams

A legendary review begins: "this book fills a much-needed gap." No, not this book. The gap is there — law students and lawyers do not know enough about finance. But no one needs the gap; rather, someone needs to fill it. We will see whether I have brought it off.

Perhaps the easiest way to explain it is historical. I wrote this book to fill a need I encountered when I began practicing business law. I had come out of law school with a good grounding in business law courses and a fragmentary but passable knowledge of accounting, but almost no knowledge of finance. I quickly learned that I had to understand something about finance in order to talk to business clients — but that I didn't need to know very much (the heavy lifting was, after all, their job and not mine).

Not willing to interrupt my life for another degree, I laid out some money for a basic finance course book of the sort used in a business school. On the premise that the best way to learn something is to teach it, I also prevailed on the dean to let me offer a course on the material in the law school at UCD.

I spent several years trying to figure out what my students needed to know and how to present it. As time passed I produced more and more "supplementary materials." One day my research assistant summoned the courage to tell me that the students pretty well ignored the (expensive) course book and relied on the supplementary materials. So I dropped the course book and started assigning merely these.

After many false starts and blind alleys, I arrived at what you see here. I would like to call it a "tentative edition," but life is always tentative so perhaps the point may go without saying. At any rate, this represents my best guess as to how best to introduce basic finance to an audience of law students. I use something very close to this as the primary course book for my own law school finance course. I have tried versions of portions at in-house seminars for a couple of national law firms. And I have used smaller fragments in programs on continuing legal education for lawyers.

Earlier versions were posted for free access on the UCD Web site. Passing cyberpilgrims told me they were using the material as supplements for law school courses in corporate finance and even (once or twice) in a business school. I believe that the material is well suited for use as a general supplement for a lot of law school courses — e.g., corporations, tax, or any place else where money crowds its way to the fore. I think it is also doable by a determined law student (or lawyer) in a hammock, although I admit I can think of other things to do with one's spare time. I should think it ought to work also as a refresher for someone who knew this stuff once but forgot it.

And even as I write this, I am making plans to present it to practicing lawyers in a continuing legal education course.

The major differences between this book and a fancy business school course book are these: First, this book is much shorter, as I have tried to pare back to essentials. Second, I have tried to focus on the needs of the audience. Some of this focus is perhaps superficial or cosmetic: When a business school book says, "Suppose you were a manager, etc.," I am more likely to say, "Suppose you have a client, etc." But I think I have gone deeper: I have tried to pay attention to things that a lawyer may care about, while business users may not.

For example, I have tried to present this material in the context that you will recognize from basic law courses. I have also tried to address some issues in regulation — usury, or utility rate regulation for example — where the lawyer will find herself on the front line. And I have tried to address the "form over substance" problem that seems to occupy so much of the attention of any lawyer, and in particular of a business lawyer.

Finally (again alert to my audience) I have tried to cut down on the math. A pre-publication evaluator asked: "Can you cut out the math?" Well, no. But I recognize that most law students are not numbers jocks (certainly I am not), and I have done what I can to make it all intelligible to the least of these. To this end, I assume that you had high school algebra, but that you have forgotten it. And I reduce the calculus to a couple of dispensable footnotes.

Up to now, I have always pretty much insisted that my students read the book with a calculator at hand. I wrote it using the TI BA-II Plus, which currently costs about $35 (Hewlett Packard has a close competitor, the HP 10). I make a point of insisting on a business calculator, rather than any old garden-variety calculator, because a business calculator will perform at least one important chore that a non-business calculator will not do. It can extract an "internal rate of return" (IRR). As you will learn later, I'm not crazy about the IRR as an analytical tool, but you have to know how to compute it anyway.

As I write this, I have almost come to believe that the calculator is an anachronism. I suspect that every one of my students has a spreadsheet on his laptop, even if she has never used it before (she will be pleased to learn that it isn't that hard). In writing this book, I have found it convenient to keep my spreadsheet up and running in background, even while the text is running on the main screen. I suspect that the reader may find it convenient to do some of the same.

Please send suggestions, corrections, brickbats, etc., to jdayer@ucdavis.edu.

December 2000

Acknowledgments

This book has required a lot of help. When I first began to teach finance a decade ago, Bernie Black was kind enough to lend me a complete set of his teaching notes, with problem sets and such. Mike Wachter kindly shared his notes as well. I have had more research assistance than I can remember: Craig Dandurand, Scott Payne, Drew Brerton, Dave Achord, Jane Takanouchi and Eric Larsen proved particularly helpful. Dave Morris and Grace Fujita collaborated to make the last push to publication. Holly Doremus, Tom Joo, Ed Rabin, Dan Simmons and Bruce Wolk provided commentary on particular topics. Keith Lundin made helpful comments, having assured me he read the entire manuscript on his Stairmaster. Eric Gustafson read it all, insisting that "data" is a plural, and that proper use of the subjunctive is the mark of an educated man. And I have benefitted from a thousand conversations with Joel Dobris. Francine Lipman expressed enthusiasm when I was still doubtful. Rex Perschbacher, as dean of the UCD Law School, provided financial and moral support. I profited, sometimes ingloriously, from the contributions of students in class at UC-Davis and also at Cardozo and Penn. I also gained from presenting some of this material to in-house law firm seminars at McDermott, Will & Emery and LeBoeuf, Lamb, Greene & MacRae; thanks, for making them possible, to Dave Gould and Ralph Mabey. James D. Cox's course book, *Financial Information, Accounting and the Law* (1980), a neglected classic of modern pedagogy, now sadly out of print, was a source of influence and inspiration. Sara Buck, Ann Graham and Sue Williams provided secretarial support. I had invaluable support at Matthew Bender from Marianne White, Rachel Soszynski, Sophie Sacca and others unknown to me. Finally, a special word of thanks to the Upper Crust Bakery in Chico, California, for providing an atmosphere hospitable to mental labor.

Introduction

The snail
Climbs Mount Fuji
But slowly, slowly.

—Haiku

Points of View

They tell the story about Clarence the tailor who, after a long life with the needle and tape measure, took a vacation in Rome. Back home, his friends asked him, "So, how was the Pope?" "Oh," says Clarence, "about a 42 long."

Everybody has a point of view. Finance is a point of view.

Summary

This book is divided into three parts, in an effort to capture three central ideas. The parts are:

I. Valuation;
II. Diversification; and
III. Leverage and Contingent Claims.

Valuation: Broadly defined, all finance is the study of valuation — the way assets (or liabilities) are valued in a marketplace. So we begin with valuation; and we begin valuation with the notion of *present value*, shorthanded as the notion that a dollar now is worth more than a dollar later. We do some elementary mechanics and a variety of applications. Not the least of our purpose is to identify the unifying deep structure that underlies a variety of deals — corporate bonds, consumer rent-to-own contracts and others. Along the way we offer some asides on "cost-benefit analysis" as a tool of public policy, and we make a few notes on the limits of the market mentality. We end with a bit on the valuation of common stocks.

Then and only then do we do a bit of accounting. We do some accounting because it is important. We leave it now because we want to see accounting in context, so we can see what it does not do as well as what it does. Equipped with the lore of accounting, we go on to consider the valuation of "projects," — a realm where accounting and traditional cash flow valuation may intertwine. We close with a few words on inflation, and the puzzle over interest rates — after all is said and done, why do things work as they do?

Having made ourselves comfortable with the idea of present value, we pause to reflect a bit on where values come from. For many students, this is the most depressing part of the course. Inevitably students will come into this course hoping to get some tips on how to make some money. This is fine; we have no quarrel with the student who wants to take care of herself. But the message here is that there is no easy money to be made — or if there is, this is the last place to look for it. Indeed, we put the point more strongly: we argue that when you stop to think of it, you realize it is amazing that anybody makes any money at all.

Diversification: Building on present value, next we make a new departure. We introduce one of the most revolutionary ideas in modern finance — so-called "modern portfolio theory," (MPT) and its principal component, the idea of diversification. We make the vital but non-intuitive point that you may be able to make your investment portfolio *safer by adding risky investments* — if these investments are suitably uncorrelated. We do the mechanics of diversification, but we also try to show how this novel but important idea worked its way into the culture of the law.

Leverage and Contingent Claims: This final explanation perhaps needs explanation most, because it brings together ideas not always treated in the same place. And the use of the term "leverage" is somewhat unconventional.

To understand what we are after, start with the job of Emma, the entrepreneur trying to finance a new project. She needs to raise money. How does she get it? Crudely, she has three choices. One, she can use *cash on hand* — the money she earned last year. Two, she can *borrow money* — take on debt. And three, she can *sell stock*.

For the time being, ignore "cash on hand," and focus on debt and stock. Note that debt and stock are different, in that holders of debt get paid first and stockholders get paid (if at all) only out of what is left. This means that whenever you have both debt and stock, stock is always more risky than debt. This need not be a problem: more risk means higher return, and the stockholder may be perfectly happy to bear the risk if he gets the better return.

The jargon label for this tradeoff is "leverage," and we explore some of the implications of leverage. But then we move on to a bigger arena. We observe that stock is a king of *contingent claim*, in that is value depends on the value of the underlying asset, and also on the size of the debt. And it turns out that once you start looking for them, contingent claims are everywhere.

People have traded contingent claims since the beginning of time. But it was only yesterday (or to be precise, 1973) that anyone came up with a good *theory* of contingent claims valuation. The theory set off a revolution. The full implications of this revolution are not fully understood yet, not even by the cognoscente. But it is changing the way we think about everything in finance.

The Corporation and the Firm

If you are reading this, chances are you have taken (or are taking) a law school course in business associations (if not, you may want to do some background reading on the corporate form — see the bibliography below). Even if you know something about business associations, it may be useful to pause and reflect on a few principles.

First, it is useful to distinguish between a *corporation* and a *firm*. A firm is a device for deploying resources. You can understand a firm best if you contrast it with another device for deploying resources: the *contract*. Suppose I want to dig an elixir well. There are two ways I might do it. One, I might sign a *contract* with someone who agrees to do the job for me, perhaps in exchange for a share of the proceeds. If I make a contract, I may not know — I may have no right to know — how he goes about his business. I simply collect my proceeds when he is done. Two, I might organize a *firm*, and do the job "directly." In a firm, I retain management and control. I may hire others to do the work for me, but they do it under my supervision. The distinction is not exact, of course. The worker in my "firm" may hold an employment "contract," and my "contract" deal may call for a lot of firm-like supervision. Still, it is a handy distinction. For our purposes, we need to note that a firm *need not be* a corporation. Lots of firms are not corporations: they may be partnerships, or sole proprietorships. But generally, all corporations are firms.

Firms present plenty of problems for the law. Many of these can be characterized as problems of *agency*. An agency problem arises whenever one person (the agent) acts in another person's (the principal's) behalf. In the nature of things, the principal and agent have different interests. The principal wants the agent to work hard and cheap. The agent wants to work less hard, and to be better paid. For example, in a large corporation you can say that the directors and managers are the agents of the stockholders. The stockholders (the principals) want the managers to increase value by working hard. The managers (the agents) want fat salaries and Friday afternoons on the golf course.

Distinct from a firm, a *corporation*, by contrast, is a device for raising money. The first principle of corporations is the idea of *limited liability*. The money at risk in a corporate deal is the money of the corporation only, not the money of its owners. Suppose I buy one share of Microsoft stock for $105. If Microsoft goes broke, I may lose my entire investment. Now suppose Microsoft goes broke owing $1 billion. My loss is still limited to my investment, the $105.

Internal Organization

A lot (but not all) of our discussion will revolve around the affairs of a large or middle-sized company that has managers and shareholders — a *corporation*, in our jargon, that is also a *firm*. It may be useful to pause for a word or two about the internal structure of this corporate firm. For example, we can imagine that our corporate firm has *shareholders* that elect *directors*. These directors appoint *officers* who hire employees and carry out the day-to-day management.

As to officers, there is no required set of titles, but most have a *president* who also functions as *the chief executive officer*, and who serves as linchpin of the corporation. There may also be a *chief administrative officer*, a *board chairperson* active in management, and any number of *vice-presidents*. But for our purposes, there are two particularly important officers that we should focus on: the *treasurer* and the *controller*. Recognizing that there is no completely fixed usage of these terms, we can generalize as follows.

The *controller* has to keep track of things. He has to figure out what came in, what went out, where it came from, and where it went. He is the beancounter's beancounter. We look to a controller for things like financial statements, audits, accounting reviews, payroll records, and tax returns.

The *treasurer* typically has a somewhat different job. She is more directly concerned with *value*. It is the job of the treasurer to *find the money* — that is, to raise the capital for investments as needed. She plays a critical role in *valuing projects* to see if they are worth doing or not. Thus, a treasurer must have a grasp on cash flow, credit arrangements, and the details of such disparate financial vehicles as pensions, insurance, and equity. This puts the treasurer at the top of the corporate money web where she may bear the title of *chief financial officer* (CFO). An awful lot of work in this course can be understood as communicating with and advising the treasurer/CFO.

Note on Who is Rich, Who is Poor

For anyone curious about the place of wealth in society, there are two questions — "How much?" and "Who?"

On the issue of "how much," some of the evidence is visceral. Most readers live in milieu where, over the last decade or so, wealth has been exploding. Real net worth of U.S. households grew by some 50 percent between 1989 and 1999.[1] At the top, the new fortunes of the high-tech zillionaires appeared to outstrip the achievements of the Rockefellers and the Rothschilds. Even below the top, there was a lot to go around. Popular folklore assured us that in 1998-99 Seattle was generating some 60 millionaires every morning. It was said that there were 10,000 millionaires at Microsoft alone.

On the other hand, the distribution of wealth was, to put it mildly, not universal. The best available data suggests that about one percent of households own about one third of the assets in the U.S. economy. The least wealthy four-fifths hold only 20 percent. And if your dream is to represent the really rich, it appears you can. According to a report commissioned by the United Nations Development Program, the assets of 358 billionaires exceed the combined annual incomes of countries accounting for 45 percent of the world's people.[2]

While the general pattern is probably clear enough, getting firm data on equality (or inequality) is tricky. One problem is what you measure. To figure out who has the money, you can measure either income (earnings, either from labor or from "rents"), or you can measure wealth (how much people have stowed away in the bank, or under the mattress, or whatever). Either way, there may be distortions — think of "land-poor" farmers and ranchers sitting on vast real estate holdings, but with cash income lower than the local bush driver.

And for either wealth or income, there are a lot of difficulties in measurement. As to income, investigators seem to have a tough time knowing just what to count. What about fringe benefits, like medical insurance, or earmarks for pensions? Or transfer payments, like welfare, or food stamps? As to wealth, perhaps the toughest job is where to find it. Regarding either income or wealth, people are notoriously cagey with nosy investigators, but with wealth in particular, the hiding of assets appears to be a major industry.

In any event, for measuring income, one popular tool is the so-called Gini Index, named after its inventor, Corrado Gini. The Gini Index is a number between zero and one. Zero represents total equality of distribution. One represents total inequality: one person has everything. Aside from the Gini

---

1 Data are summarized in James W. Poterba, *Stock Market Wealth and Consumption*, 14 J. Econ. L. 99 (2000).

2 R. Jolly, and others, UN Annual Human Development Report (1996). The number of billionaires seems to have increased since then, so the disparity may be sharper.

Index, another strategy is to simply break a society down into percentage shares and ask who gets what.

Under either standard, according to Census Bureau data, inequality in the United States decreased from the end of World War II until about 1968. Since then, it has increased, achieving its World War II level by about 1982 and continuing through the most recent reports.[3]

In a lot of other countries (but not all), inequality crept up as well. One study reported that the Gini Index for Britain went up from 0.23 in 1977 to 0.34 in 1991. On these numbers, in 1977, the richest 20 percent had four times the wealth of the poorest, and in 1991, they had seven times as much. Note that by this scale, at the end of the cycle Britain was still less "unequal" than the United States was at the beginning.

These numbers put America high on the inequality scale among rich countries and Britain, somewhere in the middle. Japan and Germany are among the most equal on this scale, with ratios of 4 to 5.5.

A more recent study[4] offers general confirmation of the earlier numbers, but adds one important outlier: Russia. This study measures income by deciles (10 percent brackets). On this scale, the richest Americans enjoy incomes a high-ish 5.67 times the poorest. But the Russians briskly outstrip them (and almost everybody else) with 6.83.

Measures of wealth, even taking account of the fact that much of it is hidden, tend to show even sharper disparities. The Gini Index for income in the United States is somewhere in the range of 0.4 to 0.505. For wealth, the comparable number is 0.793. But if you exclude houses and cars, the number shoots up to 0.966 percent. Ownership of stocks and bonds remains, as Doug Henwood says, "densely packed in the upper crust."[5]

We have already cautioned that these wealth indexes do not measure hidden wealth. These indexes also fail to measure other kinds of wealth in plain sight. For example, most workers in developed countries have a right to an annual government pension. It might be reasonable to assign a value to the present worth of that prospective future payment stream. Similarly, many workers have marketable skills that can be expected to produce income into the future. It might be reasonable to value either or both of these prospective payment streams as present assets. Neither the pension right nor the value of marketable skills will appear in any conventional data set. Including them would greatly increase the assets of many who now seem to be asset-poor.

Aside from the questions of "who" and "how much," there is a subsidiary question of "how did it happen?" Clearly we have gone through a wave of "market reforms" over the last couple of decades. The popular view seems to be that market reforms have increased wealth but aggravated inequality. Does the evidence confirm this view?

---

[3] *See* http://www.census.gov/hhes/income/incineq/p60asc.html.

[4] See data summarized in Smeedlng, *America's Income Inequality: Where do we Stand?* CHALLENGE, Sept. 19, 1996, at 39, available in 1996 WL 9035753.

[5] Henwood quotes from an unpublished Federal Reserve Board working paper that reports disparities even sharper than those set forth here. But the tendency is the same whichever set of numbers you use.

As to the first question — has the market increased wealth? — the answer has to be "yes." This answer is not unequivocal: surely the world is a dirtier, nastier place in some ways than it was in a pre-market era. And we hardly become richer if we all take out each others' appendix, even if we do it through a market transaction. On the other hand it is hard to escape the conclusion that the world as a whole has more protein, more capacity for good health care, than it ever had before. And the market must get some of the credit.

But has the market increased inequality? This question is perhaps more complicated than it appears at first blush. If we find that the market has not increased inequality, then that is the end of it. But if we find it has increased inequality, then there are at least two possibilities:

- All people have gotten richer, but some have got much richer.
- The world as a whole has gotten richer, but some people have gotten poorer while others have gotten much richer.

In fact, there seem to be real-world examples that support each of these three views. In the U.S., for example, according to fairly recent data, there seems to have been an absolute increase in inequality, with some getting absolutely poorer as others got richer. In Britain by contrast, the evidence seems to suggest that "all boats have risen at once" — the lot of the worst off has improved, even as disparities have increased. In parts of Asia (for example, Korea and Taiwan), and also in Italy, the expansion of market seems to have generated an absolute decrease in inequality.[6]

Among the most developed economies, then, the evidence is equivocal. Taking the world as a whole, it is somewhat more depressing. The UN report[7] concludes that some 20 (formerly?) third-world countries are growing and making people richer. In perhaps 100 others, growth is slow or negative. The report concludes that at least 1.5 billion people were worse off in the 1990s than in the 1980s — perhaps half a billion, even worse than in the 1960s.

A closely-related question is the impact of inequality on development. Is inequality an ally of economic development, or an adversary? Columbia University economist Roberto Perotti has explored this question.[8] Perotti identifies three areas where he thinks inequality can harm economic development. The first is education: high inequality tends to lead to low investment in education, especially at the secondary level, and especially for girls. The second is fertility: societies with high equality tend to have fewer children, and to invest more in them. The third is political stability: large gaps between rich and poor make a country more vulnerable to assassinations, coups, and such.

Gross figures on inequality tend to support this analysis. A World Bank review of evidence suggests that countries with high Gini Index numbers —

---

[6] *See Inequality: For Richer, for Poorer*, THE ECONOMIST, Nov. 5, 1994, at 19, available in WL 12754785.

[7] *See* fn.2 *supra*.

[8] Perotti, *Growth, Income Distribution, and Democracy: What the Data Say*, JOURNAL OF ECONOMIC GROWTH, June, 1996.

for example, many countries in Latin America — have developed more slowly than those like the East Asians, where inequalities are less extreme.[9]

Suggested Reading

It's hard to imagine a topic on which more worthless or silly books are written than money and finance. This is too bad, not least because it obscures some truly wonderful stuff. Some of the choices on the following list are obvious; a few perhaps less so.

If you want a readable, nontechnical account of markets and investments, read Burton G. Malkiel, *A Random Walk Down Wall Street* (7th ed. 2000).

The best possible introduction to the *American economy* is Jeremy Atack & Peter Passell, *New Economic View of American History: From Colonial Times to 1940* (2d ed. 1994). Flesh it out with the undisputed classic of *business history*: Alfred Dupont Chandler, *The Visible Hand : The Managerial Revolution in American Business* (1980).

If you want some sense of the politics of business law, start with Mark J. Roe, *Strong Managers, Weak Owners: The Political Roots of American Corporate Finance* (1995).

A good sketch of recent history of financial markets can be found in Henry Kaufman, *On Money and Markets A Wall Street Memoir* (2000) .

If you care about law and economics as it applies to corporate law, you will need to start with Frank H. Easterbrook & Daniel R. Fischel, *The Economic Structure of Corporate Law* (1992).

If you want a more entertaining *"People Magazine"* version of modern finance, you should read Peter L. Bernstein *Capital Ideas: The Improbable Origins of Modern Wall Street* (1992).

If you're going to be a business lawyer, you're going to have to know *some accounting*. Not too much — three semester hours will do it easily. If you can't squeeze it in, or if you don't want to wait, you need a copy of Robet N. Anthony and Leslie K. Pearlman, *Essentials of Accounting* (7th ed. 1999), a programmed text. It will take a little work on your part, but it's street-proven as effective in doing its job.

And for personal investing, the obvious choice is Andrew Tobias, *The Only Investment Guide You'll Ever Need (Expanded and Updated Throughout)* (1999)

A corrective to almost everything above is in Doug Henwood *Wall Street: How It Works and for Whom* (1997) .

Some Basic Web sites

Web site citations are almost an exercise in futility; they are bound to be outdated by the time the book appears, and there will be new ones that are better. But here are a few to give you a start (others are scattered through the book):

---

[9] *Measuring Income Inequality: A New Database*, WORLD BANK ECONOMIC REVIEW, SEPTEMBER, 1996.

Perhaps the best single source for data on the state of the economy is:

www.bog.frb.fed.us/releases/z1/current/data.htm.

The best of all teaching web pages is:

www.stern.nyu.edu/ãdamodar/.

A nontechnical introduction to investing from a major mutual fund firm is:

majestic.vanguard.com/EPA/DA.

It seems like everybody except an order of cloistered nuns now has a web page aimed at the personal investor. Here is a sample:

finance.yahoo.com/.

An elaborate glossary of financial terms can be found at:

www.duke.edu/c̃harvey/Classes/wpg/glossary.htm.

The dissenters' site is:

www.panix.com/d̃henwood/LBO_home.html.

The leading commercial provider of long-range price data is:

www.ibbotson.com/.

A site of cites, with a lot of references:

www.finweb.com/.

A distinctive personal site with a ton of cross references is:

www.efmoody.com/

TABLE OF CONTENTS

Page

Page

Page

Part I

Valuation

Chapter 1

PV, NPV, and Different Kinds of *r*

Lack of Money
Continues to Roll In.

—Dylan Thomas

§ 1.01 Introduction

You don't need to read a book to know what an asset is worth. An asset is worth what you get for it, less what you pay for it, known in the trade as its *net present value* (NPV). A complication is that these incomes and outflows normally come at different times, and a dollar now is worth more than a dollar later. To measure them, we need a device to locate them all at the same point in time. A corollary is that anything gets value only in terms of what you passed up in order to get it — the cost of the lost opportunity, or *opportunity cost* (more precisely, *opportunity cost of capital* (OCC)). In this chapter, we introduce both these ideas.

First, we explore the mechanics of NPV. We will see that see that you can relate any "future" value (FV) to a "present" value (PV) by defining the *percentage rate of change (r)*. So you have three components: FV, PV and *r*. The best part is that if you know *any two* of these components, you can *derive* the third.

§ 1.02 Present Value

All I Ever Needed to Know
I Learned in Kindergarten.

—Robert Fulghum

We can bet there is one thing Robert Fulghum did not learn in kindergarten: *present value*. It is our point of beginning, the linchpin to our understanding of the corporate value structure. We will do it three ways: (1) in words, (2) in numbers using a bit of basic algebra, and (3) using a calculator.

Suppose I offer you \$100, payable either today or a year from today. Are you indifferent as to when you will get the \$100? You are not indifferent. You would rather have it today. This is true independent of whether you want to use it today. Even if you have no use for the money today, you could stick it in the bank and earn interest. So if you have to wait a year, you lose the opportunity to earn interest in the interim. We can define the cost of this lost opportunity as the OCC, which we discuss at greater length in § 1.05 below.

If time is money, how can we compare the value of benefits due at different times? To compare, we factor out time. We translate values from different times into the same time frame, so we can compare them on an equal plane.

We build a simple model to see how this is done. Suppose you loan me $100 now and I repay you $120 later. Simple intuition probably tells you that you have made a 20 percent gain, but you can confirm the point easily:

$$\$120 \div \$100 = 1.20$$

Or:

$$(\$120 \div \$100) - 1 = 0.20 = 20 \text{ percent}$$

This is how we confirm that you have received a 20 percent return. We can abstract from this particular case to a general proposition. Start with the value that we possess now; call it the "present value" (PV). Then imagine the value we expect to have in the future; call it the "future value" (FV). Call the "rate of return" simply r. What we have shown is that:

$$\text{FV} \div \text{PV} = 1 + r$$

Or:

$$(\text{FV} \div \text{PV}) - 1 = r$$

To check, suppose that FV is $290 and PV is $273.59. What is r?

Note that we have *three* terms here: FV, PV, and r. So far, we have been using FV and PV to determine r. But in general, if we know *any two* of these three terms, we can compute the third. For example, we saw that (FV ÷ PV) = 1 + r. Using elementary algebra, multiply both sides by PV.

$$\text{PV}\ (1 + r) = \text{FV}$$

For example, suppose PV is $125 and r is 8.5 percent. Then, the future value is ($125)(1.085) = $135.63. So, if we know PV and r, we can derive FV. To double-check, treat FV ($135.63) and PV ($125) as "known," and solve for r. You should get 0.085, or 8.5 percent.

In this equation, the term (1 + r) is sometimes referred to as the *forward factor* (FF), i.e., the *factor* by which we multiply PV in order to go *forward* to FV.

$$\text{FF} = (1 + r)$$

So far, we have solved for FV and r. By the same logic, we can treat FV and r as "known," and solve for PV as the "unknown." That is, to solve for PV:

$$\frac{\text{FV}}{(1 + r)} = \text{PV}$$

So, for example, if FV is $140 and r is 9 percent, then PV is $128.44. If FV is $160 and r is 7 percent, what is PV?

We can rewrite the previous formula as follows:

$$\text{FV}\ [1 \div (1 + r)] = \text{PV}$$

This version conveys the same information as the previous version; both permit us to derive PV when we know FV and r. Algebraically, we have "factored out" the future value to get 1 ÷ (1 + r) (remember that to *divide* by x is the same as to *multiply* by 1 ÷ x). For example, a moment ago you *divided* $160 by 1.07 (you should have got $149.53). Note that 1 ÷ 1.07 = 0.93458, and that (0.93458)($160) = $149.53. So, to go from FV to PV, we can either (a) *divide by* $(1 + r)$, or (b) *multiply by* $1 \div (1 + r)$. We get the same result either way.

Earlier, we defined $(1 + r)$ as the *forward factor* (FF). By analogy, we can define $1 \div (1 + r)$ as the *discount factor* (DF).

$$DF = [1 \div (1 + r)]$$

Recall from high school math that:

$$\frac{1}{X} = X^{-1}$$

So DF may also be expressed as:

$$DF = (1+r)^{(-1)}$$

It is often more convenient to multiply by the discount factor than to divide by $(1 + r)$. For example, suppose you are using your hand computer. You know the *rate*, and you want to apply it to different FVs to derive different PVs. It will be convenient to compute the DF only once and then "store" it in the hand computer's memory. Then you can key in an FV and multiply by the stored DF, to derive a PV. Then you can move on to a new FV and compute again.

> **Calculator Tip:** If you have a Texas Instruments BA II PLUS, follow along while I compute a PV. I press in 1.06. Then I hit the key that says 1/x; that gives me the DF for 6 percent, i.e., 0.943. Then I hit "STO 0"; this stores my answer for later use. Now, suppose I want to discount $800. I key in $800. Then I hit the multiply key. Then I hit "RCL 0". Then "=". I get $754.72. I have discounted $800 by the 6 percent, one period DF. If I try "$1400 × RCL 0", I get $1320.75. I have discounted $1,400 by the one period DF.

We have seen that the DF at a rate of 7 percent is 0.93458. Now, consider a couple of other discount rates. Note that $1 \div (1.08) = 0.9259$, and that $1 \div (1.1) = 0.909$. Examine the three DFs. You will see that the *smaller* the rate of return (r), the *larger* is the PV, and vice versa. A moment's reflection will tell why this is so. Remember elementary fractions: $(1/3) > (1/4) > (1/5)$ and so forth. Indeed, in any fraction, the larger the denominator, the smaller the quotient.

The relationship makes practical sense in finance as well. After all, if you are the person who will receive the money, then the higher the rate, the greater the cost of delay. You may have seen a newspaper story that said, "bond prices soared today as interest rates fell." Such stories depend on the same relationship. **As *r* goes up, PV goes down — and *vice versa*.**

§ 1.03 The Centerpiece: Net Present Value

Now, the centerpiece of our valuation technique. Very often in this course we are interested in knowing the value of what we will get, *measured against what it will cost* — the present value *net of* the cost, or the *net present value*

(NPV). Can we compute NPV? We can. To see how, suppose that we pay out money today and get money back later. Start with the money we pay out today: call it "C0" (think of it as "cash at t=0" or simply as "cash out"). Think of the money we get later as a kind of FV. Then, use a discount factor to reduce FV to PV. Subtract C0 from PV. The result is NPV.

So for example, let C0 = $1,400 and let FV = $1,477. Our next job is to discount FV to PV. And here, be alert while we step lightly over a trip-wire. To discount, we need an interest rate. Based on what you have seen so far, you might say that we have an interest rate: this would be the rate that we derive from C0 and PV (that would be: 1,477 ÷ 1,400 − 1) = 0.055 = 5.5 percent.

This is true as far as it goes, but it misses the point. The point is: for discounting, what we want is not the rate that we *derive* from the *internal logic* of the deal (call it the "Internal Rate of Return," or simply "IRR"). Rather, we want a wholly separate rate that is external to the deal (call it the "Opportunity Cost of Capital," or "OCC."[1] We will say more in a moment about where we get the OCC, but for the moment, pluck it out of the air.

So, suppose it is 4.25 percent. Then the discount factor is 1 ÷ 1.0425 = 0.9592, and the PV must be ($1,477)(0.9592) = $1,416.78 Then NPV must be ($1,416.78 − $1,400), or $16.78.

NPV is the most important single valuation measure we will use in this course. We will apply it in a number of different variations, but it always comes down to this. Compute the present value of our costs. Compute the present value of benefits. Subtract the costs from the benefits.

Web site: For NPV and other topics, see http://www.timevalue.com/tools.htm.

§ 1.04 Anything is a Bargain at the Right Price

Buy on the cannons,
sell on the trumpets.

—Lord Rothschild

NPV allows us to introduce a vital distinction. The value of any asset *to the investor* is a function not only of its intrinsic worth, but also of its price. Consider Global MegaCorp, Inc., the much-admired world leader in the widget business. Global MegaCorp is old, established, well-known, and much loved by investors. The consequence is that the price of its stock is high. Would we buy Global MegaCorp at the current price? We would not. The returns come at too high a price.

Compare poor Megadur, former high-tech giant that was lately broken up by an unsympathetic judge in an antitrust suit. Investors have fled in droves from Megadur, and dumped its stock on the market at distress prices. We can see their point: the glory days are over for Megadur, and never again will it

[1] Indeed, if NPV is to have any meaning, then the discount rate must be something other than just the rate derived from the deal — otherwise the PV (the discounted FV) would always equal C0 and the NPV would always be zero!

be able to throw off the profits it yielded before. Things are bad — but not as bad as investors seem to think. Rather, we think the market has overreacted against Megadur, and that it is selling cheap. We will scoop it up in a bushel basket. In short, a general principle: anything is a bargain at the right price.

§ 1.05 Derived Rate and Required Rate: A Second Look at Opportunity Cost

—I walk to work and save a bundle
by not paying bus fare.
—You could save a lot more
by not taking a cab.

—Vaudeville shtick

A moment ago, we noted two different interest rates — one internal to the deal (IRR) and the other, exogenous, which we called the opportunity cost of capital (OCC). We need to take a second look at OCC. Abstractly, the OCC is the rate that we forego in order to take the deal before us. Consider Irving, an investor with $100 to invest. He could put it in HamCo, where it would earn 7 percent. Or he could put it in EggsCo, an entirely comparable venture, where he expects he will earn $120.

He reasons: if I invested in HamCo, how much would I have to invest in order to get $120? Since HamCo pays 7 percent, the answer is $120 ÷ (1.07) = $112.15. So the chance to invest in EggsCo is equivalent to investing $112.15 in HamCo. But it costs only $100. The NPV must be ($112.15 − $100), or $12.15. Note that the derived rate is [($120 ÷ $100) − 1] = 0.2, or 20 percent.[2]

In the classroom, we pretty much pick OCCs out of the air. But in the real world, that is where (if at all) the investor makes his money — by picking those projects that are "underpriced" in terms of their alternatives. We amplify on this point a bit in a later chapter. For now, distinguish the *derived* rate from the *required* rate and be sure you know when you are using which.

[2] Note that we are comparing two projects that are *alike* in terms of risk. We will have more to say about risk later. But for now, it is easy to grasp that (a) investors would rather have less risk than more, but (b) they will take risk if the have sufficient compensation. In other words, I might find myself with a (safe) project expected to yield $106 at t=1 and another (risky) project that is expected to yield $108. On the basis of what you have learned so far, you do not have any basis for deciding between these two; your decision would depend on a more precise notion of relative riskiness, and also on the investor's own attitude to risk. Our point is that you could not (or at least not without some cumbersome adjustments) use either one for a benchmark.

§ 1.06 Summary

It will be convenient to have a summary of some of our basic terms and the associated shorthand:

Remember these terms:

PV = Present Value
NPV = Net Present Value
FV = Future Value
DF = Discount Factor
FF = Forward Factor
OCC = Opportunity Cost
r = Rate of Return

Chapter 2
Valuation Over Multiple Periods

They say you can't do it
but sometimes it doesn't always work.

—Casey Stengel

§ 2.01 Introduction

"[A] hundred pounds payable fifteen years hence . . . in a country where interest is at six percent, is worth little more than 40 pounds ready money."[1] So said the great Adam Smith, the founder of modern economics, over 200 years ago. It is interesting that he did not specify just how much more than 40 pounds — evidently he didn't have a calculator. It is conceivable he didn't even know.[2] In this chapter, you will learn how to compute the present value of 100 pounds due after 15 years at 6 percent and so prove yourself at least as smart as Adam Smith.

We have seen how to use a present value (PV) and an interest rate (r) to derive a future value (FV), and how to use an FV to derive a PV. In this chapter, we will show how to *compound* interest over *multiple* periods. We will show how the frequency of compounding changes the value of the PV or FV. Finally, we will show a convenient formula for compounding *continuously* through time.

§ 2.02 Compounding

Just about any loan contract will provide that the borrower must pay interest. Most loan contracts also allow for *compound* interest. In this section, we explore the technique of compounding. In the last section we were dealing with three terms — PV, FV, and r. In exploring compound interest, we will use the same three terms, and we will add a fourth: "n," which represents the number of periods during which interest is compounded.

The basic insight is easy enough. Suppose the debtor borrows $1,000 and promises to pay interest computed at 6 percent a year. After one year (at t=1) the debtor owes ($1,000)(1.06) = $1060. At t=2, we might add another $60 of interest for a total of $1,120. Arithmetically, this is just fine, but it is not the way we usually do things. Far more often, the contract says that interest will be *compounded*. This means that at t=2 we will figure interest on the original principal ($1,000), *and also on the accumulated interest* ($60). So, we have ($1,060)(1.06) = $1,123.60. At the end of the third period (t=3), we

[1] Adam Smith, Inquiry into the Nature and Causes of the Wealth of Nations, Books I–III, II, the Wealth of Nations Chapter 2, § 2 (1776).

[2] The first full-fledged account of the technique appears in the work of Martin Faustmann, a German forester writing in the 1840s. *See* Martin Faustmann and the Evolution of Discounted Cash Flow (W. Linnard trans., Commonwealth Forestry Institute (1968).

compound again on principal plus accumulated interest; our new total grows to ($1,123.60)(1.06) = $1,191.02. Formally, using familiar notation, our accumulation over three periods is:

$$PV\ (1 + r)\ (1 + r)\ (1 + r) = FV$$

Note that $(1 + r)\ (1 + r)\ (1 + r) = (1 + r)^3$. Of course, we need not stop at three periods. We could continue for *n* periods. Generalizing, we can say:

$$PV\ (1 + r)^n = FV$$

As before, we can isolate the forward factor:

$$FF = (1 + r)^n$$

It is worth noting that our previous exercise was no more than a special case of today's more general rule. In that case, $n = 1$, so we were raising $(1 + r)$ "to a power of one." Since anything to a power of one is itself, we simply ignored the exponent. But for some purposes later, we will want to remember that it is there.

You can anticipate where we are going next. Just as we can go *forward* from present to future using the *forward factor* (FF), we can go *back* from future values to present values by using the *inverse of the forward factor: the discount factor* (DF). So, take our previous equation and divide both sides by $(1 + r)^n$.

$$\frac{FV}{(1 + r)^n} = PV$$

Factoring:

$$FV\ [1 \div (1 + r)^n] = PV$$

As before, it will be convenient to isolate the discount factor:

$$DF = [1 \div (1 + r)^n]$$

Which can also be expressed as

$$DF = (1+r)^{(-n)}$$

As in our previous exercise, factoring has the effect of isolating the discount factor (DF). For example, suppose the interest rate is 6.4 percent. What is the DF for two years? It is $1 \div (1.064)^2 = 0.8833$. And for three: $1 \div (1.064)^3 = 0.83019$. So, if we have an FV of $800 due at t=2, the PV at 6.4 percent is $707. For $800 due at t=3, the PV is $664.

Calculator Tip: We noted that $[1 \div (1 + r)^n] = (1 + r)^{(-n)}$. Remember also, that it is the *inverse* of $(1 + r)^n$. This suggests three different ways to punch in the digits to compute the DF:

- First, hit 1, then "divide," then $(1 + r)^n$ (make sure to get the parentheses in the right place — check the calculator manual);
- Or second, punch in $(1 + r)$. Then punch in n as a negative exponent;
- Or third, punch in $(1 + r)^n$ and then hit the "inverse" key (usually "1/x").

§ 2.03 Application: Zeroes

We can use our analytical apparatus to define a *zero-coupon bond*. What is a zero-coupon bond? Take it in components. A *bond* is a glorified IOU — a promise to pay money. Corporations "issue bonds" to borrow money. Lenders "buy bonds" to lend money. Most bonds carry the obligation to pay interest at set times, perhaps twice a year.

In the old days, the typical bond came on a sheet of high-quality rag paper including a strip of coupons representing the obligation to pay interest. In order to collect the interest, the lender (investor) had to clip off the coupon and present it to the borrower — hence, the jargon (perhaps now somewhat antique) of people who live by clipping coupons. In the electronic age, more and more of these deals are done on a computer screen instead of paper, but the jargon (and, indeed, the structure of the underlying deal) persists. Hence, "coupon bonds."

Along about 1982, some borrowers started issuing bonds that bore no coupons at all, nor, indeed, any obligation to pay interest — hence, *zero coupon bonds*, or simply "*zeroes*." Of course, no investor will advance money without the expectation of *some* kind of payment someday. But anything is a bargain at the right price. The lenders figured out that the investors would buy the bonds at a discount sufficient to compensate them for delay. For example, suppose BigCo issues a $1,000 zero payable 20 years from today in a market where the required rate of return is 10 percent. The PV of $1,000 discounted for 20 years at 10 percent is $148.64. So, we can infer that $148.64 is a "fair" price for the bond.

Web site: For more on zero coupon bonds, see http://www.investinginbonds.com/info/igzero/what.htm.

§ 2.04 Deriving *r*

You may remember Fry, the 25-year-old pizza delivery boy in Fox TV's Futurama, who accidentally got himself frozen and woke up a thousand years hence in the company of an alien, a cyclops and a corrupt robot. In episode 6, Fry discovers that his bank account of 93 cents has grown to $4.3 billion.

In this episode, we learn how to compute the effective periodic rate of return on Fry's "investment."

Recall that we are working with four variables — PV, FV, and *r*. We have learned how to derive PV and FV. Our goal now is to derive r. There remains the problem of *r*. Previously, we computed *r* as follows: we divided FV by PV to get $(1 + r)$. Then we subtracted one to get *r*.

But see what happens when we try to divide FV by PV:

$$\frac{\text{FV}}{\text{PV}} = (1 + r)^n$$

Our problem, then, is to get rid of the exponent *n*. We do so by taking the nth root of each side, as follows:[3]

$$(\text{FV} \div \text{PV})^{1/n} = (1 + r)$$

Now we can isolate *r*:

$$(\text{FV} \div \text{PV})^{1/n} - 1 = r$$

For example, suppose we know that FV is $1,020 and PV is $300, and the term is 20 years. Then:

$$(\$1{,}020 \div \$300)^{1/20} - 1 = 0.0631$$

Or 6.31 percent. Using the same technique, we can see that Fry's account earned an annual return of just 2.25 percent.

> **Calculator Tip:** Taking the nth root was difficult before calculators, but it is easy now. Using the Texas Instruments BA II PLUS calculator, you key in FV and divide by PV. Then you hit the exponent key (y^x); then n; then 1/x; equals; then subtract 1.

You can use these techniques to tease out some remarkable inferences. For example, there were 37 Elvis impersonators in the world when the King died in 1977. By Jan. 1, 1995, there were 48,000. The *San Francisco Chronicle*[4] declared that at this rate, by 2010, one in every seven Americans would be an Elvis impersonator. On the *Chronicle's* numbers, we can infer a past growth rate among Elvis impersonators of 48.9 percent per year. Extrapolate for another 15 years and you find that we can expect 18,855,620.63 Elvis impersonators by 2010.[5] This implies a United States population in 2010 of just 131,989,344 — considerably lower than the population today. Considering the general importance of the story, it is perhaps remarkable that the *Chronicle* did not showcase it more directly.

---

[3] You will recognize this from high school math as the *geometric mean*. We will have more to say about the geometric mean later.

[4] Ramon G. McLeod, *The Way We Were: Men Confessed They Like Buying Lingerie, Women Admitted They Own Shoes They've Never Worn, We're All Losing Faith in the American Dream, 1994 Was Just That Kind of Year*, S. F. Chron. Jan 1, 1995, p. 6.

[5] Presumably the odd 0.37 percent of an impersonator will be doing Groucho.

§ 2.05 Application: Short-Term Debt

In § 2.03, we used our new conceptual apparatus to help us understand a zero-coupon bond. Now, we can put our skills to work to analyze short-term debt. For example, consider your client Widge, who buys a crate of widgets from a Mandy, a manufacturer. Mandy presents Widge with a bill for $1,000. Mandy agrees that Widge can take a 2 percent discount if he pays within 30 days. Two percent of $1,000 = $20, and ($1,000 − $20) = $980. Suppose the bill arrives at t=0 and your client pays the bill at t=29. Since [(1000 ÷ 980) − 1] = 0.0204, we can say the creditor is charging 2.04 percent a month for the credit on unpaid balances.[6]

The same kind of analysis works to explain the market for U.S. treasury bills. The Treasury Department issues these bills in denominations of $10,000 or more. They are payable in 13, 26, or 52 weeks. Consider Blanche, who pays $9,500 for a $10,000 26-week bill. That works out to [(100 ÷ 95) − 1] = 0.0526 = 5.26 percent for half a year.

§ 2.06 Compounding How Often?

We have talked about compounding over multiple *periods*. We need to take a closer look at the definition of the period. The traditional deal probably called for compounding *annually,* in which case the compounding period was one year. But there is no magic in the year as a term: a moment ago, we extracted a rate for a 30-day trade discount, and another for a 26-week treasury bill. As far as the math is concerned, the period could be a minute, or a millennium. The point has practical importance because different compounding schedules will lead to different values, and you often have to be alert to make sure you understand just when compounding takes place.

For example, suppose you lend $1,000 for one year at 12 percent. At the end of the year, you have $1,000 (1.12) = $1,120. By contrast, suppose you stop the clock at the end of each *month* and compound at 1 ÷ 12 of the annual rate. At the end of the year, you then have [$1,000 $(1.01)^{12}$] = $1,126.83. Note that your *effective r* here is no longer the *nominal* 12 percent. Rather, it is [$(1.01)^{12}$ − 1] = 0.1268 = 12.68 percent.

The disparity grows as the term increases. Consider a three-year loan. At 12 percent compounded annually, the total accumulation is [$1,000 $(1.12)^{3}$] = $1,404.93. At one percent compounded monthly, the accumulation is [$1,000 $(1.01)^{36}$] = $1,430.77. (As an exercise, recompute the FV of $1,000 compounded monthly over one year at one percent a month. Then raise this product to a power of three. Compare your answer with the example in this paragraph.).

§ 2.07 Intra-Period Compounding — Nominal v. Effective

A lot of lenders and borrowers like to quote their interest rates in *annual* terms, even though the deal may allow compounding more frequently. We

---

[6] This is the rate for two weeks. What is the rate for a year? The answer is: 27.43 percent a year. Note that this is *not* simply 2.04 × 12. We will explain later. *See* § 2.07 below.

need to be alert to distinguish between the annual rate and the more frequent periodic compounded rate.

We need some notation to describe this relationship. As before, let n = the *number of periods* (most often, "years") *in a project*. Let us introduce a new term: "m," equal to the number of compounding periods *inside* a particular n.[7] Then compute the FF:

$$FF = (1 + (r \div m))$$

For example, suppose you invest $100 at an annual rate of 7 percent. If you compute interest just once a year, your FF is 1.07. FV at the end of a year will be just $107. If you compute monthly, then each month you use a rate equal to 1 ÷ 12 of 7 percent:

$$FF = (1 + (0.07 \div 12)) = 1.00583$$

So the annual rate must be:

$$FF = (1 + (0.07 \div 12))^{12} = 1.0723$$

Note that the *effective* annual rate is nearly a quarter of a point higher than the *nominal* 7 percent rate.

As far as math goes, this is perfectly innocuous; it's just a special instance of compounding. Then why do we emphasize it here? The answer is that it gives rise to confusion and misunderstanding *in practice*. More precisely: people often *state* the interest as if it were compounded annually (nominal) while *in fact* they are compounding more often and collecting the higher rate (effective). We will explore a couple of examples below, but for the moment, make sure that you grasp the distinction.

We can generalize this nominal/effective distinction to a loan that extends over a number of years. We have already seen how the FF for a multi-year loan can be defined as $(1+r)^n$. But now we are dealing with a case in which the one-year FF is no longer just $(1+r)$; rather, it is $[1 + (r \div m)^m]$. If this is the one-year FF, then the multi-year factor must be:

$$FF = (1 + (r \div m))^{(m)(n)}$$

Or, pursuing our example:

$$FF = (1 + (0.07 \div 12))^{(12)(3)} = 1.233$$

Recall that we already determined that the one-year FF for 7 percent nominal compounded monthly is 1.0723. To double-check the three-year factor, compute $(1.0723)^3$. What answer do you get?

§ 2.08 Nominal v. Effective — Discount Factors

We can turn this logic around. Earlier, we learned that the FF and the DF are reciprocals of one another, that is, DF = 1 ÷ FF. The principle ought to hold here just as it did before. So, if we have more than one compounding period per year, the DF must be:

$$DF = \frac{1}{(1 + (r \div m))^{(m)(n)}}$$

[7] Of course m can stand for "monthly," and it may be that our periodic rate is a monthly rate. But this is an aid to memory only; it could be daily, or hourly, or whatever.

Or (what is the same thing):

$$DF = (1 + (r \div m))^{-(m)(n)}$$

(Don't overlook the negative sign on the exponent). For example, if the FV is $15,000, the term is eight years, and we have a nominal annual rate of 15 percent, compounded quarterly, the PV should be $4,618.19. Confirm this result, and ask yourself, "what is the annual rate?"

§ 2.09 Application: Short-Term Debt Again

Earlier we computed the periodic rate for short-term vendor credit (2 percent, 30 days), and for treasury bills. We are now in a position to compute the effective annual rate for this short-term debt.

First, consider "2 percent, 30 days." We characterized this as a case where Mandy "loaned" $980 to get $1,000 at the end of a month. We computed Mandy's rate of return as 2.04 percent (recall that $980(1.0204) = $1,000). Now ask: what if Mandy collects the entire $1,000 at the end of one month and immediately re-lends the whole $1,000 on the same percentage terms — and does the same again at the end of each month over an entire year? How much will she accumulate? The answer is:

$$\$980(1.0204)^{12} = \$1{,}249$$

The FF is:

$$(1.0204)^{12} = 1.274$$

And the effective annual rate must be 27.4 percent.[8]

For a final example, consider the "6 for 5" or "payday" lender, familiar to anyone who was ever in the Army: he lends you $5 today for $6 on payday — a 20 percent periodic return. If he lends on the first day of each month and collects on the 30th, and if he reinvests all proceeds, then his annual rate of return is:

$$(1.2)^{12} - 1 = 7.92$$

That is a comfortable 792 percent annual return. On the same logic, what is the effective annual yield on the 26-week treasury bill?

§ 2.10 From *n* to *m*

Let us address one final manipulation. We have seen that if we know the *nominal* annual rate (r) and the periodic rate (m), then we can determine the *effective* annual rate: the formula is $[1+(r/m)]^m$. But suppose we know the effective annual rate, and want to know the nominal. We do it in two steps. First, we "extract" the intra-period compounding rate ($r \div m$). Then we *multiply by* (not "raise to a power of") the intra-period rate.

The technique for extracting ($r \div m$) is familiar. It is the same as the technique we used to extract the periodic rate from FV and PV: we take the root. Specifically, call the *effective* rate "EFF." Then:

---

[8] We assume 12 30-day months, or a 360-day year. This is a common simplification in loan contracts.

$$\frac{r}{m} = [(1 + \text{EFF})^{1/m}] - 1$$

For example, suppose the effective annual rate is 12.49 and that compounding takes place three times a year. Then the period rate is 4 percent (confirm this result).

Summary — Do Not Confuse: We are dealing with three different rates here: the periodic rate ($r \div m$), the effective annual rate (EFF), and the *nominal* annual rate (NOM). Be careful not to confuse them. So, suppose we have NOM of 18 percent compounded monthly. Then, $r \div m$ is $18 \div 12$ or 1.5 percent, and EFF is $[(1.015)^{12} - 1] = 0.1956 = 19.56$ percent.

§ 2.11 Continuous Compounding

We have seen that the effective annual rate when compounding occurs more often than once a year is $[1 + (r/m)]^{mn}$. A moment's reflection will tell you that the more frequent the compounding, the higher the effective rate. For example, suppose you want to compute interest at 12 percent over one year. Compute twice a year and you get $(1.06)^2 = 1.1236 = 12.36$ percent. Compound eight times a year and you get $(1.015)^8 = 1.1265 = 12.65$ percent. But there is no reason to stop there. We could just as well compound 1,000 times a year and get 12.74887 percent, or 30,000 times a year, and get 12.74966 percent.

More frequent compounding increases the effective rate, but note an important subtlety: while growth continues, the rate of growth gets slower and slower — the growth from 1,000 periods to 30,000 is less than a thousandth of a percent. We seem to be approaching a *limit* beyond which the *effective* rate will not grow. The question presents itself — can we define the rate at which our value would grow if we had a *nominal* rate of 12 percent, but an *infinite* number of compoundings? Or (what amounts to the same thing), can we define the accumulation at a nominal annual rate if compounding is *continuous*?

It turns out that we can. To find it, we recall the system of *natural logs* (*ln*) that we learned in high school, and deploy the *base of the natural logs*. You may remember the base of the natural logs: it is an irrational number, roughly 2.71828, usually labeled "*e*." It turns out that if you take *e* and raise it to a power equal to the nominal rate, you get the FF for continuous compounding. That is,

$$e^{(r)}$$

In our example,

$$e^{(0.12)} = 1.1274969$$

(Do not overlook the decimal in the exponent). The rate is the FF minus one. So if the *nominal* rate is 12 percent, the *effective* rate for *continuous compounding* is 12.74969 percent. Compare this result to the effective rate for 30,000 compoundings above. You can see that the difference emerges only at the fifth decimal place.

Next, consider what happens if continuous compounding extends over a period of more than one year. Earlier, we saw that the FF for one year with intra-period compounding was $[1+(r/m)^{(m)}]$ and for more than one year, $[1+(r/m)^{(m)(n)}]$ (watch the exponent). But in the case of continuous compounding, $[1+(r/m)^{(m)}]$ becomes e^r. So for continuous compounding over more than one year, the formula must be:

$$e^{(r)(n)}$$

Going back to our example, what is the FF for a nominal annual rate of 12 percent over three years at continuous compounding? The answer must be:

$$e^{(0.12)(3)} = 1.43333$$

or a three-year rate of 43.33 percent. To double-check, recall that the one-year effective rate for 12 percent at continuous compounding was 1.1274969. Compute $(1.1274969)^3$. What do you get?

Generalizing, the formula to compute the effective rate under continuous compounding is:

$$\lim_{m \to \infty}[1 + (r \div m)]^{mn} = e^{rn}$$

> **Calculator Tip:** To figure the continuous compounding rate, key in the nominal rate, (n). Then hit 2nd, and hit e^x. Then subtract one. For example, suppose the nominal rate is 6 percent. Hit 0.06, 2nd, e^x, -1, =. Rounded to five places, the calculator will show 0.06184.

§ 2.12 Continuous Discounting

We have seen how to use the continuous compounding rate to compute a forward factor (FF). You can use the same apparatus to compute a continuous compounding discount factor. The formula would be:

$$\frac{1}{e^{(r)(n)}}$$

Or (what amounts to the same thing):

$$e^{-(r)(n)}$$

For example, suppose we will get $100 in three years and the required rate is 5 percent, compounded continuously. The continuous compounding rate is $e^{-(0.05)(3)}$ or 0.8607, so the present value is $86.07. As an exercise, compute the present value under annual compounding. Before computing the answer, ask yourself whether you expect the present value under annual compounding to be higher or lower than under continuous compounding.

§ 2.13 Deriving *n*

We have been dealing with four terms: PV, FV, r, and n. We have seen that we can derive PV, FV, or r if we know all of the other three. Can we also derive n? We can, but because n is an exponent, it is a bit more tricky. We do it by extracting the *natural log* of each side of the equation, and solve the equation. For example, we know that:

$$FV = PV(1 + r)^n$$

Extract the natural log (*ln*):

$$ln\ FV = ln\ PV + n\ ln\ (1 + r)$$

Solving for *n*:

$$n = \frac{ln(FV \div PV)}{ln(1 + r)}$$

Calculator Tip: This is another calculation that is easy on your BA II Plus. Consider your client, Clyde, who just bought an IOU for $300 which will pay $800 at maturity. He hopes to get a nine percent return. To get the return he wants, how long must be the term of the note?

Do this:

- Punch in 800, then 300, then divide equals
  (You should get 2.6667)
- Hit the ln key
  (You should get 0.9808)
- Store the last number; then hit 1.09 ln
  (You should get 0.0862)
- Store it; then divide 0.9808 by 0.862

You should get 11.3815, which is the "n" you were looking for. To double check, compute $(1.09)^{11.3815}$ and multiply by $300. You should get $800.

§ 2.14 Bonus: Two Shorthand Rules of Thumb

Back in the Pleistocene Era, when people analyzed formulae by chipping with obsidian on sandstone, they developed all sorts of dodges to help themselves with the computation. In the computer age, you aren't likely to need them. But just in case you are ever called on to explain present value to a pterodactyl, here are a couple of tricks that may help you:

Seven and Ten, Ten and Seven: If you do not have a calculator handy, remember this:

Ten Percent Doubles in Seven Years
Seven Percent Doubles in Ten Years

Not exactly, but try it and see how close you get. Punch in $(1.07)^{10}$; note the answer. Then punch in $(1.1)^7$; note the answer.

The Rule of 69: At a given interest rate, how long will it take for a sum to double? For a rough guess, treat the rate as a whole number (not a percentage), and divide 69 by the rate. So, what is the doubling period for a rate of 20 percent?

$$69 \div 20 = 3.45$$

This suggests that $(1.2)^{3.45} = 2$. In fact, $(1.2)^{3.45}$ only equals 1.87575, but it's close enough for government work. So, to estimate *n*, divide 69 by the rate.

For convenience of computation, people sometimes use 70, or 72, which are even less exact, but still workable as rules of thumb.[9] A variant is the "rule of 110." It deals with the *tripling* periods — the time it takes for an investment to grow by a factor of three. The rule says: to get the tripling period, divide 110 by the rate (as a whole number).[10] So, what is the tripling period for a rate of 18 percent?

$$110 \div 18 = 6.11$$

In fact, $(1.18)^{6.11} = 2.74$, so once again, the rule is inexact, but once again, it is convenient for estimation.

§ 2.15 Background Note: *e*

You do not have to understand *e* to use it — just follow the cookbook. But if you want to know more, here is a brief sketch.

"*e*" stands for Euler, as in Leonhard Euler (1707–83), the great Swiss mathematician. As a mathematician, Euler explored this sequence:

$$(1 + (1 \div m))^m$$

Euler found the following pattern:

$$(1 + (1 \div 1))^1 = 2$$

$$(1 + (1 \div 3))^3 = 2.37037$$

$$(1 + (1 \div 2))^2 = 2.25$$

Perhaps you can see where this is taking us. The point is that as m approaches infinity, then:

$$lim_{m \to \infty} (1 + (1 \div m))^m = 2.718281828\ldots$$

As a mnemonic, some call this result 2.7 "Jackson-Jackson" — Andrew Jackson was elected president in 1828. But in fact, the repetition is only accidental: the number is "irrational," just as "Pi" is irrational, in the sense that it cannot be expressed as a ratio of two integers.

How does *e* become a part our life? Take another look at the first term in the sequence: $(1 + 1)$. Recall our FF: $(1 + r)$. If $(1 + r) = 1 + 1$, then what we are saying is that $r = 100$ percent. So, what we are saying is that $e =$ the *effective* interest rate where the *nominal* rate is 100 percent, and there is an *infinite* number of compoundings. Another way of phrasing the point would be to say that $e = e^1$.

We sometimes refer to *e* as "the base of the natural logs." A log is the power to which a particular base must be raised in order to equal a given number. For example, consider the equation $10^5 = 100{,}000$. The base is 10. The number we wish to represent is 100,000. The log is 5. You can use any number for a base, but two are familiar. So-called "common" logs work off a base of 10

[9] Math jocks will recognize this as a special application of the *natural logs*. To see that this is so, derive the rate according to the formula we learned above, using 2 in the numerator. For example, if the rate is 6 percent, you would compute $(ln\ 2) \div (ln\ 1.06)$. You should get 11.89566. To check, compute (1.06)11.89566. Note that the natural log of 2 is 0.69315, so this is the source of our "rule of 69." For more on natural logs, see § 2.15 below.

[10] What is the natural log of 3?

(as in the last example). "Natural" logs (*ln*) work off of base *e*. Logs are important in math because they make possible a lot of computations that would be impossible (or at any rate, far more difficult) without them. For example, finding *n* using the natural logs as we did in § 2.13.

Chapter 3

Annuities

—I wish I had enough money to buy an elephant.
—What do you want an elephant for?
—I don't, I just want the money.

—Schtick

§ 3.01 Introduction

We have learned how to get a present value (PV) from a future value (FV), and an FV from a PV, either with or without compounding. But so far we have worked with *only a single* future value. Suppose we were to receive *more than one* payment in the future. Now, we want to compute the value of a *stream* of payments. This stream of payments is called an *annuity.* We will start with the case of a stream of *unequal* payments. We will show a valid (if cumbersome) strategy for valuing this annuity. Then we move on to the case of a stream of *equal* payments. We develop a formula for valuing such a stream.

§ 3.02 Can You Help Paula?

But before we do the analysis, to focus your attention, here is a teaser:

You are consulted by Paula, who has a personal injury claim against BigCo. She retained Larson as her lawyer. Larson's contract provides he will get 40 percent of any award, "to be paid first out of any recovery from BigCo." After extensive pretrial discovery, BigCo offered a "structured settlement" with terms as follows: $37,559 now, $100,000 to be paid at the end of five years, and another $100,000 to be paid at the end of 10 years. Paula agreed to the award. BigCo evidently wrote a check for the $37,559, but Larson says he is keeping all the money. Paula cannot understand why. Can you help her?

§ 3.03 The Basics

One way to compute the value of an annuity is to do what we've done all along, only more so. Consider your client Clara, a clamdigger, who forecasts her income as follows:

Year	Amount
1	$2,000
2	$8,000
3	$3,500
4	$1,000

What is the PV of her projected income? We can compute it as the *sum* of the PV of each *individual component*. So, we discount each payment according to its time of receipt:

$$\frac{\$2{,}000}{1.08} + \frac{\$8{,}000}{(1.08)^2} + \frac{\$3{,}500}{(1.08)^3} + \frac{\$1{,}000}{(1.08)^4} + \$12{,}224$$

Or in tabular form:

Year	CF	× DF Formula	DF	CF×DF
1	$2,000	$1.08^{(-1)}$	0.926	$ 1,852
2	$8,000	$1.08^{(-2)}$	0.857	$ 6,859
3	$3,500	$1.08^{(-3)}$	0.794	$ 2,778
4	$1,000	$1.08^{(-4)}$	0.735	$ 735
		Total		$12,224

In the chart below, each FV on the horizontal connects to a PV on the vertical:

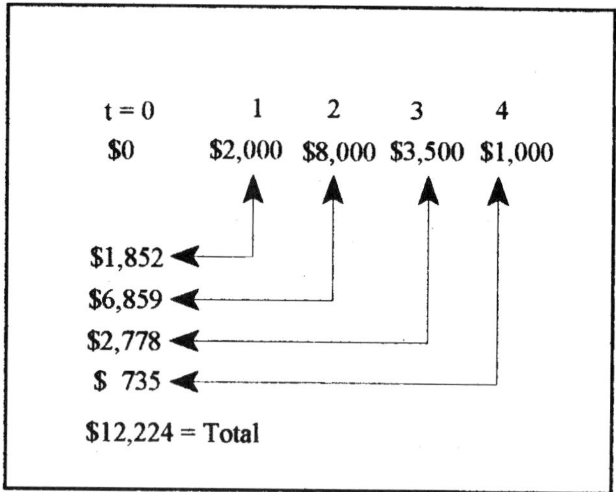

> **Calculator Tip:** You can also compute this result using the CF and NPV keys of your TI BA-II. Check the manual.

> **Another Calculator Tip:** This is easy on a spreadsheet. It's a bit more of a nuisance on a calculator because you must punch in lots of parentheses and exponents, and it is easy to get the sequence wrong. You can minimize this problem if you punch the sequence in *backwards*. Thus in our previous example, we would punch in 1000 ÷ 1.08 + 3500 ÷ 1.08 + 8000 ÷ 1.08 + 2,000 ÷ 1.08 = (to get our answer). Note that we include *no* exponents and *no* parentheses. We can dispense with parentheses because the sequence does not require them. We can dispense with exponents because we are achieving the same effect by the ordering of our entries. This process is called *backwards chaining.*

In the same way, we can define the *future* value of a series of accumulations. Your client, Clement, wants to save some money to endow a scholarship. He intends to invest the money according to the same schedule as in the clamdigger example, above. But he will value the fund at the time of the last deposit, i.e., at t = 4. How much will he have? As before, we take each payment and apply the appropriate factor, then sum the results. The main difference is that this time, we use FFs instead of DFs. Here is a summary:

$$(\$2{,}000)(1.08)^3 + (\$8{,}000)(1.08)^2 + (\$3{,}500)(1.08)^1 + (\$1{,}000)(1.08)^0 = \$16{,}631$$

Note that $x^0 = 1$, so $(\$1{,}000)(1.08)^0 = \$1{,}000$.[1]

We can summarize the results in a table:

Year	**CF**	**× FF Formula**	**FF**	**CF×FF**
1	\$2,000	$(1.08)^3$	1.26	\$ 2,519
2	\$8,000	$(1.08)^2$	1.166	\$ 9,331
3	\$3,500	$(1.08)^1$	1.08	\$ 3,780
4	\$1,000	$(1.08)^0$	1	\$ 1,000
Total				\$16,631

You can see the same result graphically in the chart below. Take each of the numbers on the horizontal axis and *multiply* by $(1.08)^n$. You get the column of numbers on the right, which total \$16,631. So we get the PV or the FV by summing the components.

[1] The careful reader will think the example perverse: why value an investment where the last contribution is made on the same day that you value the total? The answer is that this particular timing will prove convenient for analysis later. But we will investigate some other timing patterns as well.

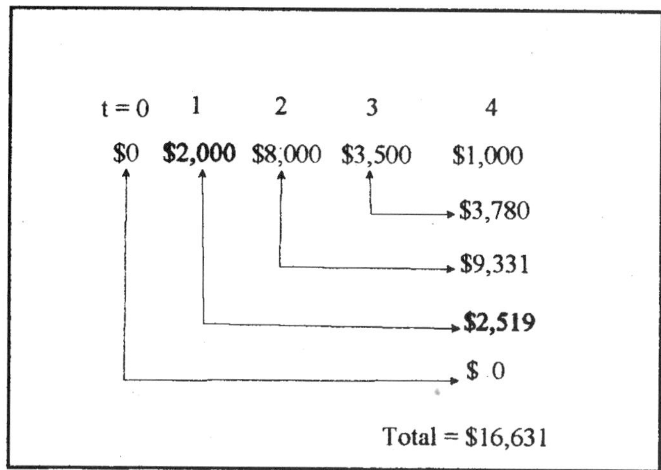

§ 3.04 A Small Simplification

The strategy of summing the components is straightforward but inelegant. Inevitably, we look for simplifications. For the example set forth above (where the payments are unequal), there is indeed one simplification. That is: if you know *either* the PV or the FV in the above example, you can compute *the other* directly. To do so, you multiply by the appropriate factor. That is:

$$(PV)(FF) = FV$$

and

$$(FV)(DF) = PV$$

Using our data,

$$\$12{,}224(1.08)^4 = \$16{,}631$$

and

$$\$16{,}630(1.08)^{(-4)} = \$12{,}224$$

The point is that once you know either the PV or the FV, you don't need to know the individual components that comprise it. You can go directly from present to future (and *vice versa*) without stopping at the way stations.

§ 3.05 A More Important Simplification

For cases like our previous example (where the payments are unequal), this is about as simple as you can get. Where the payments are *equal*, there is a far more important simplification at hand.

We do it by steps. As a working example, consider the earlier case where Clarence intended to put away money at t = 1 through t = 4, and then to value it at t = 4. Earlier, Clarence was making unequal deposits. This time, assume he is depositing the same sum in each period. The formula is:

$$FV = C(1 + r)^3 + C(1 + r)^2 + C(1 + r)^1 + C(1 + r)^0$$

Since C is a constant, we can factor it out:

$$FV = C[(1+r)^3 + (1+r)^2 + (1+r)^1 + (1+r)^0]$$

For example, suppose C = $10 and r = 8 percent. Then our series is:

$$FV = \$10\ [1.26 + 1.17 + 1.08 + 1] = \$45.06$$

This is already easier than the computation for unequal payments, but we can do much better.

§ 3.06 Geometric Series

Take another look at the series of factors ($(1 + r)^n$, etc.) The series is a *geometric series.* A geometric series is one in which the ratio between any two terms is the same. Here, as you move west, each term is (previous term)(1 + *r*). Or, as you go east, each term is (previous term) ÷ (1 + *r*). If you remember this as a geometric series, you may remember the standard device for simplifying a geometric series. For convenience, let us denote (1 + *r*) simply as "x." Then we rewrite and reorder our series as follows:

$$1 + x + x^2 + x^3$$

Now comes the tricky part. First, we *multiply* the series by (x − 1):

$$(x - 1)(1 + x + x^2 + x^3)$$

Distributing the (x − 1):

$$x + x^2 + x^3 + x^4 - 1 - x - x^2 - x^3$$

Then simplify by canceling. You can quickly determine that this series simplifies to:

$$x^4 - 1$$

Of course, this is not "our" series. It is "our" series *times* (x − 1). So, get rid of the (x − 1) by dividing it out:

$$\frac{x^4 - 1}{x - 1}$$

For example, using 8 percent as before:

$$\frac{(1.08)^4 - 1}{1.08 - 1}$$

Of course, the "ones" in the denominator cancel each other by subtraction:

$$\frac{(1.08)^4 - 1}{.08}$$

$$(1.36 - 1) \div (0.08) = 4.506$$

Let us abstract this reasoning just a bit further. Note that in the series above, we had *four* terms, but we only counted *three* exponents — so, we can generalize the original formulation and rewrite our series as:

$$1 + x + x^2 + \ldots + x^{n-1}$$

Then we want to *multiply* the series by (x − 1):

$$(x - 1)(1 + x + x^2 + \ldots + x^{n-1})$$

Distribute:

$$x + x^2 + x^3 + \ldots + x^n - 1 - x - x^2 - \ldots - x^{n-1}$$

Simplify:

$$x^n - 1$$

Divide by $(x-1)$:

$$\frac{x^n - 1}{x - 1}$$

In other words, if *n* denotes the number of terms in the series, although we start with $(n-1)$ exponents, we end up with *n* in our resulting simplification.

Now, reinstall the $1 + r$:

$$\frac{(1+r)^n - 1}{(1+r) - 1}$$

Future Value Annuity Formula: Note that the ones in the denominator cancel out. This gives us the formula for a future value annuity factor (FVAF) factor:

$$\text{FVAF} = \frac{(1 + r)^n - 1}{r}$$

Multiply this factor by your payment (C), and you have the future value of a stream of equal payments.

> **Calculator Tip:** The FVAF is easy to punch in on a standard calculator. Suppose your rate is 6 percent and your term is seven years. Key in: $1.06^7 - 1$ (note that you do not have to put the 1.06 in parentheses). Then punch the divide sign. Then key in .06, and hit "equals."

§ 3.07 Present Value Annuity Factor

The next step is to use the FVAF to compute a present value annuity factor (PVAF). We already know how to transform a future value to a present value: we *multiply* by the DF, $[1 \div (1 + r)^n]$:

$$\frac{(1 + r)^n - 1}{r} \times \frac{1}{(1 + r)^n}$$

So if we multiply the FVAF by the DF, the result must be the PVAF. Following our earlier example, we know that the four-year FVAF for 8 percent is 4.506. It is easy to determine that the four-year DF for 8 percent is 0.735. So the PVAF must be $(4.506)(0.735) = 3.312$.

Mind the Gap: Be careful to understand just what this factor tells you. It tells you the value *as of t=0* of a stream of payments that *begins at t=1* and continues to t=n. Many students trip over this one-period gap, so keep alert to avoid it (to value a series of payments *beginning at* $t=0$, see § 3.09 below).

There are many ways of arranging and simplifying this formula. We offer the following because we think it is the easiest to use with a standard business calculator:

$$\frac{(1+r)^n - 1}{(r)(1+r)^n}$$

Here is an example. Suppose you will receive nine equal payments of $800 each, where the discount rate is 7 percent. What is the present value? To find the answer, you set up the formula for the PVAF:

$$\frac{(1.07)^9 - 1}{(1.07)^9(.07)}$$

Then multiply by C, which is $800. The answer is $5,212.

> **Calculator Tip:** Follow these steps to make it easy on the calculator. Suppose your rate is 12 percent and your term is nine years. Punch in the FVAF formula as set forth above. Next, punch the divide key. Then punch open parentheses; then 1.12^9, close parentheses, then "equals."

§ 3.08 Deriving the Payment

We have seen how to derive the present value of an annuity when we know the rate, the number of payments, and the size of each payment. In summary, we defined a present value annuity factor (AF). We multiplied it by the individual payment (C). So:

$$(AF)(C) = PV$$

This a simple three-term equation: we have two "knowns," and must solve for the "unknown." On this analysis, if (AF)(C) = PV, then PV ÷ AF = C. So, if you *know* the annuity factor and the present value, you can *derive* the individual payment:

$$PV \div AF = C$$

For example, suppose someone offers to give you a lump sum of $50,000, with instructions to invest the money at 8 percent, and disperse the annuity payments in such a way that there will be nothing left after 10 years. How much should each payment be? The present value is given, and under the analysis above, we can determine the AF to be 6.71. So, the payment (C), is $7,452.

§ 3.09 Annuity Paid

Recall our definition of an annuity: (a) a finite series of (b) n equal payments, payable (c) at the *end* of each period from $t=1$ to $t=n$. We learned how to figure the future value of this annuity at $t=n$. Then we computed the present value of this future value, by applying a present value discount factor.

In both of these cases, we assumed that the first payment would be made at t=1, i.e., one time period from today. But what if the first payment was to be made *today*? That is, what if we have the same *number* of payments, but with payments that are made at the *beginning* of each period, rather than the end? This is a common enough payment stream. For example, many *leases* of real or personal property require an equal series of payments beginning at t=0. The jargon label for such a payment stream is an *annuity paid.*

Since we know how to value an ordinary annuity, it is surprisingly easy to value an annuity paid. We simply figure the value of an annuity that is one period *shorter* than the annuity paid. We then add the face value of one coupon. For example, suppose we want to determine the present value of an annuity paid of $900 for 10 years at 8 percent. First, we determine the present value of an ordinary annuity of $900 for *nine* years at 8 percent (the product is $5,622). Second, we add $900, giving us a total of $6,522. Note, we could have reached the same result by taking the value of the 10-year ordinary annuity and multiplying by $(1 + r)$.

§ 3.10 Deferred Annuity

Suppose you will receive a stream of payments for seven years, but that the first payment will be *deferred* from t=1 to t=4 — call it a *deferred annuity.* How do we specify the *present* value of this deferred annuity that begins at t=4? To answer this question, recall our procedure for getting the PV of an ordinary annuity. Our PV expressed the value *at t=0* of a series that begins *at t=1.* Apply the same logic to the deferred annuity. We can see that our calculation gives the value *at t=3* of a series of payments that begins *at t=4.*

But how do we get the PV of a value expressed as of t=3? The answer is that we apply an ordinary discount factor.

So in our example, suppose an interest rate of 8 percent. The AF for seven years at 6 percent is 5.206. This is the factor value as of t=0 for a series that begins at t=1. It is also the factor at t=3 for a series that begins at t=4. To reduce this factor from t=3 to t=0, multiply by the discount factor for three years at 6 percent. The discount factor is 0.794. So the PVAF is 4.133.

Avoid this Common Mistake: When the payment stream starts at t=4, beginning students will be tempted to discount using a factor of $(1 + r)^4$. This is wrong. When you value an ordinary annuity that starts at t=4, you get a value *as of* t=3. So, you discount using $(1 + r)^3$. Generalizing, when you take the PV of an ordinary annuity beginning at time = t, you discount from time = (t − 1).

§ 3.11 Note on Tables

In your parents' day, if you wanted to do complicated financial computations, you went down to the stationery store and bought a "ready reckoner." A ready reckoner was a booklet with page after page of numbers showing you the results of all sorts of computations. In the same pattern, standard finance books have always included "ready reckoner" style tables for computing present and future values.

In the age of computers and calculators, they are an anachronism. There is nothing you can do with a ready reckoner table of present values that you cannot do more quickly and efficiently with a cheap pocket calculator. If you do not have one yet, this is one more inducement to do so. (We do retain the tables later, however, when we come to option pricing; the math is more sophisticated, and the calculators are not so likely to fit the bill.)

§ 3.12 Paula Again

Recall Paula (§ 3.02 above). Can you help Paula? Possibly. For the moment, assume that 40 percent is a lawful contingent fee in Paula and Larson's jurisdiction. Larson took $37,559. For Larson to be within his rights, this $37,559 must be not more than 40 percent of the total award. So the total award must would have to be at least $37,559 ÷ (0.40) = $93,897. By corollary, Paula's share must be at least 60 percent of the total award. That would be $93,895 × (0.60) = $56,338.

This means that the discounted present value (DPV) of the two deferred payments must equal not less than $56,338. To get the DPV, we need an interest rate. For illustration, take a discount rate of 20 percent. In order to figure the DPV, we need to discount the first payment by $(1 + r)^5$, and the second, by $(1 + r)^{10}$. What do you get? It appears that Larson is within his rights — even though Paula gets not a penny at $t=0$.

Of course, we don't have enough information to know whether 20 percent is a "correct" rate. In order to know the "correct" rate, we would have to know the opportunity cost of capital — the rate for comparable investments. Just off hand, a 20 percent rate seems high. But in determining what is a "comparable" investment, we would have to consider the riskiness of the loan, e.g., whether the obligor is likely to meet his obligations to pay. We would also have to cope with the problem of information: you can find out just about anything you need to know about a grade A corporate bond, but you may not be able to get the relevant information about an individual obligor. So even though a 20 percent rate might seem high, both these factors may argue in its favor. On the other hand, note that the lower the rate, the more defensible is Larson's position. Do you understand why?

Chapter 4

Regulation and Disclosure

With Usura
Hath No Man a House of Good Stone

—Ezra Pound[1]

§ 4.01 Introduction

Probably governments have always claimed the power to regulate the price of money. In our society, as recently as a generation ago, regulation of the price of money was still a high-visibility topic. Lately it has receded in importance. There are probably a number of reasons, several of which we suggest below. Still, even though the topic may have receded in importance, we need to pay some attention to price regulation here now.

In this chapter we explore two topics: one, price *caps* — "usury laws" — that seek to impose an absolute limit on how much one can charge for the use of money; and two *disclosure rules*, that seek merely to assure that the borrower understands what it is she is paying.

§ 4.02 Regulating the Price of Money

Regulate the price of apartments and you call it rent control. Regulate the price of goods and you call it price control. Regulate the price of money and you call it history and you find yourself embroiled in a conflict over a way of life. After all, to the Medieval mind, usury was not just an infraction; it was a sin. You could say that the regulation of usury is the first regulation of a market economy. Or you could say — perhaps with more accuracy — that usury regulation precedes the market economy and persists as a criticism of the very idea of a market.

For "usury," as anathematized by the Pope in the Middle Ages, was not just to charge *too much* interest — usury was the taking of interest *per se*. Charging *any* interest was a foul misdeed, something a good Christian didn't do.

For most of us, it is hard even to imagine a world without interest. We wouldn't know how we could run a market economy without it. We pay (and take) interest every day, and the Vatican itself runs an investment portfolio.

As the modern economy came into being, the meaning of "usury" evolved as well. In time the animus came to fall not on interest *per se*, but on the taking of *too much* interest. But even as they abandoned the outright prohibition on interest, virtually every jurisdiction retained an elaborate system of rules limiting the price of money — controlling "usury," broadly defined.

---

[1] Canto XLV.

For economists, even these restrictions on the price of money have a bad odor. We all learn in Econ 1A (as if we didn't know it already) that a market runs on prices. Prices allocate resources (we are taught) and the price of money is an allocation tool just like any other. Money is the most fluid of commodities (according to this view) and the money market the most competitive of markets. Sovereign intervention is at best a waste of effort; at worst, it works to undermine the very purpose it hopes to serve.

This argument probably carries the day, at least the present day. Outright restrictions on the price of money seem to be in decline. The recent case law on usury is thin. But it is at best an easy triumph. America was built on a deep-seated suspicion of bankers and money men, and old habits die hard. For a politician to talk about abolishing all restrictions on the money market is like threatening to abolish Mother's Day. A couple of clicks on your web browser will carry you to a dozen Web sites detailing the (alleged?) crimes of the money market and the evils of — well, the evils of usury.

This tension may help to explain the sometimes mind-numbing complexity of our usury law. Usury is, after all, at least in part a crime among consenting adults. Any law is bound to be equivocal if it blocks a deal that both parties want to do. No surprise then that we maintain a law of usury, but a law riddled with exceptions and evasions.

California will serve as a good example. California prohibits usury in its Constitution (Article XV). Read it hastily and you might think the limitation was 7 percent. Nothing of the sort: the true limit is an "index" rate, set at 5 percent over the rate at the San Francisco Federal Reserve Bank—which is to say, high enough that you wonder why anybody bothers.

For "consumer" transactions, the California Constitution sets the rate at 10 percent. But this, too, is a deception. For one thing, the Constitution maintains a list of exceptions sufficient to protect almost anyone from whom you might be tempted to borrow.

Web site: For more on consumer loan rates, see http://www.bankrate.com/brm/default.asp.

§ 4.03 Time-Price

Overriding all these constitutional rules is another exception, in many ways the most interesting of all. This is the judge-made rule, recognized in virtually every state, called "the time-price doctrine." The rule first appears in *Hogg v. Ruffner*,[2] one of those largely forgotten Supreme Court commercial cases that have done so much to shape the face of our law.

Here is a time-price example: Crawford, the owner of Blackacre, says to Devon, "I will sell you Blackacre for $100 if you pay me today, or $110 if you promise to pay me next year." Devon says, "I accept and promise to pay you next year." A statute provides that any loan at a rate greater than 7 percent is usurious. Devon asserts that Crawford has made a usurious loan. He points to the undoubted fact that the "time-price" of $110 is 10 percent above the "cash price" of $100, and that the difference must be usurious interest.

[2] 66 U.S. 115 (1861).

Surely this argument has a surface appeal. The dollar doesn't know who owns it, and if Devon had borrowed the purchase price from a bank at the same terms, nobody would doubt that an interest rate regulation might apply.

Not so, said the Court in *Hogg*. The Court reasoned that the deal was a sale, not a loan, and that the seller had a perfect right to charge a different price for a "time sale" than he would for a "cash sale," without violating the usury laws.

The best you can say about this distinction without a difference is that it is a rule only a lawyer can love. But it is heaven-sent relief to a system that can't get along without usury laws, but can't get along with them: it sidesteps the problem abolishing usury law by defining away the question. Indeed, California carries the complication one step further. Having defined sales transactions out of the usury category, the state has adopted an elaborate batch of statutory law limiting the rate on time-price sales![3] It is likely that not one in a thousand regulated sellers (or buyers) has any idea of the arcane underpinnings of their deal.[4]

§ 4.04 Imputed Interest and Taxes

One person who is not so easily deceived about time value is the tax collector. Consider Selma, the owner of Greenacre, a parcel of real estate in the sovereign nation of Magenta, which has tax laws like our own, only simpler. She offers to sell Greenacre to Blanche for $480,000 in installments of $120,000 each over four years.

Interrupted while she is counting the money from her first installment payment, Selma answers the door and finds Tad, the tax collector. Tad tells her that a stream of four $120,000 payments looks to him like an annuity, which he proposes to analyze at the Magenta statutory rate of 10 percent. This implies a present value of $380,000. Since interest is taxable income in Magenta, he invites her to pay over tax on 10 percent of $380,384. He assures her he will be back three more times to collect more taxes as Blanche makes more payments. The amortization table looks like this:

[3] Unruh Act, Cal. Civ. Code § 1801 et seq.; (consumer goods); Rees-Levering Act, Cal. Civ. Code §§ 2981-2984.4 (auto finance).

[4] That the time-price is alive and well. *See* Walker v. Fingerhut Corp., No. C5-99-881, 2000 WL 136096 at *4 (Ct. App. Minn. Jan. 28, 2000).

t=	Balance Due	Payment	Imputed Interest	Balance to Principal	Remaining Balance
1	$380,384	$120,000	$38,038	$81,962	$298,422
2	$298,422	$120,000	$29,842	$90,158	$208,264
3	$208,264	$120,000	$20,826	$99,174	$109,091
4	$109,091	$120,000	$10,909	$109,091	$0

It happens that Blanche as a buyer may *deduct* interest paid from her taxable income in Magenta on the same terms. So the practical consequence is that the transaction, analyzed after taxes, is a good deal sweeter for Blanche, and less sweet for Selma, than you would have guessed without considering the tax effect. If Blanche and Selma intended it this way, of course, it is their business and we can have no complaint. But if Selma's lawyer let her get into this deal without thinking through the tax consequences, then he has cost her a lot of money.[5]

§ 4.05 Other Evasions

Given the fact of the money market, it is hardly surprising that the world has invented a whole variety of devices to sidestep the usury laws. We have already seen the most successful: the time-price doctrine of *Hogg v. Ruffner*, discussed above. Here are a few more.

Discounting: Early lenders discovered they could eke a little extra money out from under the usury law by *discounting* the interest. The term has a different meaning from what it means elsewhere in this book. Here is an example: the usury law of Magenta sets a limit of 6 percent. Boris wants to borrow $100 for one year. Lena says, "I will lend it to you at a 6 percent discount." Translated, this means that Linda takes 6 percent of $100 (that would be $6) and withholds it from the original loan. Obviously the effective rate here is $(6 \div 94) - 1 = 0.0638 = 6.38$ percent, but in many cases it seems to have worked.

Add-On: Retailers used to compute interest on consumer installment transactions as an addition to the original purchase price, regardless of the

[5] My friend Dan, a specialist in the tax laws of the United States, says Magenta law looks familiar to him. Of U.S. law, he comments:

Depending on the property and the amounts involved, there are two regimes that may apply. First, Internal Revenue Code Section 1274 treats payments as "original issue discount" where stated interest is less than the so-called "applicable federal rate" (a blended interest rate based on T-bills). OID is includible and deductible on economic accrual principles. In the case of a sale of a farm by an individual, the sale of a small business for less than $1 million, the sale of a principal residence, any sale of property if the total amount is less than $250,000, and certain sales of patents where the price is contingent on income from the patent, the interest element is calculated under § 483. The difference is that the interest portion is includible (or includable—the Internal Revenue Code uses both spellings) and deductible only when payments are made.

installments. Consider Carla, who wants to buy a new car for $20,000. For time payments, the dealer quotes a "10-percent add-on," bringing the total price to $22,000. The math is accurate. But if you pay off the $22,000 in equal installments over a year, your effective rate is 19.53 percent. Note that "add-on" as presented omits a vital term — the number of periods. If you are paying over two years, the effective rate is only 9.73 percent. Quoting rates as an "add-on" might have been excusable in the pre-calculator age, but there is no justification for it now. In fact, add-on is for all practical purposes outlawed as a means of disclosure under the Truth-in-Lending Act (see §4.06 below) and it seems to have fallen into abeyance.

Sale-and-Resale: Conceptually perhaps the most interesting evasion is the "sale-and-resale" device, whereby Lena will "buy" property from Boris and agree to "resell" it on defined terms. Sale-and-resale has a long, if not always honorable, history: lenders and borrowers sometimes use it to evade not just the usury laws but other rules that may constrain transactions, such as the rules governing mortgage foreclosure. Consider your client Whitman, owner of Whiteacre, and badly in need of a $200,000 loan. He agrees to "sell" Whiteacre to Melody for $200,000 cash today. The contract recites that he may "repurchase" Whiteacre if he pays $1,250 per month for 30 years.

Virtually any but the most obtuse court would recognize as the functional equivalent of a loan of $200,000, with Whiteacre serving as security (the effective interest rate is 6.58 percent). There is an abundance of precedent declaring that the substance should triumph over the form and that the court should recharacterize the transaction as subject to the laws governing usury or mortgages as the facts may dictate.[6]

For more on form and substance in finance transactions, see § 9.03 below.

§ 4.06 Disclosure: Truth-in-Lending

Aside from the decline of usury law, the most notable recent development in government control of the money market has been a great shift of focus. That is, we have moved from a focus on regulating the *price* of money to regulating *disclosure of its terms*.

The pivotal point here is the Consumer Credit Protection Act, more commonly known as the "Truth-in-Lending Act,"[7] adopted by Congress in 1969. Accepting the basic "market" premises, Truth-in-Lending makes no pretense to regulate the price of money. Rather, it mandates disclosure. It is the source of most of the boilerplate in your standard form installment contract, including the ubiquitous "Annual Percentage Rate" (APR), the (somewhat stylized) index of the price you pay for consumer credit.[8]

Back in the 1970s, there was a great flurry of litigation over the disclosure terms in consumer form contracts under Truth-in-Lending. There is less today.

---

[6] Don't overlook an important basic premise here. If the assertion in the text is true, then it must be that the law of usury (or mortgages) is *non-waivable* and that a contract seeming to sidestep the protections of these rules will not be enforced.

[7] 15 U.S.C. § 1673.

[8] Truth-in-Lending speaks not of "interest," but rather of a "finance charge." The distinction is the result of a largely forgotten political compromise that need not detain us here.

This is partly due to the fact that Congress and the courts together tightened up on the remedies, reducing the incentive to sue. Perhaps equally important, boilerplate disclosure has become bureaucratized, and most of the crude violations have been polished away.

§ 4.07 "Hidden Interest" and Regulation

Some of the issues in the regulation of money go beyond prudence and propriety to feasibility — how do you make the system work?

Take a simple example. Leander transfers Greenacre to Berowne under a contract which provides that Berowne will pay $1,000 at the end of each month for 12 months. Just about everyone would agree that some portion of the monthly payment must be directed at providing compensation for lost use of money. But how much? We have four variables at work here: C, PV, n and r. On familiar principles, if we know any three of the four, we ought to be able to derive the fourth. But here we know only two: C = $1,000 a month and $n = 12$. As to the other two, the range of possibilities is literally infinite.

To take just one example: if $r = 1$ percent a month, then the PV is $11,255. But if $r = 2$ percent a month, then PV = $10,575. On the face of the problem, there is simply no way of knowing which of these two (or indeed, any other possible combination) might be correct.

You may say, to solve this problem, we need to look behind the face of the deal and determine the "real" terms that underlie it. But this is easier said than done. Consider a fascinating case that reached the California Supreme Court. Jack La Lanne was the Richard Simmons of his generation — a health guru, with his own chain of "health spas." You could buy a membership in La Lanne-Paris Health Spa for $408, payable in cash or in 24 monthly payments of $17 each. Linda Glaire signed a contract with La Lanne and elected to pay over time, but then she sued, alleging violations of Truth-in-Lending and California usury law.

According to the evidence, La Lanne regularly assigned its contracts to Universal, a finance company. For Glaire's contract, La Lanne got $255. Glaire argued that the difference ($408 − $255) was interest and should have been disclosed as such.

On appeal, the California Supreme Court essentially bought it. At least for purposes for Truth-in-Lending, the court held that Universal was the true "creditor," and that it should have made disclosure based on what it paid for the paper.[9]

The court based its finding on the fact of a close relationship between Universal and La Lanne. Just a few years later, on facts perhaps less appealing (and over a vigorous dissent from the judge who wrote *Glaire*), the court backed away from *Glaire*, and it has not been a major factor in money market regulation since.[10]

One can sympathize with the court not wanting to get into the rat's nest of the individual deal. Yet in an important sense, the court may have had it

[9] Glaire v. La Lanne-Paris Health Spa, Inc., 117 Cal. Rptr. 541 (1974).

[10] Boerner v. Colwell Co., 145 Cal. Rptr. 380 (1978).

right the first time. The fact is that virtually every seller farms out his commercial paper within a nanosecond after the deal is finished. From the face of the consumer contract, there is simply no way to guess whether the secondary market transfer price will be the same as the original "cash price."[11] Yet this secondary market price is probably a far more accurate guide than the contract price as to the real cost of money.

Aside from characterizing the discount at 37.5 percent (which was correct as far as it went), the court made no effort to specify the real cost of money. As an exercise, the reader is invited to check it on her own (note that n = 24 and C = $17 and use $255 as PV).

§ 4.08 Applications: Installment Sales, Etc.

> This here is a stucco house
> and you are the stuckee.
>
> —George Stephens

It is easy to find familiar applications of the common annuity formula. Here is one dramatic example. Your client, Chloe just won the New Gonzo 28-state lottery with a prize of $100 million. Reading the fine print, you determine that this means $4 million a year for 25 years.[12] As an alternative, the lottery will pay her $48.79 million right now. Chloe's investment adviser, who is a careful and reliable guy, figures he can invest all her winnings so as to give a return of 7 percent per year over the same period. Should she take it?

She should take it. Invest $48.79 million now for a 7 percent return over 25 years and you get an annual payout of some $4.19 million, better than the return offered by the lottery (recall: (C)(PVAF) = PV).[13]

The same sort of analysis works to explain the typical home mortgage loan. Your client, Clemson, has found a new home that he can buy for $300,000, with a 10 percent down payment, the balance payable monthly over 30 years (= 360 months). The nominal interest rate is 9 percent a year, which translates into 3 ÷ 4 of a percent each month.[14] Setting aside the matter of the down payment, we can understand Clemson's loan as 360-month annuity at 3 ÷ 4 of a percent a month, with a present value of $270,000 (= $300,000 − $30,000). The monthly payment will be $2,172.48. By how much will his payment drop if the rate falls to 8 percent a year?

You can use the same technique to understand a retirement account. Your client, Rita, is getting ready to retire. She figures she will need $3,000 a month as living expenses, and that she will live for 20 years. Her investment adviser tells her she can get 8 percent a year. We can understand her retirement need

---

[11] For perspective, note that in the corporate bond market, we report interest rates every moment based on the trade price in the secondary market. For more on the bond market, see Chapter 6 below.

[12] For simplicity, we are computing the value of a simple annuity, where the first payment is made at t = 1, though the PV is established as of t = 0. As an exercise, you may wish to recompute using the assumption that the first payment is made at t = 0 and the PV is also established at t = 0.

[13] The lottery's payout is predicated on a return of 6.5 percent We will say more on how to derive the interest rate in Chapter 6 below.

[14] What is the effective annual rate?

as an annuity of $3,000 a month over 20 years at 8 percent a year. How much of a retirement fund will she need to achieve her objective?[15]

§ 4.09 Amortization

Daniel borrows $10,000 from Carla to build a new pizza oven for his cabin, payable in equal monthly installments over a year at an effective annual rate of 12.68 percent. His payment will be $888.49 per month, which means that the total of payments is [(12)($888.49)] or $10,661.88. At the end of one month, Carla receives a check for $888.49. Her ledger shows two accounts, one labeled "interest" and one labeled "reduction in principal." To which should she credit the payment? Here are four possibilities:

First, she might credit *all to principal* and none to interest. This method would leave a balance due of ($10,000 − $888.49) = $9111.51.

Second, she could credit *all to interest* and credit principal only after interest is paid. That would mean applying $661.88 to interest, discharging the entire interest bill, and then applying the surplus ($226.61) to principal, leaving a balance due of $9,773.39.

A third possibility is that she could *prorate* the $661.88 over the 12 payments, applying $55.16 of each payment to interest and the balance ($833.33) to principal. After the first payment, this method would leave a balance due of $9,166.67.

A fourth possibility rejects all of these. Rather, it proceeds as follows: at the end of one month, it computes the interest *for one month*. We do this by figuring the *monthly* rate, which in this case is $[(1.1268)^{1/12} - 1] = 0.01$, or 1 percent. Then, we assess interest on the unpaid balance at the monthly rate (in our case, 1 percent of $10,000 = $100), applying the payment first to interest, and then applying the balance (in our case, $788.49) to principal (reducing the principal balance to $9,211.51).

Follow the same formula in successive months, and note that with each passing month, the principal balance is lower, the sum allocated to interest is smaller, and the sum allocated to the principal is larger. The following table shows "loan amortization" under this formula for the entire loan.

[15] We note one important complication: Rita's estimate of her lifespan is only a guess. If she dies in less than 20 years, she may leave an estate; if she lives longer she may outlive her money. Of course she may find someone who will be willing (for a fee) to take the risk off her hands: for example, a commercial annuity promising to pay $3,000 a month, no matter how long she lives. For more on turning uncertainty into certainty, see Part II below.

Amortization Table — United States (Actuarial) Rule				
t =	**Remaining Balance**	**Payment**	**Finance Charge at 1% / Month**	**Reduction in Principal**
1	$ 10,000	$ 888.49	$ 100.00	$ 788.49
2	$ 9,211.51	$ 888.49	$ 92.12	$ 796.37
3	$ 8,415.14	$ 888.49	$ 84.15	$804.34
4	$ 7,610.10	$ 888.49	$ 76.11	$ 812.38
5	$6,978.42	$ 888.49	$ 67.98	$ 820.50
6	$ 5,977.92	$ 888.49	$ 59.78	$ 828.71
7	$5,149.21	$ 888.49	$ 51.49	$ 837.00
8	$ 4,312.21	$ 888.49	$ 43.12	$ 845.37
9	$ 3,466.85	$ 888.49	$ 34.67	$ 853.82
10	$ 2,613.03	$ 888.49	$ 26.13	$ 862.36
11	$1,750.67	$ 888.49	$ 17.51	$ 870.98
12	$ 879.69	$ 888.49	$ 8.80	$ 879.69

This last method seems to make economic sense, because it is the only one that relates interest to the principal obligation outstanding. Perhaps not surprisingly, it also has widespread blessing of the courts. Many opinions hold that in the absence of agreement to the contrary, interest will be allocated as in the last example. This so-called "United States rule" (sometimes called the "actuarial rule") derives from a brief passage in an otherwise interminable and impenetrable Supreme Court opinion issued over 150 years ago:

> The correct rule in general is, that the creditor shall calculate interest whenever a payment is made. To this interest, the payment is first to be applied; and if it exceed the interest due, the balance is to be applied to diminish the principal. If the payment fall short of the interest, the balance of interest is not to be added to the principal so as to produce interest.[16]

[16] Wayne, J., Story v. Livingston, 38 U.S. 359 (1839).

Calculator Note: Your TI BA II PLUS gives you equipment to figure amortization payments of principal and income under the "United States rule." You start by computing a PV, using the keys on row three. Then you can amortize individual payments by pressing 2d Amort — see your manual for details.

Rule of 78s: The United States rule is another one of those computations that is not onerous with a calculator, but would have been virtually impossible in the pre-calculator age. Therefore, it is not surprising that courts and legislatures developed an alternative scheme that offered a close approximation, but that was computationally easier. This method is called the *sum of the digits* method, or perhaps more often, simply the "rule of 78s."

Here is how it works. Add up the digits in the loan period. For a one-year period, the sum is 12 + 11 + 10 + . . . + 1 = 78. Make a fraction, where the numerator is the number of the last loan payment, and the denominator is the sum of the digits—in our case, 12 ÷ 78. Multiply this number by the total amount of interest due.

In our deal, the total of payments is $10,661.65, so the total interest due must be $661.65. We multiply 12 ÷ 78 by $661.65 and get $101.82. We subtract $101.82 from $888.49 and get $786.66. We reduce principal by $786.66. The balance remaining due is $9,213.34. Next month, repeat the same exercise, except this time, reduce the numerator by one. So in our example, our new equation would be 11 ÷ 78. Here is a table showing the amortization of Daniel's $10,000 loan under the rule of 78s:

Amortization Table — Rule of 78s				
t =	Remaining Balance	Payment	Finance Charge at 1% / Month	Reduction in Principal
1	$ 10,000	$ 888.49	$ 101.82	$ 786.66
2	$ 9,213.54	$ 888.49	$ 93.34	$ 795.15
3	$ 8,418.19	$ 888.49	$ 84.85	$803.63
4	$ 7,614.55	$ 888.49	$ 76.37	$ 812.12
5	$6,802.43	$ 888.49	$ 67.88	$ 820.61
6	$ 5,981.83	$ 888.49	$ 59.40	$ 829.09
7	$5,152.74	$ 888.49	$ 50.91	$ 837.58
8	$ 4,315.16	$ 888.49	$ 42.43	$ 846.06
9	$ 3,469.10	$ 888.49	$ 33.94	$ 854.55
10	$ 2,614.55	$ 888.49	$ 25.46	$ 863.03
11	$1,751.52	$ 888.49	$ 16.97	$ 871.52
12	$ 880.00	$ 888.49	$ 8.49	$ 880.00

You might think that the rule of 78s would have passed into history in the age of the calculator, and that the actuarial method would hold the floor. In fact, neither of these is the case. Many statutes continue to call for the rule of 78s, and many courts continue to apply it.

Meanwhile, a number of courts refuse to apply any rule that appears to "front-load the interest." Courts with this attitude tend to favor some sort of proration, such as one third of the interest for one third of the term.[17]

Other cases simply don't know what to do with the problem at all. A fascinating example is *Fox v. Grange*.[18] Nellie Fox bought a parcel of real estate from L. H. Grange, on a promise to pay $1,100 with interest on installments at 6 percent. She paid $170 down and then, over the next six years, she made payments totaling $590. After a more or less interminable string of late payments, Grange tried to cancel the contract and throw her

[17] A representative example (with a good review of case law) is In re McMurray, 218 B.R. 867 (Bankr. E.D. Tenn., 1998), where the judge refused to allow the creditor to use the rule of 78s in making his claim in a Chapter 13 bankruptcy.

[18] 261 Ill. 116 (1913).

out. Her attorney tendered $538.27 and demanded full title. The court, holding that Grange had waived any complaint about late payments, granted her plea.

The court doesn't give a clue how the attorney came up with his payoff number. But consider this analysis: after the down payment, Fox owed $1,100 − $170 = $930. Her payments of $590 over six years pencil out to an average payment of $8.19 a month. Compute monthly interest at 1 ÷ 12 of 6 percent or one-half of 1 percent per month. Construct an annuity table according to the United States rule and you find that after six years (72 payments), she has paid $306.27 and still owes $628.78. If her attorney got her title for $538.27, it looks like he saved her $90.51 — surely more than enough to satisfy his fee.

§ 4.10 What Counts as a Finance Charge?

Carmen, an auto dealer, sells cars for cash or credit. If you buy on credit, she adds: (a) an investigation charge for checking your credit; (b) a "documentation charge" for preparing the paperwork; and (c) a charge for the rent of money. Pretty clearly, item (c) is the kind of charge the drafters had in mind when they wrote laws governing the regulation and disclosure of finance charges. But what of items (a) and (b)? Carmen has a strong incentive to characterize these as "not part of the finance charge" if it is lawful to do so. Hence it is not surprising that an arcane subspecialty has developed to help determine what is, and what is not, part of the finance charge.

§ 4.11 Nominal v. Effective Again

Earlier we discussed the mechanics of intra-period compounding. We made the point that in many circles it is conventional to *state* the rate as if it is compounded annually ("nominal") while *in fact* compounding more frequently.

Under Truth-in-Lending, this practice is expressly permitted. To recall how this works, consider a case where Daniel borrows $10,000 payable in one payment, together with finance charge, at the end of one year. The finance charge is 12 percent *nominal annual*, compounded *monthly*. As we saw earlier, the *effective* rate for this transaction is $[(1.01)^{12} - 1] = .1268$, or 12.68 percent. The debtor is bound to pay not $11,200, but $11,268.25.

To confirm that this is true, compute the finance charge at one percent a month and add it to the account. Note that it is equally true if the debtor pays the finance charge on the outstanding balance at $100 per month from $t = 1$ to $t = 12$, and also repays the $10,000 at $t = 12$. Assuming the creditor can reinvest the $100 payments at the same rate, the effect is to give him an annuity of twelve $100 payments whose $t = 12$ value = $1,268.25.

The reason for adopting such an anomalous rule is perhaps historical: back in the 1960s, without computer hardware, any other scheme might have been impossible to administer. Whatever its virtues in its time, that reason surely does not hold today. But the fact remains that we continue in a realm where the mandated scheme of disclosure systematically understates the cost of credit.

Calculator Tip: On the TI BA II plus, third line from the top, you see a row of keys that let you manipulate the terms of an annuity. We deferred mentioning it until now, because the calculator respects the APR convention explained above. That is, it returns its interest (finance charge) rate in "nominal" APR terms rather than quoting the (true?) effective rate. The calculator does provide a mechanism for converting nominal into effective rates: see the Iconv key, second tier, second row from the bottom. Consult your manual for details, and feel free to use the calculator as convenient. But note that except to derive the interest rate, you have all the equipment necessary to do the job by formula already.

Chapter 5

r

> The man who says that he has no illusions
> has at least that one.
>
> —Joseph Conrad

§ 5.01 Introduction

In our first exercise, we dealt with three terms: PV, FV and *r*. We saw that if you know any one of those terms, you could derive the other two. Next, we studied compounding, where we added a fourth term: *n*. We saw that you could still derive PV or FV or *r* if you knew the remaining terms. We also saw that (with the use of logarithms) you could derive *n*. All this holds true, at any rate, as long as we are dealing with *only one* FV. But in Chapter 3, we dealt with *multiple* FVs — in the form of an *annuity* or an *annuity paid*. Again we saw that we could derive knowns from unknowns.

Through it all, we have argued that the target should be "NPV," or "net present value," a discrete sum that will offset the "cash out" against the "cash in" for a project, all reduced to present values.

There is, of course, another possible point of comparison. For every project with a PV and an FV, there is at least in principle a *rate of return* that is "internal" to the deal, in the sense that it can be derived from it — call it the "internal rate of return" (IRR).

But here is a complication. To compute NPV we had to know an opportunity cost of capital (OCC), exterior to the project, to use as a benchmark. IRR does not require that we identify an OCC. Since every project has an IRR, why not save the effort of finding the OCC and simply use IRR?

There is certainly some merit to this view, and there are plenty of cases where IRR may be the best we can do. But IRR comes freighted with a load of hidden peril. For one thing, it's not as easy to compute as NPV, nor to manipulate once computed. And it harbors some tricks and traps that can at least embarrass you and, at worst, really screw up your analysis.

Against this background, in this chapter we will show you how to determine IRR, and also show you some of the difficulties that may make it less suitable than NPV.

§ 5.02 Computing *r* — the Root of a Polynomial

Consider the case of Irving, who has a chance to invest \$100 now (at t=0) and to receive \$150 at t=1 and another \$50 at t=2. What is the internal rate of return? To try to identify it, let's set it up in an equation:

$$\$100 = \$150 \frac{1}{1 + r} + \$50 \frac{1}{(1 + r)^2}$$

For $(1 \div (1 + r))$, substitute "x," and rearrange:

$$50x^2 + 150x - 100 = 0$$

You will recognize this as a *quadratic equation*. The general form is: $ax^2 + bx - c = 0$. In our case, we know a and b and c. We are looking for x. But since x appears in the equation as x^2, we need to use the quadratic solver. The equation is:

$$x = \frac{-b \pm \sqrt{b^2 - 4ac}}{2a}$$

Using the quadratic solver, we can solve this equation without too much trouble. But what if there had been a third payoff — say, $75 at t=3? Then our equation would have looked like this:

$$75x^3 + 50x^2 + 150x - 100 = 0$$

and the math would have been (shall we say) exponentially harder. We aren't going to get into the fancy math here. Rather, we are going to leave these problems to be solved (if at all) by the use of a calculator. Indeed, any standard financial calculator will give you a set of keys for deriving *r* in situations like the examples above.

Calculator Note: Check your manual for advice on computing IRR. For example, using the TI BA II +, you will be instructed to enter a series of cash flows. Then you punch CPT IRR. The calculator gives IRR.

Web site: For more on the internal rate of return, see http://hadm.sph.sc.edu/Courses/Econ/invest/invest.html.

§ 5.03 Multiple Solutions

Next, remember an important feature of a quadratic: it may not have a single solution. It may have one, but more likely it has two. Consider the case of Charlie, who undertakes to make automated lollipop holders. The projected cash flows are:

t=1 = (minus) $10
t=2 = (plus) $24
t=3 = (minus) $14.30

What is the IRR? If you ask your TI BA-II, you will be told that it is 10 percent. To double check, we compute:

$$-\frac{\$14.30}{(1.1)^3} + \frac{\$24}{(1.1)^2} - \frac{\$10}{1.1} = \$0$$

which checks. But now, compute the value using a rate of 30 percent. What do you get?

$$-\frac{\$14.30}{(1.3)^3}+\frac{\$24}{(1.3)^2}-\frac{\$10}{1.3}=\$0$$

So you have two IRRs, 10 percent and 30 percent. Your calculator didn't tell you about the second value. Evidently your calculator has undertaken to do your thinking for you, and to throw away the implausible result. But neither result here is completely implausible. Meanwhile, suppose you are selecting investment projects under a rule that says: accept all projects with a return greater than 12 percent, reject all others. You could either (a) accept or (b) reject this project, both pursuant to the same rule.

§ 5.04 Borrowing v. Lending

Next, consider the case of Ilana, who is about to invest $100 in a defenestrator mill. She figures she can get $120 at t=1. What is the IRR? We can state the problem as follows:

$$-\$100+\frac{\$120}{(1+r)}=0$$

Solving, it is easy to see that $r = 0.20 = 20$ percent. But now consider this equation:

$$\$100-\frac{\$120}{(1+r)}=0$$

Note that this is identical to the previous equation, except for the placement of the sign. There, we assumed we *invested* (negative) $100 and *collected* (positive) $120. Here we might assume that we *borrow* (positive) $100 and *repay* (negative) $120. Surely there is all the difference in the world between *investing* at 20 percent and *borrowing* at the same rate?

Surely so. Not least, if you are *investing*, you will want the highest possible return, while if you are *borrowing*, you will want the *lowest*. You might think you would know whether you are lending or borrowing. But it is not always so obvious. An "investment" with the benefits at the beginning and the costs at the end might yield results just like the ones we present here.

Here is an example that might trip you up.[1] You are a consultant to the World Bank, which is considering whether to grow beets or corn. The per acre benefits and costs (including soil erosion costs) are set forth in the table below.

---

[1] Adapted from Colin Price, Time, Discounting, and Value 43 (1993).

	Cash Flows	
t =	**Beets**	**Corn**
1	+$4,000	+$4,000
2	+3,000	+3,000
3	+2,000	+2,000
4	+1,000	+1,000
5	0	0
6, 7, 8 . . . 1000	−1000	−2,000

Which project do you take? The IRR of beets is 7.93 percent and of corn, 13.55 percent. So if you chose simply one IRR, you would choose corn. But the inflows are identical with each project; the outflows are twice as large with corn (this must be a result of the erosion costs). So corn, with the higher IRR, is the inferior project.

§ 5.05 IRR and NPV

It is time to make a direct comparison between IRR and NPV. Your client, Claude, is considering two investments — Silk Purses and Sow's Ears. The projected cash flows are as follows:

	Cash Flows	
t =	**Silk Purse**	**Sow's Ear**
0	($100)	($100)
1	$150	$0
2	$50	$0
3	$0	$0
4	$0	$0
5	$0	$300

Can we compute IRR for these payoffs? For the Sow's Ear, the answer is an easy "yes." Recall the formula $(FV \div PV)^{1/n}$. We compute $(300 \div 100)^{(1/5)}$

− 1 = 0.2457 or 24.57 percent. For the Silk Purse, we go to a calculator or a spreadsheet and determine that the IRR is 78.08 percent.[2]

Can we compute NPV? Yes again. We compute the present value of the inflows and subtract the present value of the outflows. But to compute an NPV, we will need a *discount rate*. The discount rate is a function of the *opportunity cost of capital* (OCC) and nothing in this problem tells us what that cost might be. Consider three rates:

OCC	NPV	
	Silk Purse	**Sow's Ear**
5%	$88.20	$135.06
10%	$77.69	$86.28
15%	$68.24	$49.15

We can see that in terms of pure IRR, Silk Purse, with its 78 percent return, appears to be a clear winner. But in terms of NPV, the winner may be either Silk Purse or Sow's Ear, depending on the OCC. If your rate is low, you will favor Sow's Ear; if it is high, you will favor Silk Purse.

How can we explain this disparity? The difference is in the *timing of the returns*. Returns for Silk Purse, though smaller, come sooner. Sow's Ear is more affected by intervening interest rates.[3]

Here is another way to see the point. Suppose you want to be sure you will have $300 at t=5. Sow's Ear assures that you will get it. Silk Purse does not. Silk Purse will provide the $300 *only if* you can *reinvest* your proceeds at a rate sufficiently high to reach the $300 goal — and on the basis of the problem as stated, you have no idea at all what sorts of investments will be available to you when the time for reinvestment arrives.

For example, suppose the reinvestment rate is 10 percent. You'll have $150 to invest for four years which will give you $150 $(1.1)^4$ = $219.62. You'll have $50 to reinvest for three years, which will give you $50 $(1.1)^3$ = $66.55. Together this gives you $286.16, still shy of your goal.

On the other hand, what will you get if you can reinvest at 78.08 percent? Then you will have 150(1.7808)^4$ = $1,508.44 plus $50 $(1.78081)^3$ = $282.36. That's a total of $1,790.80. To put the point another way, if your goal is to have $300 at t=5, and if you can truly get 78.08 percent a year for five years, then you need an initial investment of only $16.75.

---

2 So says the calculator. Solving this problem as a quadratic equation, we find there is also a second solution — in this case, *negative* 128 percent. Once again, the calculator rejects the rate as unrealistic.

3 Suppose two projects, C and D. C pays $200 at t=3. D pays $300 at t=7. It is possible to figure out the rate at which the projects are equal in present value. Set up an equation like this: $\$200 \div [1 + r]^3 = \$300 \div [1 + r]^7$ and solve for r. Note that $200 = 300 \div (1 + r)^4$, so $(1 + r)^4 = 1.5$. Finally, $(1.5)^{1/4} - 1 = .1067$. So the rate is 10.67 percent.

Of course in today's market, *both* Silk Purse and Sow's Ear yield IRRs that probably exceed any credible OCC. So, if you have unlimited access to capital, you might as well take both these projects. But the *reinvestment* assumption is an issue, when comparing two alternative investments, and when you have to choose between the two. You have this same problem in milder form with a regular coupon bond. For more on the reinvestment problem and coupon bonds, see § 7.02 below on duration.

Chapter 6

Application: Coupon Bonds

> I used to think that if there was reincarnation, I wanted to come back as President or the Pope or a .400 baseball hitter. But now I want to come back as the bond market. You can intimidate everybody.
>
> —James Carville

§ 6.01 Prelude

Gutle, matriarch of the Rothschilds, the great clan of international bankers, lived on into her 90s. As the years accumulated, someone asked: "Do you think God will take her at 100?"

"Why?" came the reply. "He wouldn't take her at 86."

One purpose of this assignment is to explain this joke.

§ 6.02 Introduction

Earlier we said a word about the "zero coupon bond," where the corporation issues an IOU promising to make a fixed payment at a specific time. We started with a zero, even though it is not the most common form of corporate finance, because it is the easiest to understand. Now we will consider a device that is somewhat more complicated but far more common in practice. We will consider the "non-zero" bond, sometimes called a "coupon bond," more typically just a "bond." Like the zero, the bond is just a glorified IOU and the terms are whatever the instrument says they are. But bond finance has fallen into some highly conventionalized patterns over the centuries and it is easy to make generalizations that will hold true for a great many individual bond transactions.

§ 6.03 Bond Basics

In the typical coupon bond, the issuer promises to pay a defined sum — say $1,000, or perhaps $10,000 — at the end of the bond term. The issuer also promises to pay compensation at regular intervals — perhaps annually — for use of the money during the bond term. In the old days, the bond was a piece of paper that you had to be willing to deliver to the issuer in exchange for payment. Along the edge of the bond you would find a strip of little coupons that you would clip off and present to collect the periodic payments. The coupons are figured as a percentage of the face amount — a 9 percent $1,000 bond has a coupon of $90 a year.

The first great issuer of coupon bonds — and still the greatest — is the government. The other great issuer is the business corporation. We offer notes on the size and shape of the bond market below. For convenience, we focus on corporate bonds because it is corporate bonds that lawyers are more likely to get involved with. But most of what we say would apply to either.

To begin, let's take a moment to review some first principles of corporate financial structure. A corporation is an artificial entity, a creature of the law. Investors put up money to create corporations; in exchange they get shares of corporate stock. Managers run corporations. Their job is to find and exploit profitable investment projects.

It takes money to make money. When managers find a potentially profitable project, they will need to come up with some money to make it go. If the corporation is new, they may have enough money from the stakes of the individual investors. But if the corporation is mature and established, it may be that all the original investment stake is already hard at work. Where will managers find the new money? There are three choices:

- **Retained earnings**: Managers may have enough money left over from past successes to fund new projects. In fact, a great deal of major corporate financing goes on just this way.
- **Shareholder-investors:** Managers may go back to the original shareholders and ask for more money. Or they may offer *new* shares to new investors, in exchange for new contributions.
- **Lenders:** Managers may borrow the money. In fact, virtually every corporation does *some* borrowing, at least for short-term needs. After all, trade suppliers who leave goods on the dock and get their check at the end of the month are creditors of a sort. But managers may also borrow long-term to finance major projects through corporate bonds.

Which of these sources to use in any given case is an important question for a manager. The short answer is easy: use the source that is cheapest. We give a more detailed and presumably more helpful answer to that question later. For that endeavor, this discussion of bond pricing will serve as a building block.

At bottom, a bond is a contract — an agreement in which the corporation borrows money and makes a promise to repay. We say the corporation *issues* the bonds or *sells* the bonds, promising to pay money later in exchange for money now. The typical bond has a life of 20 or 30 years; a few last as long as 100 years.

We said that a bond is a contract. It is lawful to assign rights to payment under a contract. This rule explains the vigorous *secondary market* in bonds where buyers and sellers assign their rights to payment. But in either market, price depends on valuation, and it is to this topic that we now turn.

§ 6.04 Determining the PV of a Coupon Bond

From the preceding description, you may have identified an important difficulty in identifying the PV of a coupon bond. The point is that we are dealing with *two* payment streams. There is the stream of coupon payments (a kind of annuity). And there is the final payment for the face amount of the bond (think of it as a kind of zero). There is no single formula that will value them both at once. If you want to determine the PV of the bond as a whole, you will have to value the payment stream, and then the final payment, and then add them together.

To use a simple example, imagine a three-year bond (the typical bond extends for 10 years or more, but the arithmetic is simpler for three years and the principles are the same). It has a 9 percent coupon, which means it pays $90 at the end of each of three years, with an additional $1,000 payment at the end of the third year. What would you pay for the bond? To answer the question, first you determine the OCC. For example, choose 6 percent (recall that the OCC is exogenous and for our purposes, can be plucked out of the air). Then you value the coupon stream. Use the PVA formula:

$$\$90 \left[\frac{(1.06)^3 - 1}{(.06)(1.06)^3}\right]$$

The value is $240.57. Then compute the value of the final payment:

$$\frac{\$1{,}000}{(1.06)^3}$$

The value is $839.62. Add the two together and you get $1,080.19. This is the PV of the bond.

Next, recompute assuming that the OCC is exactly 9 percent. What is the PV? You should get exactly $1,000. The reason is that when the OCC *exactly equals* the coupon rate, then the coupon *exactly compensates* the buyer for deferred access to the face value of the bond and the present value equals the face value.

By corollary, when the OCC is *lower* than the coupon rate, the PV is *higher* than $1,000. Now, suppose the OCC is 15 percent. Note that the PV is *lower* than $1,000. What we have here is an application of the "inverse" rule from an earlier chapter: as the OCC *rises,* the PV *falls,* and *vice versa.*

We can generalize all this in a formula. Let C = the coupon payment, in dollars. Let FV = the face value, typically $1,000. Use r to denote the OCC — *not* the coupon rate, which is already embodied in C. Then:

$$PV = C \left[\frac{(1 + r)^n - 1}{(r)(1 + r)^n}\right] + \frac{FV}{(1 + r)^n}$$

Let's recap a bit of structure here. We began with three variables — PV, FV and r. Then we added n. Next, in deal with annuities, we substituted C for FV.

Now we are dealing with five variables — PV, FV, C, r, and n, all in the same item. The rule still holds — if we know *all but one*, then we can *derive* the one that we do not know.

Usually, you will know FV, C and n — they are part of the bond contract. So you'll be seeking PV or r. The equation for PV is set forth above. As we saw above, r is more difficult, although again, you can get it with a spreadsheet or a calculator.

Calculator Tip: You can do bond calculations at least three different ways on your TI BA II Plus. First, the calculator supplies a "bond worksheet." For detailed instructions, see the calculator manual.

You can also calculate the result using the PV and PMT functions (the horizontal line, third from the top). Note that you have five variables to cope with here: N, I/Y, PV, PMT, and FV. In the typical bond case you will know FV ($1,000) and PMT (the coupon) and N (the number of coupons). Starting with these, if you know PV you can compute I/Y, and vice versa. Make sure P/Y is set to the correct number of coupons per year. That is, for a single coupon of $80 per year, P/Y is one. For two coupons of $40 each per year, P/Y is two. Note that PV must carry a sign *opposite* to the signs of PMT and FV. So, if PV is negative, then PMT and FV must be positive.

Finally, you can calculate bond values using the CF, NPV, and IRR functions. Start by punching in the CFs on the cash flow keys. For CF-0, punch in negative 1,000. For CF-1, punch in the amount of the coupon. Then for F-1, punch in the number of coupons, but exclude the final coupon. Then for the next CF, punch in a single number equaling the final $1000 *plus* the final coupon. From this point, you can compute IRR if you know the PV, or PV if you know the IRR. Follow the manual.

Aside from the calculator and the pencil, some people still compute bond prices using the tables, like those included in ordinary finance textbooks. Use of the tables is usually self-explanatory. Typically, you must find an *annuity factor* appropriate to your *r* and *n*. You multiply this factor by the coupon. Then you find a *discount factor* appropriate to the same *r* and *n*. You multiply this by $1,000. Then you add the two products.

§ 6.05 Reading Bond Price Information

You can find bond prices in specialized financial newspapers and sometimes also in major metropolitan dailies. More and more, however, investors get this kind of information from the Internet. A good basic web site for bond prices is: http://www.secapl.com/secapl/quoteserver/search.html.

Meanwhile, here are a few basics about reading bond price data:

One: Bond price quotations typically lop off the trailing zero and express themselves in 100s, rather than 1,000s. This is largely a matter of inertia. But you will need to learn that a price quotation of 103.25 means that the bond is being offered for $1,032.50, and so forth.

Two: The standard quote for a bond identifies it by *coupon* and the *year* in which the final payment is due. So, consider an "8 3/8s06." The "s" is just a separator; ignore it. As to 8 3/8, recall that 3/8 = 0.375. So 8 3/8 = 8.375. But since our thousands are quoted in hundreds, we multiply by 100 and determine that the bond has a coupon of $83.75, with a final payment due in 2006.

Three: Some bond sources continue to quote the bond value in terms of its "current yield" (CY). This may *sound like* a kind of IRR, but it is not. Rather, you compute "current yield" by taking the coupon and dividing by the current price. In our three-year bond example above, then, you would divide 90 by 1080.19, giving a current yield of 8.33 percent. We already know that the true IRR is 6 percent. For comparison, where the IRR is 15 percent, the PV of the bond would be $863.01. Then the CY would be 10.43 percent.

There is a practical message here: CY tends to *overstate* IRR when bonds trade at *above* face value. It *understates* IRR for bonds that trade *below* face value.

PV	IRR	CY	
$1080	6	8.33	CV overstates when PV is low
$1000	9	9	
$ 863	15	10.4	CV understates when PV is high

The differences are modest when the market rates vary only a little from the coupon rate and when the term of the bond is long. For example, suppose a bond with a 9 percent coupon and a term of *thirty* years, rather than three. Suppose an IRR of 15 percent. The current yield is 14.85 percent. It is easy to understand why people used CY for long bonds in an age before computers when it was so hard to compute the real IRR, but there is no excuse for it today.

Closer to the mark, many bond tables quote a "Yield to Maturity" (YTM). This sounds more like an IRR — and indeed it is, almost. Unfortunately, there is one more small glitch, which we explain in the next section.

§ 6.06 YTM v. IRR — Nominal v. Effective Again

Recall our discussion of compounding. We pointed out that other things being equal, the more frequent the compounding, the more valuable the payment stream. So, start with $100 and compound annually at the rate of 12 percent; by t=1, you have $112.

But, compound semi-annually at 6 percent and you get $\$100\,(1.06)^2 = \$112.36$. We saw that the distinction had practical importance in the regulation of rate disclosure for consumer credit contracts. Specifically, the Truth-in-Lending Act lets you *quote* your rate as if you compound *annually* but actually to *compound* more often — say, monthly. In consequence, your *nominal* annual percentage rate (APR) will *understate* the true *effective* rate of your loan.

We have the same problem with bonds. Bonds may pay coupons either once or twice a year (or rarely, at other times as well). Up to now, we have assumed annual coupons. In truth, probably most bonds pay *half* the stated coupon every *half year*. But the YTM on a bond is often *quoted* as if they pay only once a year. So once again, we have a distinction between the (nominal) YTM and the slightly higher (effective) rate of return.

Recall our earlier example. We examined a 9 percent, $1000 bond and a market rate of 6 percent annually. We computed its present value at $1,080.19. It is possible — even likely — in the real world that such a bond would in fact have paid its coupon in semi-annual installments of $45 each. Traditional YTM terminology would still quote the rate at 9 percent. We would know that the true "effective" rate is $(1.045)^2 - 1$, or 9.2 percent.

On the same logic, we would have computed our PV differently. For *r*, we would have used 3 percent (not 6). For C, we should have used $45 (not $90). And for *n*, we would have used 6 (not 3). We would have derived a PV of $1,081.26. The difference here is pretty trifling: less than a tenth of 1 percent. For a comparable 30-year bond, the difference is still comparatively small: something like 0.15 of 1 percent. Still, if you are dealing in these billions, these pennies can mount up and make a difference.

§ 6.07 Prepayment Option

Suppose NewCo issues $20 million in 20-year bonds with a 7 percent coupon when the market rate is 7 percent. We can expect the bonds to trade at par, i.e., $1,000. Five years pass and rates fall to 5 percent. The value of the bond rises to $1,207.59 (check it). NewCo would love to pay off the bond for $1,000 and replace it with new, cheaper, financing. It should be clear that the bonds are worth less to the bondholders if NewCo can do it than if it cannot. Does NewCo have the right to do so?

This depends on the terms of the bond *indenture* — the contract that governs the relationship between the bond debtor and its creditors. Some bonds are *non-callable*, and NewCo must continue to pay at the old rate. Many contracts provide for *call*, perhaps with restrictions. For example, the 20-year bond may provide that the borrower can pay off the bond if it wishes, after five years but not before. The contract may provide for call only at a penalty price — maybe $1,050, for a $1,000 bond.

Does the call provision make a difference? Of course it does. Other things being equal, you're better off if you can "lock in" the current rate of return than if you risk being paid off when rates fall. So you will be willing to pay more for a non-callable bond than for a bond with a call option.

But exactly how do you value a call option? For a long time, finance theory offered no answer to that question. But one of the most important innovations in finance over the last generation has been the development of a theory of "option pricing." We shall study option pricing more carefully later. We shall see that the call option is susceptible to analysis under the new option theory.

In the meantime, there is a fudge that will help to solve the problem. In many cases, the call provision will specify that the bond is *not* callable until a certain date in the future — say, five years into the life of a 30-year bond. For example, suppose we have a 30-year bond trading at par with a provision for call after five years at $1,050.

$$\$1{,}000 = \$70 \times \frac{(1 + r)^5 - 1}{(r)(1 + r)^5} + \frac{\$1{,}050}{(1 + r)^5}$$

Solve for r (on the calculator) and you get 0.0785 or 7.85 percent, which is the *yield to call.* Is this really how it works?

Reviewing: You will want to make sure you can distinguish the *coupon* (C); *market rate* (IRR = OCC); the *yield to maturity* (YTM), the *yield to call* (YTC) and the *current yield* (CY).

A Word on Bond Rating Agencies: How do you find out how much a bond is worth? You kick the tires: you go out and talk to the president of the company, you look at the factories, you sample the product, and so forth. Information like this is valuable but it takes time, effort and energy. Given the size of the market, it is no surprise that commercial providers have emerged to offer advice on bond quality. The two biggest and best known are Moody and Standard & Poor. These two private firms undertake to grade bonds like eggs or exam papers.

At first glanced, you would think there ought to be a strong market for good-quality rating information. Indeed many investors follow the ratings. Sometimes a rule or a statute specifies that a manager may invest in bonds only if they achieve or surpass a certain grade. Companies, like students, are eager to get the highest grade possible, and for the same reasons: a high grade will improve their value in the marketplace.

Unfortunately, the record of the bond rating services is pretty grim. There are too many cases where they seem to have locked the barn only after the horse has been stolen — they have lowered the grade of a bond only after its market value had collapsed. During the great meltdown in Asian securities markets in late 1997, rating services seemed to be among the last to know. So with rating services, as with so much else, the rule seems to be: use them if you like, but don't inhale.

Web sites: Rating agency definitions can be found at:

http://www.ratings.com (Standard & Poor);

http://www.lifeofluxury.com/moodys.html (Moody's).

§ 6.08 Note On the Credit Market

The root of a capitalist economy is, perhaps, the discovery that such contract claims can be bought and sold. The place where you buy and sell such claims is the credit market. The credit market is part and parcel of a capitalist economy. Indeed, some would say it *defines* a capitalist economy. It is useful to take a look at its size and shape.

We can usefully distinguish two major classes of debt: public and private. Perhaps surprisingly, the market for public debt is older and more fully developed. England built up a large public debt during the reign of King William III and Queen Mary II (after 1688) to finance foreign wars. In the United States, Wall Street functioned as a marketplace for public debt long before it came to prominence as a place to raise private capital. Even today (as we shall see), in terms of volume, the public debt market continues to dominate.

We can also distinguish debt as a function of time: short-, medium-, and long-term. By convention, short-term debt is typically debt due within a year.

Medium-term runs from one to 10 years; long-term, over 10, with a cluster at around 30 years. Typically, the "bond" is a long-term instrument. For U.S. Treasury debt, the medium-term issues are "notes," and the short-term, "bills."

In the United States, it is instructive to subdivide the public debt. Pure federal debt totaled some $3.6 trillion in 1995, a sum equal to about 50 percent of the gross domestic product (GDP). "Munis" account for another $1.3 trillion. These munis are not, as the name might suggest, solely the obligations of municipal governments. The term also includes state debt. The common factor is that the earnings on this muni debt are not subject to federal taxes. Much more important is the $2.4 billion in debt owed by government-related agencies — notably "Fannie Mae" and "Freddie Mac," the agencies that finance home mortgage debt.

As a component of the total market, government debt has fluctuated sharply over the years. Federal government debt hit 63 percent of GDP in 1952 (when it still included much of the cost of World War II). The percentage fell for 22 years and bottomed out in 1974. It drifted up slightly during the 1970s — but then shot up again as a result of the budget deficits during the presidency of Ronald Reagan. More recently in the 1990s, fueled by a thriving economy, government debt began to fall. At this writing, there are sober adults who assert it will all be paid off by 2010.

Meanwhile, government-related debt (Fannie Mae, etc.) came out of nowhere at the end of World War II to its current level at about 33 percent of GDP, with every evidence that it will continue to grow. Formally, most of this debt is *not* guaranteed by the federal government. But the formal definition may not be the whole story. It may be that this pool of government-related debt is an institution "too big to fail," and that the government will be forced to bail it out in hard times, to avoid a total meltdown.

Traditional corporate debt has fluctuated also over the years. At present writing, corporations seem to be borrowing to beat the band — often to buy back their own shares.

Aside from government, corporate, and government-related mortgage debt, there is a wholly new debt market that has grown up in the past couple of decades. This is the market of "Asset Backed Security" (ABS). Here is a sample ABS: a bank owns a thousand claims against makers of widgets. It "pools" the thousand claims and issues bonds against the pool. As the loans get paid, the bank passes the money through to the bondholders. If some widget makers quit paying, then the pool may be worth less. But the loss falls on all the bondholders pro rata, rather than on the holder of any individual claim. For more on "securitization" as a risk reduction device, see § 27.08 below.

§ 6.09 Note: What Is a Bank?

From time to time we speak of borrowing from a bank. But what is a bank? The answer is not so obvious as it might seem. Your grandfather (or anyone with a taste for old movies) will think of a bank as a Greek-revival style building at a busy corner in the middle of downtown. There will be tellers who take deposits and a roomful of desk officers who make loans.

This is traditional "commercial banking," as we have understood it in this country for several generations. But there are lots of other things that come close to banking. And there are lots of other things that a bank may do. In fact, the traditional definition is constrained by history — but as you read this, banking is going through a transformation that is bound to change just about everything we know about it.

Reformulated, the question is not just "what is a bank?" Rather, there is a more general question: how do you go about raising and distributing money in the market place? For our purposes a unifying theme is distrust. Americans have proven themselves characteristically suspicious of "the money power." Hence the story of financial markets is a story of fragmentation and decentralization.

At the beginning of our national history, we couldn't even make up our minds that we wanted a bank. Congress chartered the "Bank of the United States" in the 1790s. President Andrew Jackson blocked the renewal of a national bank charter in the 1830s. In 1863, Congress at last authorized "national banks," but in fact they were nothing of the sort. Rather, Congress created a system of independent local banks scattered across the landscape. And along side these "national banks" there grew up an independent system of banks chartered by the individual states.

Fragmented though they were, the banks nonetheless played an important role in mobilizing capital for industry in the boom that followed the Civil War. They took deposits. They made loans. But the big-city banks also did something else less familiar to a later age: they raised money to buy stock — "investment" banking, as it came to be called, to distinguish it from its "commercial" cousin, to finance industry through "underwriting." And they traded in securities.

But alongside the great banking houses, there was another source of capital, sometimes even more powerful than the banks themselves: the insurance companies. To the consumer, the similarity between a bank and an insurer is not obvious. But a firm selling life insurance or annuities is a kind of repository for savings, quite like a traditional bank. And just like a bank, an insurance company puts its money to work through investment.

Indeed, by the beginning of the Twentieth Century, the biggest insurance companies were bigger than the biggest banks. But then in 1905, the insurance industry found itself rocked by two crippling blows: first, a wave of financial scandals, and second, a reformist mood in politics. By the end of 1906, the state of New York had prohibited insurers from owning stock, from controlling banks, or from underwriting securities. The whole affair put a constraint on the insurance industry from which it has never recovered.

For banks, the pivotal events were the market crash of 1929 and the ensuing Great Depression. The cataclysm planted two ideas: one was the notion that the culprit for the Depression was overreaching by the banks — particularly securities manipulation. The other was the notion that we needed a safety net to fend off ruin when a bank should happen to collapse. The result was two important public policies. One was the Glass-Steagall Act, which provided a framework for bank regulation that lasted until 1999. The other was the creation of a system of insurance to protect depositors against the risk of bank failure.

Glass-Steagall imposed two important limits on commercial banks. First, it put them out of the business of stock *underwriting* — investment banking. Second, it barred them from stock *dealing* — brokerage. And so we were left with the bank of the movies, accepting deposits and making loans. The system of insurance protected depositors, but not incidentally it also protected banks, This is so because an insured bank need not fear the risk of a run from panicky depositors trying to get their money out ahead of collapse.

Glass-Steagall lasted for nearly 70 years. Through much of that time, because or in spite of Glass-Steagall, the United States enjoyed the luxury of stable and dependable banking. But 70 years is a remarkable lifespan for a regulatory statute — long enough for the best of regimes to outlive its reason for being. Intellectual fashions change. So does the marketplace. And so, not least, do the patterns of regulation that purport to keep the statute in play.

Among forces that came to undermine Glass-Steagall, perhaps most important were a series of innovations that helped depositors and borrowers alike to bypass the traditional banking system. Depositors found they could put their money into *money market mutual funds*, and have all the convenience of banking, with interest to boot. Corporate borrowers discovered the *junk bond market* which gave them unparalleled access to capital. For short-term debt, merchants discovered they could replace a traditional bank credit line with the *sale of commercial paper*.

Meanwhile, the market for securities passed sideways from individual investors to the great new institutional investors: the stock mutual funds and the pension funds, which together dominate the equity market today.

A corollary pressure was the sheer matter of size. It may not seem so when you have just been denied a loan, but by world standards, American banks are not large. Hemmed in by a patchwork of regulation and a tradition of distrust, the largest American banks traditionally have been smaller than banks in Switzerland, France and Japan.[1]

As the market changed, scholars undertook to recast the familiar narrative history of Glass-Steagall. They questioned the premise that bank manipulation had caused the Depression. They suggested that the real purpose of Glass-Steagall was not to protect customers so much as it was to protect country banks and bankers. And they argued that a new view of finance undermined the traditional premises. To take just one example, they argued that a commercial bank dealing in securities might be more safe, rather than less so, because it stood to make money either by taking a deposit or by buying a security. Money market mutual funds reduce need for demand deposits.

Another force undermining Glass-Steagall was the guile and enterprise of lawyers. Long before repeal, clever lawyers had found exceptions: innovative sidesteps that freed their bank clients from the constraints of regulation, even while the regulation remained in place.

---

[1] But current events are making hash of this historical truth. A flurry of mergers are vaulting major United States banks into positions at or near the top of the world size list.

The upshot of all these forces was a revolution in banking, whereby banks do more and more things we don't remember them doing while others — insurance companies, brokerage firms, sometimes even retail megastores — act more and more like banks.

The revolution is hardly over. Yet by the late 1990s, it had built up so much steam that the actual repeal of Glass-Steagall seemed almost an afterthought. Indeed, at the moment, the great other shoe that has not dropped in the banking services is the Internet — the promised advent of cyberbanking. And here the story is ironic.

For the remarkable fact is not how much cyberspace has changed banking, but how little. Thirty years ago, law professors were talking about the disappearance of cash and the coming of an electronic financial universe. Indeed, some of this has come to pass, but its still remarkable how many people carry cash in their wallet and pay their bills with a ballpoint pen. It will be interesting to see whether the same remains true 30, or even five years in the future.

So much for the structure of banking. Almost unnoticed in the maelstrom is the matter of deposit insurance. In fact, deposit insurance has its critics: economists who argue that it encourages risk, industry insiders who argue that it unfairly burdens prudent and responsible banks. But among the public at large, deposit insurance has fans without number and almost no critics. It is inconceivable that Congress will tinker with anything so widely popular any time soon.[2]

Aside on Thrifts: Parallel to the state and federal banks, the Nineteenth Century also generated a parallel system of "building and loan associations," or "savings and loan associations," — more generally the "thrifts." The thrifts grew up as "community banks," outside the commercial mainstream. Their main reason for being was to take deposits from "wage earners" and to make loans for the purchases of homes. The thirfts are a remarkable study in grass-roots banking: it would be fascinating to compare their history to the "micro-lending" institutions on the edge of the mainstream market today. They played an important, perhaps the central, role in the spread of home ownership in the United States.

But then the story went sour: in the 1980s, a change in the pattern of regulation led the thrifts out of their traditional path and down the byway to disaster. For more on the multi-billion dollar collapse of the thrift industry see § 39.04 below.

Web site: For more on banks, see http://www.state.ct.us/dob/pages/abcs-5.htm.

---

[2] Good background on the structure of finance can be found in Mark J. Roe, Strong Managers, Weak Owners: The Political Roots of Corporate Finance (1994). On Glass-Steagall and its repeal, see James R. Barth, R. Dan Brumbaugh Jr., & James A. Wilcox, *The Repeal of Glass-Steagall and the Advent of Broad Banking*, 14 J. Econ. Lit. 191 (2000).

Chapter 7

Unequal Terms

§ 7.01 Introduction

In this chapter, we confront several problems that arise when we have annuities whose terms are unequal — for example, a three-year bond and a 20-year bond.

§ 7.02 Coping with Rate Sensitivity: Duration

If there were a Guinness World's record for big bankruptcies, one prime contender would be Orange County, California. The Orange County Investment Pool succeeded in losing something like $1.7 *billion*, more than the annual gross domestic product of many small countries. The cause of the Orange County bankruptcy is almost absurdly easy to specify.

Call it "Citron's problem," after Robert Citron, the ill-fated county treasurer who brought it all about. Citron's problem was that he "borrowed short" and "loaned long." For example, imagine that he borrowed at 4 percent and loaned at 5 percent for a 25 percent profit. That was fine until interest rates went up. Citron found himself stuck with his long-term loans, now less attractive because they carried the old low rate. On the other hand his investors, with no long-term commitment, decided to take their money and run.

Citron's problem is far from unique. In a sense it is the problem of any bank that accepts deposits (borrows short) which it uses for long-term investments. A mismatch in rates was one of the problems that brought down the savings and loan industry in the 1980s (see § 38.04). This kind of portfolio mismatch isn't inherently evil, of course: most banks make a profit most of the time. But at least you want to know what you are up against, if for no other reason than so you can price your risk accurately.

Indeed, you run across this kind of problem any time you have instruments with different degrees of sensitivity to interest rates. The problem arises with different maturities, as in the Orange County case, because instruments with different maturities may have different sensitivity to rate changes. But you get it from other sources as well. Consider two bonds with identical maturity, one a coupon bond, the other a zero. The zero is more sensitive to rate changes because it is "back-loaded" — all the cash flow comes at the end. Coupon bonds, by contrast, are not so strongly back-loaded because part of their cash flow comes in increments over the life of the bond.

On the same principle, consider two coupon bonds identical except for the size of the coupon. The higher the coupon, the more front-loading; the more front-loading, the less sensitivity to rate changes.

In the 1930s, a mathematician named Frederick R. Macaulay, with background in the insurance industry, offered a device for measuring this kind of rate sensitivity. Although it is crude and primitive, it continues in wide use, and bears his name: *Macaulay duration* (here, just "duration").

To understand duration, consider your client Isabel. Ten years ago she issued a 20-year zero at 12 percent. The PV was $1,037 [that is: $10,000 ÷ $(1.12)^{20}$]. If rates had remained stable, the PV today would be [10,000 ÷ $(1.12)^{10}$] = $3,220. But in fact, in the intervening years the market rate fell from 12 to 6 percent. So the actual implied value of the zero is [10,000 ÷ $(1.06)^{10}$] = $5,584. That's a 73 percent improvement over where you expected to be if the rate stayed at 12 percent. It gives you a whopping 439 percent over the original $1,037 value.

By contrast, suppose your original issue 10 years ago was not a zero, but rather a 20-year, 12 percent *coupon* bond. If the coupon was 12 percent and the market rate was 12 percent, then we can infer that it went to the market at face value, i.e., $1,000. If rate remains at 12 percent, then after 10 years, it will still trade at its face value of $1,000. If, however, rates fall to 6 percent, its principal value will rise to $1,442. That's an increase of 44 percent on its initial face value, which is surely a comfort, but not as much fun as the 73 percent we got on the zero.

Of course, you got the coupons all those years. To be consistent in our comparison, we need to take them into account also. This will require some guesswork. We need to ask: what sort of return did you get on the coupons *as reinvested* during this 10-year interval? Nothing in the problem dictates an answer to this question.

But we know the market rate started at 12 percent and fell to 6 percent. Let's split the difference and use a rate of 9 percent. Think of the coupons as an annuity: $120 for each of 10 years. Using our "future value annuity" factor, we can value the payment stream, as of t = 10, at $120[((1.09)^{10} - 1) \div .09]$ = $1,823. Add that to the $1,442 and you get $3,265 which is your true accumulation on the coupon bond over the 10 years.

To summarize, we got $3,265 for $1,000 on the coupon, as compared to $5,584 for $1,037 on the zero. To complete our comparison, let's extract the IRR on the two investments. First, for the coupon:

$$(3{,}265 \div 1{,}000)^{1/10} - 1 = 0.1256 = 12.56\%$$

Not bad, overall. Still, here is the return on the zero:

$$(5{,}584 \div 1{,}037)^{1/10} - 1 = 0.1834 = 18.34\%$$

That's half again as much.

The secret, of course, is in the timing. The zero is "back-loaded," so it is far more vulnerable to fluctuations in the market rate of interest. In our example, this volatility worked to the advantage of the zero, because the market rate went down. Of course, the rate might just has well have gone up, in which case the coupon bond would have come out the winner.

Now we are ready for the Macaulay duration formula (which is a lot less indigestible than it appears to be). It represents the sum of the individual payments (each "weighted by" the number of periods we have to wait for the payment) — all divided by the present value. Here is the procedure in words:

- Identify the present value of each increment, using the discount factor. For example, if the payment is due at t=3, multiply the payment by $1 \div (1+r)^3$.
- Multiply the present value of each payment by the number of time periods from t=0. So, if the payment is due at t=2, you would multiply the present value by two. If it is due at t=3, you multiply by three, and so forth.
- Add the products.
- Divide by the present value of the bond.

For example, suppose you have a three-year 9 percent coupon bond, trading at 9 percent. Multiply each cash flow (CF) by a discount factor (DF). Then multiply the resulting present value (PV) by the time period (t). The result is the *duration* of the instrument. For example, suppose you have a three-year 9 percent coupon bond, trading at 9 percent. Multiply each cash flow (CF) by a discount factor (DF). Then multiply the resulting present value (PV) by the time period (t). You get these results:

t	CF	DF	PV	PV × t
1	$90	0.9174	$82.57	$82.57
2	$90	0.8417	$75.75	$151.50
3	$1,090	0.7722	$841.68	$2,525.04
Total			$1,000.00	$2,759.11

To complete the analysis, divide the total by the present value of the bond. The duration, then, will be $2,759.11 ÷ $1,000 = 2.75911.

For comparison, suppose the market rate falls to eight percent. Recomputing the table, we get:

t	CF	DF	PV	PV × t
1	$90	0.9259	$83.33	$83.33
2	$90	0.8573	$77.16	$154.32
3	$1,090	0.7938	$865.28	$2,595.83
Total			$1,025.77	$2,833.49

Divide 2,833.49 by 1,025.77 and we find that duration has risen slightly to 2.76231. Now try it yourself: recompute duration for the same bond where the market rate is 10 percent. You should get 2.75592. Note that as the market rate goes up, duration goes down, and vice versa. Stop and ask yourself why this must be the case. Hint: note that on an ordinary coupon bond, duration will always be less than the nominal term. For example, for a three-year coupon bond, duration will always be less than 3.

For a final comparison, consider a three-year zero coupon bond. You can compute the duration by the same system we used above — but if you understand the process, you may be able to see that the duration of a zero will *always* be the same as the "t" at which its payment is due. That is: a zero of "n" years will always have a duration of "n." Do you understand why this is so? Compute a couple of examples and you ought to get the point.

Caution: We have said that duration offers an index for comparison. This would seem to suggest that if you have two instruments with the same duration, they would respond the same way to changes in interest rates — they would move up (or down) by the same amount. Unfortunately, it isn't quite that simple. We also said that duration is a crude measure and in fact, it does not capture the relationship completely.

For example, consider a 30-year 9 percent coupon bond trading at its face value, i.e., at 9 percent. Its duration is 11 (you could compute this for yourself, but it will be tedious unless you have a spreadsheet). A 9 percent zero with an 11-year term will also have a duration of 11. Now suppose interest rates climb to 12 percent. The present value of the zero will fall by 26.22 percent, while the present value of the coupon bond will fall by 24.17 percent. You would need fancier math to do a more accurate job, but duration still works pretty well as a rule of thumb.

§ 7.03 Swaps

The problem of duration also helps to explain one of the most dramatic innovations in the credit market over the past generation: the development of "interest rate swaps." A swap is just what it was in the schoolyard, only in high finance: two parties each hold rights to payment that they don't like, so they trade. Oral tradition holds that the interest rate swap was invented in 1981 with the World Bank and IBM. IBM earned its money in dollars, but it owed some loans that it was supposed to pay in Deutschmarks or Swiss Francs. Because of a shift in the international currency market, IBM saw a chance to pay off the debt on the cheap. But a direct payoff would have exposed IBM to a big tax expense.

Meanwhile, the World Bank needed to borrow money. As it happened, the Bank didn't want to borrow any more in Deutschmarks or Swiss Francs for fear it would upset the European credit market, but it was willing to borrow in dollars.

Someone at Salomon Brothers (the investment bank) asked, "Why not let them switch?" And so it came to pass. The World Bank issued $290 billion in dollar bonds, which IBM agreed to pay. For its part the World Bank agreed to take over the Deutschmark and Swiss Franc loans. Because each party was so solvent, Salomon Brothers was happy to guarantee the whole deal (and pocket a comforting fee for its trouble).

From such modest beginnings great institutions grow. By the end of 1999, there were some $46 trillion of swaps outstanding. For comparison, that is about nine times the size of the international bond market.

§ 7.04 Term Structure of Interest Rates

Your client, Boris, wants to buy a single-payment bond that costs $1,000 today and will pay you $1,259.60 at t=3. What is the IRR? Since this is a single-payment bond, we can use the single-payment rate formula, ($1,259.60 ÷ $1,000)$^{(1/3)}$ − 1 = 0.7997 = 7.997 percent. Checking, we can easily construct a table of values for the payment stream:

$$\begin{aligned} \$1{,}000\ (1.07997) &= \$1{,}079.97 \\ \$1{,}079.97\ (1.07997) &= \$1{,}166.33 \\ \$1{,}166.33\ (1.07997) &= \$1{,}259.60 \end{aligned}$$

The corresponding discount factors would be:

$$\begin{aligned} \$1{,}259.60\ (1.07997)^{-3} &= 0.7939 \\ \$1{,}166.33\ (1.07997)^{-2} &= 0.8574 \\ \$1{,}079.97\ (1.07997)^{-1} &= 0.926 \end{aligned}$$

We could double-check this schedule by looking at quoted market prices on *single-payment* bonds. For example, consider a series of $1,000 zero coupon bonds issued by ZeroCo, with maturities of three, two, and one years, respectively. On the basis of what we have seen before, we would expect to find these zeros quoted as:

t =	
3	$793.90
2	$857.39
1	$925.95

Suppose instead we find a table like this:

t =	
3	$793.90
2	$865.35
1	$934.57

The three-year bond seems correctly priced, but the one- and two-year bonds seem overpriced and (on the same logic) the spread between the two-year and the three-year price seems too small. What can be going on here? To answer the question, we will want to figure out the rates implied by this latter group of prices. We know that each bond price represents the discount factor times $1,000, and that the forward factor for each bond price is the inverse of the discount factor. So we can construct a table of forward factors like this:

$$(0.93457)^{-1} = 1.07$$
$$(0.86535)^{-2} = 1.1556$$
$$(0.79390)^{-3} = 1.2596$$

Stated differently, the price of the three-year bond seems to imply an *annual* rate of:

$$(1.2596)^{(1/3)} - 1 = 0.07997 = 7.997\%$$

Which is what we saw before. Call this rate the *spot rate,* i.e., the *annual rate* implied by the *price* of the instrument in the "spot market" — the place where instruments of this sort are traded "on the spot." On this logic, the two-year spot rate would be:

$$1.1556^{(1/2)} - 1 = 0.075 = 7.5\%$$

On the same reasoning, the one-year spot rate is simply 7 percent.

So it appears that the rate is a function of time: to extend from one year to two (and so forth), we must pay not just *more* interest, but interest at a higher *rate*. What this means is that the IRR for the three-year loan was not a single rate that applied to all three years; rather, it was the *average* of rates that apply to different components.

Let us see how this works. We know that the rate for a one-year loan is 7 percent, and that the rate for a two-year loan is 7.5 percent per year; we called each of these the "spot rate" for its term. We want to know: what does it cost to "go forward" that extra year?. To answer this question, take the two-year factor (1.556) and discount by the spot rate for the previous year (1.07):

$$(1.1556 \div 1.07) - 1 = 0.08 = 8\%$$

So the rate to "go forward" from one year to two is 8 percent. Call this "rate to go forward" the *forward rate,* to distinguish it from the spot rate.

On the same logic, what does it cost to go forward from t=2 to t=3? To answer this question, take the three-year total rate (1.2596) and divide by the two-year spot rate:

$$(1.2596 \div 1.1556) - 1 = 0.09 = 9\%$$

t =	**Spot**	**Forward**	**Total**
1	1.07	1.07	
2	1.075	1.08	1.1556
3	1.07997	1.09	1.2596

In summary, the *spot rate* is the IRR, the geometric mean of the total rate:

$$s_n = (\mathrm{FV} \div \mathrm{PV})^{1/n} - 1$$

For any particular year, the *forward rate* is:

$$f_n = \frac{(1 + s_n)^n}{(1 + s_{n-1})^{n-1}}$$

The total rate is *either*:

- The spot rate raised to the nth power; or
- The product of the forward rates.

What we have been talking about here is called *the term structure of interest rates*. The point is that different maturities will bear different rates, and the single "derived" rate (like the IRR) typically represents the geometric mean of the total, independent of the individual components.

§ 7.05 The Yield Curve

We've seen from the start that money now is worth more than money later and that most people accept compensation for delay. In this chapter, we have constructed an example in which an increase in time also generates an increase in *rate* of return. Most readers find this plausible: after all, a longer loan is more volatile than a shorter loan, in that it is more vulnerable to shifts in the market rate and, therefore, more volatile. Moreover, if short rates dependably exceeded long rates, you would have an arbitrage opportunity: you would be able to borrow long, invest short, repay the long loan and pocket the profit.

But the world is more complicated than the model. Sometimes rates go into reverse and short rates do in fact exceed long rates. A notorious example was the period around 1981, when interest rates hit some kind of a record high. Evidently investors believed that the rate structure was unstable and would not persist. Consequently they demanded (and accepted) lower rates for long-term than for short-term loans.

In fact, they were right: rates fell swiftly and sharply through the 1980s, and "the yield curve" readjusted to its traditional pattern. Indeed, one way to make some wonderful profits was to invest in fixed-income securities about 1980: you would have watched the value of your portfolio balloon while rates in the surrounding market hurtled down. The following chart shows the rate of return on instruments of different maturities for 1980 and for 1992. Here are the yields:

	March, 1980	January, 1992
6 months	15.0%	4.0%
1 year	14.0%	4.3%
5 years	13.0%	6.3%
10 years	12.8%	7.0%
20 years	12.5%	7.4%

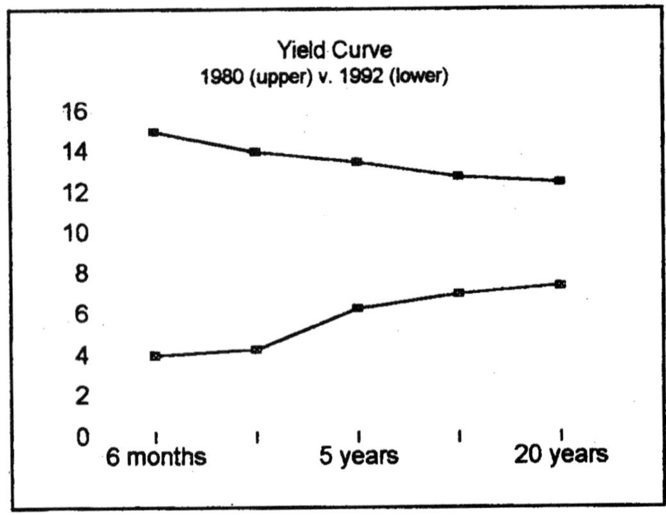

Web site: For a picture of the yield curve, see http://www.bloomberg.com/markets/C13.html.

Chapter 8
Some Second Thoughts

§ 8.01 Introduction

By now, we know enough about discounting and the time value of money to indulge in some second thoughts about our basic principles.

§ 8.02 The Limits of the Market Model

So far we have framed all value in the template of market exchange — broadly, an "economic" model of behavior. Aside from the sheer fact of its presence, there are good reasons for considering a market model. As a mechanism for organizing society, a market is *functionally* attractive to the extent that individuals can judge their own desires better than the sovereign. It is *morally* attractive insofar as in accommodates the capacity for rational choice.

But a market is at best a cultural artifact that impounds the habits and history — perhaps even the conscious choices — of the society in which it subsists. It's not just that it would be hard to endorse a "pure market" society. Rather, the point is that it's impossible to imagine what a pure market society would look like. And it is unclear who would want such a thing, could it exist.

Consider a provocative example.[1] There are any number of items that we regard as "inalienable." A classic example is the right to vote. Your spouse asks you how you intend to vote in the election today. You respond (perhaps echoing Ingrid Bergman in *Casablanca*): "Oh, I'm tired of making decisions — you decide." Most readers would regard the response as improper — improper, that is, for anyone to cede the right to vote, no matter what the terms. The right to vote is the sort of thing you can't transfer, not for love or money. It's an occasion for you to exercise your own capacity for choice.

But now, compare a different instance: love and affection. Cynics though we may be, most of us don't like to think of love and affection as the subject of a pure market transaction. We may choose to tolerate (say) prostitution as a matter of pragmatic wisdom, but most of us would regard a society with a lot of prostitution as somehow coarsened by it.

In short, we don't want you to sell sexual favors. But (at the risk of impertinence) we do encourage you to give it away. That is: a wedding is an occasion for celebration, a ritual of social solidarity in which we affirm what is best in ourselves. It's not the *traffic* in sexual favors that bothers us; it is the *market* traffic.

---

[1] Suggested by Margaret Jane Radin's *Market Inalienability*, 100 Harv. L. Rev. 1849, 1850 (1987).

Social thinkers have puzzled over this distinction for a long time. Ferdinand Tönnies, the great German sociologist, drew the distinction between *Gemeinschaft* and *Gesellschaft* — in English, inadequately translated as *community* and *society*. Tönnies' point is that there are some relationships that are purely instrumental — "society," in the parlance of the moment — and relationships that exist for the relationship itself — "community."

The line is hardly clear-cut. Students of Tönnies have used his distinction to understand (for example) the pattern of agricultural development in France. French farmers (according to this analysis) were reluctant to give up their attachment to the countryside out of a sense of community attachment, in the teeth of their "economic" interest. By the same token, probably plenty of professional commodities traders go plunging into the pit each morning energized by the sheer fun of it. And anyone who ever read a Jane Austen novel will recognize that a marriage can be romantic and economic at one and the same time. Indeed, it may be that the line *has to be* fluid and uncertain. But that doesn't make it less real.

From another vantage, consider your classmate, Clara, who locates her law office on Western Avenue in Los Angeles, midway between Olympic Boulevard and the Santa Monica Freeway. The rest of the world believes that Angelenos spend their entire lives on the freeway. There is some basis for this belief. But the true Angeleno knows that the freeways are so crowded that you are better off sticking to surface streets.

So when Clara has to go downtown to the courthouse, she has a choice — Freeway or Boulevard. Clara, of course, makes the decision on what you could perfectly well call an "economic" basis: if it is rush hour and the Freeway will be frozen, she saves time by taking the Boulevard. If construction crews have torn up the Boulevard, she might as well take the freeway. There really aren't any "non-market" forces at work here: we don't speak of her as being "loyal" to the Boulevard," or her use of surface streets as a "betrayal" of the Freeway.

Contrast Clara with your roommate Rob, who tells you that he doesn't have enough money to meet his personal taste for video games. He says he has considered assuaging his enthusiasm by robbing a bank. But (as he explains), he has weighed the costs of robbing a bank (risk of getting caught, severity of penalty, etc.) against the potential benefits (extra cash, etc.), and has decided that, on the whole, he's just as well off not to do it. Perhaps you are, on the whole, pleased that the calculus worked as it did — but as a kind of reasoning, is this really the sort of thing you want to hear from your roommate?

So there are some situations (like Clara's traffic choice) where it is perfectly all right to decide matters in sheer economic terms — indeed where it would seem odd to do otherwise. But there are others (like Rob the roommate and the decision not to rob a bank) where the "economic" analysis sounds at least incomplete, if not downright grotesque.

Here as before, the line is blurry. A parking ticket in my town costs just $7. If I let my parking meter run over, making a conscious choice to pay the fine rather than suffer the cost of going out to plug in a quarter, am I making an uncontroversial economic calculus? Or am I disclosing a culpable shortage of civic responsibility? The answer may not be obvious but the question will not go away.

A good place for exploring this topic further is the matter of *cost-benefit analysis*.

§ 8.03 Cost-Benefit Analysis and the Discount Rate

> [A] week of lead is like
> a millennium of radionucleotides.[2]

Here is a quotation from Section 1a of Executive Order No. 12,866 issued by President Clinton in 1993;[3]

> In deciding whether and how to regulate, agencies should assess *all costs and benefits* of available regulatory alternatives, including the alternative of not regulating. [Emphasis added.]

So the Clinton Administration committed itself to the use of cost-benefit analysis (CBA) as a general policy. And the order was no aberration. Indeed, it did no more than reaffirm an earlier executive order issued at the beginning of the Reagan Administration in 1981. And both orders echoed the mandate for the use of CBA in any number of federal regulatory statutes.

The widespread mandate should not obscure persistent controversy over the place and propriety of CBA. Questions persist over whether CBA should be used at all; or, if it should, how to manage the mechanics so as to get it right.[4]

The question whether CBA should be used at all parallels the discussion in the preceding section of this chapter: it is largely a question whether some things are "beyond the market." A particularly interesting case is the matter of environmental policy. There seem to be two schools of thought with regard to environmental issues, and they have trouble finding a common frame of reference. One is the school that holds environmental values to be close to sacred, in the sense that they transcend mere economics. The other is the school that approaches the issue of the environment as a problem like any other, to be tackled with the tools at hand. If you hold the latter view, then CBA is a perfectly appropriate technique.

---

[2] Albert L. Nichols, *Lead in Gasoline*, in Economic Analysis at EPA: Assessing Regulatory Impacts at 49, 78 (Richard D. Morgenstern ed., 1997). A colleague who knows about this kind of thing disagrees. She says that it depends on the intensity of use: "I'd rather wear a lead vest for a millennium than drink P32 for a week."

[3] 3 C.F.R. §§ 638, 639 (1993), *reprinted* in 5 U.S.C. § 601 (1994).

[4] For a more thorough introduction to CBA, see generally Matthew D. Adler & Eric A. Posner, *Rethinking Cost-Benefit Analysis*, 109 Yale L. Rev. 165, 176-94 (1999).

§ 8.04 Valuing Lives

> "But don't you know that people die there?" replied Charlie.
> "They dies everywheres," said the boy. . .
> "They dies more than they lives, according to what *I* see."
>
> —Charles Dickens (*Bleak House*)

One version of this problem is the matter of "valuing lives." For example, in a "Proposed Rule," the Coast Guard considered standards for immersion suits to be used in the commercial fishing industry.[5] In accompanying commentary, the author said that the proposed cost associated with the rule would total some $8.5 million per year. And he continued:

> The Coast Guard estimates that eight lives will be saved annually with reinstatement of the requirement. Economic research indicates that $2.5 million per statistical life saved is currently a reasonable estimate of people's willingness to pay to avert a fatality. Use of this figure is for ease in calculating costs and benefits of a proposed rule, and *should in no way be construed as a VALUE the Coast Guard is willing to place on HUMAN LIFE for any other purpose.*

The reader can perhaps be excused for detecting a note of panic in the tone of the beleaguered bureaucrat. We might make him feel easier if we could remind him that, however coarse it may be to value lives, still failing to value them might be even worse. It wouldn't be much comfort to the personal injury plaintiff (for example) to tell him his life is too precious to be valued in dollars. It wouldn't please the aggrieved spouse in a divorce case that she shouldn't coarsen her marriage by submitting it to the marketplace.

Aside from the larger context, there must be particular cases where CBA can serve environmental ends. For example, suppose we run an environmental cleanup agency where we have a budget of $20,000. We identify a toxic waste problem which will manifest itself at t = 25. We could take steps now that would alleviate the problem at a cost of $20,000. Or we can wait until t = 25, at which time it will cost us $100,000. At first glance, it may look attractive to take action today. But if we spend $20,000 now to save $100,000 later, we have an implicit interest rate of 6.9 percent. Suppose we can buy a 25-year zero discounted at 7 percent. The cost of such a bond should be $18,425. Clearly, we should buy the bond and use the $1,575 saving for some other project.

The question of mechanics — can we get it right? — is a much different sort of problem. Perhaps one reason why CBA has a bad name is that it seems to have been done so badly so often. Perhaps the first agency to make general use of CBA in project planning was the U.S. Army Corps of Engineers. The Corps became famously efficient at producing CBA results that suited its purposes, whatever the purposes might be.[6] CBA at the Corps has received enough public scrutiny and criticism — not to say outright derision — that one assumes they do it better today.

---

[5] *See* C.F.R. Part 28 (GCD 88-079c, May 20, 1983).

[6] *See, e.g.,* Johnston v. R.M. Davis, 698 F.2d 1088 (10th Cir. 1983) (discussing "artificially low" rates mandated by Congress for the Toltec Reservoir Project).

For another example, during the Reagan-Bush years, the Administration used cost-benefit analysis to criticize or oppose proposed agency regulations. A lot of the ammunition came from a survey by John F. Morrall III, an economist at the Office of Management and Budget.[7] The Morrall survey was widely cited and quoted.

More recently, Professor Lisa Heinzerling charged that Morrall's analysis "is in the nature of a modern urban legend, a vivid, plausible, "false-true tale," circulated broadly, embellished with local detail, and believed implicitly"[8] — but at the end of the day, misleading or downright wrong. As just one shortcoming, she shows that many of the most glaring instances of supposed bad rules were proposed but never adopted.

The question of the discount rate has proven particularly galling. There are at least two possible questions. One is — what standard should we use? One approach holds that we are looking for the OCC, just as in an ordinary market transaction. Another school embraces something that has come to be called the "Social Rate of Time Preference" (SRTP). The argument for SRTP boils down to an assertion that the OCC does not capture all the concerns that society might wish to bear.

The rhetoric of SRTP is consistent with the notion that environmental choices are in some sense beyond the market. Correspondingly, SRTP leaves itself vulnerable to the criticism that it is a concoction manufactured to justify a particular result. OCC is presented in this context as empirical, scientific, "hard." There is perhaps some merit to this criticism but it needs to be taken lightly. In fact, the difficulties of constructing a reliable OCC, both empirical and practical, are formidable enough to make OCC just as fictional as any SRTP.

You can see a version of the argument over rates at work in *Northern California Power Agency v. FERC.*[9] There, the court had to consider whether to use the average discount rate for members of society (which FERC advocated) or the cost of borrowing to municipal governments (advocated by some municipalities). The court held for the social discount rate as a principle, although it made no finding as to the validity of the particular rate in the particular case.

Aside from the question of the standard, there is still the hurdle of how to apply it. There isn't space to get into all the details here, but any survey of rates applied in practice will turn up a dismaying variety. The Office of Management and Budget has mandated a rate of 7 percent, which it said (in 1992) "approximates the marginal pretax rate of return on an average investment in the private sector in recent years."[10] But agencies use other rates; Housing and Urban Development and the Food and Drug Administration have used 3 percent, The Environmental Protection Agency used 3

[7] *See* Morrall III, A Review of the Record, Regulation, Nov./Dec.1986, at 25.

[8] *See* Lisa Heinzerling, *Regulatory Costs of Mythic Proportions,* 107 Yale L. J. 1981, 1984 (1998).

[9] 37 F.3d 1517 (D.C. Cir. 1994).

[10] *See* OMB, *Benefit-Costs Analysis of Federal Programs; Guidelines and Discounts*, 57 Fed. Reg. 53519, 53523 (1992).

percent for lead based paint, 7 percent for drinking water, and 10 percent for locomotive emissions.[11]

§ 8.05 Future Generations

Regulators also grapple with the "future generations" problem. For example, suppose we can spend $600 now that will save the life of someone 100 years from now (a "future life"). For illustration, set the value of the future life at $8 million. Should we spend the money? The arithmetic is grotesque. At a 10 percent discount rate, the present value of the future life is just $581. So simple discounting would argue that we should not do the project.

A surface difficulty with this analysis is that on these numbers, we will almost never do anything for future generations. This in itself cannot be an objection, of course: if CBA is the appropriate technique, and if our numbers are correct, then the prescribed course is not to act.

But for many critics, this misses the point. It's not just the results that argue against CBA, according to this view; it's the use of CBA in any event. For example, Professor Richard Revesz supports the use of CBA in transfers within a single generation. But he says that the question of transfer across generations "raises a different set of issues," to which the use of CBA is simply irrelevant.[12] Revesz treats cross-generational CBA as a kind of category mistake — as if it pretends (mistakenly) to postulate a single "community" of all generations, born and unborn, whose utility functions can be reconciled in a single analysis. If he is correct, of course, his approach doesn't discredit market analysis today. It simply makes the point that market analysis is not a universal nostrum for all wrongs.

§ 8.06 Now v. Later — Again

This is a good time to take a second look at our first principle. Recall: money now is worth more than money later. We set this down at the beginning, as if cast in concrete, without exceptions. The skeptical reader may already have identified cases in which the general principle will not hold. The skeptical reader is right. It is easy to identify cases in which the rule does not hold. For illustration, consider just two.

Lon, holds a winning lottery ticket. His prize is a three-week vacation in the Greek Islands. Will he take it now or later? Of course there are incidental reasons why he might want to delay: maybe he needs to wait until he can take some vacation time at work, or maybe he wants to wait until the weather is right. But setting aside these factors of convenience, there may be an inherent reason why he'd rather delay. Specifically, it may be that he enjoys looking forward to his vacation, and he'd like to savor it longer before he takes his great escape. Standard discounting theory misses this point.

[11] There is a good summary in all this from Edward R. Morrison, *Judicial Review of Discount Rates Used in Regulatory Cost-Benefit Analysis*, 65 U. Chi. L. Rev. 1333, 1336–37 (1998).

[12] *See* Richard L. Revesz, *Environmental Regulation, Cost-Benefit Analysis, and the Discounting of Human Lives*, 99 Colum. L. Rev. 942, 1042 (1999).

On the same principle, consider Candace, who is due for a root canal. Her dentist tells her (somewhat implausibly) that she can have it this month or next month, with no difference in the health of her teeth. Standard discounting theory assumes she will put it off as long as possible, and maybe she will. But we would not be surprised if she said she'd rather get it over with today so she won't have to agonize over it for the interim.

Both of these are examples where standard discounting theory will be no help at all, and we could think of others. One thing you can say about time preference is that it works pretty well *in an OCC world.* So, if my costs and benefits are measured in money, and if there is an "alternate investment" in which I can borrow or lend (as the case might require), then the standard time preference model does pretty much what it pretends to do. This is a non-trivial principle, and we will continue to rely on it through the rest of the book. But it is rather narrower than the bald statement we encountered at the beginning.[13]

§ 8.07 The First Great American Trading Scandal

Students of American history know that the founding of the Republic is bound up with the bond market. You will remember that the American Revolution was prosecuted by the Continental Congress, a weak assemblage of separate states. The Constitution creating the United States came into being only after the war. The Congress borrowed money to finance the war, but then it left the debts unpaid. Many of the claims lay in the hands of those who had worked hardest to win the war — the soldiers of the revolutionary army. They risked their lives in exchange for largely worthless pieces of paper. Other claim holders were the suppliers who had provided goods and services to keep the army in the field.

Alexander Hamilton was one of the prime movers of the project for a Constitution. Hamilton's primary goal was financial stability. It was Hamilton who induced the new United States to assume the old continental debt. Resumption breathed new life into the old continental claims. At last, the United States paid off 100 cents on the dollar.

Unfortunately, the old soldiers didn't get the benefit. Most of them had sold out on the cheap when the market was low — many in desperation for money to feed their families. The debt, meanwhile, had passed into the hands of traders and speculators.

Hamilton had served through the war as the aide de camp to George Washington. He had taken the field himself brilliantly, if briefly, at Yorktown. He understood the plight of the old soldiers and suppliers. Now he hobnobbed with bankers and stock-jobbers. His enemies accused him of ripping the fabric of society to profiteer at his old comrades' expense.

In the strict sense, the charge appears unfounded. The secondary market is not itself inherently evil. Secondary traders — even "speculators" provide

[13] For more on the limits of time preference, see Mark Kelman, Time Preference and Tax Equity (1983).

liquidity and establish prices. Moreover, for all his interest in finance, Hamilton appears not to have harbored any personal greed. Unfortunately, the same cannot be said for his friends and relatives. There is clear evidence that the secondary market for continental debt was blighted by the most blatant kind of insider trading — "speculators" who did not speculate at all but bought and sold on the strength of their inside knowledge about the intentions of the government. So many of the evils of a debt market — along with its virtues — appear to have been present at the inception of the Republic.

For whatever it may be worth, one finds echoes of the American experience in the stories coming out of the former Soviet Union after the collapse of communism. In the early 1990s, Russia in particular rushed to divest the government of the old state industries, and to put ownership in private hands. The government issued millions of vouchers to ordinary citizens to give them a chance to participate in the securities of the new private corporations. Clearly, some did. But when the dust had settled, it was clear that many of the vouchers (and the resulting securities) had wound up in the hands of market makers who got rich while the original holders found themselves left with little or nothing. Whether the episode was a net benefit is likely to remain in contention for a long time — as, indeed, the lesson of Hamilton's resumption remains in contention today.

Chapter 9

Perpetuity and "Divided Lives"

Eternity is two people and a ham.

—Universal truth

§ 9.01 Introduction

In Chapter 3, we learned how to compute the present value of an *annuity*, defined as a finite stream of equal payments. In this chapter, we will learn how to value a stream of payments that will extend for an infinite length of time, a.k.a. forever — a "perpetual" annuity, or more simply, a "perpetuity."

Since forever is a long time, students often find it implausible to suppose that there is any use for such a measure. In fact, as we shall try to demonstrate, there are good reasons for seeking to evaluate an infinite payment stream. For one, it is strictly realistic.

If you own Blackacre "in fee simple," for example, you have the right to all of the Blackacre's earnings forever — which is to say, the right to an infinite stream of payments. Even in situations where the payment stream is not infinite, it may be convenient to assume that it is infinite. The computation is easier, and the costs are not nearly as great as you might guess.

Once we have developed the arithmetic of the perpetuity, we get a useful by-product. That is, we get to analyze the problem which we shall call (for lack of a better name) "divided lives."

§ 9.02 The Arithmetic

First the arithmetic. In Chapter 3 above, we derived a formula for an annuity factor (AF) **See Ch.3**. Recall:

$$AF = \frac{(1 + r)^n - 1}{r(1 + r)^n}$$

Now we want to rearrange the formula, to offer a new insight. The content is *identical*, but the presentation is:

$$AF = \frac{1}{r} - \frac{1}{r(1 + r)^n}$$

For example, suppose we want to know the AF for five years at 6 percent. Now, take a second look at the equation above. Working out the division we can restate it as:

$$AF = 16.67 - 12.45 = 4.21$$

Recompute, but this time let $n = 15$:

$$AF = 16.67 - 6.95 = 9.71$$

And 50:

$$AF = 16.67 - 0.9 = 15.76$$

And 125:

$$AF = 16.67 - 0.01 = 16.66$$

You can see what is happening here. As n gets larger, the second "subpart" gets smaller, and the AF tends to equal the first subpart standing alone. When $n \to \infty$, then the AF becomes a *perpetuity factor* (PF):

$$PF = \frac{1}{r}$$

To get the PV of the perpetuity, we multiply C by the PF (or divide by r):

$$PF = C \times \frac{1}{r} = \frac{C}{r}$$

The perpetuity, then, can be understood as an annuity that lasts forever. It should not take any more explaining to convince you that the formula for a perpetuity is (if nothing else) much easier to manipulate than the formula for a finite annuity.

But to clarify what is afoot here, let us go back to our annuity formula and slightly reorganize it again:

$$\frac{1}{r} - \left| \left(\frac{1}{r} \right) \left(\frac{1}{(1+r)^n} \right) \right|$$

What have we done? We have split the second subpart into two separate terms. What does this version tell us? Follow $(1 \div r)$: note that $(1 \div r)$ appears in both subparts, and that the second subpart includes (among other things) a *discount factor*: $[1 \div (1+r)^n]$. Recall that we use a discount factor to bring a future value back to present value. Note that $1 \div r$ is our perpetuity. So the second subpart seems to present a *perpetuity* — minus the present value of a *second* perpetuity.

Restated, it seems to be the difference between two perpetuities, one beginning now, and one beginning in the future. Of course, the two perpetuities are the same, and this is as it should be. If the present value of a perpetuity beginning from $t=0$ is $1 \div r$, then the present value of a perpetuity beginning at $t=n$ should also be $1 \div r$ — because there is an infinite stream of payments in each of them, and there can be no relative ranking among infinities.

Students often find it implausible to assume that the perpetuity is a useful tool. Forever is a long time, after all, and most investors hold most investments for something less than infinity. This concern is understandable, but in fact, we think it is possible to show that the perpetuity is far more useful than it may at first appear. We can offer two reasons.

First, even if an investor does not last forever, an investment may. Suppose I buy Blackacre, with the intent to hold it just five years. How do I set the value? I estimate the revenues I may accrue during the five-year period. But then I also estimate the price that I will get on resale at the end of five years. In order to estimate this resale value, I have to put myself into the shoes of the prospective buyer. What will she pay? The answer is, of course, that her price will be set in the same way: the prospective buyer will estimate the revenues that she will receive while holding Blackacre, and then she will estimate Blackacre's resale price, and the cycle begins again.

Second, even if an investment does not last forever, it may be convenient to treat it as if it does. You can understand this point if you reflect again on the annuity equation presented above. Using this equation, we can see that the annuity is, in effect, the difference between one perpetuity and a second (later) perpetuity subtracted from the first perpetuity. We have also seen that the greater n is in the second subpart of our equation, the smaller is the second subpart — and, by corollary, the closer the annuity comes to approximate the perpetuity.

For example, we saw that when the rate is 6 percent, then the PF is 16.67, and when the term is 50 years, the AF is 15.76. So the AF is 95 percent of the perpetuity.

We have seen that as n increases, the AF increases. This so because n appears in the denominator of the second subpart of the equation, and not at all in the first subpart. The same is true of r: r also appears only in the denominator of the second subpart, so as r increases, AF tends to equal PF. So to continue with our earlier example, if the term is 50 years and the rate is 12 percent, then the AF is 99.7 percent of the PF (confirm this).

Summarizing, the higher the rate and the longer the term, the more the annuity approximates the perpetuity. Add to this the fact that the future is always uncertain and any prediction is bound to be an error. And recall that the perpetuity is a lot easier to compute on the back of an envelope. You can perhaps see why people often use perpetuity factors to estimate (finite) annuity terms.

Avoid This Mistake: Here is a common mistake in valuation that you can avoid. Suppose you own Blackacre subject to a bank loan which you must pay off in equal annual installments over 30 years. On this information, people who should know better will value Blackacre as if it had a 30-year life.

Wrong. The term of the loan says nothing at all about the prospective life of Blackacre. The only thing it tells you is how long the bank wants to be tied up in this deal. One way to see this is to ask, "at the end of 30 years, can we expect that some other bank will be willing to make a new loan secured by Blackacre?" If your answer is "yes," then what you are saying is that you expect Blackacre to have some positive value at that time. Extending the same logic, loan or no loan, you can perfectly well treat Blackacre as a perpetuity if the facts otherwise justify.

Multiplier: Finally, a word about jargon. You will meet a lot of people who profess not to measure perpetuities, but rather to measure values in "multiples of earnings" — this business is worth "ten times earnings," or "12 times earnings," and so forth. God bless'em, but they are doing the same thing we are. Recall that (1 ÷ 0.08) = 12.5. So, to say "we are valuing this business as a perpetuity at eight percent" is equivalent to saying that "we think this business is worth 12.5 times earnings."

As a corollary, if someone uses a multiplier, you can infer the interest rate she used. For example, suppose the enterprise earns $2 million a year and the witness values it at eight times earnings. Since (2)(8) = 16, the valuation is $16 million. On the other hand, 2 ÷ 16 equals 0.125, so the implied rate is 12.5 percent.

This suggests a useful rule of thumb. We have already pointed out that the *higher* the interest rate, the *lower* the factor and, other things being equal, the lower the ultimate valuation. We could just as well say, the *lower* the factor (or, as we call it here, "the multiple"), the lower the ultimate valuation. Restated: when you argue for a *high* rate and a *low* multiple, you are arguing for a *low* valuation. By contrast, when you argue for a *low* rate and a *high* multiple, you are arguing for a *high* valuation.

§ 9.03 Divided Lives

As a by-product of our analysis of the perpetuity, we are now in a position to understand another approach to valuation. Recall the annuity formula as set forth above:

$$\text{PVAF} = \frac{1}{r} - \frac{1}{r(1 + r)^n}$$

We said you could think of this formula as two perpetuities, separated by a minus sign. Another way of putting it is to say we have a perpetuity (1 ÷ r) minus a "residual" — the residual being the present value of the perpetuity that survives after the annuity. Let PVA = "present value of the annuity." Let PVP = "present value of the perpetuity." Let PVR = "present value of the residual." Then:

$$\text{PVA} = \text{PVP} - \text{PVR}$$

The associated factors would be:

$$\text{PVAF} = \text{PVPF} - \text{PVRF}$$

As we said above, the higher the n, the smaller the residual, and when n = infinity, the residual becomes vanishingly small. But there are a variety of situations where n is not infinitely large and the residual is not vanishingly small. These are situations were we may have two valuable interests — the annuity and the residual perpetuity. In effect, we may divide the life of the perpetuity — hence "divided lives." We consider several aspects of this problem of divided lives.

[A] Leasing

Perhaps the most obvious example of the problem of divided lives is the matter of leasing. Consider the situation of Landor, who owns Blackacre with a perpetual income stream estimated at $100 per period. At a rate of 10 percent, we can say that Blackacre is worth $1,000.

Tess tells Landor that she'd like to buy the use of Blackacre for seven years. What should Landor charge her for the privilege? As a good first guess, we can value the right as a seven-year annuity. Using the formula we developed above, we could value the annuity at $487. Landor would retain the residual, with a PV of $1,000 − $487 = $513. This is a standard deal with a familiar nomenclature. You wouldn't have to be a law student to recognize Landor as the Landlord and Tess as the tenant.

The same logic might apply when MegaMotor undertakes to offer its new Piranah sports car on lease for a three-year term. The arithmetic might be a bit more tedious because the Piranah presumably will not last forever and so the remainder is not a perpetuity, but the general logic is the same: annuity in the hands of the lessee, residual in the hands of the lessor.

None of this is arcane. Indeed, the law offers well-recognized rules for sorting out the rights of "owners" (lessors, landlords), as distinguished from those of tenants or lessees. We say that Landor, the "owner," holds a "fee simple," an "estate in land." Tess, the "tenant" gets a mere "chattel real." On the same principle, accountants put "ownership" interests on the balance sheet, but leave leases "off balance sheet." The Bankruptcy Code treats leases differently from "sales." The Uniform Commercial Code has an article governing sales of goods and a separate article governing leases (the Tax Code treats leases differently also, but this may be a sidetrack; the Tax Code does *everything* its own way).

This is perhaps plausible at first glance. But on closer scrutiny, it seems hard to justify. For one thing, the "owner" of a lease is an "owner," just as much as the owner of the underlying interest — the only difference is that what he "owns" is a finite, rather than an infinite, term. For another, consider the case of Greenacre and Whiteacre, which are alike in every respect. You can lease Greenacre for 99 years for $12,000 a year (payable at year end). You can buy Whiteacre for $100,000. Assume an r of 12 percent. Apply the "divided lives" equation; we can see that the present value of the term is $99,998.86, and of the residual, just $1.34. It is hard to believe that great distinctions should turn on such trifling numbers.

Two Practical Wrinkles: Finally, a couple of wrinkles that aggravate the lease/sale confusion in practice. First, suppose your client is considering a three-year lease on a new Belcher forklift truck for his factory. Of course, no one knows what the truck will be worth at the end of three years, but a reasonable guess is that it will be worth $20,000. The lease includes a clause that provides:

> At the end of the lease term, the truck will be appraised by an independent appraiser. The lessee has the option, but not the obligation, to buy the truck at the appraised price. *Provided, however* that if the appraised price is less than $20,000, the lessee is obliged to pay the lessor the difference between $20,000 and the appraised price, in addition to all other obligations in this lease.

As far as your client is concerned, there is no earthly reason for calling this deal a "lease." The lessee has the opportunity to enjoy any increase in the value of the property, and the obligation to pay its entire cost. If anything counts as full ownership, this would seem to qualify. Statutes and accounting rules pretty much reach the same result, although sometimes they come at it back-handed. Nonetheless, you continue to see documents with terms like these that bear the name of "lease."

Second, a somewhat more common, and more complicated, contract is the one where the lessee has the option to buy the truck at the end of the lease term at a pre-defined price (for instance, $20,000), but does *not* have the obligation to cover any shortfall. This option right may be valuable in itself. A full valuation of the lease contract would require that we value this option as well as the lease term. It can be done, but we have not yet studied the tools necessary to the job. You might want to consider this issue later in the course when we study options and contingent claims.

Background: There is a good general introduction to federal law on consumer lease disclosure at:

http://www.bog.frb.fed.us/pubs/leasing/d-form.html.

[B] Rent-to-Own

There is a curious footnote to the topic of leasing. That is the growth of the "rent-to-own" industry as a means of merchandising consumer goods. The customer "rents" furniture, appliances, television sets — sometimes even jewelry — for a weekly rental payment. Beyond the week, there is no obligation to continue: the "renter" can surrender the item at any time for any reason, or for no reason.

But if he fails to "make the prescribed number of renewals" (translated: keep up the payments), he will lose the item and all that he has paid.. From information on the industry's trade association Web site, it is clear that this is a business for people low on income and low on sophistication: substantially none of their customers have household incomes in excess of $75,000, and fewer than 10 percent are college graduates.

Consumer activists think it is an abomination: a device to prey on the vulnerable or the unprotected. The industry for its part says the rent-to-own stores respond to "a growing consumer need for acquiring the use of household products without incurring debt or jeopardizing the family's credit."

And that is the linchpin: "without incurring debt." For the industry has pretty well succeeded in persuading the legislatures and the courts that these open-ended "keep it or walk away" transfers are not credit transactions. Not being credit transactions, they are exempt from standard usury and credit disclosure laws. Ironically at this point, the industry has succeeded in selling the legislatures of most states on a system of statutory regulation that pretty much leaves the rent-to-own industry intact as an exception to standard consumer credit law.

[C] Life Estates and Remainders

We can apply the same logic to a problem beloved of all first-year law students: sorting out the rights of the "life estate" versus the "remainder." In the last section, we noted that the annuity factor is the perpetuity factor minus the residual factor:

$$PVAF = PVPF - PVRF$$

Rearranging:

$$PVPF = PVAF + PVRF$$

In words, we are saying that the perpetuity always equals the sum of the annuity plus the residual — no more, no less. But the *relative* proportions will change. For example, consider a 20-year annuity. If the rate is 4 percent, then the factor equation is:

$$25 = 13.5903 + 11.4097$$

If the rate is 10 percent:

$$10 = 8.5136 + 1.4864$$

But now, compare the relative proportions. In the 4 percent case the annuity is 13.5903 ÷ 25 = 54.36 percent of the whole. The residual is the remaining 45.64 percent. If the rate is 10 percent, then the annuity is 85.14 percent of the total, while the residual is just 14.86 percent.

For a practical example, consider your client Ned, who holds the vested remainder in Blackacre behind Annie, his aunt, the life tenant. Blackacre is worth $1 million. Mark, a market maker, has offered to buy the remainder outright for $200,000. Is it a good deal?

To answer this question, Ned borrows a life expectancy table from a neighboring insurance office and determines that Annie is likely to live another 18.35 years. Now, everything turns on the rate. At a 5 percent discount rate, Ned's remainder is probably worth 40.85 percent of the total of $408,485 and Mark's bid is far too low. At 15 percent, it is worth only 7.69 percent of the total or $76,948 and Mark's offer is generous.

For another example, consider your client Otho, who owns and occupies Dingly Dell, his home in the sovereign republic of Magenta, a nation whose tax laws are somewhat like our own, only simpler. The Magenta Revenue Code says that Otho can deduct the value of any gift to charity from otherwise taxable income. Otho wants to give the home to his old law school (a charity) when he dies. A fund-raiser from the law school tells Otho that he can put money in his pocket if he makes the gift today.

Here is how: Otho makes an outright gift of Dingly Dell to the school, but he retains a life estate himself. The house is worth $850,000. Tad, the tax collector consults his actuarial table and determines that Otho has a life expectancy of 14 years. Tad applies the "regulation rate" of 9 percent. On these numbers, Tad determines that Otho has given away 29.92 percent of the total value, or $254,359. It happens that Otho has other income totaling $300,000 on which he would otherwise have to pay tax at a 31 percent rate. Offsetting the deduction against the other income gives Otho an immediate tax saving equaling 31 percent of $254,359, or $78,851.

Chapter 10

Application: Common Stock

Took it All.

—Henry Watterson[1]

§ 10.01 Introduction

We turn now to the task of valuing that most familiar of all investments — common stock. In one sense, this job ought to be easy. Common stock is the residual claim. So the common stockholder gets whatever is left, like Henry with the cashbox in the quotation above.

Of course it isn't that easy. Among other difficulties, earnings may fluctuate and so estimating the size of the residual is no simple matter. We leave aside this problem of fluctuation for a moment, expecting to return to it later (see Chapter 23 below). A more urgent problem arises because of the nature of the corporate structure. Oversimplified, shareholders elect directors who appoint managers, and managers decide how to deal with the earnings. They may pay them out to shareholders in the form of dividends. Indeed, they may sometimes pay dividends even if they do not have earnings. Or they may retain the earnings for use in the company.

So anyone constructing a model of share value must consider, first, the problem of estimating earnings, and second, the question of what the managers do with the earnings once they get them.

§ 10.02 A Crude Model — Value as a Function of Earnings

In this context, we begin the job of constructing a model to estimate share value. Based on our prior knowledge, a crude but serviceable model suggests itself. That is: estimate earnings per share to be expected periodically, beginning at t = 1. Call these "EPS." Note that EPS works just like C in our earlier perpetuity formula, C ÷ r = PV. For reasons that will become apparent later, redefine PV as "P_0." Then:

$$P_0 = \frac{EPS}{r}$$

So, if EPS = \$4 and r = 8 percent, then PV = \$50.

Continuing to apply the perpetuity analysis, we know we can say either that PV is EPS either *divided by r* or *multiplied by* 1 ÷ r. In our example, 1 ÷

[1] Henry Watterson, the owner and (great) editor of the Louisville Courier-Journal, liked to take his walking-around money out of the company till. His bookkeeper told him, "Henry, it is your paper and so it is your money, but it would make my life easier if you would leave me a note telling me what you have taken." Henry grunted his assent. Next week, the bookkeeper found the till empty except for a note, which said, "Took it all. (Signed) Henry."

(0.08) = 12.5 and 12.5 x $4 = $50. This 12.5 is the term that we previously identified as the discount factor (DF). So:

$$(EPS)(DF) = PV$$

Rearranging:

$$DF = \frac{EPS}{PV}$$

In our example, $4 ÷ $50 = 12.5. Market observers often use the discount factor, so defined, as a crude measure of share value. They call it the "price-earnings ratio," or simply the "PE." So if LittleCo, with earnings of $4, trades at $50, we say it has a PE of 12.5.

People often quote the PE as an index of share value. There are many difficulties with using the PE as a measure of share value, some of which we discuss below. For the moment, note just one: the PE works on the assumption that earnings will remain constant, *and* that they will remain available to shareholders. At least for most corporations, nether assumption is even remotely plausible.[2]

§ 10.03 As a Function of Dividends

Here is a second possible measure. Recall that the manager may pay a dividend to shareholder, and that the dividend may be less (or sometimes, more) than the earnings. Define this dividend, payable periodically beginning at t=1, as "Div_1." Since it is the dividend and not the earnings that reach the shareholder, we could use our perpetuity model, but refined so as to value not earnings but dividends.

$$P_0 = \frac{Div_1}{r}$$

We could call it (although the term is not widely used) a *price-dividend* ratio, on the model of the PE, above. But this price-dividend ratio has the same difficulties as the PE. And it has some new difficulties of its own. Specifically, it tells us nothing about what becomes of the earnings *other than* dividends. These also, after all, belong to the shareholder, and should be valued accordingly.

§ 10.04 Dividends Plus a Residual

As a third attempt, we could break our analysis into two parts. We could estimate dividends "up to a point" (say, one year). Then we could estimate the present value of the residual beyond the point. For example, suppose we are thinking about buying the stock now, at t=0, the day after the last dividend, and we expect to sell it at t=1, the day after the next dividend. Call the dividend at time = t, "Div_t." Call the selling price at any time = t "P_t." Then the price we should be willing to pay today at t=0 should be:

[2] You may have noticed that the PE ratio is just the "multiple" under a new name. *See* § 9.02 above.

$$P_0 = \frac{Div_1 + P_1}{1 + r}$$

For example, suppose the next year's dividend will be $10, and we expect the price after payment of that dividend to be $105. Let the rate ($r$) be 15 percent. Then we should be willing to pay ($115 ÷ 1.15) today.

But what determines P_1? Recall that P_1 is what we should expect a rational investor to pay as of t = 1. Using the same analysis we used above, we could say that P_1 would impound (a) the dividend due a year hence at t = 2, plus (b) the residual value after the payment of that dividend — both brought back to their "present" (that is, t = 1) value.

So:

$$P_1 = \frac{Div_2 + P_2}{1 + r}$$

We could substitute the material to the left of the "equals" sign for P_1 in our previous equation. Then we would say:

$$P_0 = \frac{Div_1}{1 + r} + \frac{Div_2 + P_2}{(1 + r)^2}$$

This works if we assume Div_2 to be $10.50 and P_2 to be $110.25. Then:

$$P_0 = \frac{10}{1.15} + \frac{10.50 + 110.25}{(1.15)^2}$$

Dividing through, you get ($8.70 + $91.30) = $100. We could, of course, continue this analysis for P_3 and so forth — indeed, for any number of time periods out to some arbitrarily chosen "horizon" (call it H). Let the Greek letter σ (sigma) designate the sum of all the individual payments from t = 1 through to the horizon. Then, we could state a general formula for the value of a share:

$$P_0 = \left[\sum_{t=1}^{H} \frac{Div_t}{(1 + r)^t}\right] + \frac{P_H}{(1 + r)^H}$$

So, we get the sum of dividends plus the horizon price. But the further out on the horizon you go, the smaller the horizon component (the future price) becomes relative to the total value, and the larger the sum of dividends component becomes. As we get closer and closer to infinity, the present value of the horizon price becomes infinitely small until we can ignore it. Then we have:

$$P = \sum_{t=1}^{\infty} \frac{Div_t}{(1+r)^t}$$

This is better than the earlier equations because it recognizes: (a) that the dividend may change over time, but (b) that in the end, the value to the shareholder is the discounted present value of all the dividends.

§ 10.05 Note on Stock Price Information

For most of us, the problem is not finding stock price information — it is figuring out how to avoid it. Flip on the morning news and your reporter is giving you yesterday's high and low prices. Some stations even ribbon stock prices underneath their regular programming, almost as if they were as important as football scores. Sources proliferate, and we would not think of trying to instruct you on how to read all of them.

The information content will vary, but any listing of a stock price will have to begin with either the *name* of the company, or perhaps its *ticker symbol* — a shorthand code name, harking back to the days when stockbrokers watched the prices roll into their offices on narrow pieces of ticker tape. By definition, you will also get a *current price*. Chances are you will also get some information on past prices. For example, you are likely to get a report of the high and low prices for the last trading day, and sometimes also for the last *year*. Many also give you the PE, computed as the earnings per share (EPS) for the past 12 months, divided by the most recent share price. You may also get a number for the *dividend*, if any — typically the sum of all dividends paid during the past 12 months.

Chapter 11

Application: Growth Stock

Where are the customer's yachts?

—William R. Travers[1]

§ 11.01 Introduction

At the end of the day, all the residual earnings belong to the shareholders. But the problem with stock valuation is that the manager may pay out all the earnings, or less, or more. A useful model of stock valuation will try to cope with the matter of retained earnings. To cope with the problem, consider the conversation recorded by a fly on the wall at the annual meeting of Consolidated Widget, Inc.

Report from the Boardroom at Consolidated Widget, Inc.:

It had been a good year for Consolidated Widget. When they closed the books on December 31, the accountants showed a clear profit of $100 — a return of 10 percent on the asset base of $1,000. Over caviar and Dom Perignon, the directors gathered to consider what to do with the money.

"More research and development," said Randall. "Widgets are changing, and if we don't get on board, the train will leave the station without us."

"I agree about the market," said Calvin, "but why do the work when someone else has already done it for you? There's a nice little widget works down the street that has a lot of cutting-edge products. I think we can pick it up for a song."

"Aren't you both being a bit presumptuous with someone else's money?" asked Orville. "This company belongs to the shareholders. Pay the earnings to them as a dividend and let them decide."

"Dividend, schmividend," said Uriah. "We should reward ourselves, but we should do it as a favor to the shareholders. After all, a well-paid manager is a happy manager. If we get good compensation, we will do better work."

[1] Gazing at New York harbor and admiring a squadron of brokers' yachts. Reprint, Fred Schwed, Where Are the Customer's Yachts? (1995).

§ 11.02 Earnings, Dividends and the Function of the Manager

In the Consolidated Widget boardroom, as between Randall, Calvin and Uriah, who is right? On the information given, you can't tell. The answer is: management should do *whatever is most productive for shareholders*. That means: if management can use the money to make more money for the shareholders than the shareholders can make for themselves, then management ought to retain the money and take advantage of its investment opportunities. Indeed, if this is the case, and if shareholders understand what management is doing, then we can expect shareholders to reward management for *not* paying the dividend. By the same logic, if shareholders have better investment opportunities than managers, then managers ought to pay the money back.

If you read the financial pages, you will quickly see that this debate over how to spend corporate earnings is no mere academic exercise. Consider Intel, the computer chip maker. For a decade, Intel paid no dividend at all, but plowed all its earnings back into research and development. The stock price soared. Why? We can infer that investors were delighted not to get a dividend, because they figured the managers were doing better with the money than the investors could have done on their own.

Finally, one year Intel paid a tiny dividend — and apologized. Not to worry, Intel told its investors, we still have enough money to sustain our valuable research program. In fact, the market was not delighted. The stock price sagged. Apparently investors took the dividend as a sign that Intel might not be as productive in the future as it had been (all this took place a number of years ago; it might be interesting to ask whose judgment was vindicated by Intel's continued apparent success).

In the flush 1990s, stories like Intel's became commonplace as countless Internet companies piled up losses while they watched their stocks soar. When analysts began to complain that Amazon.com wasn't showing a profit, founder Jeff Bezos responded that he certainly hoped not; his business plan depended on piling dollars into investment for growth, and any effort to sidetrack them to investors would mean opportunity lost.

But not all stories have a happy ending. Consider Ford Motor Company. When Ford introduced the Taurus in the mid-1980s, the company revolutionized the car market, earning itself a bundle. Flush with the success of the Taurus, Ford had the money, the talent and the experience to pull off a repeat, revolutionizing the car business into the Twenty-First Century. Did Ford seize this opportunity? It did not. Ford put its engineers on short rations while it blew the winnings on costly and improvident mergers. By the early 1990s, Toyota had Lexus, Nissan had Infiniti, and Ford had — the Taurus. In retrospect, it was pretty clear that Ford would have been better off just giving the money back to its shareholders.

Indeed, the issue of investment policy is one of the great questions about the role of the large public company in modern society. Are managers too short-sighted, passing up good growth opportunities so shareholders can get a short-term fix? Or are they too improvident, pouring too much into costly follies at shareholders' expense? You can see that either way, it is important to have a good measure of what constitutes "growth" in corporate earnings.

§ 11.03 Defining Growth

In short, we want managers to retain earnings if they will "grow." To make sense out of this statement, we need to know how to measure "growth." Here is an example. Your client is Zyplonics, Inc., the world's leading maker of lemons out of lemonade. Zyplonics will have earnings per share (EPS) next year (t = 1) equal to $4 per share. Taking account of Zyplonics' risk, class, etc., the market demands a return (r) on Zyplonics stock of 16 percent. If Zyplonics retains no earnings, then Zyplonics pays out all earnings in dividends (Div). Assuming no growth, then we can value Zyplonics as a perpetuity with a value (P_0) (EPS_1) $\div r$ = (Div_1) $\div r$ = $4 ÷ 0.16 = $25 per share.

But Zyplonics has a chance to invest in a project to develop a new elixir well. The project will require Zyplonics to withhold 60 percent of its EPS_1 earnings from dividends, and plow them back (PB) into new project. The return on investment (ROI) will be 20 percent of the t = 1 PB, beginning at t = 2 and continuing forever. Starting at t = 2, Zyplonics will resume a 100 percent payout (PO) of earnings. Note that this all implies a growth (g) in earnings between t = 1 and t = 2 as follows:

$$g = \frac{(EPS_1)(PB)(ROI)}{(EPS_1)}$$

In our example, our t = 1 earnings will be $4 and we will plow back 60 percent (or $2.40). On that $2.40, we will get a perpetual return of 20 percent (or 48 cents).

$$g = \frac{(\$4)(0.6)(0.2)}{(\$4)} = 0.12$$

Our t = 2 earnings will be:

$$EPS_1\ (1 + g) = \$4\ (1.12) = \$4.48$$

Recall that these earnings from t = 2 to infinity will be paid out in full. So to value Zyplonics, we begin by valuing this perpetuity. The value is:

$$\$4.48 \div (0.16) = \$28$$

But this $4.48 EPS begins at t = 2, so the perpetuity must be its value as of t = 1. In order to know its value today, we must discount it for one period. Thus,

$$\$28 \div (1.16) = \$24.14$$

But then we must value the t = 1 dividend. Recall that our PB was only 60 percent of t = 1 earnings. By definition, then, our PO must be:

$$(1 - 0.6) = 0.4 = 40 \text{ percent}$$

As of t = 0, that sum would be worth:

$$\$1.60 \div 1.16 = \$1.38$$

Summing the two, we get a current share price:

$$\$1.38 + \$24.14 = \$25.52.$$

So withholding earnings at t = 1 leads to an increase in share price from \$25 to \$25.52, or by 52 cents.

To double-check, suppose management followed the same reinvestment strategy, except that its ROI was *only 16 percent*, rather than 20. In this case, EPS at t = 2 will be:

$$\$4 + [(\$4)(0.6)(0.16)] = \$4.384$$

The t = 1 share price will be:

$$\$4.384 \div (0.16) = \$27.40$$

The t = 0 value is:

$$\$27.40 \div (1.16) = \$23.62$$

The shareholder is also entitled to the t = 1 dividend of \$1.60, whose t = 0 value is \$1.38, as before. So the total t = 0 value is:

$$\$1.38 + \$23.62 = \$25$$

This is the same as the share price without reinvestment. The reason is that the *required rate of return* (r) on Zyplonics stock is 16 percent. If the ROI is *also* 16 percent, then managers are doing no better than investors can do for themselves, and they add nothing to investor value by retaining and reinvesting. They lose nothing either, of course, which is why the share price remains at \$25.

To see if you understand, try computing the value of a share if the ROI is *lower* than 16 percent — say, 10 percent. If that is true, then of course the present value of the "growth" company will be *lower* than \$25 per share. Nobody ever plans it that way, of course. On the other hand, we might read in the paper that management announced a reinvestment program and the price of stock fell. In that case, we could infer that investors thought the reinvestment program was a loser even though management liked it.

To avoid confusion, remember that we are juggling *three different "rates"* here. We have r, the required rate of return on our stock. We have ROI, the return on investment of our plowback. And we have g, the rate of growth. Make sure you understand which rate you are talking about when.

§ 11.04 Perpetual Growth

If we can compute growth in this way for one period, it is easy enough to see how we might extend the analysis to multiple periods. For example, suppose we knew Zyplonics would grow not for one year only, but for two years. It would be easy to set up a framework where we measure the individual intermediate dividends for t = 1 and t = 2, and then for the perpetuity thereafter. But this is cumbersome. Naturally we want to find some way to simplify if we can.

Here is one important simplification. Suppose we know EPS_1, and r, and g. Suppose we assume that both g and r will remain stable *forever*. In this case, EPS $\div$ r = our share price. If we do not pay out all earnings, it turns out that we can state the present value of the perpetuity as:

$$\frac{Div_1}{(r-g)}$$

There is a perfectly straightforward proof of this relationship in § 11.14 below, but if you are willing to take it on faith, you can ignore it for now without loss of continuity. Note that the numerator here is Div_1, not EPS_1, and note that Div_1 no longer equals EPS_1. Rather, $Div_1 = (EPS_1)(PO)$, the percentage of earnings that is paid out in dividends. Note further that the denominator is the rate of return *minus* the growth rate. Do you find this counterintuitive? Perhaps you will be more comfortable if you remember that the smaller the denominator, the larger the quotient — so subtracting growth yields an increase in share price.

Here is an example. We know that Zyplonics, above, has an r of 16 percent, and that t=1 earnings will be \$4. We know that a 60 percent PB and a 20 percent ROI will yield a g of 12 percent. If PB is 60 percent, then Div_1 = \$1.60. So:

$$\frac{\$1.60}{(0.16 - 0.12)} = \$40$$

To check your understanding, recompute assuming that ROI is 16 percent. You should be able to satisfy yourself that P_0 = \$25. Then recompute, assuming that ROI is 10 percent. You should get a P_0 of \$16.

What if g = 16 percent? In that case, $(r-g)$ will equal zero. But \$1.60 divided by zero is *infinity*. This doesn't seem right — and it isn't. So, $Div_1 \div (r-g)$ works only if the growth rate is *smaller than* the required rate of return. But since we should be skeptical of a high growth rate anyway, this isn't a big problem.

Continuing our analysis, let's continue with our original assumptions, except this time change the *plowback ratio* — increase it to 70 percent. What will be the impact on our share price? Recall that g = PB x ROI. So, $g = 0.7 \times 0.2 = 0.14$ — higher than before. Our payout ratio will change as well. Since PO = (1 − PB), and since PB equals 70 percent, then PO equals 30 percent and Div_1 will equal \$4 × 0.3 = \$1.20. The stock price will be \$1.20 ÷ (0.16 − 0.14) = \$60. This is a lower dividend but a higher share price than before, but this makes sense when you recall we are investing a higher proportion of our earnings at the 20 percent rate.

Here is something else we can learn from this equation. Recall that the value of the no-growth Zyplonics was $(EPS_1) \div r$ = \$4 ÷ (0.16) = \$25. If the "growth" Zyplonics is worth \$40, and no-growth Zyplonics is worth \$25, how shall we account for the difference? It must be that \$40 − \$25 or \$15 represents the *present value of growth opportunities* (PVGO). We can express this relationship in various ways. Here are two:

First, the t=0 price must equal the "basic" share price plus the present value of growth opportunities:

$$P_0 = \frac{EPS_1}{r} + PVGO$$

$$= \$25 + \$15 = \$40$$

Rearranging, we can see isolate earnings per share as a percentage of share price:

$$\frac{EPS_1}{P_0} = r \times [1 - \frac{(PVGO)}{(P_0)}]$$

$$= \$4 \div \$40 = (0.16)\ [1 - (\$15 \div \$40)] = (0.16)\ (1 - 0.375) = 0.10$$

In words, earnings per share equals 10 percent of share price, or 62.5 percent of the rate of return.

A 36,000 Dow? In early 2,000, the Dow Jones Industrial Average was trading between 10,000 and 11,000, riding the crest of the most spectacular runup in history. The mood of the financial press was edgy: no one was ready to panic, but there was a widespread sense it couldn't last forever.

Not so James K. Glassman, the financial columnist. Glassman argued that we could look forward to a 36,000 Dow — nearly four times the current level.[2]

We won't try to weigh the evidence for Glassman's optimism here, but we can ask: under what circumstances could he be right? Consider DowCo, a hypothetical stock that tracks the Dow. It trades at $125. All agree that the predicted growth rate for DowCo is 4 percent. The dividend is $10 a share. Recall our model:

$$\frac{\$10.50}{(0.12 - g)} = \$105$$

Solving for r, we get 12 percent. So if 12 percent is in fact what the market demands by way of return for DowCo, then everything checks. But what if investors are in fact willing to accept a lower rate of return for DowCo — say, 6.2 percent. Then:

$$\frac{\$10.50}{(0.12 - 0.091)}$$

The indicated value of a share of DowCo is about $450, some 3.6 times its earlier price. So, we can anticipate that once investors come to price DowCo as a function of their true required rate, the price will rise to some $450 a share.

Of course, the same logic would apply if we were correct in our estimate of a (high) rate of return, but incorrect in our estimate of growth.

§ 11.05 Relating Growth and Earnings

Here is another way to see how growth increases value. Recall our first growth example in § 11.03 above. Zyplonics looked forward to EPS of $4 per year as a perpetuity. But the company chose to plow back 60 percent of its t=1 earnings, or $2.40. In exchange for that $2.40, Zyplonics bought a 20 percent ROI — a perpetuity of 48 cents, beginning at t=2. Adding our "original" earnings of $4 a share, this gave us a total of $4.48 per year forever.

[2] *See* James K. Glassman & Kevin A. Hassett, *Dow 36,000*, Atlantic Monthly, Sept. 1999.

We noted that the advance from \$4 to \$4.48 constituted a one-time growth rate of 12 percent.

Another way of looking at the same deal is to isolate the string of 48-cent "coupons" that we bought with the \$2.40 investment. We receive payment on the first ticket at t=2. So capitalized as of t=1 we have:

$$(\$0.48) \div (0.16) = \$3$$

Seen in this light, we can say that we spent \$2.40 to get \$3.

In our earlier example, we assumed that there was no more growth after the first increment. But suppose instead that we can *continue* to plow back and reinvest between t=2 and t=3, just as we did before between t=1 and t=2. That is, suppose at t=2 we have earnings of \$4.48, from which we will pay out 40 percent (\$1.792) and retain 60 percent (\$2.688).

$$(\$2.688)(0.2) = \$0.5476$$

We can capitalize this return at the 16 percent rate, giving us \$3.36. So we have spent \$2.688 to get \$3.36. This is a net present value of (\$3.36 − \$2.688) = \$0.672 or 67.2 cents. Recall that last year's perpetuity was only 60 cents, so this year's constitutes an increase of 12 percent.

Now take a second look at the \$3 value that we acquire by reinvesting at t=1. What did it get us? It got us a permanent 60 cent gain, which can be *capitalized* at the 16 percent rate, and which will *grow* at the 12 percent rate. In other words, the PVGO must be:

$$(0.6) \div (0.16 - 0.12) = \$15$$

Which is what we are looking for, the PVGO, the relationship between earnings and growth.

To double-check our reasoning, assume that we plow back not 60 percent of earnings, but 70 percent. That is, we reinvest:

$$(0.7)(\$4) = \$2.80$$

which earns:

$$(\$2.80)(0.2) = \$0.56$$

If this 56 cents is a perpetuity then its NPV is:

$$(0.56 \div 0.16) - \$2.80 = \$0.70$$

Note \$0.56 ÷ \$4 = 0.14, so g in this example is 14 percent. Growth is larger because we have been able to reinvest more money at the (high) 20 percent ROI. Trusting that the investor will continue to invest 70 percent of earnings at a 20 percent ROI, then we can see that the PVGO is:

$$(0.7) \div (0.16 - 0.14) = \$35$$

If P = 70 percent, then PO must equal (1 − 0.7) = 0.3 = 30 percent. So Div_1 must be (\$4)(0.3) = \$1.20. If r is 16 percent and g = 14 percent, then:

$$Div_1 \div (r - g) = \$1.20 \div 0.02 = \$60$$

Recall also that $P_0 = (EPS_1 \div r) + PVGO$. So here: \$60 = \$25 + \$35, which is exactly what we get when we discount dividends by the growth adjusted rate of return.

§ 11.06 Note on Estimating Components

Suppose you want to use the formula $d_1 \div (r - g) = P_0$ to learn more about a security. You can find d_1 and P_0 easily enough: just look them up in the newspaper. But what about r and g? They are not so readily available. Since we have here a *single* equation with *two* unknowns, we cannot derive the unknowns from the equation. On the other hand, if we knew *either* r or g, then we could derive the other. How do we do it?

The abrupt answer is: we pay a securities analyst. Anybody can manipulate the model, but they get their fingernails dirty coming up with the data, and the measure of their success (and their paycheck) is the accuracy of their forecasts. For a less abrupt answer — you will learn something about estimating r in a later chapter, when we study the Capital Asset Pricing Model (CAPM) and its kin.

As to "*g*," there is no simple cookbook: you make your best guess, depending on your forecast for the health of the economy and of the company. One *crude* measure is to extrapolate from past growth (but recall the "Elvis Impersonator" analysis, § 2.04 above). On the other hand, *if* you believe past performance is a guide, you may be able to put it to work. Suppose you know that the $t = 0$ dividend is \$3. You determine that the dividend 5 years ago ($t = -5$) was \$1.75. You can determine the periodic growth rate by taking the geometric mean, the same way we did to price a zero-coupon bond. Recall:

$$(FV \div PV)^{1/n} - 1 = r$$

So $(\$3 \div \$1.75)^{(0.2)} - 1 = 0.1138$ or 11.4 percent. Many analysts will use this sort of extrapolation for lack of anything better, but you ought to be able to recognize just how crude it must be.

The "geometric mean" is a form of "average." Can we save time by simply adding up the past prices and taking an arithmetic average? We cannot. Consider the past prices of GroCo:

t=	Price
0	100
1	50
2	75

In words, we have a 50 percent decrease (100 to 50) followed by a 50 percent increase (50 to 75). The "average" change is therefore zero — hardly a helpful datum for a stock whose price has fallen by 25 percent. But:

$$(75 \div 100)^{1/2} - 1 = -0.134 = -13.4 \textit{ percent}$$

Note the minus sign. To confirm, note that $1 - 0.134 = 0.866$, and that $100(0.8666)^2 = 75$. The geometric mean is altogether more helpful.

§ 11.07 A Two-Stage Model

In our previous example, we treated growth as perpetual and constant. Most newcomers regard this assumption as wildly unrealistic. It is perhaps not quite as unrealistic as it first appears, for a couple of reasons.

First, in a healthy, expanding economy, we can expect *most* companies to grow: that is how a growing economy becomes what it is.

On the other hand (this is the second reason), remember what happens when you measure the residual perpetuity after a finite series: the longer the finite series, the smaller the present value of the residual — and the less consequential the error. So even if growth is not "perpetual," still if it lasts for "a long time," our perpetuity formula may offer a reasonably good guess.

But even if you accept these two points, still there remains the question of the *size* of the growth estimate. In our previous example, we used a figure of 12 percent. The *economy* may grow at 2, 3, maybe 4 percent. If this is the *general* rate, then isn't a *particular* rate of 12 percent almost certainly too high? Almost certainly yes. If someone tells you he can sustain 3 percent growth forever, you might give him a second look. If he says he will get 12 percent forever, hold on to your wallet.

But there is more to be said on the issue. Even though no company can expect to do 12 percent *forever*, still a lot of companies go through *phases*. We might expect an "early" stage — a kind of "corporate adolescence" — during which we can plow back a large portion of our income and enjoy a high growth rate. We might expect a later stage during which our opportunities would still be attractive, but less numerous, leading us to reduce our plowback ratio (and correspondingly, our growth rate). We can value such a company. We do the job in separate parts. First, we value the individual dividends of the high-growth stage:

$$\frac{\text{Div}_1}{(1+r)} + \frac{\text{Div}_1(1+g_h)}{(1+r)^2} + \frac{\text{Div}_1(1+g_h)^2}{(1+r)^3} + \ldots + \frac{\text{Div}_1(1+g_h)^{n-1}}{(1+r)^n}$$

You can probably follow the notation. "Div_1" is the dividend at t = 1. It yields "g_h" which is the growth rate for the high-growth period. Naturally "n" equals the number of periods of high growth. Note that in this formulation, "g" always lags one digit behind "r." That is because we start compounding growth one period later. Note that in all terms of the equation above, the numerator is just a fancy way of defining the dividend for the period in question.

This series will give us the present value of the dividends in the high growth period. Then we value the low-growth "perpetuity." We already know how to value a perpetuity. With adaptations to suit, the formula would look like this:

$$\frac{\text{Div}_1(1+g_h)^{n-1}(1+g_l)}{(r-g_l)}$$

We can recognize "g_l" as the growth rate for the low-growth period. The numerator of this equation is the dividend for the period $t=n$ multiplied by $(1 + g_l)$ — that is, the dividend for period $t=n+1$. The denominator is the familiar $(r - g)$, using the low-growth rate. Taken together, the quotient gives us the present value *as of* $t=n$. But we need the present value as of $t=0$. How do we get it? Easy enough: we multiply by the appropriate discount factor, which is $1 \div (1 + r)^n$. That is:

$$\frac{\text{Div}_1(1+g_h)^{n-1}(1+g_l)}{(r-g_l)} \times \frac{1}{(1+r)^n}$$

Or simply:

$$\frac{\text{Div}_1(1+g_h)^{n-1}(1+g_l)}{(r-g_l)(1+r)^n}$$

Combining the equation for the dividend stream and the equation for the perpetuity, we get the total value:

$$\frac{\text{Div}_1}{(1+r)} + \frac{\text{Div}_1(1+g_h)}{(1+r)^2} + \frac{\text{Div}_1(1+g_h)^2}{(1+r)^3} + \ldots + \frac{\text{Div}_1(1+g_h)^{n-1}}{(1+r)^n} + \frac{\text{Div}_1(1+g_h)^{n-1}(1+g_l)}{(r-g_l)(1+r)^n}$$

Let's do an example. DivCo forecasts its t = 1 dividend to be \$1.40. DivCo expects to be able to increase that dividend at a satisfying 25 percent rate, but only for two years. After that, growth will fall to 6 percent, where it can be expected to remain indefinitely. The required rate of return is 11 percent. What is the value of a DivCo share? Compute it this way:

$$\frac{\$1.40}{1.11} + \frac{(\$1.40)(1.25)}{(1.11)^2} + \frac{(\$1.40)(1.25)^2}{(1.11)^3} + \frac{(1.40)(1.25)^2(1.06)}{(.11-.06)(1.11)^3}$$

$$= \$1.26 + \$1.42 + \$1.60 + \$33.90 = \$38.19$$

The box below charts the components of the price. Undiscounted values of the dividends are along the horizontal at top. Discounted values are on the vertical at left. Note that the t = 4 value becomes a t = 3 perpetuity before being discounted to t = 0. Note also that if dividends have been growing at 12 percent, then the t = 0 dividend must have been \$1.12.

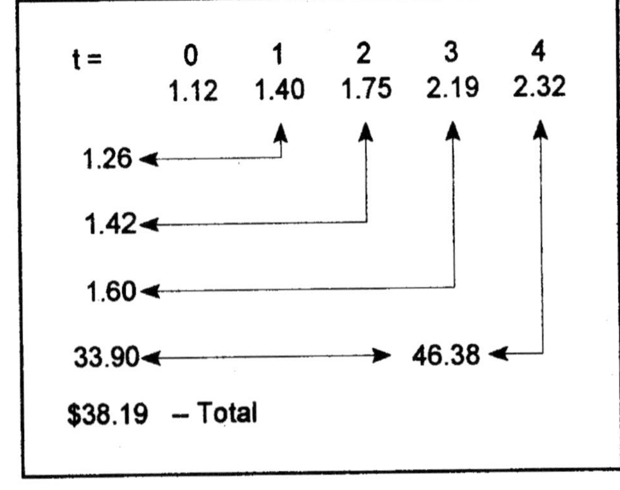

§ 11.08 Growth Patterns — a Comparison

Here we have a graph and a chart that show the "same" security with different growth rates. In all cases, we assume a t=0 dividend of $1.12, and a required rate of return at 11 percent. If the dividend were to remain forever stable, the value of the share would be $10.18. Using these assumptions, we compute the value with: (a) supernormal growth (at 25 percent) through t=3, followed by normal growth at 6 percent; (b) perpetual normal growth at 6 percent; (c) zero growth; and (d) *negative* growth at 6 percent.

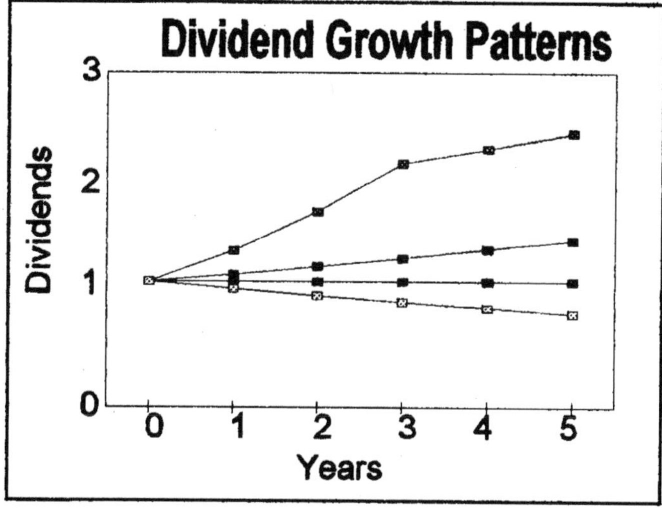

t=	0	1	2	3	4	5
Supernormal Growth Dividends	1.12	1.40	1.75	2.19	2.32	2.46
PV	1.12	1.26	1.42	1.60		
$Div_4 \div (r-g)$				46.38		
$\frac{[(Div_4 \div (r-g))]}{(1+r)^3}$	*33.90*					
Total PV	38.19					
Normal Growth Dividends	1.12	1.26	1.34	1.42	1.51	1.60
$(Div_{(t+1)}) \div (r-g)$	25.20	26.80	28.40	30.20	32.00	
Zero Growth Dividends	1.12	1.12	1.12	1.12	1.12	1.12
$(Div_{(t+1)}) \div r$	10.18	10.18	10.18	10.18	10.18	
Negative Growth Dividends	1.12	1.05	0.99	0.93	0.87	0.82
$(Div_{(t+1)}) \div (r-(-g))$	6.18	5.82	5.47	5.12	4.82	

Web site: A classroom exercise that applies stock and bond valuation models is: http://www.arbor.edu/~rlewis/mgt646/Beatrice49.htm.

§ 11.09 Principal v. Income

We've been trained to think of investing in terms of the distinction between "profits" (or "earnings" or "interest") on the one hand, and "return of capital" on the other. One consequence of the growth model is that it makes the distinction hard to manage. The dollar doesn't know who owns it and, correspondingly, the investor doesn't care where his money comes from. He just wants to know how much.

Difficult though it may be to draw the line, still there will be many cases in which we have to do it. For example, tax laws may distinguish between "ordinary income" and "capital gains" — with a tax advantage for capital gains. So the investor has a powerful motivation to nudge his returns out of the category of income and into the category of capital gain. The difficulty is that the capital value is nothing more than the discounted present value of the future income.

For a further example, consider the will of Wilma, who left her widget factory in trust to pay "income to Alfa for life, remainder to Betty." Your client Tess is the trustee, with the obligation to carry out the terms of the will. Tess determines that she could continue to operate the business at the current level and earn $40,000 a year indefinitely. Or she could withhold and reinvest

$24,000 a year, in which case she figures income would grow indefinitely at a rate of about 12 percent a year.

Clearly the business is worth more in the aggregate under the second (reinvestment) strategy than under the first (stable income). Betty the remainderwoman will press for reinvestment; Alfa the life tenant will want income. Which must the trustee choose? This is one of those questions on which it is self-defeating to generalize, but the short answer would seem to be that the trustee must favor the income beneficiary even to the extent of diminishing overall value.

The matter is dealt with at length in the Uniform Principal and Income Act. The reader is invited to make her own decision as to how well it solves the problem presented here. Perhaps the simple answer is that Wilma (or her lawyer) made a mistake by writing the language into her will to begin with: she should have found some other way to specify who gets what out of her estate.

An illustration of the general problem is *Holmes v. Hrobon*, where Thomas made a will in which he left his laundry business to his wife for life, with the remainder to his "legal heirs." He specified that his "wish that the said trustee shall continue my linen and laundry business as long as the same may be profitable." But before figuring income due to the wife, the trustee peeled off some of the gross revenues and used them to buy competing businesses. He argued that expansion was "necessary to keep pace with the increase or progress and continued operation of the business of the plant." But the court disagreed; it held that trustee had no authority to charge the costs of expansion against the life tenant.[3]

The lesson here is one that ought to be familiar to an advance law student: as an estate planner, you need to step up to the plate and face these issues head-on in advance, rather than brushing them off and leaving them for the courts to sort out late.

§ 11.10 Other Securities: Hybrids

Up to now we have distinguished "debt" and "equity," but there is no reason to stop there. We can slice the pie into any number of pieces, a few familiar, others more exotic.

For example, lawyers are accustomed to distinguishing between debt that is secured by particular items of property — a mortgage for real estate, or an Article 9 Uniform Commercial Code security interest for personal property.[4] The main point of having security is that the secured creditor gets to go to the head of the queue — to the extent of the property in which he holds a security interest, he gets first dibs.

---

[3] 93 Ohio App. 1, 103 N.E.2d 845 (1950); *see also id.*, 158 Ohio St. 508, 110 N.E.2d 574 (1953).

[4] Be on guard against a potential source of confusion here. "Securities" — stocks and bonds and the like — have, strictly speaking, nothing to do with "security interests," — interests in property to secure repayment of loans. One can imagine a security — say, a corporate bond — that includes a security interest — say, a collateral trust — in which it is easy to get tongue-tied. In practice, the distinction is usually tolerably clear.

But this is only the beginning. Creditors may also agree *by contract* among themselves to subordinate some claims to others. You will often find contract-subordinated debt — behind "regular" debt but ahead of equity — on the balance sheet of a company near bankruptcy and scrambling for new money to keep going.

In much the same way, you can subdivide equity. Aside from ordinary (common) stock, most people have heard of *preferred stock*, where the holder has a contract right (a "preference") to some kind of payment stream, ahead of ordinary equity. The name is perhaps misleading. For the ordinary investor, preferred stock is not "preferable" to much. It isn't as safe as debt (i.e., further down the ladder). It isn't as rewarding as common (you don't get to participate in growth). It exists more or less by institutional accident: old-fashioned regulated utilities issued preferred stock because it helped them to increase their capital base (and therefore their "return on capital"). And corporations like to buy other corporations' preferred stock because they get a tax break on the dividends.

Just as you can subdivide the categories, so also can you blur the line between categories. Plenty of corporations issue "convertible bonds," (and some "convertible preferred stock"). You can guess the drift: the holder gets the right to payment on a bond, with the option to convert the debt to equity. If the value of the stock stays low, he'll keep his right to the bond payment stream; if the value of the stock goes up, he'll exercise his conversion right and walk away with the shares.

Further, just how would you categorize a "variable rate bond," where the coupon fluctuates as a function of some exterior market index? U. S. government Series E bonds are an example: the interest is set at 90 percent of the average five-year Treasury rate for the preceding six months. If you ever read John Galsworthy's *Forsyte Saga*, you may be familiar with *consols* — a kind of perpetual bond. They have never caught on in the United States (where the government taxes them like equity, even though they act like debt). But they are common in Europe and Canada, and they were a rock of stability for the British upper middle class (i.e., the Forsytes) in the Nineteenth Century.

The deals we have spoken of so far are all *contractual.* Some creditors get priority by *statute* — most notably the tax collector, but also wage claimants and others. Indeed, the Bankruptcy Code mandates an elaborate ladder of priorities for distributing the assets of the debtor who is insolvent. Other creditors get priority by virtue of winning a lawsuit and getting a "judicial lien." Neither of statutory priorities nor judicial liens can be thought of as sources of "business finance" in any conventional sense, but the lawyer who is planning the deal will need to think about them to complete her analysis.[5]

[5] Complication on complication: the Bankruptcy Code provides that the bankruptcy trustee and the creditor may make deals for "post-petition financing." *See* 11 U.S.C. § 364. If he does the deal right, the post-petition creditor may get a priority position for his post-bankruptcy loan. These Section 364 loans are hardly a major source of corporate finance, but they are an important niche market for bankers and lawyers alike.

§ 11.11 The Blurring of Categories (Substance Over Form)

More Bridges are Necessary for a Good Merchant
Than a Lawyer can Make.

—Luca Pacioli[6]

It is time to reassess a theme that has pursued us from the beginning of this book. Call it "the blurring of categories." A lot of a lawyer's job involves getting things into the right category. Was it a sale or a lease? A stock or a bond? Or more precisely — a lot of her work involves either: (a) manipulating the deal to fit it into a category or (what is not at all the same thing) (b) manipulating the category to fit the deal.

This is what courts do, for example, when they say they are reaching for the "substance" of the deal as distinct from the "form." Of course we all want to get past the form to the substance. And there are well-recognized cases where the court does just that. Earlier, we remarked on the fact that we can expect most courts to recognize usury in disguise behind a sale/resale. Article 9 of the Uniform Commercial Code can be regarded as a great triumph of substance over form: the Code applies to any deal *intended* to create a security interest, *including* — and then it names a long list of deals previously thought of as distinct, all of which (per the Code) will be treated alike because they are alike in substance, whatever the form.[7]

Yet it isn't always so easy. For example, a real estate "mortgage" is a deal "intended for security," just as much as an Article 9 security interest. Yet half a century after Article 9, there is little pressure to unite mortgage law with the law of chattel security.

Why not? It is wonderful to speculate on possible reasons. Maybe it is simply cultural: maybe real estate lawyers come from different law schools, go to different churches, play different games than personal property security lawyers. Maybe there are sinister economic forces at work: for example, maybe there is a "recording lobby" that doesn't want to lose control over its mortgage recording turf. On the other hand, maybe there are distinctions that amply justify the distinction. For example, one salient feature of real estate is that it doesn't move.[8] Is this fact, largely inarguable, sufficient to justify the different legal regimes. Or is it (favorite lawyer phrase) a "distinction without a difference."

A venerable example is the matter of sale versus lease. We saw earlier that the distinction between sale and lease is less a square corner than a slippery

---

[6] As quoted in J. Giejsbeek. Ancient Double-Entry Bookkeeping, 27 (1914).

[7] *See* UCC § 9-102:

> (1) Except as otherwise provided in Section 9-104 on excluded transactions, this Article applies
>
> > (a) to any transaction (regardless of its form) which is intended to create a security interest in personal property . . ..
>
> (2) This Article applies to security interests created by contract including pledge, assignment, chattel mortgage, chattel trust, trust deed, factor's lien, equipment trust, conditional sale, trust receipt, other lien or title retention contract and lease or consignment intended as security.

(Quoted from the 1972 text. The revised Article 9 does not pick up this language. Presumably after a generation, there aren't many lawyers left who remember the old forms.)

[8] But for Mark Twain's story of how Tom Morgan's ranch slid downhill onto his neighbor's place, see Roughing It 240-3 (1891).

slope (see § 9.03 above). Yet the distinction persists. The Uniform Commercial Code distinguishes sale and lease. The Bankruptcy Code makes a lot of the distinction. Tax lawyers make the distinction, although perhaps for different reasons and in different ways. For their part, accountants insist on the distinction — though again, perhaps for different reasons, and clearly in different ways.

But sale/lease is surely no more than an example. Surely the same sort of problem haunts the distinction between debt and equity. We will see a more dramatic instance later, when we consider the issue of contingent claims in Part III below.

Where is all this taking us? There isn't a tight moral here, but we can offer an insight, or a caution. It is this: the more you deal with the structure of finance, the more the category lines tend to blur: the more any "asset" comes to appear as the center of a force field of positive and negative cash flows. And the more you recognize (to garble the simile) that you can slice'em and dice'em into a more or less infinite number of pieces. This fact is either a problem or an opportunity, depending perhaps not least on the state of your digestion.

§ 11.12 More About the PE Ratio

Earlier we introduced the PE ratio: we saw that it was no more than the discount factor for a perpetuity, which we have studied earlier. We remarked that market observers use the PE as a way of describing stock price behavior. The PE certainly has a lot of intuitive appeal. But the appeal may be deceptive, for several reasons.

In the first place, note that the PE doesn't really measure value: it merely restates what we already knew. It is accurate only because it is definitional, in the sense of "all bachelors are single men."

Even conceding that the PE is only a definition, we might consider using it as benchmark for comparison. Suppose NewCo is trading at 60 or 70 times earnings while the average for the market as a whole is 20. We can see at a glance that NewCo is somehow out of line with the market as a whole. Surely this must tell us something.

But what does it tell us? The trouble is that there are any number of reasons why NewCo might be out of line with the market, and they tend to cancel each other. To see that this is so, first recall our formula for a perpetual-growth stock: $Div_1 \div (r-g)$. If the PE is large, then we might infer that the denominator of our growth equation is low. And the denominator may be low if growth is high. So we can infer that a high PE implies that the market expects NewCo to enjoy strong growth.

So far, so good. The trouble is that there are any number of other explanations, equally plausible. For example, it may be simply that the earnings of NewCo have *fallen* recently, and the market has not yet assimilated the decline. Or it may be that the earnings are *cyclical*, and we are reading data from the bottom of a cycle.

On the same reasoning, consider OldCo, trading at six or seven times earnings. Maybe OldCo is an old, sluggish company with low growth prospects.

Or just as plausibly, maybe OldCo is an undiscovered jewel, capable of churning out attractive returns on modest investment. Or maybe last year was the only good year OldCo will ever have.

There are any number of other possible explanations. The point is that the PE alone is consistent with almost any story, and so tells us very little about how the stock might behave.

Finally, recall that the "E" in PE is *accounting* earnings. And we have already seen that accounting rules are not carved in stone. There is abundant evidence that companies may try to tweak the accounting numbers so as to hit an earnings target. This problem afflicts us in many contexts, of course, but it is perhaps particularly acute here because both investors and managers seem so focused on the PE as a measure.

There are any number of cases where managers have engaged in questionable accounting practices solely to tweak the PE. In a notorious example back in the 1980s, General Motors found itself embarrassed by falling earnings. The company simply reestimated depreciation so as to reduce expenses, and thereby boosted its earnings back to a more tolerable level.

A more sinister difficulty with PE ratios is that they tend to be self-fulfilling. If all the analysts figure that BigCo "should" have a PE of, say, 15, then they will buy or sell as the price trend seems to dictate until BigCo's PE reaches the declared ratio — and lo, the analyst is vindicated as a seer. The trouble is that the very concept of the PE lets the analyst evade the heavy lifting of his trade: estimating risks, forecasting cash flows, and the like.

Despite all this, PE ratios will remain with us and investors will continue to use them. You know that when a stock is selling at 427 times earnings (as Netscape was in the fall of 1995), then the market is at least a little frothy. You might have known, when the Japanese PE hit 70 a few years back, that it was likely for a fall (indeed it was, and indeed it did).

Current PE Ratios: as of this writing (summer, 2000), the composite PE of stocks in the Dow Jones Industrial Average is about 20, and of the (broader) Standard & Poor 500 Index, about 28. Both are far above historic means, but some 20 percent below their level of the previous year.

§ 11.13 Why?

Whoever you are, you have at least a vague notion of "the capital market." It is the place where investors buy and sell stocks and bonds. It runs around the clock in New York, London, Zurich, and Tokyo. It is the place where bells ring, lights flash, and people do a lot of yelling.

But if you want flashing lights and bells, you go to a gambling casino. There are plenty of gambling casinos. So why bother with a capital market? What does the market offer that you cannot get in Las Vegas or Atlantic City? The standard answer is — the market allocates capital. Investors have capital to invest, and managers have projects that need capital. The market brings these two parties together, and by bidding and asking, everyone finds out which projects are most worthy.

This is the standard story, and it is at least partly true. But on close scrutiny, it does not hold up very well. The fact is that lots of people raise capital without using the capital market. Meanwhile, much of the trading on the market has little to do with the raising of capital.

Start with the trading on the stock exchanges. Let us distinguish between *primary* trading — buying stocks or bonds in new enterprises, or for new projects — and *secondary* trading — the resale of stocks and bonds already issued. Secondary trading may be a good thing, but it is not the raising of new money. So, most of the noise you hear from the floor of the stock exchange has nothing to do with the issuance of new securities.

Indeed, there is plenty of evidence that when entrepreneurs need new money, they do everything they can to avoid going to the market. Doug Henwood collects data showing that large corporations fund over 90 percent of their capital needs internally — i.e., with "last year's earnings," rather than with new issues of stocks and bonds.[9] Others will disagree with that number, depending in part, on exactly what you measure and how you measure it. But there is no quarrel with the general tendency.

Other evidence points in the same direction. Consider the "initial public offering" (IPO) of LittleCo, the well-known Silicon Valley garage startup. It has been growing nicely for the last couple of years. Now LittleCo decides it is time to offer its stock to the public. This can be a big event in the life of the company. When the market is hot, the chances are that investors will be eager to buy the shares of LittleCo. The old investors who got in before the IPO will find their wealth soar as the value of their old shares rises.

But this is the catch. Most such IPOs are not about raising *new* capital at all. Virtually every IPO comes from a company that *already is* operating, and that *already has* capital. The purpose of the IPO is to allow the *original* provider to bail out at a profit — really a "secondary" transaction, and not an "initial" offering at all.

Something similar happens with bonds. You might think that when a company issues bonds, it is raising capital — but close scrutiny will show that in many cases, the company is issuing bonds so it can buy back stock. In other words, the bond issue simply replaces one capital source with another. Indeed, between 1981 and 1996, U.S. corporations retired $700 billion *more* in stock than they issued. In a good many of these cases, companies issued bonds to retire the stock.

None of this is conclusive, of course. There are great difficulties in measuring and evaluating evidence in this field. And there may be quarrels over the inferences. After all, even if this evidence is true it may prove merely that markets work in ways more subtle than our inquiries can capture. But capital markets are hugely expensive (at least in gross) and hugely disruptive of non-market life. If and insofar as they serve the purpose of allocation, they may earn their keep. But it is always a worthwhile question whether they are really worth all the effort.

---

[9] Doug Henwood, Wall Street: How It Works and For Whom 72-76 (1997).

§ 11.14 Appendix: Infinite Series with Constant Growth — Proof

Here we prove that $d_1 \div (r-g) = P_0$. You do not need this proof in order to follow the argument in the chapter. We proceed the same way we proceeded to prove that $C \div r = P_0$. That is, we find the sum of an infinite series. We want the sum of:

$$P_0 = \frac{d_1}{(1+r)} + \frac{d_1(1+g)}{(1+r)^2} + \frac{d_1(1+g)^2}{(1+r)^3} + \ldots + \infty$$

Where $r > g$, $d_1 > 0$. Rewriting:

$$P_0 = \frac{Div_1}{(1+r)} + [\frac{Div_1}{(1+r)} \times \frac{(1+g)}{(1+r)}] + [\frac{Div_1}{(1+r)} \times \frac{Div_1(1+g)^2}{(1+r)^2}] + \ldots \infty$$

Now, let a =

$$\frac{Div_1}{(1 + r)}$$

and let x =

$$\frac{(1 + g)}{(1 + r)} < 1, r > g$$

We have seen that such a series simplifies to:

$$\frac{a}{(1 - x)}$$

So:

$$\begin{aligned} P_0 &= \frac{a}{(1 - x)} \\ &= \frac{[Div_1 \div (1 + r)]}{1 - [(1 + g) \div (1 + r)]} \\ &= \frac{Div_1}{(1 + r) - (1 + g)} \\ &= \frac{Div_1}{(r - g)} \end{aligned}$$

Which is the result we wanted.

Chapter 12

The Least Accounting You Can Get Away With

Accounting is a series of political decisions
which we now call accounting principles.

—Herbert Miller[1]

Life must be understood backward.
But . . . it must be lived forward.

—Kierkegaard[2]

§ 12.01 Introduction

It is said that if a boy watches too much of the Discovery Channel, he may never get a date. We have somewhat the same attitude towards accounting. You probably need a little accounting as part of a sound basic lawyer's education. But too much may be — oh, okay, "harmful" is too strong a word. But it may not be a good use of your resources: as the economists would say, it's a matter of comparative advantage.

Ideally, we think you should have about three college units of accounting, with adequate basic mechanics, focusing on the user of financial information. We can't offer you three units of accounting in this class without crowding out everything else. However, you need to know at least the rudiments of accounting to understand some important points about finance. In this chapter, we offer what we think is the least amount of accounting you can get away with.

There are three major points in this chapter. First, you will encounter some of the basic framework of accounting — balance sheet, income statement and statement of cash flows. Second, you will meet the tension between conceptual accounting definitions and straight cash flow reporting. Third, you will get an introduction to the distinction between "accounting profit," and a broader measure of return on assets.

§ 12.02 The Balance Sheet

If we know anything about accounting, the chances are we know that the firm produces a *balance sheet*. The balance sheet is a "snapshot" that shows, for any given moment in time, what the firm *owns* (its assets) and what it *owes* (its liabilities). Here is a balance sheet:

---

[1] In Gary John Previts & Barbara Dubis Merino, A History of Accountancy in the United States: the Cultural Significance of Accounting 388 (1998).

[2] Soren Kierkegaard, Soren Kierkegaard's Journals and Papers (edited and translated by Howard V. Hong & Edna H. Hong), Journal IV A 164 (1967).

Balance Sheet
LittleCo, Inc
Dec. 31

Assets		**Liabilities**	
Cash	$3,000	**Accounts Payable**	$9,000
Accounts Receivable	$2,500		
Inventory	$10,000		
PP&E	$30,000	**Long-Term Debt**	$25,000
		Net Worth	$11,500
	$45,500	**TOTAL**	$45,500

"Cash" explains itself. "Accounts receivable" are rights to payment in favor of LittleCo, against customers to whom LittleCo sold goods. "Inventory" is the stuff that LittleCo buys and sells. If LittleCo is a maker of widgets, then we would expect the inventory to be a warehouse full of widgets. "PP&E" stands for "property, plant, and equipment." That would include the tools, machines, etc., that LittleCo needs to run the business — also real estate, if LittleCo has any.

"Accounts payable" is the conceptual mirror image of accounts receivable. This is short-term debt that LittleCo owes to suppliers and suchlike. We would expect it to be repaid in 30 days or so. Long-term debt might be a 30-year mortgage that LittleCo borrowed from the bank to buy its real estate.

This leaves "net worth," as the *residual* term, being the sum of the assets (what the firm owns) minus the liabilities (what it owes). You can also call it the "equity," or "owner's equity." Since net worth is a derived term, it follows that assets (on the left) *must* equal liabilities plus net worth (on the right); it's definitional, like saying that all bachelors are single.

§ 12.03 Income Statement

Slightly less well known, but perhaps more important, is the second major accounting document, the *income statement*. Here is an income statement for LittleCo, produced to accompany the balance sheet above:

Income Statement **LittleCo, Inc.** **Jan. 1–Dec. 31**	
Sales	$33,000
COGS	18,000
SG&A	8,900
Depreciation Expense	1,000
EBIT	$5,100
Interest	2,250
EBT	$2,850
Tax	798
Net Income	$2,052

Read it from the top. "Sales" is self-explanatory: this is the total of our gross revenue from operations, i.e., without deducting expenses. "COGS" is a much-used acronym: it stands for "cost of goods sold." "SG&A" stands for "selling, general and administrative expense." "Depreciation expense" is another deduction; we'll discuss it more later. "EBIT" stands for "earnings before interest and taxes." It's a subtotal: to get it, we start with sales and then subtract COGS, SG&A, and depreciation expense.

Finally, note that long-term debt shows on the balance sheet as $25,000, and interest at $2,250. We know that 2,250 ÷ 25,000 = 0.1, so the overall *rate* of interest must have been 10 percent. If you understand "EBIT," you can probably decipher "EBT," which means "Earnings Before Taxes" — but after interest. We figured taxes at an (arbitrarily chosen) rate of 28 percent, to get our "bottom-line" net income, also known as "earnings" or "accounting profit." For more on the relation between accounting profit and NPV, see § 12.07 below.

We said the balance sheet was a *snapshot* at a *point in time*. Note that the income statement covers a *period of time* — a *movie*, as it were, distinct from the snapshot on the balance sheet. This income statement extends for one year, beginning from the time of the last balance sheet. With the old balance sheet and the income statement, we are in a position to construct a new balance sheet for a new year. All other things being equal, it would show assets of $45,500 *plus* the new earnings of $2,052, or $47,052 Since liabilities remain unchanged, the net worth will be $47,052 − $9,000 − $25,000 = $13,052.

Note that in this example, we didn't say anything about "dividends." This is not necessarily surprising; some companies pay dividends to shareholders every year; some do not. But suppose LittleCo had chosen to pay a dividend of $1,000 in cash to its shareholders. We'd simply deduct the $1,000 from net income before we totaled up the new balance sheet.

§ 12.04 Some Particular Accounting Rules

There are a number of accounting rules that can serve as illustrations of the accountant's strategy — and of its problems. We examine four.

[A] Depreciation

Consider the matter of *asset values*. Suppose you bought a forklift truck in 1995 for $50,000. You put it on your 1995 balance sheet at its $50,000 purchase price. Assuming you know your way around the bargain barn, this probably isn't too troublesome a judgment. But what do you do when you come to 1996? You might say "revalue it." But how? You can't really know how much it is worth unless you sell it — and that, by definition, is what you do not want to do.

Accountants have a standard strategy for dealing with a problem of this sort. They require us to "depreciate" the truck. For example, we might decide that: (a) the truck will last for 20 years; and (b) at the end of 20 years, it will be worthless. The accountant might say: all right, we want you to *deduct* $2,500 ($50,000 ÷ 20) each year to represent the reduction in value of the truck. You'll charge the $2,500 to the income statement each year as *depreciation expense* (compare the depreciation expense on the income statement for LittleCo).

And you'll show the *value* of the truck as the original purchase price, less the accumulated depreciation. In the current example, after three years, you would have had three annual $2,500 depreciation charges and your balance sheet would show a value of $50,000 gross less $7,500 in accumulated depreciation for a net asset value of $42,500.

That's easy enough once you get the hang of it, but take a closer look at what is — and is not — going on. In the first place, note that this is *almost all guesswork*. Okay, the $50,000 price was not guesswork, but who knows whether this truck will last for 20 years, or 30, or 10? And why divide the $50,000 *pro rata*? Why not take a bigger deduction in the earlier years when the machine is new and the value is high — or, for that matter, a bigger deduction in the later years, when it is probably decaying faster?

Second, note what we are *not* doing in this example. From the look of things, you might think we were setting up some kind of "sinking fund," or "blocked account," or special lockbox, where we keep the depreciation money, to make sure we have money available when the truck wears out. But in fact, we are doing nothing of the sort. Not one penny changes hands. However much cash we had before, we still have it now.

Third, and perhaps most important, assume that we will replace the truck at t = 20 for a cost of $50,000, and that we want a sinking fund to provide for the replacement. Do we need to set aside $2,500 a year? We do not. A sinking fund like this can be analyzed as a kind of annuity. In an earlier section, we learned how to define the cash flow (C) necessary in an annuity to yield a particular FV. For example, suppose the interest rate is 9 percent. To check your own recollection, compute C. **Hint:** The FVAF is 51.16.

But then the fact remains — why would we want $50,000 at t = 20? There's not the slightest guarantee that a forklift truck will *cost* $50,000 at t = 20

— or, for that matter, that we will want any forklift truck at all. The real question ought to be — what *at any given moment in time* is the best use of our resources? Should we buy more trucks? Or sell some of our present stock? Or get out of the business altogether? On the basis of the data available, we have no idea whatever.

As a corollary, note something else that we do not do with the asset value: we do not "mark to market." That is, we make no effort to adjust balance sheet values to current market prices. Of course it is likely that a second-hand forklift will be worth less than a new forklift. But maybe not as much as — or maybe more than — you would guess from the depreciation schedule. And in some cases, old may be worth more than new — a mint condition 1965 Ford Mustang is probably worth a lot more today than the day it rolled off the lot. The point is — for the most part, we simply don't care.

Definitional Note: suppose your asset is not a forklift truck, but something "intangible," like a patent or a copyright. Economically, it may play the same role as the forklift — it is a capital asset that you expect to use in producing other income. Do you get to *depreciate* the patent? No, you do not. Instead, you *amortize* it. There are differences in the details, but for our purposes you can think of *depreciation* and *amortization* as the same thing.

One person who seems to have understood the analytical difficulties of depreciation was the late Supreme Court Justice Louis D. Brandeis, who died in 1941. Brandeis encountered the problem most notably as the court struggled with the problem of public utility rate regulation. Brandeis thought the entire scheme of rate regulation (as it existed in his time) was unsound. For his critique of depreciation, see especially *United Railways & Electric Co. of Baltimore v. West.*[3] For more on the problem of rate-making, see § 17.06 below.

[B] Inventory

We encounter a different kind of problem if we consider accounting for *inventory*. Suppose at t = 0 we have 200 pieces of inventory which we bought for (and carry on our balance sheet at) $60,000, or $300 each. Suppose that during the next year we *buy* another 150 pieces of inventory — but this time, they cost us $350 each, or $52,500, for a grand total of $112,500. Meanwhile, during the year, we *sell* 200 pieces of inventory. When it comes time to assemble the income statement, the question arises — which did we sell? Did we sell the old stuff (so-called "first in, first out," or FIFO accounting)? Or did we sell the new stuff first, using the old only when we ran out of new ("last in, first out," or LIFO)?

It is easy to see that the choice makes a big difference to our income statement. Suppose our gross revenues were $100,000 and our selling and administrative expenses were $35,000. If we use FIFO, our COGS sold is $60,000 and we show a $5,000 profit. If we use LIFO, our COGS is $67,500 (150 × $350 + 50 × $300), and we show a $2,500 loss!

We should emphasize that this has just about nothing to do with which items come out of the warehouse first. If you are selling dairy products, you

[3] 280 U.S. 234 (1930).

put the oldest out front, so it will go first and you won't get stuck with spoilage. If you are selling coal in the cellar, the latest to arrive will be the earliest to sell — but it has been around since the Pleistocene Era, so what's the big deal? The question is — what kind of story do you want to tell? If you want to show how smart you are, buying up cheap and selling expensive, then FIFO supports your account. If you want to caution the investors that you'll have heavy replacement costs, then LIFO tells the truth.

[C] R & D

Your client, Forrest, laid out $50,000 cash for a forklift truck. Forrest must report the decline in the cash account, but he gets to put the truck on the balance sheet, and (for the moment, at least) he is no worse off. On the other hand, suppose he invests $50,000 to develop a new formula for elixir. If he succeeds, then presumably he will have an asset worth at least as much as a forklift truck (or at any rate, that is the hope). Can he therefore include $50,000 in asset value on your balance sheet for research and development (R&D)?

The short answer is "no." He must charge off the R&D as an expense at the time it is made. There is an obvious reason for this rule, which you can see if you think about what would happen if it were different — then, any time the firm made a costly mistake it would write it up as "research!" Not a good way to build value. Most research (unlike most forklift trucks, we hope) goes to waste.

That's all well and good on its own, but it creates distortions. Imagine two companies, OneCo and TwoCo, identical except in one respect. OneCo *developed* its technology by spending $50,000 on (successful) R&D. TwoCo *bought* its technology from another company in a market transaction for $50,000. As you can guess, OneCo will show its technology at a value of zero, while TwoCo will show $50,000 in its asset account. The point of this exercise is not to knock the R&D rule, which is probably a pretty good one, at least taken in isolation. The point is that you probably can't satisfy all your needs at once.

Another problem where accounting tradition runs aground on financial analysis is the matter of *goodwill*.

[D] Goodwill

> We are not here to sell a parcel of boilers and vats,
> but the potentiality of growing rich
> beyond the dreams of avarice.
>
> —Samuel Johnson[4]

"Goodwill" has a specific meaning in accounting lore. Suppose BigCo buys SmallCo. The assets of SmallCo are a cash register and 10 widgets. The fair market value (FMV) of the cash register is $100. The FMV of the widgets is

[4] The great critic and lexicographer, hyping the sale of his friend's brewery. http://www.xrefer.com/entry/248692.

$250. But BigCo agreed to pay $650 for SmallCo as a whole. Tessie the treasurer of BigCo records the cash register at $100 and the widgets at $250. But what should she do with the remaining $300? A leading accounting text summarizes:

> If the total purchase price paid by the buyer exceeds the FMV of the seller's identifiable net assets, the excess is called *goodwill*. Theoretically, goodwill represents a buyer's anticipated excess earnings or purchased net assets, above and beyond the earnings reflected by the fair market value of the acquired net assets. Excess earnings may result from superior management of the net assets or operating synergies that result from combining the acquired net assets with the buyer's existing net assets.[5]

We quote the definition because we think it reflects the frame of mind of the accountant, in contrast to the perspective of finance. The point is that the investor just isn't likely to think of it in the same terms as the accountant. What the investor wants to buy is a prospective stream of cash flows. The particular (disaggregated) sources don't make any difference. Again, this doesn't mean that the accounting principle is wrong. But it does create a tension that you may have to cope with in law.

§ 12.05 Tax Accounting v. Investor Accounting

It ought to be clear by now that accounting rules are not carved in stone — managers have a lot of discretion over how, and when, to record expenses and income. This fact leaves managers caught in a crosswind. Consider the dilemma of Fiona, the chief financial officer of ExpenCo, a public company whose shares are listed on the New York Stock Exchange. Fiona knows that investors will reward high earnings with high share prices. So she is impelled to manipulate the accounting rules any way she can to minimize expenses and maximize earnings. On the other hand, ExpenCo must pay a tax on income, defined as gross revenue minus expenses. Fiona knows that *low* earnings mean low taxes — and so (when it comes to tax time), she is impelled to *maximize* expenses so as to minimize tax!

It shouldn't really matter: investors should be smart enough to see through the cosmetics, and to recognize that an increase in tax expense actually helps them because it takes dollars away from the roughnecks at the Internal Revenue Service and puts them back in the hands of ExpenCo. And indeed there is some evidence that investors do in fact get the point (see Chapter 18 below). But executives like Fiona are never comfortable with analysis: they always fear that investors will punish them for minimizing taxable income by running down the share price. So the topic remains a hot-button issue among tax accountants.

For our purposes, we need to note just two important tax rules. First, with regard to *depreciation*, the rule is that the company gets to keep two sets of books. Tax depreciation bears not the slightest relation to "investor" depreciation. Indeed, the disparity is so regularized that the accountants even provide

[5] E. Richard Brownlee, et al., Corporate Financial Reporting: Text and Cases 360 (2d ed. 1994).

rules for reconciling the tax books to the investor books. We will have more to say about depreciation accounting later in (see § 13.02[A] below).

With goodwill also, you get to keep two sets of books. For accounting purposes, you amortize the goodwill ("write it off") over a reasonable time, not to exceed 40 years. Since a longer period means a lower annual expense deduction, it seems likely that most companies just take the 40 years. For taxes, you spread it over 15 years.

For inventory, a different rule applies. Call it "live by the sword, die by the sword." The rule is that ExpenCo can use any (lawful) form of inventory reporting for tax purposes — but that it must use the same rule for reporting to investors. In other words, if you want to choose an inventory rule that maximizes your expenses and minimizes your income for tax purposes, you're going to have to live with the same rule in your inventory accounts.

§ 12.06 Statement of Cash Flows (Herein of EBITDA)

The sum of the inquiry so far is that accounting values are based on accounting concepts that may or may not serve the interests of investors. As modern finance theory has evolved, investors have voiced increasing criticism of accounting principles. They argue that accounting principles are too conceptual, not enough related to investor concerns. Better to forget about traditional accounting concepts and to concentrate on the one thing that cannot be understood — that is, to concentrate on cash. Accountants have sought to respond to this sort of criticism (at least in part) by generating another financial statement — the so-called *Statement of Cash Flows* (SCF).

[A] The Mechanics

Accountants typically create the tax-flow statement by a kind of "reverse engineering" from the income statement and the balance sheet. To understand it, we can do the same. Consider TiniCo, that began business a year ago with $10, all cash. After a year, we look at the income statement. We note gross revenues of $25 and expenses of $23, for a bottom-line net income of $2. This is the number we report to the investors as "earnings."

But on a more careful look, we see not all the $23 of expenses was paid in cash. Rather, $4 of the $23 is an expense allowance for depreciation. So we know that (other things being equal), we have $4 more in *cash* than you would guess from our statement of *income*. On a second look, we notice that not all of our gross revenues were *paid* to us in cash. Rather, we find that at the end of the year we held $7 worth of outstanding accounts receivable. Since we had no receivables at the beginning of the year, this amounts to an *increase* in receivables (from $0 to $7). Since receivables are not cash, it also means that in terms of *cash* we are $7 *poorer* than we would have guessed from the income statement.

An increase in receivables translates into a reduction in cash. One way to hang on to cash is simply not to pay our debts. So, suppose on a third look we find that our "accounts payable" have increased from $0 to $6. Then we know we are $6 richer than the income statement disclosed.

We can summarize these data in a truncated statement of cash flows:

Statement of Cash Flows
TiniCo, Inc.
Jan. 1–Dec. 31

Cash, Jan. 1	$10
Net Income	2
Plus Depreciation	4
Minus Increase in Receivables	<7>
Plus increase in Payables	6
Cash, Dec. 31	$15

More precisely, we should call this the statement of *operating* cash flows, because it represents results of ordinary day-to-day operations only. A full-blown cash flow statement would also include a section on cash flow from *investing*. For example, if we bought a new factory for $22, the investing section would show a negative balance of $22. The full cash-flow statement would also include a section on cash flow from *financing*. So, if we borrowed $19 in a long-term bond issue (to help pay for the new plant) we would show a positive balance in the financing section of $19.

Active investors, being "finance types," tend to love the statement of cash flows. Consider Lance, the guy in the $2,000 suit with the Porsche and a Rolex the size of a grapefruit. Lance isn't really interested in the niceties of depreciation accounting (except as it may affect taxes). What he wants to know is: how much cash will the business throw off? If he has an annual report, he turns to the cash flow statement first.

If he doesn't have one, he will sketch one of his own on the back of an envelope. Here is how he will proceed: he'll start with "EBIT" (defined above, see § 12.04) and then he'll *add back* depreciation. That will give him a rough measure of cash flow: call it "EBITD" (though heaven knows how you would pronounce it). On the same principle, he could add back amortization — call it EBITDA, which is a tad more pronounceable.

[B] Example: Time-Warner

To see EBITDA at work, consider a watershed in the history of cash flow valuation: the 1991 deal that joined Time Inc. and Warner Communications into a media conglomerate, Time Warner.[6] The merger partners forecast that the new company would yield some $2.3 billion in accounting earnings before interest and taxes. But interest would eat up $1.4 billion. Anticipated capital expenses were about $500 million. That left only $400 or $500 million — not enough to cover expected depreciation and amortization charges. On a traditional net income basis, the deal was a loser.

[6] This account is based on Richard M. Clurman, To the End of Time: the Seduction and Conquest of a Media Empire, 256-58 (1992).

The negotiators feared that the market would punish the stock if they presented the deal as a loser. So they prevailed on the regulators (specifically, the Securities and Exchange Commission (SEC)) to let them present it in terms of EBITDA. This was a first: the SEC had never before allowed EBIT to be used in just this way.

As it happened, the financial press was not distracted. Financial press reports ignored the EBITDA presentation and told the story in terms of traditional net earnings. "Time Warner Takes It on the Chin," said the Sunday New York *Times*. *Fortune* magazine (ironically, owned by Time Warner) included the deal in a list of "Five Largest Losses."[7] But aside from the financial press, what was the response of the market? This is harder to say — it is often hard to disentangle one event that may influence a stock price from all other factors at work at the same time. But at least in the long run, you would have to say the market took it in stride. Time-Warner flourished as a merged conglomerate — capping its next decade of growth with a new mega-merger, this time with AOL.

[C] EBITDA in Court

Courts occasionally find themselves confronted with the task of estimating cash flows in litigation. A good example is *Steiner Corp. v. Benninghoff.*[8] Steiner was a 100-year-old textile company. Over 93 percent of the shares belonged to members of the Steiner family. The Benninghoffs, minority shareholders, were the descendants of former employees.

The Steiners, as controlling shareholders, undertook to merge the firm into a holding company, and to cash out minority shareholders. The Steiners set the cash-out price at $840 a share. Believing they were being underpaid, the Benninghoffs sued. In a 13-day trial, each side presented valuation experts to shore up their case. Experts on both sides used estimates of future EBITDA as points of departure for their analysis. In the end, the court valued the company at $1,407.02 per share and granted judgment awarding the Benninghoffs an additional $2.4 million plus interest.

Web site: A skeptical account of EBITDA is at: http://www.fortune.com/fortune/investor/2000/07/10/str.html.

§ 12.07 Accounting Profit v. Return on Capital

It is time for another critical inquiry into the concept of "accounting profit." Take another look at our income statement. Recall how we derived "operating income," also known as "EBIT." Note that only after EBIT do we deduct interest. This fact is innocent enough in itself, but it harbors an issue that lies at the heart of accounting theory. Namely: is interest an expense?

---

[7] *Id.*

[8] 5 F. Supp. 2d 1117 (D. Nev. 1998).

[A] Mechanics

The *accounting answer* is: yes, interest is an expense. You deduct it after EBIT, but still before figuring net income or "profit." From the standpoint of the shareholder or "owner," this makes sense: what goes to pay interest is not available for the residual claim.

But put the issue in a larger context and the answer is not so obvious. Consider your client, Manfred, the manager of LittleCo. He has identified an opportunity to invest in a profitable new project on LittleCo's behalf. It takes money to make money, and Manfred will have to raise some new money to take on this profitable project. Where will he get it? Consider two choices:

- He can borrow money — from the bank, or via public debt, or whatever.
- He can issue new shares.

Which source should he use? Either one will cost him. If he borrows, he'll have to pay interest. If he goes after equity, of course he doesn't have to promise a specific repayment. But he can't expect to get a good price for his equity unless investors think that LittleCo has a promising future, and will be able to pay dividends someday.

You can see this in a simple example. Suppose LittleCo needs $100. Manfred can borrow $100 from the bank with interest at 10 percent. There are five shares of LittleCo outstanding today. The question arises: how much will a buyer pay for a new LittleCo share? If a buyer will pay $100 for a new share, then Manfred can get his new money in exchange for only one new share. If buyers will pay only $10 a share, then Manfred can't raise his $100 unless he is willing to issue 10 new shares. Equity looks a lot more attractive to Manfred in the first case than in the second.

So the short answer to our question is: he should use whichever source is cheaper. If debt is cheap, he should borrow money. If equity is cheap, he should issue equity. Recognize either debt or equity as a source of capital: his job is to minimize his cost of capital, so as to maximize asset return.

Perhaps you can see this most easily if you consider the case of the large public company with bonds and stock, both of which trade in the secondary market. It is easy to imagine an investor who holds both bonds (debt) and stock (equity) in the same company, and who gets a return from each.

Or consider Lance, the high-rolling investor, who wants to buy the whole company. He isn't really interested in the debt-equity mix. If the debt is too expensive, he can pay it off. Or if debt is cheap, he can borrow more. Note that this is equally true from the standpoint of the equity owners of the private company who aren't in the securities market and who aren't planning to sell. For them too, the real issue is the source, and not the cost, of capital. So, we need to draw a basic distinction:

- Return on *assets*: the money available to satisfy *any and all* claims — debt and equity together.
- Return on *equity*: the money available to satisfy equity, after debt.

Net income — "accounting profit" — is a lot closer to "equity return" than it is to "asset return. Of course, anything can be a correct answer to the right question, so neither of these is intrinsically more important than another. But you need to keep in mind that "accounting profit" is not a good measure of asset return — indeed, it doesn't even try to be.

[B] Example: Slavery and Return on Capital

Here is a dramatic illustration of how a famous scholar confused asset return and equity return.

We all know that slavery is wrong. But was it profitable? Specifically, consider the Antebellum South. Did the slave owners make a profit from the management and sale of slaves? The question is important, quite independent of the evil of slavery itself. For example, it may help explain the cause of the Civil War. If slavery was unprofitable, then the Civil War cannot have been "about" slavery. It might have been "about" foolish pride, or neighborhood suspicions, or "preserving the Union" — but not slavery. Correspondingly, if slavery was very profitable, the Civil War must have been (at least in part) about slavery, the abolition of slavery, and freeing the slaves.

For a long time, the settled wisdom was that slavery was not profitable, and indeed, that at the time of the firing on Fort Sumter, the slave system was getting ready to collapse on its own. One of the most influential sources leading to this conclusion was a study by Charles Sydnor published in 1933. Sydnor estimated that the yield on capital investment in slaves was just 2.4 percent, far lower than the yield on secure private bonds.

Sydnor developed his analysis by fashioning an income statement for a hypothetical investment in 50 slaves. He put the cost of slaves at $30,000 and the cost of land at $6,000. He allowed for "depreciation" on land at 3 percent per year, and on slaves at 6 percent per year. He set the market interest rate on borrowings at 6 percent. Here is his income statement:

Income Statement	
Sales Income (63,200 lbs. of cotton @10¢/lb)	$6,320
Expenses	
Supplies	$1,000
Wages — overseer	300
Depreciation — land	180
Depreciation — slaves	1,800
Interest — land	360
Interest — slaves	1,800
Total Expenses	$5,440
Net Profit	$ 880

Of course, $880 ÷ $36,000 = 0.024 = 2.4 percent, so Sydnor's numbers appear to add up. But there is a critical error here. Before reading on, pause for a moment and see if you can spot it.

Did you see the error? What Sydnor is trying to estimate is the *return on assets*. And from that standpoint, interest is not an expense; rather, it is *income*. Recalculating, we can see that what *all* investors get out of the investment is ($1,800 + $360 + $880), or $3,040. This suggests a real return on investment of 8.4 percent, well above the rate for bonds. So it appears that slavery, however reprehensible, might have been profitable in narrow economic terms.[9]

§ 12.08 Accounting Profit and NPV

It is time for a direct assessment of the relation between accounting profit and NPV. Consider your client, Irving, an investor who bought all the equity of (debt-free) OpCo for $1 million. After one year, Irving determined that OpCo had yielded $100,000 in positive cash flow from operations. But the accountants recorded large depreciation charges and his reported net income was only $40,000. He thereupon sold the business for $1.2 million.

How can we evaluate these numbers? Restricting ourselves to the income statement, we could say that his *accounting profit* is 4 percent ($40,000 ÷ $1,000,000). His cash flow statement suggests a *cash-flow return* of 10 percent ($100,000 ÷ $1,000.000). But a dollar doesn't know who owns it. What Irving got out of the deal was the cash flow ($100,000) plus his gain on resale ($200,000), which suggests an overall IRR equaling 30 percent.

But which is the NPV? The answer is that none of these is the NPV. In order to know his NPV, we will have to know his OCC, which is not given in (and cannot be derived from) the example. Suppose that Irving, in order to buy OpCo, had passed up a deal that offered a 35 percent return. Then we could say his OCC is 35 percent. Discount $1.3 million at an OCC of 35 percent.

As is so often the case, it appears that NPV is the superior measure of profitability. Yet it has to be conceded that accounting profit persists as a highly visible measure of investment performance. If you doubt it, consider how much attention the financial press pays to the announcement of "earnings" by major corporations. "Earnings" are no more than accounting profits, subject to all the vagaries and limitations suggested above. Yet stock prices rise and fall on earnings announcements.

What is going on here? One theory is that it is an illusion: that investors are not fooled by earnings numbers, and can decode them by techniques such as those suggested above. Yet if this is true, then why so much fuss over the earnings number? Another theory is what cynics call the "greater fool" theory of investing — the idea that *I* may see through the earnings distortions, but that I know *you* will not, and that I pay attention to earnings numbers not because *I* believe them, but because I think *you* will. Given the high visibility of accounting information, it is hard to believe that there are really so many fools left.

---

[9] *See generally* Charles S. Sydnor, Slavery in Mississippi (1933), summarized and discussed in Jeremy Atack & Peter Passell, A New View of American Economic History: from Colonial Times to 1940, 327 (2d ed. 1994).

In any event, as if to complicate matters further, consider the fortunes of America Online (AOL) during its phenomenal rise to prominence in the mid-1990s. AOL adopted accounting policies which were, by conventional measures, "aggressive," though not outright illegal. There is good reason to believe that the market punished AOL stock for its aggressive accounting — and rewarded the company (via a higher share price) when it stopped. Yet, for this to be true, it must be that the market was punishing AOL not because it was misled, but precisely because it was not misled at all! We will have more to say about all this when we consider the theory of "efficient markets" (see Chapter 18 below).

Enough about markets. What about the courts? In deciding, for example, damage cases, do courts use accounting profits, or NPV? The answer is that overwhelmingly they rely on accounting profits; they almost never apply anything like NPV. A benign explanation is that "accounting profit" is more predictable and therefore reliable: accounting data are there for the taking, while OCC is elusive and therefore subject to manipulation. Another argument might be that "accounting profit" is probably what the parties intended.

But another interpretation is conceivable. Thus, it may be simply that the lawyers didn't understand NPV, or think to explain it to the judge. Indeed, a review of the case law gives rise to a strong inference that there is an element of culture lag here — that modern financial analysis is simply slow in penetrating to the trial court.

But there are reasons to believe this pattern has changed. We've already noted the recent explosion in financial reporting. One corollary may be an increase in sophistication among investors about NPV. One straw in the wind may be the strategy of "the sage of Omaha" — Warren Buffett, surely one of the nation's most successful investors, explaining why he had essentially missed out on the computer boom.

Buffett argued that there are some industries which, taken as a whole, use more capital than they yield — even if they may give rise to some transitory profits. One example, said Buffett, is the airline business. Apparently there is good evidence that the airline business, taken over its entire history (through 1992), used more capital than it returned to investors. Buffett says:

> Sizing all this up, I like to think that if I'd been at Kitty Hawk in 1903 when Orville Wright took off, I would have been farsighted enough, and public-spirited enough—I owed this to future capitalists—to shoot him down.[10]

§ 12.09 The History and Structure of Accounting

Drive east for a couple of hours out of Florence in Tuscany and you come to Borgo San Sepolcro, a little city famous for at least three things. One is a tasty dried mushroom, splendid as an appetizer. The second is what may be the world's greatest painting — the "Resurrection" of Piero della Francesca, a longtime resident and sometimes city councilor. And the third is a statue of Luca Pacioli, the father of modern accounting.

---

[10] Quoted in "Mr. Buffett and the Stock Market," Fortune, Nov. 22, 1999.

Pacioli illustrates George Stigler's rule that the man who gets credit for a discovery is not the first discoverer, but the last. Indeed, Pacioli didn't claim to be a discoverer at all. But his book, *Everything About Arithmetic, Geometry, and Proportion*, is the first organized treatise on double entry bookkeeping, so by general assent he enjoys the honor of paternity.

It is no accident that Pacioli wrote in the height of the Italian Renaissance, during the great commercial boom that gave rise to so many of our modern financial institutions (bankruptcy — Italian "banca rotta" was invented more or less in the same time and place). What is perhaps more remarkable is how little has changed since Pacioli's time. Not that he needs to, but the fact is that a modern accountant could pretty much recognize most of what Pacioli taught some 500 years ago.

Indeed, for the next chapter in the history of accounting after Pacioli, you have to wait nearly 400 years until the great boom in capital formation that followed the American Civil War. The protagonists this time were mostly Scotsmen — "whisky, golf, and accountants," according to one version, are the Scots' great contributions to world culture. In any event it was Scottish accountants who standardized accounting and turned it into a profession — and then spread out over the planet to apply its principles..

The profession has matured and centralized over the years to the point where only a tiny handful of firms dominate the profession worldwide. In the United States, there are now just five major firms: Arthur Andersen, PricewaterhouseCoopers, KPMG, Ernst & Young, and Deloitte & Touche. The list varies somewhat in other countries but the general drift is the same.

The profession continues to evolve in two important ways. First, the major accounting firms are all trying, with greater or lesser success, to expand into business consulting. Indeed, just a few years ago Arthur Andersen (the accounting firm) spun off its consulting business into a wholly separate firm, Andersen Consulting.

The other change is that accountants continue to expand into what lawyers once thought of as law practice. The consequence is a major turf battle between the two professions. At this writing the result remains unclear, but a couple of points need to be noted. One is that in almost every other country, the accountants are already well established in services that U.S. lawyers think belong to them — Andersen partners like to say that they are the biggest law firm in every country except the United States (recall that no other country, excepting possibly Israel, relies on lawyers as much as we do).

The other is that in the United States, major law firms seem to be looking for ways to "build alliances" with accounting practices — a pretty sure sign that the old barriers are crumbling, and that the troops inside the fortress are scrambling to make peace with the invaders.

Important as accounting may be, it wouldn't be nearly as important as it is had it not been for one more event. That is the coming of the New Deal securities regulation in the United States in the 1930s. With the Securities Act of 1933 and the Securities Exchange Act of 1934, Congress created a web of regulations that governs the market for securities even today (a remarkable run — nearly 70 years is impressive longevity for any regulatory regime). The basic premises are simple enough: the securities laws undertake not to govern the *content* of securities offerings, but to regulate *disclosure*.

And who plays the central role in disclosure? Of course it is the accountant. The oversimplified explanation is that you cannot sell shares in a public company unless you produce (inter alia) an *annual report*. The report must bear the bearing the certificate of an *auditor*. The auditor is an "accountant's accountant." He does not keep the books himself, but he examines the books. For the report to be acceptable to the SEC, the auditor must give his opinion that the books were kept according to *Generally Accepted Accounting Principles* (GAAP) (for more on the "substantive law" of accounting, see § 12.10 below. So accountancy moves out of the realm of private agreement and becomes a component of federal law.

As the gatekeeper for mandated disclosure, the SEC plays a powerful role in shaping accountancy doctrine. In principle, the SEC could (though in practice it does not) make itself the accounting rule maker. But the SEC's chief accountant remains one of the most influential people in the accounting world.

The central role of disclosure has probably made accountants a lot of money. But it is a devil's bargain, and it has brought a lot of them to grief. Just about any time an investment goes under, the aggrieved investor looks for someone to sue, and the accountant, with his deep pocket, will be high on the list.

Of course there is no end of controversy over the propriety of all this securities litigation (and in any event, Congress and the courts have more or less bolted up the floodgates lately). Suffice it to say that if the accountant allows the manager to ship bricks under the guise that they are computer inventory, he probably deserves whatever trouble he gets into. For present purposes, we might content ourselves by looking for problems that help to keep the accountant on the spot.

One is structural. The accountant is *hired by* managers. But his reports are *directed to* investors. Managers and investors have conflicting interests. The accountant is bound to feel pressure from his (nominal) boss, the manager, to undermine the interest of his (real) employer, the shareholder.

A second problem concerns the accountant's conception of his job. Go back to the beginning of our discussion: recall that the accountant looks *backwards* to figure out where things came from and where they went. For resource management and control, this is wonderful: accountants have taught us all how to understand how a business has done. But finance looks *forward*, asking how things will go in the future. To set the backward-looking accountant down into a forward-looking valuation job is necessarily to put him in a false light.

You can't blame accountants for not being able to forecast the future — after all, who can? But you can expect that they are bound to have headaches as long as they find themselves cast into a role they are not even temperamentally suited to perform. For a third reason why accountants get into trouble under disclosure laws, see the next section.

§ 12.10 Where Do Accountants Get Their Rules?

We said above (to take one example) that you can't capitalize R&D. But who says so? In short, where do accountants get their rules?

The flip and unhelpful answer is that they come from "Generally Accepted Accounting Principles" (GAAP), mentioned above. But this begs the question. Where do you find GAAP? A more helpful answer is that there is a kind of "common law" of accounting, just like there is a "common law" of — well, of law, such as you study in law school. And like our own common law, GAAP today is at least in part memorialized in a code. For GAAP, the "code" is the collected pronouncements of the Financial Accounting Standards Board (FASB, pronounced "Fazz-B"). FASB is a self-created accounting professional entity, not unlike the American Law Institute, propounder of the Restatements. It has term members with salaries, and a research staff.

Web site: For FASB, go to http://www.rutgers.edu/Accounting/raw/fasb/.

FASB pronouncements are authoritative when FASB speaks, but FASB doesn't cover everything. The SEC sets at least some accounting rules through its role as regulator. And there are some pre-FASB pronouncements still extant in the work of the (old) Accounting Principles Board (APB) and, from before that, some Accounting Research Bulletins.

FASB was born in 1973 in the heat of conflict. The old APB found itself the butt of criticism. The SEC was making noises like it just might want to take over the job of accounting rule making for itself. Faced with the threat of a federal takeover, the accounting profession created a committee under a distinguished lawyer and former SEC Commissioner, Francis M. Wheat. Wheat's committee produced "the Wheat Report" which led to the regime we have today.[11]

The Wheat Report bought independence for the accounting profession, but freedom came at a price. The trouble was that by keeping their flexibility, the accountants left themselves with no defenses when they need them. That is: at least part of the reason why accountants get into securities litigation is that they don't have any clean, flat, unbreakable rules to point to when management presses them to fudge the books. At the same time, they don't have any clean, flat, crystal-clear defense when the aggrieved investor shows up with her lawyer.

Most accounting rules come from FASB and its predecessors, but the SEC also retains a critical (if secondary) role. This is so because the SEC gets to prescribe the form of accounting documents filed with it.

Web site: The criteria for SEC filings are set forth in its Regulation S-X, available at: http://www.sec.gov/smbus/forms/regsx.htm.

The courts, of course, inevitably retain the power to make their own decision as to what counts as an accounting standard. In a famous case, the Second Circuit upheld a criminal conviction against the testimony of eight independent accountants that the conduct was not inconsistent with generally accepted accounting principles.[12]

[11] American Institute of Certified Public Accountants, Establishing Financial Accounting Standards, Report of the Study of Accounting Principles (1972).

[12] United States v. Simon, 425 F.2d 796 (2d Cir. 1969).

Chapter 13

Valuation of Specific Investments

Frankly my dear, I'm going to build a dam.

—Rhett Butler (attr.)

§ 13.01 Review: Backwards and Forwards

Let us summarize what we have done so far. We began by setting forth a primitive definition of present value (PV) and of net present value (NPV). We concluded that NPV equals the present value of all expected receipts less the present value of all expected costs. We specified that "cost" did not just mean out-of-pocket expenses, but also includes "opportunity cost" (OCC), i.e., opportunities foregone to get our expected benefits.

We moved on to develop a few simple formulas for defining PVs and NPVs: we created "discount factors" (DF) and "forward factors" (FF) to translate future values to present, and present values to future. We defined a "simple annuity," an "annuity paid," and a "perpetuity." And we showed how to relate the OCC to PV by defining the OCC as our "required rate of return" (RRR), and using this rate to specify our DFs and FFs. Armed with this background, at last we applied some of our learning to various types of investment securities such as stocks and bonds.

After this initial exercise in valuation, we turned our attention to the task of learning some basic accounting. Our purpose was twofold. One was to master a bit of accounting on its own terms. But another was to understand accounting in comparison (or contrast) with finance.

We are now equipped for a more ambitious task. We want to learn how to value particular investments — in the jargon of the trade, "projects." The task will require us to deploy our basic valuation techniques, along with our knowledge of accounting.

§ 13.02 Three Basic Rules

We speak of valuing a "project." The term is purposely abstract. We mean to include any possible investment opportunity. We could be seeking lost treasure like Humphrey Bogart, or smuggling gold ingots like Alec Guinness. Or we could be doing something more drab like buying a new forklift truck. In any case, we will follow three rules.[1] They are:

- Only Cash Flow Matters.
- All Costs are Opportunity Costs.

[1] This organization follows Richard Brealey & Stewart C. Myers, Corporate Finance (6th ed.).

- Ignore Sunk Costs.

All of these rules are stated or clearly implied in what has gone before. We can add force by putting them to work.

[A] Only Cash Flow Matters (The Example of Depreciation)

In an earlier section, we made a brief inquiry into the principles of accounting. We saw that accounting values do not strictly correlate with cash values; the accountant may record a gain in wealth before the enterprise receives any cash, or she may *not* record wealth *even though* the enterprise received cash. In particular, we examined the concept of depreciation. We saw that accounting depreciation deductions are conceptual only, and do nothing whatsoever to change the cash position.

For example, suppose LittleCo buys a forklift truck for $100,000 cash. The accountant will record the cash payment, but she will not record any decline in wealth. Rather, she will offset the $100,000 cash reduction with a $100,000 increase in asset value. At the end of the year, she will record depreciation. Suppose she decides to fully depreciate in equal increments over 10 years. Her depreciation deduction for each year will be $10,000. She will record this as a "depreciation expense," and it will go to reduce asset value, but no cash will change hands.

So far, this is review. But now we can introduce a complication. There is a case where depreciation *will* affect cash flow, and where we should consider depreciation in project valuation. The issue arises any time that the depreciation will affect taxes.

Recall some first principles of taxation. LittleCo is a corporation. It must pay the corporate income tax. Its income is its earnings less its expenses, as defined by tax law. Tax law allows LittleCo to count depreciation as an expense.[2] So (tax) depreciation may reduce taxes and thereby increase cash flow.

Here is an example:

LittleCo has $200,000 in income net of all expenses except depreciation. For convenience, we will assume it is all cash. LittleCo's marginal tax rate — the tax on the last dollar it earns — is 34 percent. So LittleCo faces the prospect of computing its tax as ($200,000)(0.34) = $68,000. LittleCo's after-tax income on this analysis will be $200,000 − $68,000 = $132,000. Assuming LittleCo pays its taxes in cash, its after-tax cash flow will be the same.

But now, assume LittleCo is also entitled to take an expense deduction for depreciation in the amount of $150,000. If LittleCo takes the deduction, its taxable income will be $200,000 − $150,000 = $50,000. Its tax will be

[2] The amount of depreciation we take for tax purposes very likely will differ from the depreciation allowance shown on our general books and records. In other words, we may keep "two sets of books," one for taxes and one for reporting to investors. This is entirely lawful. Contrast the rather different situation where we keep "two sets of books," one to show to investors, and the other to tell the truth. This may give rise to civil liability, and may even be a crime, but for present purposes that is beside the point.

($50,000)(0.34) = $17,000. Its after-tax income will be $50,000 − $17,000 = $33,000.

But in this case, its after-tax cash flow will not be the same. For convenience, again assume that LittleCo pays all its taxes in cash. Then its after-tax cash flow will be $200,000 − $17,000 = $183,000. So by taking the deduction LittleCo, while reducing its reportable income, has increased its cash flow by $183,000 − $132,000 = $51,000. We can define this $51,000 as the *depreciation tax shield* — the amount of cash saved by taking the deduction. In valuing the cash flows from the asset, we will want to take account of the depreciation tax shield, even if we would ignore simple depreciation.

We can generalize this into a formula. Let T = the tax rate. Let Dep = the nominal dollar amount of the depreciation deduction. Let CF = the total cash flow from the business. Assume that all expenses *except* depreciation are paid in cash Then:

$$CF = (EBIT + Dep)(1 - T) + T(Dep)$$

In words, the after-tax cash flow with the depreciation will be: (a) the after tax cash flow without the deduction, plus (b) the nominal dollar amount of depreciation multiplied by the tax rate. Item (b) therefore denotes the amount of cash that the taxpayer puts back in his pocket by virtue of the depreciation deduction. Call it the "tax shield." Denote the tax shield as TS. Then:

$$TS = T(Dep)$$

Using our numbers:

$$CF = (\$50{,}000 + \$150{,}000)(1 - 0.34) + (0.34)(\$150{,}000) = \$183{,}000$$

$$TS = (0.34)(\$150{,}000) = \$51{,}000$$

It is helpful to be able to isolate the tax shield because often we will want to know just how much tax relief a particular depreciation deduction is buying.

Surplus Depreciation: It is entirely possible that a particular asset will generate a greater sum in depreciation deductions than we expect to report in income. For example, suppose LittleCo buys a new widget smasher that will increase cash income next year by $40,000 (independent of depreciation tax), but will generate a depreciation deduction of $75,000. With a tax rate of 31 percent, the tax shield will increase LittleCo's cash flow by: (a) $12,400, if LittleCo offsets depreciation only to the extent of our new income, and (b) $23,250, if LittleCo can deduct the all the depreciation.

Which do we get? The short answer is that we get to deduct depreciation only to the extent of other income — so, $12,400. The prospect of "surplus depreciation" may tempt us to invest in an asset that generates a (paper) loss if we need the deduction to offset other income. Tax rules also allow us to "carry back" and "carry forward" otherwise surplus deductions, but this is a complexity beyond our scope here.

Repeating: only cash flow matters. But depreciation may generate a cash flow if it reduces our taxes.

[B] All Costs Are Opportunity Costs

Ten years ago, your client Harry bought an apartment house for $300,000. After expenses, last year Harry netted $30,000 from the apartment house and he figures he can look forward to the same sort of return indefinitely. Harry figures 8 percent is a pretty good return, so as a rough-and-ready estimate, he figures the apartment house is worth $30,000/0.08 = $375,000. That is a gain in capital value of 25 percent.

Is this analysis correct? It is not. In fact, Harry's apartment house is plugged in between two giant high-rise office buildings. Either adjacent owner would cheerfully pay Harry $800,000 to get him out of the way so they could tear down his little old apartment house and expand their big hotel. By *not* selling the $375,000 property and passing up the $800,000 sale, Harry is bearing the cost of a very expensive lost opportunity — call it an *opportunity cost.*

To cast it in traditional NPV terms, suppose Harry could have invested $300,000 at t=0 to get $800,000 now. The implied return on this investment is 167 percent. Treat this rate as his OCC and the t=0 value of Harry's $375,000 (payable at t=1) becomes just $140,625. Subtract his $300,000 investment and you have an NPV of *negative* $159,375. Not a good investment at all.

Harry probably understands this point, and indeed, the chances are he sold out and retired on the profits without ever consulting you. But it is surprisingly easy to find examples of lost opportunity cost in real life. For example, consider Penn Central, the old northeastern railway system. When it collapsed into bankruptcy in the early 1970s, it was losing money hand over fist. It emerged several years later as a highly successful real estate company. What happened? Penn Central abandoned its old, unproductive rail lines and sold the underutilized underlying real estate. No one was willing to pay enough for rail services in those days. But the tracks ran through some of the most highly developed urban areas in the country. Once the managers made the real estate available for its most profitable use, the money began to roll in.

At the level of your own checkbook, suppose you have a $10,000 balance earning no interest. Suppose you have a credit card, with a $10,000 balance accruing interest at 1.5 percent per month. Every month you leave the money in the checkbook, you bear an opportunity cost of ($10,000)(.015) = $150.

If opportunity cost is so easy to understand, why is it so easy to miss? One reason may be that standard accounting conventions conceal this kind of disparity. Recall that accountants value most assets at *original* cost, not at current market value. So, consider SlowCo, whose balance sheet shows that it has assets of $1,000 and liabilities of $300, implying a net worth of $700. Its profit and loss statement reports net income of $84 last year, which implies a 12 percent net return to equity. However, the books do *not* show that managers passed up a chance to sell the whole company for $2,000. After paying off the $700 debt, that would have left $1,300 on the table for shareholders.

[C] Ignore Sunk Costs

The rule of sunk costs teaches: that was then, this is now. Or: wake up and smell the coffee. Consider Lockheed Corporation, the defense contractor. Lockheed spent $1 billion trying to develop the Tri-Star airplane before it became clear that the project was not nearly as promising as the original planners had hoped. Some analysts at Lockheed argued for abandoning the project. Others said that it would not make sense to abandon a project after having spent so much money. So Lockheed continued to spend and aggravated its losses. In the end, Lockheed only avoided bankruptcy thanks to a huge taxpayer bailout.

Likewise, consider the North Florida Canal. The United States Army Corps of Engineers spent $100 million on the first stages of the canal, and had to admit it looked like a loser. But the Corps argued that it was desirable to spend *another* $300 million on the project. Why? Because otherwise the $100 million spent already would be wasted.

Both Lockheed and the Corps ignored the principle of sunk costs. The real question was not, "how much have we spent?" but rather, "what do we get if we spend another dollar?" In each case — Tri-Star and North Florida Canal — the proponents would have saved money by stopping their projects, even at a loss, before losses aggregated further.

For contrasting evidence on the same point, consider the original Saturn automobile. General Motors spent millions developing the Saturn as a new-age consumer-friendly car. The Saturn got high ratings from auto enthusiasts, and generated a lot of satisfied customers. Unfortunately, it became clear early on that GM could not sell the car at a price high enough to recoup its large capital investment.

Does this mean that GM should have abandoned the project? Not at all. The question was, "what could GM do with the investment if it did not go forward?" If the "salvage value" was lower than the value in current production, then GM should keep manufacturing the Saturn, even if it was a loser. The evidence is muddy, but there is good reason to believe that GM made the right decision *not* to abandon Saturn, because the alternative would have been worse.

In all these cases, an economist would say we should decide "at the margin" — what is the value of the (marginal) next dollar? We can rephrase it as: where do we go from here? Or again: ignore sunk costs.

§ 13.03 The Rules at Work: An Example

Let us try to put these ideas together in a working example. Five years ago, your client NewCo bought a defenestrator for $100,000. NewCo expected to use it for 10 years, and undertook to depreciate it (for both accounting and tax purposes) on a straight-line basis — that is, at $100,000 ÷ 10 years, or $10,000 per year. It has a current book value of $50,000.

Recently, a competitor began selling a new high-tech defenestrator, and the market value of NewCo's current product has fallen to just $7,500. The corporate tax rate is 25 percent. NewCo could put the machine to a new use, in which it will earn (pre-tax) $2,500 a year for five years, after which it would be worthless. The interest rate is 6 percent.

Should NewCo keep the defenestrator, or sell it? To answer that question, analyze the costs and benefits of the project, keeping in mind our three rules. First, discount the payment stream from the new project. Since we want to *discount cash flows only*, make sure to deduct taxes: \$2,500 (1 – 0.25) = \$1,875. So:

$$PV = \$1{,}875 \left[\frac{(1.06)^5 - 1}{(0.06)(1.06)^5} \right] = \$7{,}898$$

But if we keep it, we pass up the chance to sell it today, so there is an *opportunity cost* equal to the sale price of \$7,500. That would give us a net of (\$7,898 – \$7,500), or \$398. Note that we do not offset the \$50,000 undepreciated original cost, because we *ignore sunk costs.*

Are we done? We are not done. There will be tax consequences from the sale. We have a "tax basis" of \$50,000, embodied in the undepreciated book balance. If we sell for \$7,500, we can compute a *loss* (for tax purposes) of (\$50,000 – \$7,500), or \$42,500. Assuming we have other income on which we would otherwise have to pay tax, then this is an *offsetting deduction* that will reduce our tax liability by (\$42,500)(0.25) = \$10,625. We cannot get this tax benefit unless we actually sell the old defenestrator. So, our true opportunity cost is not just \$6,500, but (\$7,500 + \$10,625) = \$18,125. Setting this off against our prospective \$7,898 income stream, we find that the true NPV of keeping the project is *negative* \$10,227.

Are we done now? We are not done. We know that if we keep the widget, we forego the right to take the deduction for loss on sale. But if we keep the widget, we *do* retain the right to *continue to take depreciation deductions* according to the original schedule. We said we had a right to a deduction of \$10,000 per year. At 25 percent, the associated tax shield is \$2,500 a year. For consistent measurement of opportunity costs, we must recognize that if we *sell* the old defenestrator now, we *lose* the right to this \$2,500 per year for five years.

The opportunity cost of selling the defenestrator, then, is not \$1,875 a year, but rather, (\$1,875 + \$2,500), and the value of our annuity becomes \$18,429. So, if NewCo keeps the defenestrator, it gets \$18,429. If NewCo sells the defenestrator, it gets \$18,125. In sum, then, the project shows a positive NPV of \$304 (\$18,429 – \$18,125). For a summary chart, see below.

Note how sensitive this comparison is to the choice of interest rate. At 7 percent, the PV of the annuity stream is \$17,938, and the advantage tips in favor of sale.

Keep	**Sell**
\$7,898, PV of new use	\$7,500 sale proceeds
\$10,531, PV of depreciation tax shield	\$10,625 offsetting deduction on sale
\$18,429	\$18,125

Tax-Driven Deal: Thus, taxes can affect the decision whether or not to invest; they can make the difference between positive and negative NPV. A theoretically ideal tax system would not cause people to make investments that they otherwise *would not make*, and would not cause people to forego investments that they otherwise *would make*. But, in real life, our tax system does have those consequences.

Financing Cost: Note that we have not said anything about the cost, or even the method, of financing the project. The reason is that if we have done our job right, the financing cost is already impounded in our opportunity cost.

§ 13.04 More on Depreciation and Taxes: MACRS

If you do not like paying income taxes, you can fight for a reduction in your tax rates. Numerically, you can achieve the same result if you ignore the rate and try to increase deductions. So, for example, suppose you have income of $100 on which you must pay a tax at a rate of 25 percent (or $25). You would rather pay only $20. You can achieve this result if you can reduce the rate from 25 to 20 percent. Or, you can achieve the same result, even without a change in the tax rate, if you increase your deductions by $20 so that your taxable income is only $80.

From a strategic standpoint, campaigning to increase deductions has an additional advantage. Tax *rates* are highly visible. They make good sound bites on the evening news. To understand tax *deductions*, you have to be a specialist. Not surprising, therefore, that lobbyists seeking to reduce taxes figured out early on that if they had to choose, they would rather concentrate on increasing deductions. That way, they could lighten their burden, yet still retain the privilege of complaining about high rates.

A moment's reflection will show you how the logic of deductions stands traditional accounting on its head. In traditional accounting, managers provide information for *investors*. Managers are motivated to paint a rosy picture and to minimize bad news. In tax accounting, managers provide information to the *tax collector*. Managers want to tell the tax collector they never earn a dime. Not surprisingly, over the years we have evolved to the point where everybody keeps two sets of books: one for investors, and one for taxes. There are even rules on "reconciliation," where the accountants tell the investors how the tax books differ.

Starting around the end of World War II, the great battlefield for the tug-of-war with the tax collector was the topic of depreciation. Accountants and lawyers poured illimitable energy into speeding up the depreciation deductions, while the Internal Revenue Service worked just as hard to slow them down. The campaign reached a kind of resolution in 1986 when Congress enacted the so-called Modified Accelerated Cost Recovery System (MACRS).

As an innovation, MACRS was good for the *system* because it reduced the deadweight cost of haggling over depreciation. And, it was good for *taxpayers* because it gave them a better deal on deductions than they would have received under straight accounting. MACRS allows a faster write-off than ordinary accounting rules in at least two ways. First, for many assets it shortens the depreciation period. Second, it "front-loads" the deductions in the early years. For example, autos and light trucks qualify for depreciation over six years. They get this right even if the vehicles will last as long as 10 years.

Under MACRS, each year, you get to deduct a percentage of the original purchase price. For the six-year class, the percentages are:[3]

Year	Percentage
1	20.0%
2	32.0%
3	19.2%
4	11.5%
5	11.5%
6	5.8%

To see how MACRS works, consider the case of LittleCo, which just purchased a new truck for $100. The truck will last for 10 years with no salvage value. LittleCo's discount rate is 12 percent and its marginal tax rate is 36 percent. Absent MACRS, LittleCo would depreciate the truck "straight line" — i.e., in equal increments over 10 years. What is the depreciation tax shield if LittleCo uses straight-line depreciation? This is easy enough to compute: the sum is $20.34.[4]

What happens if you use MACRS? The results are shown below:

Total Depreciation	Year	Percentage Deduction	Deduction for the year	PV (r = 12%)
$100	1	20.0%	$20.00	$17.86
$100	2	32.0%	$32.00	$25.51
$100	3	19.2%	$19.20	$13.67
$100	4	11.5%	$11.50	$7.31
$100	5	11.5%	$11.50	$6.53
$100	6	5.8%	$5.80	$2.94
Totals			**$100.00**	**$73.82**

3 Students learned in accounting may recognize it as a version of double-declining balance with no salvage value and a half-year convention.

4 Think of it as the present value of a 10-year annuity. You can figure a $10 coupon and take 36 percent of the present value. Or you can simply figure the present value of a $3.60 coupon.

This is the present value of your total depreciation deductions under MACRS. To get the PV of the tax shield, multiply by the marginal tax rate (here, 36 percent) — you get $26.57.[5] That is an improvement of some $6.23 over the tax shield with straight-line depreciation.

If available, MACRS is almost always preferred to straight-line depreciation. We can think of only two cases where you would not want to. One is where you will not have any income against which to set off the deduction. The other is where you expect tax rates to spike up later. In either of those cases, you might want to "save" the deductions for later years when you would have more to worry about.

Web site: A more detailed introduction to MACRS is at: http://www.taxpoint.swcollege.com/taxpoint_2001/student/m10/m10-2.html.

§ 13.05 A Hidden Cost: Working Capital

[A] The Problem

Your client, Wembly Widget, is the president and majority stockholder of WidgetCo, Inc., a maker of premium high-end widgets. You had the privilege of drafting his incorporation papers just three years ago, and it has made you proud to see him through a period of spectacular growth: such a hard worker, and such a nice man. Therefore, it came as a shock to you when Wembly called to say that investigators from the Department of Labor were climbing all over his books and records and muttering the words "felony" and "fraud." Your dismay was not assuaged by a confidential conference with Wembly, wherein he expanded on his story.

Yes, it was true, he maintained a 401(k) retirement program for his employees and, well, yes, it was true that he had fallen behind in meeting his obligation to pay over payroll deductions to the plan administrator. He had not intended to, he assured you, and you could not say he had taken the money to line his own pockets (indeed, he had not drawn anything but the barest living expenses out of the company for a year and a half).

But the bank was nipping at his heels, and the vendors were threatening to withhold essential supplies, and those payroll deductions were just too, too tempting . . . and well, yes, he had pretty much done what the government snoopers suspected. As a matter of fact, as he somewhat abashedly let slip late in the meeting, there was also a little matter of withholding taxes. Once again, he knew he was supposed to collect and pay them over on his employees' behalf, and again, well, yes, he had taken the money for ordinary operating expenses.

Sighing, you undertook to explain to Wembly that his worst fears were well founded and that he was indeed at risk of criminal prosecution — and, that for what it was worth, he had probably piled up some debts that would not be dischargeable in bankruptcy. Together, you undertook the slow task of

---

[5] You could have reached the same result by taking 36 percent of the undiscounted depreciation deduction for each year and then totaling.

trying to conduct a defense for Wembly, or at least to minimize his misfortune. But as you worked, you felt a persistent buzz in your ear that kept asking, "what is a nice guy like Wembly doing in a situation like this?" In this section, we consider one possible answer: the problem of *working capital.*

[B] The Mechanics

Let us start with the core of the business. WidgetCo is a retail widget store. To attract customers, WidgetCo lays in a stock of widgets. To buy the widgets, WidgetCo borrows $100,000 from BigBank at 5 percent. When WidgetCo sells a widget, it can pay back some of the loan.

But what of the time between purchase and sale? WidgetCo's money is tied up in the inventory, where it is not yielding any current income. However, the meter is still running at the bank. Somehow, WidgetCo will have to scrape together enough to pay the 5 percent interest, whether it has any sales or not.

How to feed the meter at the bank: this is the problem of working capital. More broadly, we define working capital as the wealth that is tied up in the business and not earning any income. Inventory (as above) is the obvious example. The amount of working capital tied up in inventory can be a major item, particularly for a business that needs to keep a great variety of items in stock, or for a business that sells "big-ticket" items, like cars or boats (in mid-1998, Boeing had 18 airliners backed up on the tarmac, waiting for completion and delivery). But working capital pops up in other places as well. For example, suppose WidgetCo sells a widget to a good customer who says "bill me." Widget bills him, and he pays in 30 days. Because of competitive pressure, Widget feels it can't afford to charge interest for this short-term credit. But the short-term credit is another form of wealth tied up in the business, so another form of working capital.

But this matter of "credit" working capital works both ways. WidgetCo sends bills to its customers, but it also gets bills from its suppliers. If WidgetCo can *delay paying its suppliers* (without cost), then it has put money in its own pocket. This may be no trivial sum. Sears, the retailer, gets supplies from thousands of vendors. Sears traditionally paid its bills in 30 days. Along about 1980, interest rates went through the roof, and Sears found itself in a short-term credit crunch. Sears simply started delaying payment to 45 days. The change saved a lot of money for Sears — and it dumped a great cost on the suppliers, who had to scramble around to find a way to cover their own working capital costs in the interim.

You can get a good first approximation of working capital by looking at the balance sheet. The accountants separate assets into "current" and "long-term." They do the same with liabilities. "Current assets" include inventory, receivables, and suchlike. "Current liabilities" include short-term payables. You can define "working capital" as current assets minus current liabilities, or (CA-CL).

It is tempting to ignore working capital because it would seem to balance out in the long run. But this is likely to be a mistake. In a close case, working capital can make the difference between profit and loss. And — perhaps of greater importance — working capital needs tend to grow precisely when the business is growing, so an enterprise poised for takeoff may find itself starved for oxygen.

The simplest way to account for working capital is to record a cash outflow at the beginning of the project when the investor puts working capital into the business, and then to record an inflow at the end of the project when the investor gets his money back. Note that even if the sums are the same, the PV of the return inflow will be lower than the PV of the outflow because the inflow will be discounted. Thus, suppose the investor puts in $1 million of working capital at t=0 and takes out the same million at t=5. Assume a rate of 2.3 percent per period (or 12 percent for five periods). The PV of the t=5 repayment is $829,857 and the cost of working capital is ($1,000,000 – $829,857) = $107,143.

For a more complicated business, you would need more complicated accounting. A good rule of thumb is to figure working capital as a percentage of gross revenues. For example, in the widget business, it is common to estimate working capital at 8 percent of gross.

But working capital needs will vary over time. For example, our client Winona is thinking of taking a flyer in the widget business. The project will last for six years, after which she will liquidate. Experience has taught us that working capital needs in widgets equal 8 percent of gross revenues. The discount rate is 10 percent. We estimate revenues (and derive working capital needs) as follows:

Working Capital Needs				
t=	**Gross Revenue**	**Change from Previous Year**	**Change in Working Capital**	**Total Working Capital**
1	$12,500	$12,500	$1,000	$1,000
2	$14,000	$1,500	$120	$1,120
3	$16,000	$2,000	$160	$1,280
4	$19,000	$3,000	$240	$1,520
5	$25,000	$6,000	$480	$2,000
6	$26,000	$1,000	$80	$2,080

To figure working capital needs, proceed as follows. Start with the $1 million change in working capital for the first year. That is Winona's working capital contribution for the first year. Since this sum will be in use throughout the year, we will be cautious and value it as of the *beginning* of the year. So we give it its t=0 value, or $1 million. Then go on to the $120,000 change in working capital for the second year. Determine the PV from t=1 (note that we continue to lag behind). The result is $120,000 ÷ 1.1 = $109,091. Continue through the six years. Confirm that you get these values:

t =	Changes In Working Capital	Present Value At 10%
1	$ 1,000,000	$ 1,000,000
2	$ 120,000	$ 109,901
3	$ 160,000	$ 132,231
4	$ 240,000	$ 180,316
5	$480,000	$ 327,846
6	$ 80,000	$ 49,674
	Total	$ 1,799,968

Then, at t=6, we liquidate the entire business, which is to say, we recover the working capital of $2,080,000. The PV of $2,080,000 from t=6 is $1,174,106 (confirm). Subtract your total working capital ($1,799,968) from your recovery ($1,174,106) and you get negative $625,862, which is your working capital expense for the six-year project.

Aside from working capital, Winona was careful about estimating her costs and revenues from the projects. She expects to pay $2,000,000 for a widget maker, and to sell it for $200,000 at the end of the project. Assuming all of her revenues and expenses except depreciation are cash, here is a chart of her cash flows:

t=	Capital Cost	EBIT (1 − t)	Dep	Total CF	PV at 10 %
0	($2,000,000)				($2,000,000)
1		$100,000	$200,000	$300,000	$272,727
2		$200,000	$320,000	$520,000	$429,752
3		$400,000	$190,000	$590,000	$443,276
4		$500,000	$120,000	$620,000	$423,468
5		$600,000	$120,000	$720,000	$447,063
6	$200,000	$300,000	$60,000	$560,000	$316,105
				Total	$332,391

On these figures alone, the project looks like a modest (although scarcely a sensational) success. It is a good thing you remembered working capital, though. From this estimated NPV of $332,391, subtract working capital of $625,862, and the project now shows a net loss of $293,471.

§ 13.06 Cannibalizing

We need to warn against one other potential pitfall in costing. Consider the case of WidgetCo, a firm that makes the best widget in town. It sells for $1,000. WidgetCo perceives there is a market for a low-priced widget, and that it is the company to produce it. WidgetCo puts together plans and forecasts and they plunge into the market. Thousands of new customers beat a path to their door, and the project is a success. Except, unfortunately, that most of their *new* customers are their *old* customers, who desert the high-priced brand for the low-priced junior partner. Offsetting their losses against their gains, the managers at WidgetCo wish they would never had the idea in the first place.

What they have done is cannibalize their own product. When they did their projections, they failed to take account of the impact of the new project on their existing business. It is an easy mistake to make, and as the example shows, it can be fatal. Of course, sometimes it makes good sense to bid in two segments of a market — Texas Instruments, in addition to the BA II Plus, makes the cheaper BA 35. Evidently, TI satisfied itself that the customers for the BA II Plus and for the BA 35 are not the same. Otherwise, they would be wasting money by producing both and competing with themselves.

Chapter 14

Valuing Money (Herein of Inflation)

We're not for Inflation
We're not for Deflation
We're for Flation

—Political Slogan

A nickel isn't worth a dime any more.

—Yogi Berra

§ 14.01 Introduction

In this chapter, we study changes in the price and value of money — inflation (or deflation). We examine how inflation can distort estimates of cash flow, and we show how to avoid the distortion. Then, we discuss measures of inflation, chiefly the Consumer Price Index (CPI). Finally, we show why a reliable measure of inflation is, for all practical purposes, impossible.

§ 14.02 Real v. Nominal Interest Rates

Inflation is easy enough to define in the abstract. Suppose you spend every penny you earn. Then the boss gives you a 10 percent raise — say from $1,000 to $1,100 a week. But you find that rent groceries, clothing, movie tickets, whatever, have all risen by 10 percent. Your *nominal* income has increased by 10 percent but your *real* purchasing power is no better than it was before. You need ($1,000)(1.1) = $1,100, just to keep current.

But at least you are no worse off. Suppose that all prices had risen *except* the price of your labor: you have just $1,000 to buy stuff that now costs $1,100. You can buy just $1,000 ÷ $1,100 = 0.909 or 90.9 percent of your needs. But, in either case, an *increase* in the general price level translates into a *reduction* in the purchasing power of money. Welcome to the world of *inflation*.

We need to worry about inflation in investing. Suppose we require a 4 percent return. Then, for every $100 invested, we want to get ($100)(1.04) = $104 if purchasing power remains constant. But if there is inflation, then we will need enough to compensate us for the change in purchasing power as well. So, suppose that inflation will run at 6 percent. Then, in order to meet our goal, we would need not just $104, but $104 times a factor for inflation. Generalizing, let q = the real return; let i = the rate of inflation; and r = the total nominal rate. Our threshold rate (the return we must get in order to induce us to invest) must be not less than:

$$(1 + i)(1 + q) = (1 + r)$$

How do we apply this principle in capital budgeting? Do we use real rates? Or nominal rates? The answer is: it does not matter — as long as we are consistent. This means:

- If our estimates are "real" flows, discount at the "real" rate.
- If our estimates are "nominal" flows, discount at the "nominal" rate.

To see that this must be so, compare these two sets of equations, first:

$$PV = \frac{(\text{Real FV})(1 + i)}{(1 + q)(1 + i)} = \frac{\text{Nominal FV}}{1 + r}$$

And then:

$$PV = \frac{(\text{Real FV})}{(1 + q)}$$

See that to compute the nominal numerator, we multiply the real numerator by one plus the inflation rate. We discount by the nominal denominator, which includes both real and inflation components. In the second equation, inflation cancels out of both numerator and denominator, leaving us to discount only by the real rate.

Web site: A variety of inflation calculators can be found at: http://www.jsc.nasa.gov/bu2/inflate.html.

For example, suppose we expect cash flows in *real* dollars of $1,000 in each of the next five years. Our required *real* rate of return (q) is 7 percent. The estimated inflation rate (i) is 4 percent. In column three below, we show the real income discounted at the real rate, $(1 + q)^n$. In column four, we show the nominal return, which is the real return *multiplied* by $(1 + i)^n$. In column five, we show the nominal return discounted by $[(1+q)(1+i)]^n$. Note that columns two and four are the same.

t =	Estimated Income (Real)	Discounted (Real) $[1/(1+q)^n]$	Estimated Income (Nominal)	Discounted (Nominal) $[1/\{(1+i)^n(1+q)^n\}]$
1	$ 1,000	$ 935	$ 1,040	$ 935
2	$ 1,000	$ 873	$ 1,082	$ 873
3	$ 1,000	$ 816	$ 1,125	$ 816
4	$ 1,000	$ 763	$ 1,170	$ 763
5	$ 1,000	$ 713	$ 1,217	$ 713
	Total	$ 4,100		$ 4,100

Pitfall: This is straightforward enough, but there is one common pitfall. Suppose we expect cash flows of $1,000 (real) in each of the next five years in the previous example. We also expect to have depreciation tax shields of $1,000 in each of the five years. Use the same rates as before: 7 percent required real (q), and 4 percent inflation (i). We have already shown how to compute the present value of the expected cash flows. How do we handle the depreciation? The trick is to remember that the depreciation cash flow is *already stated in nominal terms*. So, you must discount by the *nominal rate*.

Nominal	**Discounted Nominal**
$ 1,000	$ 899
$ 1,000	$ 808
$ 1,000	$ 726
$ 1,000	$ 652
$ 1,000	$ 586
Total	$ 3,670

To get the total net worth of this project, add this $3,670 to the $4,100 computed above.

Computing Rates: We are dealing with three terms here: q, i, and r. On first principles, if we know any two, we can derive the third. So to compute a nominal forward factor (OFF) the equation would be:

$$\text{NFF} = (1 + q)(1 + i) = (1 + r)$$

We know that the discount factor (DF) is the inverse of the FF, so it follows that the nominal discount factor (NDF) is the inverse of the nominal forward factor:

$$\text{NDF} = \frac{(1 + r)}{(1 + q)(1 + i)}$$

We can manipulate these equations to get other useful results. For example, if we know the OFF and the real rate, we can isolate the inflation rate:

$$i = [\frac{(1 + r)}{(1 + q)}] - 1$$

On similar logic, if we know the OFF and the inflation rate, we can isolate the real rate (check this).Or if we know the real rate and the inflation rate, we can compute the nominal rate:

$$q + i + (qi) = r$$

For example, if the real rate is 6 percent and the inflation rate is 4 percent, then [(1.04)(1.06)] gives us 1.1024, the nominal rate, r. Checking: (1.1024 ÷ 1.06) will give 1.04 and (1.1024 ÷ 1.04) will give 1.06. Note that, although we *multiply* and *divide* to make these relationships, the results are not much different from what they would be if we were to *add* or *subtract:* (0.04 + 0.06) = 0.1, which is less than one quarter of 1 percent off the actual rate. Most people use the add-and-subtract version as a "back of the envelope" calculation.

§ 14.03 The Consumer Price Index

In this section, we examine a common measure of inflation. We will see how it works. Then we will explain how this measure (and indeed *all* common measures of inflation) is defective in principle.

The measure we want to consider is the Consumer Price Index (CPI). The CPI comes from the Bureau of Labor Statistics (BLS), a U.S. Government agency. The BLS computes the CPI monthly, measuring price changes for a fixed "basket" of goods and services. The index treats 1982–1984 as a base. The base period gets a value of 100. Using this base, the CPI at the end of 1991 was 140.1. The index is saying: it cost $1,401 to get what $1,000 would have bought in 1982–1984.

The BLS also provides "historical" data, going back to 1926. You can use various index numbers to construct comparisons between years. You can compare purchasing power for any two years if you know the nominal purchasing power for either of them, and the CPIs for both. For example, let E = the "early" year, and L = the "late" year, and S = "salary." Then:

$$S_L = S_E \left[\frac{CPI_L}{CPI_E} \right]$$

For example, suppose you know your father earned $8,400 in 1965. The CPI for 1965 is 31.5. What would it take to have comparable purchasing power in 1991? Compute the value of 140.1 ÷ 31.5 and multiply by $8,500: the product is $37,805.

On the same logic:

$$S_E = S_L \left[\frac{CPI_E}{CPI_L} \right]$$

For example, the CPI for 1990 is 130.7. The law firm of Nasty, Brutish & Short started new associates in that year at $75,000. For 1963, the CPI is 30.6, and a comparable firm hired its associates in that year at $15,000. Which associate is better off?

There are many other ways of measuring inflation. The BLS also computes *producer price indexes* (PPI). Both the CPI and the PPI include prices for food and energy, but economists believe these prices tend to be unstable and distracting; they therefore often factor out food and energy to get a reliable fix on true price movements. The government also produces a set of *Gross Domestic Product Deflators*, which derive in part from the PPI and the CPI. Other numbers measure *particular* aspects of purchasing power. For example, many observers watch the data on *average hourly earnings*, or the government's quarterly *Employment Cost Index* to estimate the cost of labor.

But there is a fatal defect in all these indices. To understand it, consider this example. Suppose you buy just two items, beef and soybeans. At t=0, you pay $1 a pound for each. Your total budget is $100, so you spend $50 on each. Now, suppose that at t=1, the price of beef goes to $1.50, while the price of soybeans remains at $1. How will you spend your money now? If you continue to spend half your money on each product, you will get 50 pounds of soybeans (as before) but only 33.33 pounds of beef ($50 ÷ $1.50 = 33.33).

If you continue to buy half beef, half soybeans, you will buy 40 pounds of each. There are many intermediate possibilities. There is no way, in principle, of inferring from the t=0 data alone what you will do with the t=1 prices.

Now, suppose the BLS picks you as the typical consumer and constructs its t=0 CPI on the assumption that you buy beef and soybeans in a ratio of 50:50. At t=1, what should BLS do? It has two choices. First, it may *keep its index constant* — in which case it is no longer representing the buying habits of the typical consumer. Or second, it may *adjust its index to represent the new consumption pattern* — in which case it is no longer making a real comparison.

In practice, every inflation index falls victim to one of these distortions. The CPI, as a typical example, will use the same index for a few years (during which time it becomes increasingly distorted), and then it will "adjust" the index (after which it is no longer making real comparisons).

There are other problems with a CPI. For example, how do you define the "typical" consumer? In Seoul, your measure would have to include lots of kimchi; in Mexico City, lots of tortillas. What do you do in Los Angeles, where your population has lots of Mexicans and lots of Koreans? Second, how do you measure *quality*? It is likely that *every* new car today is better than *any* new car was 30 years ago. If the consumer pays twice as much for a car today — and if the car is in fact more than twice as good as the old one — then his real cost may have *declined* rather than risen.

Similarly, how do you measure *new products?* Computers and cellular telephones did not exist a generation ago; today they are everywhere. Even if the CPI does include them, it is likely to include them too late — i.e., only after they have come into broad general use. So, there is a systematic bias towards underestimating their value.

As a matter of practice, the CPI also omits several items that some users might consider important. For one, it does not consider *taxes*. Moreover, it does not count *investment* property. This exclusion may have special relevance at the current writing (in mid-1998). The stock market is at record levels, while the CPI seems to advance at a snail's pace — supposedly a combination made in heaven. But if we included the cost of investing in the CPI, the numbers would look far less favorable.

None of this is news to students of the CPI, and there is a plethora of secondary literature on how one might account for the distortions. Meanwhile, there is fairly wide (though not universal) agreement that the CPI tends to *overstate* inflation. Thus, the CPI is slower to pick up cost *reductions* (from quality improvements, new products and the like) than it is to pick up cost *increases*.

§ 14.04 Deflation

We have concentrated on price *inflation*, but there is no reason in principle why prices cannot move the other way. For example, we might go to the store and find it costs us only 97 cents to buy the goods that cost us a dollar last year. The price change is $[(97 \div 100) - 1] = -.03$, or *negative* 3 percent.

So, we have price *deflation*. Few people alive today have experienced general price deflation, but it is not impossible in practice. In the United States, prices drifted down more or less steadily from the end of the Civil War to the end of the Nineteenth Century. Of more current interest, some economists believe we may be drifting into another deflationary cycle — or indeed, that when you take account of distortions in price indices, that a deflationary cycle has already begun.

§ 14.05 Who Cares?

It is worth a moment's time to reflect on why all this matters. It is true that if all prices went up and down at the identical rate it would not matter. Recall our first example, where you got a 10 percent raise, and found that you had to pay 10 percent more for everything you bought: the price change was, in the end, invisible.

But inflation (deflation) never works that way. Always, some people are affected more than others. For example, suppose you buy a house with a 30-year fixed-rate mortgage whose payments take 25 percent of your income. Suppose there is an unanticipated[1] increase in the CPI and the general level of prices — including the price of your labor — grows by a factor of four. You have found yourself paying quadruple prices with your quadruple wages — but not for your mortgage, where your payment was locked in at the beginning. You gain, and the mortgagee loses. Generalizing, *inflation helps debtors and hurts creditors, and vice versa.* Whether a particular society tolerates inflation or not may depend on whether it is dominated by debtors (who are happy to repay their old debts with worthless money) or the reverse.

On the other hand, it is traditional that inflation hurts people on *fixed incomes* — typically pensioners or government employees — insofar as their inflows fail to compensate for the increasing price levels.

§ 14.06 Inflation Accounting

Inflation also presents distinctive problems to students of accounting. Suppose LittleCo has $100,000 in cash. It spends $50,000 at t=0 to buy a new forklift truck, so its t=0 balance sheet shows two assets: cash, $50,000; and forklift truck, $50,000. Now suppose at t=1, we find that DebtorCo could sell the forklift truck for $56,000. This might signal nothing less than a dramatic increase in value — perhaps the market is afflicted with an unanticipated shortage of forklift trucks. Under standard accounting rules, we do not mark up the value of the forklift to represent the increase in value. But it is easy to imagine a system where we did so. Should we shift to such a system of "value accounting?"

Before you decide, consider this alternative. It may be that the price of the forklift has risen because the value has risen, but it may be that the price has risen because the value of *money* has *declined* through inflation. If that

[1] The qualifier is important. If inflation were anticipated its effect would be impounded in the original mortgage.

is the case, then the purchasing power of the forklift remains unchanged, and you might not want to change the bookkeeping entry at all. At a minimum, you would need some device for distinguishing between "real" and "nominal" increases in value.

The problem is aggravated when you consider the problem of the cash. With the forklift, we use the cash price as an index of value. But the cash is the index itself. Consider the case where there has been a general increase in prices. You certainly would not want to mark up the cash value. If anything, you would want to mark it *down*, to make it clear that cash no longer has the buying power it had at t=0.

There is no good way to solve this problem. To explore the alternatives in more detail, consider the case of Harry's Repair Shop.

§ 14.07 Inflation Accounting: Harry's Repair Shop

To consider the effect of "general" and "particular" price changes, consider this problem. Harry opens Harry's Repair Shop, Inc., on Dec. 31, 2000. He invests $33,000 in cash in exchange for common stock. He borrows $11,000 from FinCo on a five-year note. He buys Blackacre with $18,000 cash, which he intends to use as a site for his shop. He does one repair job for which he bills $800. The job was all labor; the customer furnished all parts. Presumably, his balance sheet at the close of business looks like this:

Balance Sheet
Harry's Repair Shop
Dec. 31, 2000

Assets		**Liabilities**	
Cash	$33,000	**Payable**	$11,000
Receivables	800		
Blackacre	18,000	**Net Worth**	$40,800
TOTAL	$51,800	**TOTAL**	$51,800

The next day, Harry wins the lottery and decides to take a year-long trip around the world. He leaves immediately and returns on December 31, 2001. He learns that there was 12 percent inflation during the year. He learns that his land has appreciated in value to $24,000. What will be his new balance sheet? If we use *conventional accounting principles*, it will be:

Balance Sheet
Harry's Repair Shop
Dec. 31, 2001

Assets		**Liabilities**	
Cash	$33,000	**Payables**	$11,000

Receivables	800		
Blackacre	18,000	**Net Worth**	$40,800
TOTAL	$51,800	**TOTAL**	$51,800

In other words, just what it was on December 31, 2000. In the jargon of the trade, we use *historical costs* and *nominal dollars*.

Historical Costs, Constant Dollars: Nominal dollars ignore the effect of inflation. Suppose instead, we recast our balance sheet to keep dollars *constant* through time, independent of inflation. We will key it to the value of the dollar for December 31, 2001. The 2001 balance sheet will show:

Balance Sheet
Harry's Repair Shop
Dec. 31, 2001

Assets		**Liabilities**	
Cash	$33,000	**Payable**	$11,000
Receivables	800		
Blackacre	20,160	**Net Worth**	$42,960
TOTAL	$53,960	**TOTAL**	$53,960

Note that we have left the "financial" assets alone. Since 2001 is our benchmark, we must declare them at face value. But Blackacre, a non-financial asset, will sell for "inflated" dollars. So, we benchmark Blackacre at its inflated dollar price. The 2000 balance sheet will show:

Balance Sheet
Harry's Repair Shop
Dec. 31, 2000

Assets		**Liabilities**	
Cash	$36,960	**Payable**	$12,320
Receivables	896		
Blackacre	20160	**Net Worth**	$45,696
TOTAL	$58,016	**TOTAL**	$58,016

What have we done here? Start with cash. Recall that inflation was 12 percent. We took our 2001 number and multiplied by 1.12. This is how we convey the notion that we had 12 percent more buying power (for the same number of dollars) back then. Since it is denoted in dollars, we do the same thing with the receivables. Taking both together, the message is that we have lost value by holding onto our money. For whatever consolation it may be, note that we also adjust upward our *payables* by the same formula. So, if we have less, we also owe less. For Blackacre, no restatement is necessary. Since it is a non-financial asset, we assume it neither gains nor loses value.

Current Cost, Nominal Dollars: This time, we ignore the *general* price change, but recognize *specific* changes. Again, let us start with 2001:

Balance Sheet
Harry's Repair Shop
Dec. 31, 2001

Assets		Liabilities	
Cash	$33,000	**Payable**	$11,000
Receivables	800		
Blackacre	24000	**Net Worth**	$46,800
TOTAL	$57,800	**TOTAL**	$57,800

Here we have marked up Blackacre to its current market price. The "financial" assets stay the same. See what a nice net worth we show. The 2000 balance sheet will show:

Balance Sheet
Harry's Repair Shop
Dec. 31, 2000

Assets		Liabilities	
Cash	$33,000	**Payable**	$11,000
Receivables	800		
Blackacre	18,000	**Net Worth**	$40,800
TOTAL	$51,800	**TOTAL**	$51,800

Note that we are back to the original balance sheet.

Current Cost, Constant Dollars: Can we put these two together? Can we account for general and specific price changes at the same time? We can. Start with 2001:

Balance Sheet
Harry's Repair Shop
Dec. 31, 2001

Assets		Liabilities	
Cash	$33,000	**Payable**	$11,000
Receivables	800		
Blackacre	24000	**Net Worth**	$46,800
TOTAL	$57,800	**TOTAL**	$57,800

We treat the "financial" assets at benchmark nominal values. We mark up Blackacre — but not just for inflation. Instead, we mark Blackacre up to the price it would fetch in today's market. The 2000 balance sheet will show:

Balance Sheet
Harry's Repair Shop
Dec. 31, 2000

Assets		**Liabilities**	
Cash	$36,960	**Payable**	$12,320
Receivables	896		
Blackacre	20160	**Net Worth**	$45,696
TOTAL	$58,016	**TOTAL**	$58,016

This is the same as current cost, constant dollar. Note that we have marked up the financial assets to recognize what *would have been* required to keep values constant. We list Blackacre at its 2000 value, but stated in 2001 dollars — i.e., what Blackacre would have been worth had we not corrected our 2001 balance sheet for inflation.

Chapter 15

Rents, Profits and Competition

If there is a $5 bill
on the sidewalk in your neighborhood,
someone has already picked it up.

—Economist Joke

§ 15.01 Introduction

In this chapter, we begin an inquiry into the question, "where do net present values come from?" We make the point that it is hard to make a buck. We also explore the concept of "economic rents," as a device for identifying and isolating NPV.

§ 15.02 Competitive Markets

Let us review some of the basics. Suppose you will get $162 (FV) at t=1, and that the discount rate (r) is 8 percent. You know, then, that the present value (PV) is $162 ÷ 1.08 = $150. Suppose you can buy this package for $135. Then you know that the NPV is ($150 − $135), or $15. As we might say, while the *required* rate of return is 8 percent, the *expected* rate of return is 20 percent.

All this is familiar. But there is a trap here: if this investment is really worth $150, how come you can get it for $135? If you can do it, blessings on you. But it is hard to see how you will get away with it. For one thing, suppose you *already owned* this right to $162 at t=1. Assume 8 percent is the right rate. You would not *sell* for $135. No, you would insist on something very close to $150. And why not? On the facts as stated, you can expect to get no less.

Or consider the view of the buyer. Suppose he would be willing to pay $150, but suppose he offers $135. If he acts very quickly, he might get lucky. But if it is worth $150 to the buyer, then there is a good chance it will be worth $150 to some other buyer as well. And once the first buyer offers $135, chances are someone else will come along to bid $136, or $137. And then the first buyer will have to bid $138, and so it will go until the price goes to $150.

When you stop and think about things this way, you wonder how anybody makes any money at all, ever. If there is an opportunity out there, we can expect someone to try to grab at it. And unless we get up very early, and are very alert, the chances are good it will be gone before we get there.

§ 15.03 Trust the Market

One teaching of this bleak insight applies to the job of project evaluation we pursued in an earlier assignment: when in doubt, trust the market. For example, your client, Mildred, sets out to build the world's greatest banjo pick.

She will need real estate, equipment, raw materials and employees. What will it cost to buy all these components? It will cost what the market says it will cost. So count on the market price. You are more likely right than wrong.

This may sound like a truism, but people get it wrong. Here is an example. Mildred has done her homework on banjo picks. She has scheduled the project for a 10-year life. She has totaled up the costs and benefits for all components except the real estate. She calculates an NPV of *negative* $500,000.

But she will also need a factory building. She has identified a good prospect — a sturdy old fortress that looks like it will last to the next ice age. It will cost $5 million on top of her other costs, which seems to suggest that her NPV is even worse than she thought. But she takes a second look. She decides she can resell the building at the end of 10 years for $12 million. At your chosen interest rate, that translates into a PV of $7 million. So, her (revised) estimated NPV is: [($7 million − $5 million) − $500,000], or $1.5 million.

Does this make sense? Well, we can never say never, but think about it: if that building really has a PV of $7 million, why is it selling for $5 million? And if Mildred is so clever at real estate, why is she wasting her time on banjo picks? Indeed, if she is this good at buildings, why doesn't she just skip the banjo picks (whose NPV is, after all, negative) altogether? At the very least, she should ask herself, "What is so special about my knowledge that makes me think I can second-guess the real estate market — and not just second-guess it, but second-guess it for a 10-year, $5 million gamble?"

Here is another example — a grim story, but strong enough to reaffirm the point. The subject is slavery in Brazil in the late Nineteenth Century. There is reason to believe that the "appropriate" rate of interest for "investing" in slaves was 25 percent per annum. A healthy 25-year-old male slave had a life expectancy of about 20 years (i.e., to age 45). You could rent one at Rio for 330 million reis per year which must, therefore, have been his annual earning capacity. Under these conditions, what would be the worth, to his owner, of a healthy 25-year-old slave? For the answer, it would be fair to use the "simple annuity" formula ($c \div r$) since the 25 percent rate is so high that the residual after 20 years really is not worth worrying about. On this logic, the answer would be 1,320 million reis.

But in 1884, such a slave in the Rio market sold for only 700 million reis. What could account for the discrepancy? Here is a possible answer: Brazil was to abolish slavery in 1888. Hence, the remaining effective earning power for his owner extended, not over 20 years, but over only four, or less. Treating the earning power as a four-year annuity at an annual rate of 25 percent, the present value turns out to be 779.33 million reis. Turning it around, the PV of 700 million reis seems to apply an n of just about 3.43 years. In other words, the market seems to have been accurately pricing the remaining value, to the owner, of the slave. The spooky part is that while abolition was widely discussed in 1884, the 1888 abolition date had not yet been announced.

Does this example in any way "justify" slavery? Of course not. Quite the contrary, you could take it as a grim reminder of just how much markets may know.[1]

---

[1] Summarized in Robert Fogel & Stanley Engerman, Without Consent or Contract: The Rise and Fall of American Slavery (Technical Papers) (1st ed. 1992).

§ 15.04 Commodity Prices

Now consider another example. Your client, Harry, is planning to make defenestrators. To make defenestrators, you need elixir, a mineral that one digs out of the earth. The market for elixir is highly competitive — many buyers, many sellers, and lots of price information. There are elixir deposits all over the world. Most of them lie under pieces of scrub land, far from anywhere, that no one wants for any other purpose, so storage costs are negligible. Extraction costs are also negligible. Elixir sells for $20 a barrel. The price has been rising at 5 percent a year as long as anyone can remember. The OCC for the defenestrator project is 6 percent.

Harry sets out to estimate his elixir needs for the next 10 years. He figures he will need a million barrels a year. He undertakes to fashion an annuity formula like our basic annuity formula, but adjusted to take account of growth. His equation looks like this:

$$C(1+g)\left[\frac{1}{(r-g)} - \frac{(1+g)^n}{(r-g)(1+r)^n}\right]$$

Using numbers from this project:

$$\$20{,}000{,}000\ (1.05)\left[\frac{1}{(.06-.05)} - \frac{(1.05)^{10}}{(.06-.05)(1.06)^{10}}\right]$$

The product is $189,910,871 (check it — if you doubt the formula, double-check it by computing out the separate components with a spreadsheet). But there is a flaw in this reasoning. Consider this analysis. Suppose growth continues at 5 percent from t=0 to t=1. Then the t=1 price of a gallon of elixir will be $21. At 6 percent, the PV would be $19.81. Do you see the problem? If the value achieved by not selling today is only $19.81 and the value achieved by selling is $20, then you might as well sell today.

Since the elixir market is highly competitive, we can infer that there are sellers ready to extract their elixir and put it on the market if the price is right. As more product is brought to market, we would expect the price of elixir to drift down from $20 to $19.81. In the meantime, there is a gap in the market. The jargon calls it an *opportunity for arbitrage* — a chance to make 19 cents by selling for $20 a product whose opportunity cost is just $19.81.

But there is another way to interpret this data. Opportunities for arbitrage are unlikely in competitive markets. Indeed, a competitive market may be defined as one in which there are no opportunities for arbitrage. If this is the case, then the t=0 price of $20 must represent the *exactly* discounted present value of t=1 price. This will be true, of course, if the expected increase in price for the next year is not 5 percent, but is 6 percent. Then we can expect the spot price to increase from today's $20 to $21.20. Discounted at 6 percent, the present value is today's $20.

Of course it would also be true if the growth rate was *in fact* 5 percent, but if we were wrong in picking our discount rate. If both discount rate and growth rate were each 5 percent, then once again we can derive a market-clearing PV price of just $20.

If this logic follows for any *one* year, then it must follow for *each and all* future years. Generalizing: the t=0 price must represent the discounted present value of the "market's best guess" as to *any* future spot price.

What is the implication of this proposition for cash flow planning? The implications is this: when estimating the cost of elixir, *we don't need to do any discounting*. The reason is that *the market has already done it for us*. So, we can figure the PV of *all* our future elixir costs as simply: ($ 20)(1,000,000)(10) = $200,000,000.

The same logic would hold, of course, if the PV of the t=1 price, properly discounted, turned out to be *higher* than the t=0 price. Then elixir owners would be motivated to hold their product *off* the market, until the t=0 price rose high enough to induce them to release it.

We will revisit the issue of market pricing and "trusting the market" later, when we explore the "efficient capital market hypothesis" (ECMH). But, for now, you just have to look back over the previous examples to see the importance of picking the right discount rate; a half a point off may make the difference between recommending a winner and putting your job (or your client's job) on the line by backing a sure loser. If the market is willing to lend a helping hand in valuation, take it.

§ 15.05 Economic Rents

What we have said so far amounts to this: a competitive market, *by definition* is a market in which there are no NPVs — that is, because they have all been bid away. Now we turn to the flip side of the coin: we try to identify situations where positive NPVs can be found. We start with David Ricardo, the first great economic theorist. Ricardo wrote in England, just after the Napoleonic War. There were great farms in England, but masses of people survived (if they did survive) on the edge of starvation. Ricardo asked, "Why are so many poor?"

In response to his own question, Ricardo reasoned like this. Suppose there are two kinds of farm land, "good land," where you can grow wheat at $1. a bushel, and "bad" land where it can be grown for $1.25 a bushel. Suppose there is more demand for wheat than can be satisfied from the good land, but not so much as to require all the bad land. Ricardo argued that on assumptions like this, the price of wheat would fall to $1.25 a bushel: that is the price you would need to induce the owner of the "bad" land to put his land into production. At this price, the owner of the "bad" land would just cover his cost. He could not really expect to do better, otherwise *other* owners of "bad" land would cut their prices and undercut him.

But if the market price settled at $1.25, what of the owner of the good land? The answer is that he would make a quarter per bushel because his costs were 25 cents lower than the costs of the farmer with the bad land. Ricardo called that quarter a "rent." He is using the term in a somewhat special sense, of course: we think of the rent as any charge that any landlord extracts from any tenant, and his use is far more narrow. Since Ricardo was an economist, we call his rent an "economic rent."

Ricardo didn't believe that the landowner had any particular moral claim on it, and he had no trouble in proposing a remedy that would make it vanish. Ricardo's remedy: improve competition. Specifically, Ricardo saw England as hemmed in by high protective tariffs that kept out cheap foreign wheat. He felt the way to ease the lot of the poor was to the lower the tariff, increase competition, and thus wipe out the economic rent.

Ricardo talked as if his analysis applied to land only. Later in the century, other economists saw that if it worked for land, it worked for anything. Any time anyone can command a price above cost, he has a rent. For example, suppose you build a *better mousetrap*. As the saying goes, the world may beat a path to your door. You may be able to price above marginal cost and enjoy economic rents — at least until someone else learns to copy your product, and drives the price down. Or maybe the government will allow you to put a *patent* on your better mousetrap. Then the government becomes your ally in protecting your economic rent, and competition be hanged.[2]

Or you might just be born lucky. Do you remember Two-Head Gruskin, who used to pitch for the Sycamore Skyhooks in the old Three-Eye League? Two-Head could watch both first and third base the same time. Had he not suffered from an unfortunate indecisiveness, he surely would have dominated the game. Best of all for Two-Head, he had it all to himself: no one else could imitate his natural advantage and no one could enjoin him from exploiting it. In a sense, you could say that Two-Head had the ideal "economic rent," more advantageous even than Ricardo's good land.

One important way to enjoy economic rents is to make your product just a bit different from everyone else's. There is a lot of cheese in the world, but do not tell that to the cheese makers around Parma, Italy. They make the only real "parmigiana," and they fight fiercely to maintain their brand identity. No wonder that a good Parmesan cheese can sell for $15 or $20 a pound.

One important corollary needs to be noted here. In order to enjoy economic rents, you have to be the *first* person to capture the advantage. The *second* owner — that is, the person who buys *from* the person with the rents — cannot expect to enjoy it. The reason is that the benefit of the rents will be impounded in the price he pays. To live like a lord, you had best be born a lord. To reap the profits of the computer chip, you must invent the computer chip (or what might not be the same thing, you must be the first to package and sell it).

Lately economists have pressed the analysis of economic rents to a whole new plane. They have seen that not just entrepreneurs seek rents. Laborers seek rents, through labor unions. Even governments seek rents, through imposing government monopolies and the like. Indeed, on this generalized model, it seems that the only way to get onto Easy Street is to enjoy an economic rent. Just about all of us want an Easy Street address. So you can picture all of us as we spend our nights and days trying to conjure up an economic rent — hence *rent-seeking behavior*, one of the great buzzwords of modern economic thought. If you believe the economists, we all do it, just about all of the time.

---

[2] Economists distinguish between economic "rents" and "quasi-rents," but it is a subtlety we gloss over here: for our purposes all revenues over costs are "rents."

And so, at least on this model, we go our merry way, trying to construct our little rent nests invulnerable from the ravages of competition. It is easy to see how this analysis bristles with issues of policy. Thus, as consumers, we all gain when price is bid down to cost. And it must be true at least in part that competition brings out the best in us, helping us to stretch our limits beyond where we thought we could go. On the other hand, competition is terribly wasteful. If ten people enter a race and one wins a prize, then the other nine may have spent their resources for nothing.

Moreover, the ethics of the reward system are not completely self-evident. We may be grateful that Two-Head Gruskin was not a capitalist buccaneer — but what did he do to earn his economic rent, aside from being born with the right genes? We may all think that the inventor deserves some kind of patent protection for his invention. But how much, and for how long?

These are urgent questions, but time forbids us from searching too deeply into them here. We must restrict ourselves to a narrower subset of issues. Our point of departure will be to recognize that "net present value" is just another name for "economic rent." We need to give a little time to the question of how people identify and exploit these opportunities for gain. We need also to look more closely at the "paradox of rents" — the idea that once you know rents are available, they disappear. We will also say a bit about what happens when rents do *not* disappear — when there are "mispricings," such that two identical assets sell at different prices.

§ 15.06 An Example: Defenestrators

> The fuzzy side is always up
> And 80 percent of the product is beige.
>
> —Former Carpet Salesman[3]

Consider this problem arising in the defenestrator industry. The industry is highly competitive. This means that there is no practical limit to the number of buyers and sellers in the marketplace. It also means we must take the price that the market dictates; if we try to go higher, someone will undercut us and we will not sell any product at all.

Up to now, there has been only one kind of plant in the defenestrator business, so you can infer that everyone in the business has the same cost structure. You can build one of these defenestrator plants for $100,000. It will produce 100,000 units a year and will last forever. Operating costs (i.e., costs excluding debt service) are 90 cents a unit. The market rate of interest is 10 percent.

Question: what is the price of a defenestrator *today*? From the information on hand, you *already know enough* to answer this question. Remember, we are in a market where we take the price the market gives us, and where no one can try to capture an economic rent without someone else undercutting him and driving him out of business.

Once you have figured out the answer to this question, you are ready to go on. We will return to the defenestrator industry later, to consider what

[3] Explaining why he left the business.

happens when someone comes up with a more efficient manufacturing plant. But we need at least one other concept before us.

§ 15.07 Note: Cab Fare

So you've had enough of law school and you are thinking of taking up a new life behind the wheel of a New York City taxicab.[4] Before you clean out your locker, check out the grim economics of the taxi business. You lease your cab by the day. You pay $100 or more up front every day to take the cab out of the garage. You pay for your gas. You bear all the risks, not least the risk of slack demand. If you are unlucky, a shift may net you as little as $20 or $30.

If you want to drive your own cab, you have to buy a taxi medallion. If you had the foresight to start, say 30 years ago, you bought your medallion for perhaps $35,000. After all these years, the chances are you own your medallion free and clear, and with pluck and luck you make a modest living. Moreover, you can look forward to a nice profit on resale at retirement, for the current price of a medallion runs upward of $275,000. Perhaps you can do it if you can find a partner who will share the financing costs and who will be willing (like you) to drive 12-hour shifts every day.

The profit, in short, goes to the medallion owner, more precisely to the owner who had the good luck to buy the medallion when prices were low. The current price represents the discounted present value of the prospective future cash flows, net of the few coins left behind for the lessee-drivers. What we have here would seem to be a classic instance of "economic rents," just like the "unearned increment" that British landed proprietors used to enjoy before the abolition of the corn laws 160-odd years ago. The price of medallions has ascended by some 87 percent since the modern leasing system began back in 1979. The executive of a medallion-financing firm claims that as an investment, medallions have a better record than the stock market: the market has risen only a paltry 11 percent or so a year since the 1930s, while medallions, he says, have appreciated at a rate of 18 percent.[5] There is nothing that offers so much consolation as a cozy relationship with an economic rent.

[4] Most of the figures in this note come from Howard Husock, *New York's Unsung Taxi Triumph,* City J., Summer 2000, available at: http://www.city-journal.org/html/9_4_new_yorks_unsung.html.

A more thorough analysis is in Bruce Schaller & Gorman Gilbert, *Villain or Bogeyman? New York's Taxi Medallion System,* Transp. Q., Vol. 50, No. 1, Winter 1996, available at: http://www.users.rcn.com/schaller.interport/taxi/taxi2.htm.

[5] Andrew Murstein, president of Medallion Financial, as quoted in the Fin. Times, Apr. 8, 1999, available at: http://www.medallionfinancial.com/news_articles_financialtimes040899.htm.

Chapter 16

Salvage

If there were a back door,
it wouldn't be a shrine. . .[1]

What's our Exit Strategy?[2]

§ 16.01 Introduction

As we have seen, all costs are opportunity costs. One implication is, in deciding whether to stick with a project, we always consider what we could otherwise do with the assets. If the assets are better deployed in another use, we should quit and pursue the other use. If the other use is inferior, then we should stick with the current use. This is the principle of salvage value. In this chapter, we explore the meaning and implication of salvage value.

§ 16.02 Salvage Value

When Francis Lowell built his path-breaking cotton textile mill at Waltham, Massachusetts, in 1814, he hit on a revolutionary solution to his labor problem: farmers' daughters. Lowell recognized that the rock-strewn hills of rural New England was not good farmland in any event. With his highly productive new mechanized factory, it was easy for him to offer wages better than the earnings that they could scratch off the farm. Work was hard and their fathers made sure they stayed closely supervised to preserve their moral well being. But work on the farm had been harder and at least as lonely. And after a few years in the mills, the daughters could return home with attractive dowries. Participation by women in the labor force grew from substantially nothing at the turn of the Nineteenth Century to as high as 25 percent by 1832.

Unfortunately, ideal as they were as workers, there simply were not enough farmer's daughters to meet the demands of the booming textile industry. By the early 1840s, the mill owners were scouring the world for a new labor force. And they got one: the Irish, driven off the land at home by the potato famine, fled to the New World and into the mills. The changeover was swift and dramatic. Before 1845, the mill weaving rooms were 95 percent Yankee. By 1855, they were 60 percent Irish.

Inevitably, the new surge of immigrants provoked a kind of bidding war, driving down wages and driving up the demands imposed on the laborers. But a closer look shows a fascinating counter-trend. As Irish immigrants made

[1] Maurey Maverick, the Congressman to San Antonio, during the 1960 presidential campaign, answering a question from candidate John F. Kennedy. They were at the Alamo.

[2] Warren Buffett, the second richest man in the United States. He made virtually all his money as an "outside investor," taking positions in companies which he felt were undervalued by the market.

themselves available to work more cheaply, the farm women did not cut their wage demands. Instead, they went back to the farm. Farmwork may have been less attractive than millwork at high wages, but at low wages, it made sense to go home. Indeed, female participation in the labor force began to drop as the women left the mills and continued down to a nadir around 1890 before it began the rise that continues today. As to the wages of laborers — though they fell overall, it seems they would have fallen even further if the women had stayed in the competition.

Hard as their lives may have been, the women had one important advantage in the competition for manufacturing employment: they had an "exit strategy," a second-choice outlet for their productive capacity that they could turn to when mill wages fell too low. The exit strategy saved the women from the worst misfortunes of the Irish laborers. Yet ironically, you might say it worked to the advantage of the Irish as well, insofar as it took the women out of the competition.

The farm women were lucky to have an exit strategy. Not so lucky were some of the investors who, about the same time, poured their money into the building of canals. Investors hoped that the canals would provide a vital network of transport. Unfortunately for the investors, they barely finished financing the canals before the technology that made canals possible found itself swept aside by a newer and better technology — the railroads.

By the late 1850s (as Atack and Passell say), no one with any sense would have built a new canal.[3] But did canal traffic cease? It did not. The cost to *build* a canal was prohibitively high. But the cost to *operate* a canal was trivial. You could cover your operating costs with a fee that was entirely competitive with railroad prices. Meanwhile, the *salvage value* of the canal was negligible — what else could you do with it? Better to leave the canal in place and get what you could out of it than to go to the added expense of tearing it up and starting over.

This is what Warren Buffett, America's second richest man, has in mind, when he asks about exit strategy. Buffett (who understands a lot of things) seems to understand that there is a difference between a $20 million investment with a $20 million salvage value, and the same investment with no salvage value at all. An exit strategy saved the farm women when mill wages declined. The lack of an exit strategy cost the canal investors dearly.

The canal story is a chapter in a larger story. You could say that the history of transportation — canals, railroads, subways, etc. — is, in a sense, the history of salvage problems. *Most* American railroads have gone through bankruptcy, many more than once, as owners found they paid more for assets than the salvage market would compensate.[4]

---

[3] Jeremy Atack & Peter Passell, A New Economic View of American History from Colonial Times to 1940, 155 (2d ed. 1994). Atack and Passell provide admirable summaries of the research on both canals and factory women. They are the source of most of what is presented here.

[4] But it does not always end that badly. One of the largest and most successful bankruptcy reorganization cases of all time involved the Penn Central Railway. By the time Penn Central filed for relief in 1970, its transport business was floundering. But its right-of-way ran through the heart of some of the most densely populated and productive portions of the nation. The reorganizers transformed a sluggish

Sophisticated finance types understand that the exit strategy — the right to change one's mind, as it were — is a valuable asset in itself, and ought to be valued in its own right. As we shall see later, it is a kind of "option." Option theory gives us specific guidance on how to go about pricing such an option. We will not trouble ourselves with the full exploration of option theory now. But the next example does give you a chance to think through some of our new learning, with particular reference to salvage value.

§ 16.03 The Welcome Home Inn

The Welcome Home Inn is having a hard time of things. The Inn has 250 rooms, which it rents for $100 per day. But no hotel can be 100 percent full, 100 percent of the time. Management dreams of occupying 200 rooms per day, but lately the Inn has been averaging only 150.

LittleBank holds a $25 million mortgage on the property at 8 percent, which means that debt service is $2 million per year. The debt is "nonrecourse," which means that LittleBank can look only to the motel property for satisfaction and has no recourse against any other person or asset. Other fixed costs (taxes, insurance, basic utilities, etc.) are $2 million per year. The Inn has been deferring some maintenance projects to defer costs. Variable costs equal $40 per room per night. In other words, potential annual income and expenses are as follows (in millions):

Average Occupancy	Fixed Cost	Variable Cost	Total Cost	Revenue	Net Profit (Loss)
150	$ 4	$ 2.19	$ 6.19	$ 5.475	$ (0.72)
200	$ 4	$ 2.92	$ 6.92	$ 7.300	$ 0.38
250	$ 4	$ 3.65	$ 7.65	$ 9.125	$ 1.48

So, at an average occupancy of 150 rooms per year, Welcome Home Inns gets $5.475 million in revenue. It must pay $2.19 million to cover variable costs and $2 million to cover fixed costs other than the mortgage. That leaves only $1.29 million per year for the mortgage. If it had $2 million, it could sustain a mortgage of ($2 ÷ 0.08), or $25 million. Using the same logic, the biggest mortgage this property can sustain is ($1.29 ÷ 0.08), or $16.125 million.

Something has to give. Welcome Home does not have enough revenue to pay expenses and service debt. And even if LittleBank forecloses on the

and uneconomic railroad into a highly profitable real estate development company. Penn Central may not be alone. In Kentucky, I met a man who operated a soybean farm 10 miles long and 20 yards wide, courtesy of changing transportation needs. Finally, as a child growing up in rural New Hampshire, I remember that the old right-of-way provided a pretty good playground, although I admit I was not in a position to pay a lot for it.

mortgage and takes the property, it still does not get enough value to cover its loan. There are five possibilities:

- Raise occupancy. At current costs, the break even point is an average occupancy of 182.65 persons per night throughout the year. But raising occupancy almost certainly involves catching up on some of the deferred maintenance, so costs would almost certainly increase.
- Cut operating costs. Fixed costs, like taxes and basic utilities, are probably hard to change. Variable costs like services may be vulnerable, but in the typical hotel, it is unlikely that you can cut variable costs very much without affecting service. This hotel is already suffering from deferred maintenance. It is likely that further cuts in operating cost will result in further deferral of maintenance.
- Cut prices. The problem says nothing about what would happen if you cut the rack rate from $100 to, say, $85. Note also that even if you keep the rack rate the same, at *any* price over $40, it is worthwhile to fill those otherwise empty rooms (I like to use this one to show my students how to get a discount at a hotel in the off season).
- Cut the mortgage. At current occupancy levels, there is $1.29 million available for debt service. At the 8 percent rate, this implies a capital cost of $16,125,000.
- Sell. At what level of occupancy should management call it quits? How would this answer change if management undertook one of the other suggestions above?

§ 16.04 Defenestrators Again

Now we are ready to reconsider the problem of the defenestrator industry. Recall we were in a business where anyone could cover cost, but no one could make an economic rent. We saw that for $100,000 anyone could build a plant that would make 100,000 units a year, and that operating costs were 90 cents a unit. The rate of interest is 10 percent.

Under these conditions, it should be clear that the price of a defenestrator is $1. Reason it like this: since our plant costs $100,000 and the rate is 10 percent, we will need $10,000 a year to service debt. We can produce 100,000 units a year. At that rate of production, we will need to collect 10 cents per unit for debt service. Since operating costs are 90 cents a unit, then we will need to charge (.90 +.10), or $1 a unit at full production just to cover cost. If we charge any less (or produce any less, or both), then we will not cover cost. If we charge any more, then we will not sell any at all.

But here is a stroke of good luck. You have just discovered a new technology that will produce defenestrators at an operating cost of 85 cents a unit. You can build a plant — but only one plant — for the new technology for $100,000. Just like an old plant, it can produce 100,000 a year and last forever.

Right now, you are the only one in the business with the new technology. You figure you can maintain your advantage until t=2. You know that after t = 2, everyone else will learn how to produce defenestrators as cheaply as you do. You know that after t = 2, the industry will be competitive, just as it is today. This means (definitionally) that no one will make an economic rent, and prices will just cover costs. But in the interim, you can expect demand to be sluggish — i.e., not everyone will be able to sell all the defenestrators they want to.

The question is: with your two-year lead on new technology, how do you make an economic rent? Or to put it in familiar language, how do you maximize your NPV? To answer this question, you are going to have to give some thought to your pricing policy. Remarkably, you are not a price-*taker* any more, stuck with whatever the market dictates. Instead, you are a price-*searcher*, with some leeway to set a price on your own. This does not mean you can set just *any* price. Remember that the market is sluggish, which means that if you go too high, you will not sell any at all. By contrast, clearly you can undercut your competitors and still make a profit (because your technology is cheaper). Indeed, since demand is sluggish, if you do cut your prices below the historic price, you will drive some competitors out of the business.

Which brings us to our final datum: salvage value. The current salvage value for an old defenestrator plant is $60,000. As of t = 2, you expect the salvage value to be $57,900.

With this information, you ought to be able to calculate the economic rent (the NPV) of the defenestrator project. To help you think through the problem, consider these questions. First, note that as of t = 2, others will be able to build competing "new-technology" plants just like yours, and the market will return to competition. Ask yourself — what will be the price of defenestrators after t = 2?

To answer this question, recall what it means to be in a competitive market — i.e., a market where there are no economic rents. Then ask yourself — what will be gross value of any new-technology plant as of t = 2? Note once again, that the answer follows from the definition of competitive market. Then ask yourself — what will be the price of defenestrators after year two? Correct answers to the previous two questions should impel you to a correct answer for this question.

The next question is — Would you expect an existing, old-technology plant to be scrapped at t = 2? The answer is clearly "yes" isn't it? Note that no plant — old or new — can sell product at any price above the market price. But at the market price, an old plant does not produce enough to service all its debt. Compute the sum that *would* be available if you used the old plant in the widget business. Treat this amount as a "coupon," and value the old plant as a perpetuity. Now compare the salvage value.

So, with a head start on new technology, you have an advantage for two years, but no longer. Moreover, you can charge a price above marginal cost and still compete. But what price? It cannot be *more than $1*, the current price, or competitors with old technology will undercut you and drive you out of business. The price cannot be less than 85 cents, or you would not even cover per-unit variable costs. If you charge less than 95 cents, you will not be able to cover debt service. What you want (we can see) is a price that will make the present producer *indifferent* between (on the one hand) taking the $60,000 salvage value today; and (on the other hand), the present value of staying in the business and getting the salvage value at t=2. What we want is a strategy that will drive prices no lower than necessary to capture our share of the business. As an equation, it looks like this:

$$\$60{,}000 = \frac{[100{,}000\ (p - 0.90)]}{(1.1)} + \frac{[100{,}000\ (p - 0.90)]}{(1.1)^2} = \frac{\$57{,}900}{(1.1)^2}$$

Solve for p. That is the "indifference" price. Go the least bit below it, and you drive out potential competitors. Go above, and you risk having someone undercut you.

§ 16.05 Reality Check: Real Estate Appraisal

As a benchmark for all this market theory, it may be useful to compare a little courtroom practice. Consider the case of a mortgagee making a loan secured by an interest in real estate. The mortgagee will want to know something about the value of the real estate in order to know whether it is prudent to make the loan. For example, he will want to know something about the value of the property to know what kind of security he has against repayment. In lieu of direct market values most mortgagees get appraisal opinions from professional appraisers.[5] Indeed, property appraisal is a recognized enterprise, with its own professional organizations, learned journals, and the like. At the same time, appraisal values are notoriously elastic, and it will be a rare case in which parties are not able to come up with competing appraisals where valuation is in dispute

To study the role of the appraisal opinion, consider your client, Blanche, who is buying the Whiteacre, an apartment house, from Selma for $500,000. Blanche will pay $100,000 down, and finance the rest with a loan from LoanCo. But LoanCo will loan no more than 80 percent of the value, so Blanche must satisfy LoanCo that Whiteacre is in fact worth what she is paying for it.

Amos, an appraiser, agrees to provide an appraisal for a fee. To carry out his analysis, he uses the standard form "Small Residential Income Property Appraisal Report," mandated for this sort of case in the lending industry. The form calls on the appraiser to give the value indicated by *three separate* approaches — "sales comparison," "income," and "cost." As to sales comparisons, the appraisal form calls for data on *comparable properties*, defined as "the most current, similar, and proximate competitive properties to the subject property in the subject neighborhood." The form specifies that "this analysis is intended to evaluate the inventory currently on the market competing with

---

[5] The alert reader may notice that there is a market transaction in this case — i.e., the purchase for which the purchaser is borrowing the money. Why doesn't the lender simply rely on the purchase price? The answer is that the incentives are wrong. Precisely because he is financing the purchase with borrowed money, the purchaser is not motivated to value as carefully as he would if he were buying with his own money. Since he doesn't bear the "downside" risk of loss, he is motivated to overvalue. For more on this topic, see the discussion on "games debtors play" in § 34.02 below.

the subject property . . . and *marketing time trends* affecting the subject property" [emphasis added].

The form also provides space to furnish information on "market conditions," including "growth rate, property values, demand/supply, and marketing timing" as well as the "prevalence and impact in the subject market area regarding loan discounts, interest buydowns and concessions, and identification of trends in listing prices, average days on the market and any other changes over past year." The form specifies (in bold type) that "Race and the racial composition of the neighborhood are not appraisal factors."

To figure the cost of replacement, the form calls for a gross price computed using a construction cost per square foot, together with a justification for the square-foot cost chosen. To compute value as a function of income, the form calls for an estimate of rents, together with a "gross rent multiplier."

Chapter 17

Profits in the Market Model

The last thing you want
is a job where you get paid what you're worth.

—Iron Law of Economics

§ 17.01 Introduction

In this chapter, we explore some of the difficulties in the concept of "profit." We examine the notion of "earnings" as developed by accountants. Then we compare (and contrast) the notion of "economic rents." We introduce the (paradoxical?) notion that in a competitive market, there *can be* no profit. That is: the very *definition* of a competitive market is one in which no one does any better than to break even. To press our analysis, we try to understand the possible meaning of "profit" as the term is used in the Uniform Commercial Code.

§ 17.02 The Puzzle of Profit

Everyone *seems* to know what a profit is: businessmen go into business "for profit." Accountants assemble statements of "profit and loss," and the like. Thus, Alpha, Betty and Charlie contribute $150 each at t=0 (totaling $450) as the original investment in ABC, Inc. ABC does business for a year. At t=1, suppose ABC shows gross income of $220 and expenses of $180.40 for net earnings of $39.60 (for simplicity, assume that all revenues and expenses are in cash). The t=1 balance sheet will show assets of $450 (the original capital) plus $39.50 (the earnings) or $489.50. As a return on *income,* we have a yield of ($39.60 ÷ $220), or 18 percent. As a return on *assets*, we have a return of ($39.60 ÷ $450), or 8.8 percent.

Accountants and others often refer to "net earnings" as "profit." Many investors look to "return on income" or "return on assets" as measures of performance. But we have been taught to look not for accounting measures, but for "net present value" (NPV), also known as "economic rent." For a short-hand definition of NPV, let C_o = (negative) cash out and C_i = "cash in."

$$NPV = C_o + \frac{C_i}{1 + r}$$

Do the ABC accounting numbers permit us to measure NPV? They do not. In order to compute NPV, we would need to know, first, the t=1 cash value of the t=0 capital contribution. We would add that to the (cash) earnings to this asset value to get C_i. Then we would need to know appropriate discount rate, which would be the opportunity cost of capital required by the original investors when they made their contribution. For example, suppose the t=1 asset values total $450, the same as the t=0 value, so that C_i = ($450 +

\$39.60), or \$489.60. Suppose the OCC is 20 percent. Then the PV is (\$489.60 ÷ 1.2), or \$408, and the NPV is (\$408 − \$450), or −\$42. In percentage terms, our NPV return is [(\$408 ÷ \$450) − 1] = −0.0933, or (negative) 9.3 percent.

To explore the problem further, we invite you to consider how you would cope with the problem of measuring "profit" in a familiar law context. Then, we add a note on the economist's model of the market.

§ 17.03 "Profit" Under the Uniform Commercial Code

You have probably already met Section 2-708 of the Uniform Commercial Code, defining seller's damages for breach of contract. Section 2-708(1) provides that the measure of damages is "the difference between the market price at the time and place for tender and the unpaid contract price." But Section 2-708(2) sets a separate rule that applies "if the measure of damages provided in subsection (1) is inadequate to put the seller in as good a position as performance would have done."[1] In that case, then the measure is:

> the profit (including reasonable overhead) which the seller would have made from full performance by the buyer, together with any incidental damages . . . due allowance for costs reasonably incurred and due credit for payments or proceeds of resale.[2]

This section has perplexed courts and scholars for a generation. Given your new analytical skill at finance, see if you can make sense out of it now.

For starters, consider the case of Selma, a seller of widgets. She has fixed costs that remain constant over any number of units sold. These would be costs like lease payments and salaries. She has variable costs that — well, they vary, depending on how many units she sells. This would include materials, wages for temporary employees and the like. Variable costs always increase as production increases, of course — but at some point, they will start to increase *relatively faster* than production. This will happen, for example, when the business gets harder to manage, or supplies get dearer. Here is a cost chart for Selma's widget business, showing her costs for different levels of widget sales — six up to 12:

Selma's Cost Chart							
# of Units	6	7	8	9	10	11	12
Fixed Cost	50	50	50	50	50	50	50
Variable Cost	53	54	61	76	110	164	240
Total Cost	103	104	111	126	160	214	290

How much will Selma sell, and how much money will she make? Of course, you can't tell, because you don't know the price of widgets. But basically, it

1 UCC § 2-708(2).

2 *Id.*

boils down to two possibilities. One is that Selma functions in a competitive market — a market with a more or less infinite number of potential buyers and sellers. If that is the case, Selma is a price taker, and pretty much takes what the market gives her. Suppose the market price is $16 per widget. How many widgets will Selma sell? Look at this chart, and see if you can find it:

Competitive Market — Price Taker							
# of Units	6	7	8	9	10	11	12
Net Income (Gross Income Less Total Cost)	−7	8	17	18	0	−38	−98

The answer is obvious, isn't it? Selma will sell nine widgets. She will not sell 11 or 12 unless she wants to go broke in a hurry. She could sell six and go broke (albeit more slowly). She could sell ten, but why bother? At seven, she makes a profit — but at eight, she makes a bigger profit, and at nine, a bigger profit still. So, nine it has to be. Of course, if the price is any higher or lower, there will be a different story. She might be able to make more money selling more widgets. Or she might not be able to make a profit at any number of widgets. For the moment, the point is that price is something she is pretty much stuck with.

In this market, suppose Selma does, in fact, get nine contracts to sell, and that one of them cancels. This being a competitive market, she is, indeed, able to get a new customer at the market-clearing $16 price. What are her damages? Section 2-708(1). does not seem to offer much help (figure it out: the contract/market formula would give her *nothing*, would it not?). Is this, then, perhaps, a case for "lost profits" under Section 2-708(2)? Maybe, but think of it this way — in this competitive market, the only limit on Selma's sales are her costs. There is an unlimited supply of *potential* customers, but on the numbers above, she'll be willing to sell only nine. On this reasoning, any "subsequent" sale she makes simply fills up her nine-sale dance card. To give her "lost profits" on top of that would be to give her a double recovery. Or would it?

To help you analyze the problem, consider this approach. Many older commentators say that as long as Selma has an unlimited *supply*, then Selma ought to have "lost profits," because the "new" contract is not really a substitute for the contract that was broken. But doesn't this fail to take account of the fact that Selma's profits are limited, not by total supply, nor by total demand, but by her *costs*? In "real life," how likely do you suppose it is that a seller is really selling at the limit set by her costs? How likely do you think you are to find anything like a "competitive market?"

§ 17.04 Note on Traditional Contract Doctrine

UCC Section 2-708(2) did not just spring forth like Athena from the brow of Zeus. It has a history in the pre-Code common law of contract. It may be helpful to recall the doctrinal framework. In your first year of law school, you were taught that the measure of damages for breach of contract is "the value of the promised performance."

For example, suppose Spade promised to deliver a widget to Marlow in exchange for $7, and that Spade broke his promise, and that Marlow bought a "substitute widget" for $10. In the case of *Marlow v. Spade*, then Marlow will win damages in the amount of ($10 – $7), or $3. Ignoring costs of litigation, this award gives Marlow what he expected to get when he went into the deal — call it the "benefit of the bargain," or the "expectancy" measure. But courts did not always give these "expectancy" damages.

Maybe you read the famous old case of *Flureau v. Thornhill*,[3] where the court restricted the plaintiff-buyer to out-of-pocket expenses he incurred "in reliance" on the promise. Teachers offer *Flureau* as an illustration of the "reliance rule," said to be an alternative to the "expectancy rule," but they do not always offer any convincing account of when to apply one rule and when to apply the other. Some people say that *Flureau* is the "English rule," without any explanation as to why the English should embrace a different contract law than the United States. Finally, *Flureau* involved *real estate*, so some say it is the "real estate rule," without really explaining why we should treat real estate different from other goods.

But there is another possible approach, linked to notions of the market. Widgets (surely you know by now) are a fungible commodity, traded widely in a highly competitive market with lots of buyers and sellers, all with broad, equal access to information and so forth.

Think back to the moment when Spade offered a widget to Marlow in exchange for $7. In a competitive market, at that moment, the chances are pretty good that if Marlow had not bought from Spade for $7, he would have been able to contract with Humphrey for a virtually identical widget for a virtually identical price. If Marlow does contract with Spade, you could say that he is *passing up* a chance to contract with Humphrey. If Marlow later has to pay $10, you could say that this is an expense he bears *in reliance* on Spade's promise. On this account, *Marlow* is not an "expectancy" action at all!

Now, look again at *Flureau,* the "real estate" case. There may have been a competitive market for widgets in the Eighteenth Century, but there was certainly no such market for real estate. No one thought of real estate as "fungible." There wasn't anything like a national listing service, or a system of commercial brokerage. Many properties really counted as "unique." Indeed, there is good evidence that people did not treat real estate as a "commodity" at all, but rather as a kind of national heritage, part of a pattern of government. For all these reasons, you would not think of a real estate deal as entailing an "opportunity cost" in the same way that *Marlow* created an "opportunity cost."

On this reading, *both Flureau* and *Marlow* are really "reliance" cases, and the rule of expectancy damages seems to disappear. Does this analysis assist at all in telling you how to cope with Section 2-708(2)?

---

[3] 2 Black. W. 1078, 96 Eng. Rep. 635 (K.B. 1776).

§ 17.05 Final Note on Economic Theory

Students of economics will have recognized the theory that underlies most of the last several sections: it is a vulgarized version of *marginalism*, the analytical foundation of just about everything that has happened in economics since 1870. Marginalism holds that you can understand the economy by focusing on behavior *at the margin* — specifically, at the *last* dollar spent, sought or owned.

We saw a stark example of marginalism in our discussion of David Ricardo and his notion of rents. We need to elaborate on this analysis now. Suppose there are five parcels of corn land, labeled A through E. Production costs per bushel on each parcel are as follows:

Parcel	**$ / Bushel**
A	1
B	2
C	3
D	4
E	5

Which land will be deployed in corn production? As we saw earlier, the answer depends on the market price of corn. If corn sells for $3 a bushel, we can expect parcels A, B, and C to be deployed in corn production. The owner of A will make a profit of ($3 − $1), or $2, while the owner of B will make a profit of ($3 − $2), or $1. The owner of C will make no profit. The owners of D will not plant corn because their costs would exclude their profit. If the price rises to $4, we can expect D to go into production. If it falls to $2, we can expect C (and D) to leave.

Ricardo developed his model at the beginning of the Nineteenth Century. It was not until around 1870 that a number of other economists undertook to generalize the point. As the historian Herbert Hovenkamp says, they developed "a general theory of consumer demand, a theory of value, a theory about production and consumption, and a theory of costs," all based on the analysis of pricing at the margin.[4] In general, as Hovenkamp explains, they saw that "only marginal, not total value, is relevant," and that "business firms, whose goal is to maximize profits, also equalize marginal utilities, which they measure as marginal expenditures and marginal revenues."

This marginal revolution has become so much part of the substrata of our thought that it is hard to imagine what life would be like without it. But to

[4] *See* Herbert Hovenkamp, *The Marginalist Revolution in Legal Thought,* 46 Vand. L. Rev. 305, 313 (1993).

understand just how revolutionary it was, it might be useful to consider what economists believed before 1870. This job is not easy, because the point is that economists did *not* have a precise or coherent theory of value before 1870 — which is precisely why marginalism proved so successful. But oversimplified, the practical fact is that most economists accepted some version of what has come to be called the "labor theory of value" — the idea that value was somehow a function of the effort imputed into the product.

One person who fell under the spell of Ricardo's economics was Karl Marx. Readers with even the haziest recollection of college Marxism will recall the distinctively Marxist notion that it is the workers who add value to the product, and the managers and capitalists who rip them off. But the labor theory of value is not a Marxist doctrine only. In some version, it is part of the intellectual equipment of anyone who believes that the laborer is worthy of his hire.

The trouble is that no one has ever come up with a workable method of defining the labor contribution. Is it measured by effort? Or by need? Or by the worthiness of the product? Or by something else? In default of a good answer, marginalism succeeded by sidestepping the question.

Perhaps the critical difference between marginalism and its predecessors is that labor theories tended to look backwards to the creation of the product while marginalism looks forward. Of course, that is what we have been doing throughout these materials, as we defined value in terms of prospective return, as we ignored sunk costs, as we set prices at the margin. But it was not always so. On this issue, as on so many others, the law reflects the thinking of its time. And it is easy to identify many areas where the law *did* recognize some version of premarginalist value theory.

One such version is the so-called "wage-fund doctrine." As Hovenkamp explains, the wage-fund doctrine "held that at any given time the total fund available for the payment of wages was directly related to the amount of capital that had previously been invested in the enterprise."[5] Hovenkamp points to *Adkins v. Children's Hospital* as an opinion that relies on the wage fund doctrine.[6] Another is the notion of "par value" in corporate stock. Most students of corporate law have learned how courts once turned to capital contribution as a measure of corporate value, and how they have rejected that standard in favor of the valuation models we study in this course.

§ 17.06 Tariff Regulation: A Requiem

A quarter century ago, in half a dozen or more major industries, we lived in a nation of regulated monopolies, under a system of "tariff regulation." If you sold airline or railroad tickets, or natural gas pipeline space or telephone access, or electricity, the government set your prices (tariffs). If you wanted to raise your prices, you had to ask the regulator. You had to justify your request as necessary to give you a "fair rate of return."

Today that old system of tariff regulation has mostly vanished. It would be fascinating to speculate on just what it was that brought about such a gale

[5] *Id.* at 345.

[6] 261 U. S. at 557 (1975).

of deregulation, so unexpected, and in so short a time.[7] There are probably a lot of reasons, but here is one: incoherence. In the world of modern economic and financial theory, regulators found that they couldn't justify what they do.

The core of the problem lies in one Supreme Court case — a case now largely forgotten, but one which ruled our life for a couple of generations. The case is *Smyth v. Ames*.[8] It set the benchmark for rate regulation, and it harbored the seeds of its own destruction.

In *Smyth* the Supreme Court struck down a system of state railroad regulation.[9] Speaking for the court, Justice Harlan said that rates must preserve "the fair value of the property being used." He said that in computing fair value, the state must consider (among other things) "*the probable earning capacity* of the property under particular rates prescribed" (emphasis added).

Smyth became the benchmark for rate regulation and continued so until at least 1944. But it is unintelligible: it says that fair value is based on earning capacity — but then it makes earning capacity depend on fair value! This is a vicious circle from which there is no escape. To try to use it as a basis for rate regulation is to offer no basis at all.

Critics understood the logical defect in *Smyth* from the start. As a principle of regulation, the Court finally abandoned it in 1944.[10] But *Smyth* lives as an illustration of the principle that history has a sense of humor. The irony is as follows: the most aggressive critics of *Smyth* were the progressives, who for the most part favored *more* regulation rather than less.[11] Their real foe was not *Smyth* as doctrine, but rather the judicial control of rate regulation. They wanted to move regulation out of the hands of the (restrictive) courts, into the hands of the (presumably more tolerant) regulatory agencies.

They failed to grasp that in destroying *Smyth*, they destroyed the only plausible contender (however insufficient) for the role of regulatory rule. *Smyth* may be incoherent, but it seems to carry an enduring superficial appeal. Without *Smyth* there was no good fallback for regulatory policy.[12]

Gold-Plating: "Circularity" may be the strongest criticism to be leveled against tariff regulation, but it is not the only one. For another important

---

[7] Joseph D. Kearney & Thomas W. Merrill, *The Great Transformation of Regulated Industries Law,* 98 Colum. L. Rev. 1323, 1328 (1998).

[8] 169 U.S. 466 (1898).

[9] It's an aside, but we ought to take a moment to recall that railroad rate regulation was a hot-button issue in the politics of the 1890s, somewhat akin to Medicare or Social Security reform today. Appearing in Smyth as a proponent of the regulatory scheme was William Jennings Bryan, thrice an unsuccessful candidate for president of the United States).

[10] FPC v. Hope Natural Gas. Co. 320 U.S. 591 (1944).

[11] Under Smyth, "since the earnings are determined, in large measure, by the rate which the company will be permitted to charge; and, thus, the vicious circle would be encountered." (Brandeis, J., dissenting in Missouri ex rel. Southwestern Bell Telephone Co. v. Public Service Commission of Missouri, 262 U.S. 276, 292 (1923)). *Compare* Justice William O. Douglas, "The heart of the matter is that rates cannot be made to depend upon 'fair value' when the value of the going enterprise depends on earnings under whatever rates may be anticipated." Hope Natural Gas, 320 U.S. at 601. Indeed, there is some reason to suspect that Justice Harlan may have understood the problem himself. He agonized over the opinion. The result is uncharacteristically turgid and unreadable, as if he knew himself that he hadn't brought it off.

[12] For an expanded version of this account, see Barbara Fried, The Progressive Assault on Laissez Faire: Robert Hale and the First Law and Economics Movement (1998).

criticism, consider the benchmark for rate-of-return regulation: we seek to grant a return on *capital*. But capital is only one resource that you might use in producing a product. You might equally well use labor. Now, consider the choice of the manager, beholden to shareholders. If he uses capital, he can build the cost into his rate base. If he uses labor, he has no such opportunity. It doesn't take rocket science to conclude that the return-on-capital rule will bias the manager to favor capital as a resource even when it is less economic than labor. Call it the problem of *gold-plating*.[13]

[13] Also called the Averch-Johnson (or simply "AJ") effect, after its expositors. *See* H. Averch & L. Johnson, *Behavior of the Firm Under Regulatory Constraint,* 52 Am. Econ. Rev. 1053 (1962). AJ is sometimes misread as holding that the manager will favor capital at the expense of labor. But this is a misunderstanding. He may simply use too much of both.

Chapter 18

Efficient Capital Markets

> The truly melancholy part of the policy of systematically making a nation of gamesters is that tho' all are forced to play, few can understand the game. . .
>
> —Edmund Burke[1]

> Gotta Run. Potatoes.
>
> —Michael Lewis.[2]

§ 18.01 Introduction

In a previous chapter, we considered the case of an investment opportunity that offered a positive net present value or (what is the same thing) an above-market return. We saw that there was a puzzle inherent in such an opportunity. The puzzle was: why did it exist at all? If it was such a great deal why hadn't someone else scooped it up? Or at least, why hadn't competitive bidding driven the price up to the point where the return was no more than "normal?" Indeed, we suggested that people have powerful motivations to seek out "economic rents" of this sort, and that most of us spend much of our lives engaged in such "rent-seeking behavior."

We left the impression that rent-seeking is, to put it mildly, a highly competitive game. This would explain the man on the telephone quoted in the epigraph above. The occasion was the time of the Chernobyl nuclear disaster. The Ukraine has a big potato crop, right? And radioactivity from Chernobyl will spoil the Ukrainian potatoes, okay? So potato prices worldwide will shoot up, got it? Okay, gotta run . . .

In this chapter, we present a stronger, more ambitious version of this intuitive anecdote. Our new version is the so-called "Efficient Capital Market Hypothesis," (ECMH). Broadly, ECMH asserts that securities markets impound all available information that may affect the price of securities — and by corollary, that there is no identifiable way systematically to beat the market.

ECMH has been part of the ruling paradigm of finance theory for more than a generation, and perhaps remains so. Lately, it has come under attack. For purposes of exposition, we will lay out the meaning of ECMH first in the next section. Later, we will summarize an approach that may unseat it.

---

[1] Reflections on the Revolution in France 311 (Pelican Classics ed. 1968).

[2] Michael Lewis, Liar's Poker: Rising Through the Wreckage on Wall Street (1989). The book is Lewis' rollicking account of his career with a great investment banking house during the good times of the late 1980s. Lewis recounts how he was on the telephone with another trader at the time of the first reports of the Chernobyl nuclear disaster. The quoted line was the response of his conversation partner when he heard the news.

§ 18.02 Efficient Markets

First, a word on definition. We need to be more precise about what we mean when we say there are no unexploitable opportunities. Most importantly, we do *not* mean that all prospects will work out as expected. In *any* case something may come along to botch our plans and to confound our hopes. All we mean is that current price levels have impounded all *available* information, and that no person's guess is (systematically) better than any one else's. There is a jargon term for this state. When a market price *impounds all available information* that might affect that price, we say the market is *efficient*. This may seem like a slightly perverse or unusual use of the word *efficient*, but stick with it for now — in this discussion, it will make our life a whole lot easier.

Next, let us specify the nature of our inquiry. Our problem is empirical. If we say, "markets are efficient," then we are making an assertion about the state of the world. The assertion is either true or not, as the evidence may dictate.

Taken in this light, let us note a few basic facts about efficiency and efficient markets. First, in deciding whether a market is efficient or not, it is of no relevance to show that some investors guess wrong. Recall, we never said that prices impound *all* information — only all *available* information, which is a different story.

Second, note that *whether or not* markets are efficient, lots of investors *act as if* they are not efficient. If you ever went shopping at a garage sale, you were banking on market inefficiency: trusting that your time and effort and energy would yield above-marginal returns through the discovery of hitherto undiscovered bargains. If you ever sat up nights puzzling over the balance sheet of a public company, trying to decide whether to invest in its stock, you are doing the same thing.

Third, note an interesting sort of game strategy in the world of efficient markets. If *I* am skeptical about market efficiency, then I want *you* to believe in it. After all, the more you believe, the less effort you will spend in rent-seeking. And the less effort you make, the less competition I face, and the more opportunities remain on the table for me.

There is a curious paradox lurking in this last proposition — call it "Grossman's paradox."[3] Grossman's paradox says markets are efficient if and only if *not everyone believes* they are efficient! The reason should be obvious. I will go rent-seeking only when I think it is worth my while. Insofar as I identify positive NPVs, my activity tends to drive prices towards their "efficient" level. However, if the markets are already efficient, I am wasting my time.

---

[3] The market will break down for lack of trading as it approaches perfect efficiency because as all traders become perfectly informed, they no longer trade because the prices, reflecting perfectly their information, are no longer advantageous. Informed traders will only step in to trade opposite uninformed traders who, in essence, pay the price of the transaction cost. Hence, the norm should be an "equilibrium level of disequilibrium," in which securities prices reflect new information rapidly, but not so quickly that market professionals cannot earn a positive return. it;See Sanford Grossman & Joseph E. Stiglitz, *On the Impossibility of Informationally Efficient Markets,* 70 Am. Econ. Rev. 393 (1980).

This calls attention to another important insight about the motivations of investors. For a market to be efficient, it is by no means necessary that all players be rational rent-seekers. Prices may reach efficient levels even if some (or many) players are irrational — indeed, even if they are deceived. The famous case of *SEC v. Texas Gulf Sulphur Co.*[4] offers an instructive instance. Texas Gulf Sulphur (TGS) was a mining company. TGS started drilling an exploratory hole in November. It discovered minerals and began quietly to buy land. In April, a mining newspaper published a story confirming that the hole was a major strike. The day before the announcement, TGS stock closed at 29⅜. A month later, it stood at 58¼ — a gain of nearly 100 percent. Obviously, the market responded to the news.

But back in November, before the drilling began, the stock closed at 17⅜. In other words, the stock went up by 75 percent in price before the discovery was ever announced! In fact, TGS insiders were quietly buying TGS stock prior to the announcement — an activity that, as the court found, violated the securities laws. Though it may have been wrong, their activity clearly helped to make the price more efficient. Indeed, if efficiency is your goal, the way to achieve it would be to let the insiders trade freely!

Finally, note a problem of definition. Before we talk about efficiency in "the market," we really ought to clarify what sort of "market" we have in mind. There are markets and markets, after all. And you really would not expect the same kind of "efficiency" from the market in garage sale antiques as you would in the market for, say, pork belly futures on the Chicago Board of Trade.

Taking all these limitations into account, let us turn to the question of efficiency in organized securities markets — the major exchanges where stocks and bonds are bought and sold. Plenty of people go rent-seeking on the exchange, hovering over their computers, huddling with their brokers, doing whatever it may take to find a positive NPV. Is all this activity worth it?

A generation ago Eugene Fama, then a young doctoral student, undertook to answer this question. For his dissertation, he sought to review all the available evidence on market efficiency. Fama's conclusion: the activity is not worth much. Organized securities markets are efficient in the sense that they impound available information, and so they are no place to go looking for bargains.

In its simplest sense, Fama's insight may seem almost trivially self-evident. After all, if IBM is trading at $50 and you know it will be worth $100 next year, you are not going to wait until next year to buy. You will buy now and drive the price up. Trivial or not, Fama's contention set off an uproar. After all, his work seemed to question the purpose of the entire organized brokerage industry (although on close reading, it is clear that Fama himself never goes that far). Why bother to hire a stock-picker if you can do just as well shooting darts or letting your pet monkey pick them for you? In any event, Fama's assertion quickly claimed a place at the center of the finance agenda. This is ECMH.[5]

---

[4] 401 F.2d 883 (2d Cir. 1968).

[5] For Fama's early work, see Eugene Fama, *The Behavior of Stock Market Prices*, 38 J. Bus. 34 (1965); *Efficient Markets: A Review of Theory and Empirical Work*, 25 J. Fin. 383 (1970)

Following Fama, discussions of efficiency typically identify three sub-categories.

- *Weak* efficiency focuses on security *prices*. Weak form efficiency asserts that the price pattern of a security is random, such that you cannot extrapolate a future price from the record of past prices. Weak form efficiency has the virtue of being testable — all you need is a record of prices and a fairly hefty computer.
- But no one supposes that people buy and sell based on bare price alone. No, investors use balance sheets, 10-Ks, CNN, whatever, all to try to inform their decisions. So, *semi-strong* efficiency asserts that prices impound *all available public information*. It is hard to come up with a *comprehensive* test of semi-strong efficiency, but there are many studies that try to relate security prices to *particular* news events — e.g., company announcement of dividend changes.
- Cold-eyed students, remembering cases like *TGS*, recognize that it is irrational to limit the search to *public* information — after all, *non-public* information may drive prices, even if illegally. Hence, *strong-form* efficiency asserts that prices impound all public *and non-public* information.

Since 1965, there has been a cascade of research seeming to support or disconfirm the hypothesis of market efficiency — together with a smaller, more recent body of research seeking to challenge it (see Chapter 19). Most of the attention has focused on semi-strong. Weak is after all somewhat trivial in the sense that no one thinks that investors are driven by the information impounded in past prices only. Research on strong is perhaps more interesting, at least insofar as it focuses attention on the fact that prices are driven in part by the trading (often illegal) of "insiders" privy to information not available to the market as a whole. Semi-strong, by contrast, occupies the vast middle ground in which we suppose many traders to operate.

For lawyers, the issue is most likely to present itself in litigation over alleged "mispricing." Suppose an investor buys stock at $100 and watches it fall to $60. He sues for fraud. Whether he succeeds in his action may depend on whether the $100 price "impounded" false information. The question entails a judgment as to whether the market was "efficient" in the sense described here. The U.S. Supreme Court faced the question in *Basic, Inc. v. Levinson,*[6] and came down on the side of efficiency. A divided court held that the trader may rely (in the words of Justice Blackman) "on the integrity of the price set by the market."

Basic involved negotiations over a prospective merger. Basic held merger talks with Combustion while denying that it was holding talks, and denying that any merger was in prospect. But then it changed its tune and accepted an offer at $46 a share. Former shareholders who had sold out the pre-merger price sued under Rule 10b-5 under the 1934 Securities Exchange Act. The Court held that they were entitled to rely on "the integrity of the market" in

---

[6] 485 U.S. 224 (1988).

making their deal. The Court quoted with approval from a district court opinion in another case:

> Thus the market is performing a substantial part of the valuation process performed by the investor in a face-to-face transaction. The market is acting as an unpaid agent of the investor, informing him that given all the information available to it, the value of the stock is worth the market price.[7]

Justice Blackmun doesn't name it but he seems to have been adopting a version of "semi-strong efficiency" here: he seems to assume that the market goes beyond mere share price to assimilate "public" information (like the public denials), but not "secret" information (like the fact of the negotiations themselves). His opinion has come in for a lot of criticism from professors, as having reached out to embrace a novel and unproven theory. But in fairness to Justice Blackmun, the case gave him an issue he couldn't really duck: either he found that the market was efficient, or he found that it was not. And either decision entailed a fairly sophisticated guess about the state of the world.

A more unsettling criticism is that the Court may have misunderstood the way the market impounds information. Justice Blackmun seemed to assume that the price popped up because the market had learned some new information. On closer observation, however, we see that the problem is more complicated. In fact, the price did not just pop up on receipt of the merger announcement. Rather, it had been creeping up over the months prior to the announcement.[8]

What can we make of this slow price drift? At first guess, we might say that the market was assimilating the information about the merger, though poorly. A second guess might be that the market was *fully* assimilating information — about the *possibility* of a merger! So, suppose a merged WidgetCo would be worth $40. As the curtain rises, WidgetCo is trading at $10, whence it drifts slowly up to $17.50. The market may be telling us that there is a 25 percent chance of a merger that will increase the value to $40.[9]

Web sites: For more on the history of ECMH, see:

http://www.proinvest.com/home/emh.htm.

For Fama's recent thoughts on efficiency, see:

http://www.dfafunds.com/The_Firm/About_Dimensional/Philosophy/History/Chicago/fama.html.

§ 18.03 Efficient Markets and the Accounting Paradox

Critical scrutiny of *Basic* invites attention to a paradox that runs through the controversy over efficiency. The paradox involves the controversy over accounting disclosure. Recurrently, critics of the accounting progress will argue that investors are harmed to the extent that some particular type or item of information is "undisclosed." Defenders of traditional accounting rules

[7] In re LTV Securities Litigation, 88 F.R.D. 134, 143 (N.D. Tex. 1980).

[8] 485 U.S. at fn. 4.

[9] For an insightful critique of Basic, see Jonathan Macey & *Geoffrey Miller, Good Finance, Bad Economics,* 42 Stan. L. Rev. 1059 (1990).

will argue that disclosure of the disputed information will upset securities prices. Yet the very fact of the dispute is an anomaly; it depends on the predicate that the "undisclosed" information is already known. This is awkward for both sides. If a particular type of information is so well understood as to motivate a demand for disclosure, why do you need more disclosure? On the other hand, if it is already well known, why resist disclosing it?

A classic instance is the dispute over "FASB 106." Recall that FASB is the the *Financial Accounting Standards Board,* the agency that promulgates *Generally Accepted Accounting Practices,* (GAAP).

FASB 106 bears the title of "Employers' Accounting for Post-Retirement Benefits Other Than Pensions." That is: things like retiree medical expenses. A company may pay out expenses like this in any given year. And it may be obliged by contract to pay such expenses in the future. Up until a few years ago, most companies accounted for these expenses on a "cash basis," charging off the expenses when paid, but not booking the future liability, on the premise that it was not yet due. Conceptually, this was probably wrong; good accounting practice requires that all expenses be "recognized" when incurred, no matter when paid. So, the companies probably should have been taking the deduction from the time the obligation was incurred, no matter when the cash went out. But as long as the numbers were not a big deal, nobody paid much attention.

At last, as retiree medical expenses mushroomed, FASB took notice. In December 1990, after agonizing discussion, FASB promulgated Standard 106. It prescribed that companies must deduct retiree medical expenses as accrued, no matter when paid. FASB prescribed that public companies must conform to Standard 106 for fiscal years beginning after December 15, 1992.

From the regulated public companies, the response was dramatic. Throughout 1992, the financial press overflowed with stories warning about the baneful effects of FASB 106, arguing that it would savage corporate profits. As presented, the warnings were plausible: the numbers were big, and, relative to profits, the charges would indeed make an impact. Managers howled with pain, while investors' hearts (allegedly?) beat faster. After all (the proponents asserted) it was time these numbers got out on the table.

Such, for example, is the tenor of an article in *Barron's,*[10] the influential market news weekly, distinctive for the care and comprehensiveness of its coverage. The author, Jack T. Ciesielski, also a writer for an accounting newsletter, presented a survey showing the dimensions of the hit on companies in the Dow Jones 30. He offered estimates on the hit in store for balance sheets and income statements, with breakout data on earnings per share and percentage of equity.

You can guess where this is going. For if Ciesielski knew, then *everybody* knew — at least after he published in *Barron's*. Or, at any rate, if the readers of *Barron's* knew, then this was precisely the sort of information that would be — no, strike that — *has been* assimilated in market prices. If that is the

[10] Jack T. Ciesielski, *How FASB 106 Will Whack Corporate Earnings,* Barron's, Sept. 28, 1992 at 15.

case, how could FASB 106 make a difference? Suggested answer: it cannot. And this presents the accounting paradox. If the information was, for all practical purposes, in the public domain, then why did management struggle so hard to keep it secret?

Ciesielski did not make it clear where he got his information, but it is easy to infer the answer. Companies like these attract a following of inquisitive people who want to know what they are up to. Forget the amateurs with the 10-share holding who drop in for coffee at the Investor Relations office. More important are numerous professional analysts who devote a large chunk of their time and energy to studying these companies, making their own best guesses of what the numbers might be. Analysts use a panoply of tools to marshal clues, rumors, hunches — and okay, espionage.

So, there is always a body of knowledge about these companies that does not depend on the bare bones of the accounting documents. One way or another, analyst information made its way to Ciesielski in time to put it in *Barron's*, some four months before the starting gun for compliance. But if all this information is so easily available, it undercuts the first premise. Specifically, if the market already knows this information, what is the point of requiring companies to provide it?

Accounting data is not entirely irrelevant, of course. A bank loan agreement may provide that a company maintain a specified "accounting ratio" — a balance sheet ratio of assets to liabilities — as a condition of its loan. Or, a regulated utility may find itself bound by accounting numbers in getting rate approvals. But the use of accounting numbers in formal roles such as these does not resolve the puzzle, it only aggravates it. After all, if accounting numbers are so irrelevant to underlying business dynamics, why would anyone use them as a basis for triggering loan defaults or utility rates?

The FASB 106 episode is dramatic, but hardly unique. Since the beginning of modern financial regulation, *regulatees* have resisted pressures for this sort of mandated disclosure. Yet there is abundant evidence (at least for public companies) that disclosure is an irrelevancy: that, if the information is true, the market already knows, and, if false, that the market is not fooled. Once again, this only deepens the problem: if information is so irrelevant, why would the regulatees care?

§ 18.04 Note: Sir Isaac Newton, Charles Ponzi, John Maynard Keynes, and the Idea of "Speculation"

> If you want to know what God thinks of money,
> just look at the people he gave it to.
>
> —Dorothy Parker

They say that during the great market runup of the Seventeenth Century, the scientist Sir Isaac Newton, believing values to be inflated, cashed out all his investments and took his money off the table. Later, as the market continued to soar, Sir Isaac changed his mind and reinvested. "When the whole world is crazy," he is said to have said, "it does not pay to be sane."

You can guess what happened next. The market dropped (like an apple, one is tempted to say) and Sir Isaac (along with countless others) lost everything he had.

Sir Isaac's plight (if the story has any truth in it) presents a challenge to any student of market behavior. Is there *any* principled strategy, in market analysis, to distinguish between the crazy and the sane? Or is the market its own answer to the question, transcending such paltry human aspirations at rationality?

One way to get a handle on the puzzle might be to consider the career of Carlo Ponzi, a onetime forger, sign-painter, and hotel waiter, who, in 1920, as "Charles Ponzi," found himself at the epicenter of one of the most spectacular — and crudest — financial frauds in American history. That would be the original "Ponzi scheme," to which he gave his name.

Ponzi began his route to infamy with an arbitrage play. By his own account (and some part of this, at least, appears to be true) he discovered an anomaly in rules governing international postal reply coupons. He "wrote a man in Spain," he told the New York Times, about a proposed investment project,

> [A]nd in reply received an international exchange coupon which I was to exchange for American postage stamps with which to send a copy of the publication. The coupon in Spain cost the equivalent of about one cent in American money, I got six cents in stamps for the coupon here. Then I investigated the rates of exchange in other countries. I tried it in a small way first. It worked. The first month $1,000 became $15,000. I began letting in my friends. First, I accepted deposits on my note, payable in ninety days, for $150 for each $100 received. Though promised in ninety days I have been paying in forty-five days.[11]

Fifty percent in 45 days looks attractive by any measure (as a refresher, try figuring the compound annual rate). Ponzi set up shop in Boston in 1919 with a firm called (this is not a joke) the Securities Exchange Company. By May, 1920, he had enough money to buy a $35,000 home in the banker's colony of suburban Lexington. A skeptical observer might well have wondered how anyone could make that kind of money off a penny stamp — and the answer, of course, would have been that he could not. Virtually from the start, it appears that Ponzi kept the scheme going by the simplest of dodges: he used new money to pay old. That is, he paid his "50 percent" to early investors not from proceeds of actual investments — of which he had substantially none — but from the funds provided by later investors. This works up to a point. But the most elementary arithmetic will show that you can keep it going only by exponential expansion. Start with $1. Figure how much you will need to cover each successive cycle:

[11] N.Y. Times, Jul. 30, 1920, at 1, col. 7.

$ 1
$ 1.50
$ 2.25
$ 3.38
$ 5.06
$ 7.59
$ 11.39
$ 17.09
$ 25.63
$ 38.44

So, by the tenth cycle, you would need to take in nearly 40 times your first round contribution just to keep current.

Ponzi's scheme did not last, of course. By the end of July, he was raking in money at the rate of $200,000 a day. But on July 26, the State Attorney General announced (on the scantiest of legal authority) that he intended to take action against the firm. The decision provoked panic-stricken investors into a multi-million dollar run on the assets of the firm. Against all reasonable expectations, Ponzi stemmed the tide for yet another couple of weeks. But by August 7, his bank balance was down to $13,391.32, and by August 13, Ponzi was in jail (on a charge of mail fraud).

Oddly, for all its notoriety, Ponzi's scheme was not the worst financial disaster in financial history. Creditors in the end got something like 37 cents on the dollar from his bankruptcy estate. Ponzi himself served a prison sentence and died broke.

But a troubling problem remains. Ponzi's family, in an effort to fend off liability, at one point considered trying to defend him on an assertion of "financial dementia." The real question is: what about the dementia of the countless thousands of investors who clawed their way into Ponzi's offices to leave their money with him during the frothy summer before the crash? It begs the question to say they were captured by a "herd mentality." The puzzle remains: why would a *herd* act this way, any more than an individual?

One possible reply is that Ponzi, among his other vices, was a liar who did his best to deceive everyone. Maybe, although it is hard to believe that so many people could be fooled so easily. But that raises the next question: how to account for all the schemes that run on Ponzi logic with no deception at all?

Example: did you ever send a chain letter? "Send this to six of your friends now and get (a thousand letters) (a million dollars) (unlimited love and affection) in just six weeks." Ponzi logic, no? If you send the letter to six of your friends, then, by the tenth round, to keep the game going you will need 60,466,176 recipients. The love-and-affection chain letter may be harmless enough, and most kids outgrow it after they leave junior high school.

But how different is it from those business franchises where your profits depend not so much on what you sell, but on the number of sub-franchisees that you sign up in your area? Or the schemes to breed, chinchillas, ostriches, or whatever the animal of choice may be, where the profits are supposed to come not just from selling flesh or fur, but rather from selling breeding stock to other breeders? Individual deals will stand on their own terms of course, but chinchilla breeding obeys the same mathematical laws as international postal coupons, and it just is not that hard to get chinchillas to breed.

And we need not restrict ourselves to chinchillas or chain letters. Along about 1980, a string of retirement homes for ministers' wives put itself in the protection of the Los Angeles bankruptcy court. The evidence made it clear that directors had been taking "capital contributions" from new residents and using them for ordinary operations. No one had the stomach to put a lot of ministers' widows back on the sidewalk (and the bank didn't want them) — but isn't it fair to say that the directors and managers were using Ponzi logic?

Which brings us back to Sir Isaac. If the folklore is true, he may have lost his shirt, but what exactly was wrong with the posture? The great John Maynard Keynes argued that the market was like a beauty contest where the prize goes not to the handsomest contestant, but to the person who guesses which contestant everyone *else* will think most handsome.[12] Does this mean the market is all Ponzi logic? Not necessarily. Maybe *everyone else* really does know who is the most handsome, and will reap their rewards accordingly.

Or maybe the music will stop and leave everyone at the party, like Sir Isaac, scrambling for a secure corner. They say that one never recognizes a "speculative bubble" until it is over. If this is true, is there *any* way to tell the speculators from the prudent investors?

---

12 John M. Keynes, The General Theory of Employment, Interest and Money 156 (Macmillan 1936),

Chapter 19

An Exploration of Market Efficiency: Dividends

Do you want your pizza cut in six slices or eight?
Cut it in six. I'm not hungry enough for eight.
—Yogi Berra

§ 19.01 Introduction

Earlier, we considered the effect of information on asset prices and whether (or to what extent) asset prices may impound the effect of (anticipated) good or bad news. We also considered how taxes (as a particular example of bad news) may affect the prices of assets. In this chapter, to explore the meaning of market efficiency, we turn to a problem that is much discussed, if not necessarily well understood. This is the matter of *dividend* payments on common stock.

More precisely, we will consider the question whether the payment of dividends will change the value of a stock investment. We will suggest that under defined assumptions, *it should make no difference* whether the stock pays dividends or not. In deciding whether this proposition is true, we will want to know (inter alia) whether the market is *efficient* in the sense used here. If dividends should not, and do not matter, then we can infer that the market is efficient, in the sense that investors are fully informed. If dividends should not matter and *do* matter, then it may be that the market is not as efficient as we might otherwise suppose.

§ 19.02 Dividend Irrelevance

We have examined the basic mechanics of the dividend problem. The corporation invests assets and (if it is lucky) accrues "earnings." So long as it remains solvent, the corporation *may* pay out earnings to shareholders in the form of *dividends*. But earnings are not the same as dividends and (at least in the ordinary case) nothing *requires* the corporation to pay out any particular dividend, or any dividend at all. And we have seen already, if the manager can invest the money better than the shareholder, the sensible manager will forego the dividend to invest the money, and the sensible shareholder will reward the manager.

But large public companies maintain regular, consistent, dividend policies. Why? Some historians relate it to the growth of "popular" investing in the early part of the Twentieth Century. On this view, the first time large numbers of investors came to the capital market was during World War I when they bought bonds under the "Liberty Loans" program to promote the war effort. Before the war, only some 350,000 Americans bought bonds; at the crest of the Liberty Loan campaign, holders numbered some 4 million. Liberty bonds yielded only a ho-hum 3.5 percent return. But they did provide a regular yield, and they reassured millions that it was safe to go fishing in the investment pool. After the war, managers needed new money for corporations. They did not want to borrow, because borrowing would have put them under the thumb of the banks. Previts and Merino pick up the story from there:

> After [World War I], corporate managers adopted a new strategy that helped to free their firms from bankers' control. . . . Corporations began to pay regular dividends, akin to interest, in order to attract people who had invested in Liberty Bonds during the war into the equity market. The strategy worked brilliantly. Small investors purchased equities in unprecedented numbers. Corporate managers found themselves awash in cash, and the corporate sector went from a net cash surplus of $3 billion in 1921 to $9 billion in 1929. . . .[1]

By the 1930s, there was an ingrained notion that a "good corporation" was a corporation that paid dividends. The great Benjamin Graham, co-author of the classic treatise on securities analysis, gave his endorsement (if qualified) to the dividend model.[2]

In 1961, two professors turned the classical argument on its head. Franco Modigliani and Merton Miller (MM) argued that under specified conditions ("clean test tubes"), *it should make no difference* whether the corporation pays dividends or not.[3] In summary, MM argued that if the company chose not to pay a dividend, the value of the potential dividend should still be impounded in the share price. MM also argued that if the investor wanted a different level of payout, he could get it by buying or selling shares. Note that this is an "efficiency" argument, in that it assumes that investors have accurate knowledge about the company's resources whether or not it pays a dividend.

Consider three firms: StayCo, DivCo, and HoardCo, identical except for their dividend policy. Each firm has total assets of $1 million made up of $100,000 cash, $900,000 "other" Each firm has 10,000 shares outstanding, worth $100 each. The management in each company believes it has identified a new project with a positive NPV, although no one, including management, has any idea how positive the NPV might be. In order to fund the positive NPV project, each company will need to have $50,000 in cash. None of the firms has any debt. There are no taxes. The three companies chose to fund the positive NPV project in three different ways, as follows:

StayCo pays out $5 per share in dividends, and funds the project with the remaining $50,000 in cash.

DivCo pays out $10 per share in dividends or $100,000. It then has to sell more shares to raise the cash to fund the NPV project.

---

[1] Gary Previts & Barbara Merino, A History of Accountancy in the United States: The Cultural Significance of Accounting 250-1 (1998), citing R. Sobel, The Great Bull Market (1968).

[2] Benjamin Graham & David Dodd, Security Analysis 325-38 (1st ed. 1934). Graham and Dodd was revised and reissued several times but happily, Whittlesey House has reissued the first edition. A careful reading of Graham and Dodd will show that this best of all books on investing is more nuanced than we sometimes remember, and that modern theory may be less revolutionary than we thought. But in the end, Graham does come down on the side of dividends.

[3] Franco Modigliani & Merton Miller, *Dividend Policy, Growth and the Valuation of Shares,* 34 J. of Bus. 411 (1961).

HoardCo pays out no dividends at all. It invests $5 per share in the new project, and puts the other $5 per share into a bank at the opportunity cost of capital, where it neither makes nor loses money.

Let us look at these three different strategies in order to see if the choice of a dividend policy has any effect on the company or its investors.

StayCo: $5 Dividend: StayCo will pay a $5 dividend tomorrow reducing corporate wealth (ignoring the NPV) to $950,000 and reducing share value to $95. But the investor has both the share (worth $95) and the dividend (worth $5), so his wealth position remains unchanged at $100.

DivCo: $10 Dividend + Sell More Shares: Paying the $10 dividend will reduce DivCo's corporate wealth (ignoring the prospective positive NPV) by 10 percent, from $1 million to $900,000. But, as before, the shareholder has both the share and the dividend so his wealth remains unchanged at ($90 + $10), or $100. DivCo still needs $50,000 to fund its positive NPV project. But it can raise this money by issuing and selling new shares in the open market. In an efficient market, the sale of shares will neither help nor hurt current shareholders, as we will explain in a moment. DivCo may fear that the issuance and sale of new shares will damage him because it will dilute his relative position in the company. But he too has an alternative: he can buy shares to restore his position from the new offering.

HoardCo: No Dividend + Hoard Cash: HoardCo will invest $50,000 in the positive NPV project, and will invest the balance at "the market rate," perhaps in treasury bills where its return will be no better and no worse than the return available to any other investor. The investor may want cash. She can get it by selling shares.

§ 19.03 The Share Price

This model assumes that the company or the investor is able to adjust a position by buying or selling shares. But this is tenable only if the share price is "fair," i.e., if the share price leaves existing investors neither better nor worse off. In an efficient market, the trade in shares should indeed be fair in that sense. To see that this is so, consider the case of DivCo, which paid out dividends totaling $100,000 [($1000 a share)(100 shares)]. DivCo retained "other" assets of in the value of $900,000 (ignoring the prospective NPV), so the equilibrium share price was $90. DivCo needs to raise $50,000 to fund the new project, and it undertakes to do so by selling shares. What must be the share price?

The answer is that the price of the new shares must be $90, just like the price of the old. To see that this is so, consider what would happen if the price were either higher or lower than $90. First, if the new shares sold at $100, then DivCo would need only 500 shares ($50,000 ÷ $100) to raise $50,000. The new issue would leave DivCo with 10,500 shares, with assets (ignoring the NPV) worth $950,000. We can see that $950,000 ÷ 10,500 = $90.48. This means that the new shareholders would have paid $100 per share for stock worth only $90.48. At the same time, they would have made a gift of 48 cents a share to the old shareholders.

On the other hand, suppose the new shares sold for $75. DivCo would need 667 shares ($50,000 ÷ $75). But $950,000 ÷ 10,667 = $89.06. This means that new shareholders would be paying $75 to get an asset worth $89.06, and old shareholders would be paying 94 cents a share to enjoy the ride. A manager who lets this happen probably cannot look forward to long tenure in office.

If DivCo issues new shares at the current market price of $90, then it will need to issue 556 new shares ($50,000 ÷ $90). Neither new nor continuing shareholders are helped or harmed by the new issue.

Similar logic applies to investors. DivCo pays $10 a share in dividends; StayCo pays $5 and HoardCo, nothing. Suppose an investor holding 100 shares of HoardCo wants a "DivCo" dividend. Can she get it? She can. Her HoardCo stake is worth $100 × 100 = $10,000. If she sells 10 shares, she will have her $1,000.

The same logic works the other way around as well. Suppose an investor with 100 shares of DivCo prefers no dividend. She can take the $1,000 DivCo dividend check and use it to buy DivCo shares from the new issue, or on the open market.

§ 19.04 A Possible Criticism: Control Premia

There is one objection to this analysis that may be important in a few cases. Many analysts believe that share price will rise above the "ordinary" market price if the shares at stake would give the investor *control* of the enterprise. For example, suppose there are 100 shares outstanding, selling at $1 each. "Control" analysis argues that it will cost you more than $51 to buy 51 shares because the 51-share stake will give you a majority stake and the corresponding power to control the minority.[4]

Such "control premia" might be regarded as a kind of market efficiency and, therefore, not relevant in a clean test-tubes analysis. There is also a good deal of controversy as to whether and to what extent they really exist. If a potential for a control premium is indeed present in a particular case, then the presence will distort the analysis of share buying and selling that we set forth above.

§ 19.05 MM Summarized

Now we have seen what MM intend when they argue that dividends are "irrelevant." They mean that the investor should not care whether she gets dividends are not, so long as managers are working to maximize share value. On this premise, the manager should return the earnings to investors if he cannot earn a return at least equal to what investors can earn on their own. He should retain them if he can earn a return better than what investors can return on their own — and investors will reward him with higher share prices if he does so.

Meanwhile, if any individual investor wants cash, she ought to be able to get it even without dividends by selling her shares. On the other hand, if she

[4] In practice, you can do it with a lot less than 51 percent. Since most shareholders don't vote, and since those that do tend to follow management instructions, a stake as low as 5 or 10 percent may control.

wants to retain her investment position, she ought to be able to do so even when the firm pays dividends by using her dividends to buy new shares.

We have said that MM assume "clean test tubes." This means, for example, that we assume managers do what they are supposed to do and serve investors rather than seeking merely to fatten their own purses. It means that investors have perfect information. It means that there are no distortions for taxes. Of course, no one assumes that the world is in fact a clean test tube. But MM adopt a strategy like the strategy of the hard scientist: they pose their abstract model. Then they ask: how should we adjust our model to take account of the "imperfections" in the world that we know.[5]

§ 19.06 Dividend Irrelevance and Taxes

Now we are ready to relax one of the clean test-tube assumptions. Specifically, we have assumed a world with no taxes. But there are taxes, and they may affect dividend policy. We need to examine these tax effects, to see how they will change our model.

There are two important problems related to taxes. One is the matter of different *kinds of payout*. For instance, the tax law may provide separate tax schedules for equity and for debt. The other is the matter of different *payees*. For example, some payouts will be taxed at two levels (both the corporate and the shareholder level), some only at one level. Moreover, not all shareholders are alike; not everyone pays the same rate.

Let us work through an example. Your client Alice owns one share of stock in TaxCo, Inc. Alice's marginal rate of personal income taxes (T_p) is 28 percent (the marginal rate is the rate she has to pay on the last dollar earned). TaxCo has $100 per share in earnings (E) beyond what it needs for new projects. *Either* Alice or TaxCo could earn an 8 percent return on available investments. The corporate income tax rate (T_c) is 34 percent. Suppose TaxCo pays out the entire $100 in dividends. Under these assumptions, the money Alice gets to keep will be:

$$(E)(1 - T_c)(1 - T_p) = \$47.52.$$

Now, suppose the company does *not* pay any dividend, but simply keeps the money and reinvests. For the moment, assume that TaxCo reinvests at the opportunity cost of capital, so that the investor is neither gaining nor losing, at least not in terms of the raw return. TaxCo will have to pay the first-year tax, leaving it with ($100)($1 - T_c$). But Alice will not have to pay any individual income tax on the money because it is not paid out, i.e., not received as income. During the second year, the company will not pay any tax on the original ($100)($1 - T_c$). But, it will pay tax on any money it earns from the ($100)($1 - T_c$). How does TaxCo compute its tax? Suppose the company invests a given sum and gets a return (r). The company gets to keep only $r(1 - T_c)$. At the end of the first year, TaxCo will have:

[5] Indeed, one of the intriguing attributes of MM's argument is its novelty as a strategy of analysis. MM were among they very first to apply the strategy of the hard sciences to an investment problem. In this, they were path-breakers. But today, virtually all academic analysis of investments goes forward on a model that seems (at least) to imitate the hard sciences.

$$[E(1 - T_c)][1 + (r[1 - T_c])]$$

If TaxCo keeps the money for n years, the sum in the hands of the corporation at the end of the n years is:

$$[E(1 - T_c)][1 + (r[1 - T_c])]^n$$

All this says is that when r is taxed the *true* growth rate is the *after-tax* growth rate. So, suppose the pre-tax growth rate is 8 percent, and the tax is 34 percent, as in the previous example. Then:

$$[100\ (1 - 0.34)][1 + (0.08[1 - 0.34)]^{10} = \$110.41$$

Suppose TaxCo pays this sum to Alice at t=10. She does not get to keep it. No, she has to pay individual income taxes. So her net at t=10 would be:

$$\$110.41\ (1 - 0.28) = \$79.49$$

Using 28 percent, Alice would receive $79.49.

But this is a t=10 value. To determine the t=0 value, we must discount, using a discount rate. But which rate? There are three choices:

- Use the "benchmark" 8 percent rate.
- Use the corporate after-tax rate of [(0.08)(1 − 0.34)] = 0.0528, or 5.28 percent.
- Use Alice's after-tax rate of [(0.08)(1 − 0.28)] = 0.0576, or 5.76 percent.

The correct answer is — use Alice's after-tax rate of 5.76 percent. To see that this is so, ask this question: what rate would you use if you wanted to figure Alice's "forward" accumulation from t=0 to t=10. Clearly, the answer would be her personal after-tax rate. Since this is the rate we would use for the forward factor, we should use the same rate in computing the discount factor. So the PV would be:

$$FV \div (1 + [r\ (1 - T_P)]^n) = \$79.49 \div (1 + [0.08\ (1 - 0.28)]^{10}) = \$45.41$$

Thus, [$79.49 ÷ $(1.0576)^{10}$] = $45.40. Note that her original position, under a "dividend" policy, was $47.52. Alice is *worse* off when the company pursues a no-dividend policy and keeps the money.

Can this be right? It can be right. Note that TaxCo has a higher tax rate than Alice, 34 percent v. 28 percent, and this higher rate is reflected throughout the above computations. Just to double-check your understanding of this point, you might reverse the tax rates (TaxCo = 28 percent; Alice = 34 percent) and recompute.

A Change in Tax Rates: To understand in full the importance of tax policy, it is useful to consider the effect of a change of tax rates. Take the case of StableCo, which will have pre-tax earnings (EBT) of $100 every year. StableCo has no growth opportunities and expects to pay out all available earnings as dividends. The tax rate is 36 percent for corporations and 28 percent for individuals. Irving, an investor, requires an after-tax return of 7 percent. What value will Irving put on StableCo? To answer this question, first determine Irving's dividend net of individual and corporate tax.

$$Div = EBT\ (1 - T_c)\ (1 - T_p) = (\$100)\ (0.64)(0.72) = \$46.08$$

Since this dividend will continue indefinitely, we can treat it as a perpetuity. So the value of the share to Irving is $46.08 ÷ 0.07 = $658.29.

Now, suppose that Congress unexpectedly drops the corporate tax rate to 32 percent. We recompute the dividend equation keeping everything else constant. The value to Irving rises to $699.43, a pleasant 6.25 percent return in investment value. Note that this gain flows to the shareholder who holds the share *when the tax cut is first disclosed.* After the tax cut is disclosed Irving, a rational investor, will no longer agree to sell the stock for $658.29. He will demand the higher $699.43 price, and so the original holder, not the buyer, will enjoy the gain. Is this an arbitrage opportunity? No, it is not, because the *after-tax* rate of return is identical.

The Tax-Free Investor: For further insight into the role of taxes, note that not all investors pay tax on earnings. For example, consider Freelandia, a (non-profit) college that may invest its endowment fund in stock. The corporation that issues the stock will pay taxes as usual on its income, but Freelandia as investor pays no tax on the investment. How will this fact affect the price of the stock?

To answer this question, assume that the tax-free investor has the same required rate of return as the taxable investor — in our example, 7 percent. Then, we can capitalize dividends the same way — except that the dividend rate will be higher. So, if the corporate tax rate is 36 percent, then earnings that reach the (tax-free) investor will be $100 (1 − 0.36) or $64 and the capitalized value will be $64 ÷ 0.07 = $914.28 — a whopping 39 percent improvement over the value to the taxable investor.

What does this imply for the market? It implies that stock prices will be higher than they would be with no tax-free investors. Freelandia can bid nearly 40 percent more than the taxable investor for new issues — or for stock already issued in the hands of taxable investors. The effect will be that stock prices in general will rise until tax-free investors like Freelandia satisfy their taste for stock.

§ 19.07 The Agency Problem

We have said that in a world of clean test-tubes, it should make no difference whether managers pay out dividends or not, as long as they are acting so as to maximize all possible returns. But there is another place where it may be useful to relax the original assumption. That is: many observers do not trust managers to maximize the value of the cash in their hands. Far more important is the risk that the cash will burn a hole in their pocket and they will waste it in foolish projects to maximize their personal power, or just as a form of self-flattery.

The world is too full of examples. Ford built up a cash hoard of billions from the success of the Taurus. They spent $2.5 billion of it to buy Jaguar and found themselves with little more than a rusty nameplate. Gulf stock was trading at $40 a share in the mid-1980s; over the preceding five years, Gulf had spent $90 a share on explorations and investment. Flush with oil money, Sohio bought Anaconda Copper and Arco bought Kennecott Copper; both found out that: (a) copper was not a very good business, and (b) they did not understand it very well anyway. Novell bought WordPerfect and Quattro Pro and then dumped them at distress prices.

In perhaps the biggest folly of all, Texaco tried to take over Getty Oil. The company found itself on the business end of a lawsuit from Pennzoil, a competitor, alleging that they had unlawfully snatched away an opportunity that rightfully belonged to Pennzoil. A jury brought in a verdict that exceeded $10 billion (in a resulting bankruptcy they settled for $3 billion)[6] At this writing (Fall, 2000) we are in the midst of the greatest wave of corporate mergers in history. But if the past is any guide, many of these deals will unravel at the investors' expense.

Hoarding is not evil per se. Boeing usually operates awash in cash. But Boeing needs a lot of cash when it sets out to develop a new airplane. Boeing does not like to have to go hat in hand to the bankers. Better to keep a bankroll of its own and save the freedom of motion.

The problem of cash hoarding can be seen as a specific example of a more general problem: shareholder-manager *agency costs*. Shareholders cannot watch managers very closely; therefore, they cannot veto bad spending proposals. Limiting the amount of cash that managers have to play with is an imperfect but important substitute for oversight.

§ 19.08 Closely-Held Corporations

What we have said so far makes sense for *public* companies, where there is a *separation between ownership and control.* It may be useful to reflect for a moment on the behavior of *closely held* corporations, including *family* corporations. An important distinction is that in closely-held corporations, the investors are also the managers. In the case of the "ordinary" closely held corporation, the investor is subject to double taxation, just as in the large public company. But since managers are also the owners, they have an obvious strategy to try to avoid double taxation. The strategy is to pay out all earnings *as salaries* to the (shareholder) managers. Salaries are deductible as business expenses and thereby avoid both individual and corporate taxes.

Not surprisingly, the tax collector tries to block this end-run around the tax law. The Internal Revenue Code imposes a tax on "accumulated earnings." In *Steiner Corp. v. Benninghoff*, the court explains the accumulated earnings tax:

> An accumulated earnings tax may be imposed, under I.R.C. § 531, when a company, "for the purpose of avoiding the income tax with respect to its shareholders . . . permit[s] earnings and profits to accumulate instead of being divided or distributed." I.R.C. § 532(a).

[6] Texaco/Pennzoil offers a curious footnote in the history of efficient market theory. When the verdict was announced, the price of Pennzoil stock rose, and Texaco fell. This is to be expected; after all, one was richer and the other poorer. The oddity is that Texaco fell by less than the amount that Pennzoil rose. Can we account for the discrepancy, or is it evidence that markets are not, in fact, efficient? One possible explanation is that investors expected the difference to be dissipated in the costs of appeals, etc. *See generally* David M. Cutler & Lawrence H. Summers, *The Costs of Conflict Resolution and Financial Distress: Evidence from the Texaco-Pennzoil Litigation*, 19 Rand J. Econ. 157 (1988).

That is, the tax may be imposed when a company chooses not to make distributions to its shareholders because its shareholders (or at least its controlling shareholders) prefer not to receive dividends — and consequently be liable for income tax on those dividends — at a given time. Instead, they would rather let the value of the stock appreciate and either pass that gain on to their heirs with a stepped up basis at death, or sell the stock and pay tax at the capital gains rate rather than the higher personal income tax rate applicable to dividends. To the extent that such earnings are retained to provide for the "reasonable needs of the business," however, no accumulated earnings tax will be imposed.[7]

Another response to the problem of double taxation is the so-called "Subchapter S corporation." Subchapter S is a kind of hybrid corporation, granting the investor direct pass-through of earnings (without double taxation) as in a partnership, with some of the advantages of the corporate form (notably, limited liability).

§ 19.09 Stock Repurchases

We saw above that for many taxpayers there is a tax on dividend income. This tax induces managers to find ways to pay out money to shareholders without calling it a dividend. One way to circumvent the dividend label is to repurchase shares. By definition, a share repurchase is not a dividend, yet it has the same effect; it puts money in the shareholder's pocket. You can guess the catch here. You do not get favorable tax treatment if you admit that you are doing something just to avoid taxes. So you cook up all sorts of reasons for the stock repurchase besides tax avoidance.

For example, you are doing it because it is a good investment. This proposition is perhaps more complicated than it looks at first blush. Look at the case of two companies, BuyCo and PayCo, each with 10,000 shares worth $100 each, or $1 million. Each has $50,000 burning a hole in its pocket. BuyCo sets out to buy back ($50,000 ÷ $100) = 500 shares. In one respect, they have given away some money to some shareholders and not to others, but, on the other hand, they got rid of $50,000 worth of claims also, so when the dust settles, shares are still worth ($950,000 ÷ 9500), or $100 a share. Compare PayCo, which paid a dividend of $5 per share, or $50,000 in total, to its shareholders. After the dividend each share is worth ($950,000 ÷ 10,000), or $95 per share. But each shareholder has $5 in cash. The firms are identical. The *only* difference is the number of slices that the ownership pie is divided into.

But, suppose management thinks its shares are, in fact, worth 10 percent more than market, say $1.1 million. It pays out ($100)(500), or $50,000 to those shareholders getting out. The surviving pool is ($1,050,000 ÷ 9500), or $110.53 per share for the survivors. Or, suppose management thought the shares were really only worth $950,000. It pays out $50,000 to 500 departing shareholders at $100, and retains only $900,000 for the 9,500 remaining shareholders or $94.74 per share. Translation: the company says it buys its stock because it

[7] 5 F. Supp. 2d 1117 (D. Nev. 1998).

is a good investment. Usually, it is nothing of the sort — just a push. If it is a good investment, it is the kind of good investment that favors continuing stockholders over departers.

Chapter 20

Arbitrage (Herein of Short-Selling)

Honey, if this moment were a stock, I'd short it.

—Saul Steinberg[1]

§ 20.01 Introduction

Okay, so this fellow goes running into the loan office and says, "I'm going to Europe for a month. Can you loan me $5,000?" The loan officer is not too crazy about the deal but he does not want to get a reputation as a naysayer, so he sidesteps. "Well," he says, "what about collateral?" "No problem," says the borrower, "I have my Mercedes parked out in the street." The loan officer perks up his ears a bit. He follows the borrower outside and sure enough, there is a fine, spanking new Mercedes, worth $50,000 easy. "OK," he purrs, "$5,000 against a $50,000 car will do it. But of course I will need interest." And again the buyer says: "No problem."

So, the borrower takes the $5,000 and vanishes. A month later, sure enough, he shows up at the loan desk and says, "I'm ready to pay off." The loan officer says "Sure, just give me a minute now," and pulling out his calculator, he figures — let us see, the usual rate is 12 percent a year, for one month that would be $47.44. Throw in a little pocket change for my trouble. "That will be $5,050," he says. Borrower whips out a roll of bills and counts out one hundred and one 50 dollar bills. Somewhat bemused, the lender hands over the keys to the car.

"Hey wait," he says as the borrower heads for the door,

"Can you tell me why you needed to borrow $5,000 for a month?"

"Can you tell me," says the customer, "any place else where I could store a new Mercedes for a month for $50?"

Welcome to the world of arbitrage.

§ 20.02 Arbitrage

Suppose two shares of stock in IBM. Each gives its owner the same ownership share in IBM, with the identical rights to vote, to enjoy dividends, and so forth. One sells for $75, one for $135. This is an *opportunity for arbitrage* — a case where "the same" asset is selling at two different prices. You arbitrage this opportunity by buying the low priced, or selling the high priced, and waiting for the prices to adjust. A person who engages in arbitrage is an *arbitrageur.*

---

[1] Financier, to his third wife, Gayfryd, at the million dollar party she threw to honor his 50th birthday in 1989. At this writing (summer 2000), Steinberg's empire indeed seems to be unraveling; stock in his flagship Reliance Group Holdings is trading at about 25 cents a share. *The Fall of the House of Steinberg,* http://www.nymag.com/page.cfm?page_id=3421.

The lore of finance is full of stories of successful arbitrage. Back in the Nineteenth Century, the great J. P. Morgan ran banks in London and New York. They say he noticed that the identical bond would trade at different prices on opposite sides of the Atlantic. He started buying in one market, selling in the other, as the circumstances might dictate.

Our Mercedes parking example is a more subtle and elegant case. The "lender" never saw himself in the business of running a parking lot. The creative stroke of the "borrower" was to recognize that lending and parking were "the same" and thus to uncover an opportunity for arbitrage.

In the 1980s, the term took on a somewhat broader meaning. The decade witnessed a frenzy of capital market activity as investors hustled to buy, sell, merge, restructure, and liquidate the securities of public companies. Not surprisingly, that market generated a breed of investors who tried to anticipate where the next deal was coming from so they could buy the securities and get caught in the updraft. Since the term "arbitrage" has no narrow, precise meaning, it seems fair enough to call these investors "arbitrageurs," or, as they came to be known, simply "the arbs." By the way, quite a few of them were able to score so well because they were trading on illicit information: in the end, some of the arbs went to jail.

The basic arb strategy is primitive. If you think the stock is too cheap, buy it. If you think it is too expensive, sell. But consider this pairing: Fandango and TangleCo are two natural resources companies, each investing in the development of elixir, a new remedy with tremendous prospects for curing bunions and flat feet. So far as you can tell, there is no basis on which to discriminate between the two companies: each seems to have competent, responsible management, a productive workforce, up-to-date equipment, and the like. Yet, Fandango bonds trade at $95, while TangleCo bonds trade at $101.

What to do? Well, first of course, you have to satisfy yourself that these two companies really are identical. This is, ultimately, a judgment call to be made based on all the evidence, and nothing we can say will dictate the final decision. But at last, you decide they are identical. What then?

One's first thought is to say: Fandango bonds must be underpriced, so buy Fandango and wait for the price to drift up to $101. This appears consistent with the evidence. But think again. It is just possible that Fandango bonds are *rightly* priced and that the problem is with the bonds of TangleCo, which are *over*priced. If this is the case, buying Fandango bonds may not do a bit of good: TangleCo bonds may drift *down* from $101, while Fandango bonds stay just where they are.

If you think TangleCo is overpriced, of course you should sell whatever TangleCo bonds you hold now before the price goes down. But what if you do not own any TangleCo bonds? Is there a strategy that lets you exploit this arbitrage opportunity? There is. You *short-sell* the TangleCo bonds and wait for the price to go down.

Here is how it works. You *borrow* some TangleCo stock with a promise to repay (say) next month. You *sell* the stock you just borrowed and pocket the $101. Next month, when it comes time to repay the loan, you cover your short sale by purchasing TangleCo stock in the open market. This works fine if TangleCo behaves and drops in price to, say, \$97. You sell at \$101, you buy at \$97, you get to keep the difference of \$4 (\$101 − \$97). Of course, if TangleCo misbehaves you could be in bad trouble. You might have to cover at \$105, say, or \$110, or \$200, or \$1,000. But you, of course, pick only securities that do their duty.

To cover all bases, you want to do both of these together. Buy Fandango ("go long," on Fandango, in the jargon of short sales) and short TangleCo. On these facts, chances are that *one* of your judgments is correct. You simply wait and see what happens. You liquidate one of your positions at a profit, and the other at "no loss."

Does it all sound too good to be true? Of course. Start with the basic premise — that Fandango and TangleCo are "the same." This was, after all, a judgment call on your part, and like all judgment calls, liable to error. It may be they only *appeared* to have the same products, management, etc. And if they are in fact different, then there is no reason to expect the kind of price equilibrium you anticipate. Which is to say, you might wind up losing money on both.

Short-selling has a bad name, for two reasons. One, it is risky. In our TangleCo example, the investor makes a \$4 profit on an investment of exactly nothing (except the cost of borrowing the TangleCo stock), which translates into an infinite rate of return. Or it could just as well turn into an infinite loss. Allowing this kind of behavior introduces an element of volatility that some people think we should exclude.

The other reason why short-selling has a bad name is that short-sellers are, in the nature of things, merchants of bad news. They make money when the stock goes down. They are always rooting around trying to find out what is wrong with an investment. The mere presence of the short-sellers lurking around a stock is likely to put managers into a fury.

But advocates of short-selling argue that this misses the point. Information is valuable to investors, they argue, and it costs time, effort, energy and money. Short-sellers have the motivation to seek out the needed information, and to rationalize securities prices accordingly. Moreover, they argue, borrowing the *stock* to get *cash* is very little different from borrowing *cash* to get *stock*. No one seems to think there is anything disreputable about borrowing cash to buy stock. Why should they complain about short-selling, which amounts to the same thing?

Arbitrage is important for the theory of finance for reasons beyond the obvious. As an empirical assertion, it is intuitively plausible. But in the construction of theory, it plays a far more vital role. Finance theorists tend to assume (at least for purposes of analysis) that arbitrage is impossible. Building on such a premise, they will argue that such-and-such a train of events will lead to "an opportunity for arbitrage;" and is therefore impossible. The argument is interesting in a sinister way. It seems to be "analytical," self-contained and thereby scientific. But the assertion of the non-existence of arbitrage, however plausible is only empirical; it is true or not true only as the evidence will dictate. An arbitrage *argument* may be persuasive if the facts support it. An arbitrage *proof*, by contrast, is a contradiction in terms; you don't prove something simply by assuming that it is true.

Having denied the possibility of an "arbitrage proof," we will offer a few of them later in this book. See Chapter 31 below.

§ 20.03 Commodity Pricing: An Arbitrage Proof

In an earlier assignment, we argued that if there is a ready market for a commodity with no storage and transaction costs, then the "spot" price *must* equal the present value of the forward price, discounted at the risk-free rate. Here we develop a proof of this notion, using short-selling and the logic of arbitrage.

We imagine a market in which there is risk-free borrowing and lending, and where we can make both "spot" and "future" investments. We can "go long" (give cash for the right to receive the asset) or "go short" (take cash for the obligation to deliver the asset). Suppose the risk-free rate is 7 percent, and a unit of our asset costs $100 at t=0.

Assume there is no arbitrage. Here is one possible portfolio. Borrow $100 risk-free. Spend the $100 to buy one unit of the asset. Contract to sell the unit with delivery and payment at t=1. Store the unit pending future delivery. The t=1 price will be $107 (we will explain why in a moment). At t=1, deliver the unit, collect the money and repay the loan. The cash flows are as follows:

	t=0 cash flow	**t=1 cash flow**
Borrow R_f	$ 100	$ (107)
Buy asset and store for t=1 delivery	$ (100)	
Deliver and receive payment		$107
Net	$ 0	$ 0

In an arbitrage-free market, here is a second possible portfolio. Sell one unit short, receiving $100 cash now in exchange for a promise to deliver at t=1. At t=1, collect risk-free investment proceeds and cover short at a cost of $107 (we will explain why in a moment):

	t=0 cash flow	**t=1 cash flow**
Invest R_f	$ (100)	$107
Short asset for t=1 delivery	$100	
Cover short		$ (107)
Net	$ 0	$ 0

In this model, we have assumed that the forward price of a unit is the spot price times 1 + *r* (in our example, ($100)(1.07) = $107). Why do we make this assumption? We make it because in an arbitrage-free market it *must* be so. It must be so because any other price would yield an opportunity for arbitrage. To see that this is so, consider what will happen if the forward price is $109. Then we will proceed as in our first example above — borrow, buy and store. Here are the payoffs:

	t=0 cash flow	**t=1 cash flow**
Borrow R_f	$100	$ (107)
Buy asset and store for t=1 delivery	$ (100)	
Deliver and receive payment		$ 109
Net	$ 0	$ 2

Note that our t=0 payoffs are the same as they were before, but our t=1 payoffs yield a $2 arbitrage profit.

By contrast, suppose that the forward price is $105. Then we follow the strategy in the second example above — short the asset and invest risk-free. This is the payoff matrix:

	t=0 cash flow	**t=1 cash flow**
Invest R_f	$ (100)	$107
Short asset for t=1 delivery	$100	
Cover short		$ (105)
Net	$ 0	$ 2

Once again, the t=0 payoffs are the same, but the t=1 payoffs yield an arbitrage profit of $2.

§ 20.04 Market Completeness and The Spanning Set

One remarkable feature of short-selling is that it opens up investment possibilities that may not otherwise exist. As such, it helps to make markets "complete."

Here is how it works. Imagine that the future will hold two possible contingencies, either sun or rain. In this world, there is only one security, "x." It will give us a gain of 100 percent if next year is sunny, but only 20 percent if it rains. That is, if the share sells for $100 today, we can expect a price next year of either $200 or $120 next year.

This share is infinitely divisible, so an investor can buy any part of a share that she wants. Suppose an investor wants a gain of $50 if it is sunny next year, or $10 if it rains. Note that she can get it by buying one half a share today. Or suppose she wants a gain of $200 (sun) $40 (rain). She can get it by buying two shares today (and so forth). But suppose our investor wants a portfolio that will give her a gain of 100 percent in sun, or *60* percent (not 20) in rain. Note that there is no combination of x *alone* that will offer this set of returns.

Now, suppose that in addition to x, there is a second security, "y." It will give a return of 50 percent in sun, and a *loss* of 40 percent in rain. Of course, y alone will not yield our investor her desired percentage return, no more so then x. But, can we achieve this result by acquiring these securities in combination? We can. To see that this is so, set up this pair of equations:

$$100x + 50y = 100$$
$$20x - 40y = 60$$

In words, we have set up a pair of equations that represent the available securities and the desired percentage returns. Is there a solution to this pair of equations? There is. Recall high school algebra. As stated, we have two unknowns (x and y), so we have an infinite number of solutions. Our strategy is to isolate one of the unknowns and solve for that unknown, and then solve for the other unknown. For example, we can see that (20x) (5) = 100x. So, multiply the entire bottom line by 5:

$$5(20x - 40y) = 5(60)$$

$$100x - 200y = 300$$

Then subtract the top line from the reconstructed bottom line:

$$100x - 200y = 300$$

$$-(100x + 50y = 100)$$

$$-250y = 200$$

So by subtraction, we have eliminated x and thereby isolated y. Solving for y is a simple matter of dividing out 250:

$$y = -0.8$$

Now we go back and substitute our solution for y in the original equations. We now have a set of equations with only one unknown, x. We can solve for x:

$$100x + [(50)(-0.8)] = 100$$

$$100x - 40 = 100$$

$$100x = 140$$

$$x = 1.4$$

To double-check:

$$20x - [(40)(-0.8)] = 60$$

$$20x + 32 = 60$$

$$20x = 28$$

$$x = 1.4$$

What does this tell us? It tells us to construct a portfolio that consists of 1.4 shares of x and *negative* 80 percent of a share of y. We get a negative position by making a short sale of y. To confirm that this works, try to figure out how you assemble a portfolio that will yield 100 in *either* sun or rain.

Do not be misled here: we have described the *payoffs* of this portfolio. But we have said nothing about the *odds* that a security or a portfolio will move up or down (50-50? 90-10? Or some other combination?). And perhaps most important, we have said nothing about what it will *cost*. As we shall see later, investors care a lot about the odds of different possible returns. For the moment, suffice it to say that if the investor wants to reduce the range of her payoffs, she will probably have to pay for the privilege.

In the real world, is it possible for the investor actually to assemble packages of "shorts" and "longs" like the example we set forth above? Sometimes, but not always. On the other hand, you have seen why it may be important to *look* for relationships of this sort, and so you can infer that investors will be motivated to try to find them, or to concoct them if they cannot be found.

§ 20.05 Noise: Efficient Markets Revisited

> There is no other proposition in economics which has more solid empirical evidence supporting it than the Efficient Markets Hypothesis.
>
> —Michael Jensen[2]

Students taking a first course in finance hear a lot about ECMH.[3] The idea is at least a classroom convenience, in the sense that you have to start somewhere. And most professors grew up in an academic milieu where the idea enjoyed fairly widespread acceptance (witness Professor Jensen, above).

Lately, however, the idea has come under strain. Part of the strain is a simple matter of evidence. For example, take the classic illustration that two shares of IBM cannot trade at different prices. But maybe they can. There is no direct evidence of IBM, but an important new study analyses the curious case of the linked oil companies, Royal Dutch and Shell. Though they are nominally separate, Royal Dutch and Shell operate under an agreement whereby they split all profits on a ratio of 60:40. If market values truly price away arbitrage, then the market capitalization of the two securities ought to subsist at a level of 1.5:1. In fact, it does nothing of the case.[4]

Aside from the bald empirical fact of cases like Royal Dutch/Shell, scholars have developed a more sophisticated critique of ECMH.

Before outlining the critique of ECMH, it is probably useful to start by examining some of the more obvious arguments against it, which turn out, remarkably, to be fairly weak. For example, students will note the presence of hugely successful investors in the world — Warren Buffett, say, or Peter Lynch, or George Soros, who seem to have accumulated billions investing for themselves and others. Surely this cannot be all chance?

In fact, it might be chance. ECMH does not say that everyone will get the same return. In every race, someone has to come first, and there is nothing about the performance of a Warren Buffett inconsistent with the notion that they are statistical outliers (indeed, Buffett and Soros have been having some spectacular troubles of late).

In the same vein, students will say that they've seen and heard individual investors who, while they may not have the pile of a Buffett, seem to have piled up a pretty good return in the market. Again, this might be good luck. Moreover the evidence is not necessarily reliable. People talk about their successes and hide their failures. In order to know how well they are doing, we would need more than just talk.

We may also observe investors who seem to win by sheer hard work. They turn their computers on before the coffee water boils. They keep a stack of

---

[2] *Some Anomalous Evidence Regarding Market Efficiency,* 6 J. Fin. Econ. 95, 95 (1978).

[3] This section draws heavily on Andrei Shleifer, Inefficient Markets: an Introduction to Behavioral Finance (2000). Eugene Fama, the man who "invented" ECMH, has weighed in as an important critic of his own former assertion. *See, e.g.,* Eugene Fama, *The Cross-Section of Expected Stock Returns,* J. Fin. 57 (1992).

[4] *See* Leonard Rosenthal & Colin Young, *The Seemingly Anomalous Price Behavior of Royal Dutch Shell and Unilever nv/plc,* 13 J. Fin. Econ. 123 (1990).

annual reports on the bedside table. And they seem to make some headway. Here also, we need to take account of chance and luck. But we can add two other problems. For one, recall that all costs are opportunity costs: if investors are getting superior returns by dint of hard work, we need to offset the kind of returns they would get by investing the same kind of hard work elsewhere. It may be, in terms of opportunity cost, that they would do as well by slinging hash at McDonald's.

And second, there is the bugbear of risk. Investors expect higher returns when they run higher risks. It may be that the seemingly high returns are no more than ordinary compensation for a high level of risk. For more on the risk-return tradeoff, see Chapter 23 below.

But even if we can explain away so much evidence, still there may be good reasons *in principle* to doubt that markets are as efficient as we sometimes say they are. Recall a first principle of the model of efficiency. The model does not assume that *all* investors are "rational." Rather, it assumes that "rational" investors, even if only a partial subset of the universe, drive the market price.

But if this is the model, then it must be: (a) that irrational behavior is "random," in the sense that individual irrationalities cancel each other; or (b) that rational investors can "arbitrage away" they errors of the irrational. In fact, neither of these assumption seems plausible.

Start with arbitrage. Suppose two assets, HiCo and LoCo, alike except in price. Standard arbitrage theory says that one of these must be mispriced, but it does not say which one. If you buy LoCo, on the theory that it is underpriced, you may stand by dismayed while the price of HiCo drops to meet it. If you short-sell HiCo on the theory that it is overpriced, you may have a comparable frustration as the price of LoCo rises. The arbitrage move is to buy LoCo *and* short HiCo, trusting that you will win on one, though you may do no better than break even on the other.

This is fine if arbitrage is possible, but there are many cases where arbitrage is not possible. Suppose, for example, that the whole market seems underpriced. You can buy and hold and hope that you are right. But you have no offsetting hedge to protect you against error. This may be a winning strategy if your perception is correct, but it is at best a judgment (informed or otherwise) and it is not arbitrage.

Go on to the possibility of random error. In fact, there is a good deal of empirical evidence that our irrationalities are *not* random — that we systematically overestimate some kinds of risks and underestimate others. If errors are not random, they will not self-cancel. Rather, they will be reflected systematically in market price. The "rational" trader has no choice but to seek to anticipate and estimate their effect.

Finally, consider the Darwinian proposition that reason triumphs as noise traders fall out of the game. Even if this is true, what assurance do we have that they will not come back to the game, once they have accumulated a new stake? Or, perhaps even more likely, that they will be replaced by a new cohort of noise trader, just as enthusiastic and just as refractory as their predecessors?

A trader can anticipate and try to cope with all these possibilities, of course. He can bet his hunch that the market is underpriced. He can try to anticipate and capitalize on "systematic error." He can seek to estimate just how persistent are the noise traders and what it will take to outlast them. But as he does all this, he is no longer acting as rational market player. Rather, he is acting as a noise trader himself, and is vulnerable to all the risks that he sought to avoid.

Web site: For reasons to doubt ECMH, visit http://www.investorhome.com/anomaly.htm.

§ 20.06 Note: Ed Thorp and the Big Casino

Ed Thorp can tell you the difference between the little casino at Las Vegas and the big casino in Wall Street: when you win at Vegas, they throw you out. Thorp learned that first hand when, as a young mathematician, he created a revolutionary system of card-counting and dealt himself into a small bundle of money. He tells all about it in his book, *Beat the Dealer* (1962), which he wrote before turning his hand — or more precisely, his mind — to finance.

The casinos had it right, really: Thorp is not a gambler. He is better understood as an arbitrageur, perhaps *the* arbitrageur. Understanding how Ed Thorp made his fortune can help you understand how to make money in the market, and how not to.

You would not think opportunities for arbitrage would exist in anything so dynamic and fluid as the modern securities market: there are plenty of players, plenty of opportunities, plenty of information — all the qualities you would think you would need to assure that assets found their "true" price. But, however dynamic the modern securities market may be, there are those who say that opportunities for arbitrage have never been better. For accompanying the growth in trading and liquidity, we have witnessed a virtual explosion of "new" securities — the so-called "derivatives," an almost infinite array of alternative cash flows, sliced and diced to meet every financial taste. Given the dizzying array of new choices, it is perhaps not surprising that comprehension levels are slow in catching up.

Lawyers have a lot to do with this process, of course; in the 1980s in New York, they used to say there were three ways to make partner: one was to invent a new security and no one remembered the other two. But it was really the mathematicians who did the most to create the derivatives revolution, and so it is perhaps not surprising that it was the mathematicians who were among the first to understand it. Thorp, perhaps remarkably, has not insisted on keeping his secrets to himself. He matched his early monograph on blackjack with a newer study on investment, *Beat the Market*, which he published in 1967.

But the boneyards of expectation are littered with the remains of those who bet on a sure thing, and so here: there are certainly ways that the arb opportunity can go wrong. The most important risk is in the nature of arbitrage itself: arb opportunities are like Elvis sightings — reported far more often than confirmed. A bitter, but still relevant gambling proverb may be helpful here: if you go into a strange poker game, you look around for the sucker and if you do not see him, you get out, because you are it. If something looks too good to be true, it probably is.

Often this is good advice, but Ed Thorp ignored it to his profit, and to the profit of investors who put their money in his limited partnership, where for a long time he turned in returns of close to 20 percent a year. It did not just happen, though; he started with superior analytic ability and fleshed that out with a lot of hard work, pouring over mountains of data to try to understand the shape of the emerging market before anyone else did.

And, in the end, his own first principles caught up with him: he withdrew from the money management business. He said he had to because everyone now knew what he once knew. His ideas were so widespread that, well, not that *anyone* could make money with them, but that *no one* could make money with them, or at least that, no one except those with the lowest transaction costs.

This is what he told the press, at any rate: there is a full account in the Wall Street Journal.[5] Maybe he was kidding — someone else, or himself. A year later, he was back in action. This time the focus was on warrants — a kind of call option — on the Japanese stock market, hedged against the Nikkei 225, the Japanese equivalent of the Dow Jones Industrial Average. Exotic? Sure. In a few years, the rest of the world will catch on. But by then, presumably, Ed Thorp will have found something else.

---

[5] Jonathan Clements, *Money-Manager Math Whiz Calls it Quits,* Wall Street J., March 15, 1990 at C1.

Chapter 21

Monopoly Pricing

What I love, of course,
is a big castle and a big moat
with piranhas and crocodiles.

—Warren Buffett[1]

§ 21.01 Introduction

Let us start with a story. At the beginning of the Nineteenth Century, the Mississippi River became the central transportation route for European invaders into the American heartland. Crews would float goods downriver on simple flatboat rafts (the young Abe Lincoln crewed such a raft). The upriver trip was harder. Different crews (the job took special talents) would shove, push, haul and drag keelboats up against the current. The rafts were simply broken up for scrap. The raft crews made their way home, or went off into the great world for new adventures. The cost of a downriver shipment (from Louisville to New Orleans, 1810 to 1819): some $16.55 a ton. For the upriver trip, several times as much — perhaps $100 a ton.

The steamboat changed all this. Robert Fulton first demonstrated a steamboat on the Hudson River in 1807. The steamboat made its first serious foray onto the Mississippi in 1815 — upriver, where it proved vastly superior to the keelboats. Steady improvements in design cut freight costs by a factor of 20 in less than four decades. Both upriver and downriver costs fell. Upriver transport remained more difficult and expensive in relative terms, but steamboats were so much more efficient on the upriver run that they drove keelboats virtually off the river.

But the price pattern, on closer scrutiny, presents a puzzle. While upriver transport remained more costly, the price pattern for customers was just the opposite. You paid substantially more for the easy downriver run than you did for the expensive upriver portion.

Can you guess why? Maybe the material in this chapter will help you.[2]

§ 21.02 Selma Again: Profits Under Monopoly Pricing

Earlier, we considered the position of a seller in a competitive market. We described her as a *price-taker*, and we tried to show how, in a competitive

[1] America's second-richest man, on his theory of investing. Buffett explains that he likes businesses with a "strong franchise." A "franchise," in Buffett's lingo, is a product or service that people will seek out and ask for by name, even if it is priced above the competition. Probably Buffett's most successful "franchise" investment has been Coca-Cola.

[2] There is an excellent summary of the available evidence on river transport pricing in Jeremy Atack & Peter Passell, A New Economic View of American History: From Colonial Times to 1940 156-58 (2d ed. 1994).

market, prices are driven down to a point where there are no "profits," in the sense of economic rents.

But there is another possibility. That is, our seller Selma may be a *monopolist*. In that case, she may be better off than if she was in a competitive market. She is no longer a *price-taker*. But that does not mean she can charge anything she wants. What it does mean is that she is a *price-searcher* — able to search out the otherwise hidden "reserve prices" of her customers, and to run her own price up accordingly. How does this work?

Consider the following chart. The top two lines show the number of units she can sell at the defined "monopoly price." The third line shows total revenue — number of units times price per unit. The fourth line repeats the same cost data we saw in § 17.03 below.. The fifth line shows net profit at the monopoly price (revenue minus cost). The last line we will explain in a moment.

Monopolistic — Price Searcher							
Number of Units	6	7	8	9	10	11	12
Monopoly Price	$ 23	$ 22	$ 21	$ 20	$ 19	$ 17	$ 16
Total Revenue	$ 238	$ 154	$ 168	$ 180	$ 190	$ 187	$ 192
Total Cost	$ 103	$ 104	$ 111	$ 126	$ 160	$ 214	$ 290
Net Profit at Monopoly Price	$ 35	$ 50	$ 57	$ 54	$ 30	$ (27)	$ (98)
Net Profit with Monopoly & Price Discrimination	*	*	$ 57	$ 62	$ 47	$ 10	$ (50)

How can we read this chart? Start with our earlier competition example. We saw there that if the market price is $16, Selma maximizes her profit by selling nine units. That gives her total revenue of $144 (16 × 9), minus total cost of $126, for a profit of $18. Recall that in a competitive market, she could not exceed the market price or someone else would undercut her and she would have no sales at all. But, if she holds a monopoly, her options are different. Now, she can run the price up to $20. She will still sell nine units, for total revenues of $180 (20 × 9). Since her costs remain constant at $126, she makes a profit of $54.

This is the classic monopoly situation. Note that she *could* sell 10 units and still make a profit — but a profit of only $30, not $54. This reduction in total sales marks the "deadweight loss from monopoly" — the reduction in total sales that come about because it is no longer in Selma's interest to sell out to the point where marginal revenue equals marginal cost.

Indeed, rather than *increase* production to 10 units, she will do just the reverse. She will *reduce* production to just *eight* units, increasing her profit from $54 to $57 (and increasing deadweight losses accordingly). On the other hand, she *will not* go all the way down to seven units, because that would reduce her profit to just $50.

But there is still more to the story. Suppose she is selling eight units at $21, for a net profit of $57. We can see that there is *one* customer who will not pay $21, but who *will* pay just $20. Selma, therefore, wants to learn how to *price discriminate*. That is: she *produces* nine units at a total cost of $126. She sells *eight* at the $21 price for a total revenue of $168 — and sells a *ninth* at $20, for a grand total revenue of $188! Subtract the $126 total cost and you get a net income of $62.

Now, take another look at the Uniform Commercial Code section on lost profits. Suppose Selma has contracts to sell eight units at $21. One of her customers cancels. The same day, she sells a ninth unit at $20. Under UCC § 2-708, what is her recovery? Should she get (a) $21-$20, (b) "lost profits" (perhaps $57 ÷ 8 or $7.13), or (c) something else?

In any of these cases, would you think it right to bypass UCC § 2-708 and go to § 2-709?

Bonus: If these problems seem too easy for you, you might like this one. Suppose Blanche, a builder, has a contract to build a machine for Otto, the owner, for $100,000. She expects to spend $80,000 on the job. Presumably, if Otto canceled before work started, Blanche has a right to the contract price ($100,000) less the expenses saved ($80,000). But suppose Blanche has done half the work when Otto cancels. She is able to dispose of the "work in progress" at a junk price of only $50,000. She figures she saved $10,000 in variable costs — wages, etc. What is Blanche entitled to under § 2-708?

Reprise: There is really only one key point to remember: we assume that every seller is going to sell as many units as are cost-justified. Is this assumption justified? If so, what are the implications for rules governing seller's damages? If not, what assumption *is* justified, and what does it tell you?

§ 21.03 Final Note: Explaining the Price Puzzle in Mississippi River Transport

If you understand the logic of monopoly pricing, you can figure out the puzzle in the Mississippi River transport pricing problem, posed above. We asked: if it was so much cheaper to carry goods downriver than upriver, why is it that shippers paid less to carry goods upriver than downriver?

The answer is, of course, a fairly straightforward matter of supply and demand. Demand for places on downriver steamboats came from farmers in the heartland, shipping goods to the grain markets of Europe. Demand for places outran the supply of placers, and steamboat operators could be "price searchers," setting prices above marginal costs and extracting economic rents. There was not nearly as much demand for backhaul places on the upriver runs. So, steamboat owners counted themselves lucky to get any price above marginal cost, even without economic rents. The practical result was that customers paid less for the expensive upriver run than they did for the cheaper downriver passage.

Note: we said that steamboating destroyed keelboating for the upriver run. Remarkably, steamboating did *not* destroy downriver rafting. Indeed, more than twice as many flatboats reached New Orleans in 1846 as reached there in 1816. The reason seems to be that flatboating, though using an obsolete technology, remained cheap. The capital investment was negligible, compared to the cost of building a high-tech steamboat. For building and crewing the flatboats, you could use the abundant supply of off-season farm labor, including young men probably not unwilling to grab a chance at a frolic in the big city.

Indeed, in one sense it appears that steamboating actually *reduced* the cost of flatboating. Remember that the flatboat operators had no more use for their crews after they reached New Orleans. But some, at least, would want to return home. In 1815, the return trip might take several months. After the coming of the steamboat, the time fell to just 10 days. Steamboats thus made flatboats more competitive, rather than less so.

Part II

Diversification

Chapter 22

Harry's Wonderful Money Machine

> Put all your eggs in the one basket
> and WATCH THAT BASKET.
>
> —Mark Twain[1]

§ 22.01 Introduction

The Theory of Investment Value (1937) by John Burr Williams is a classic in investment analysis. Williams outlines a strategy for picking stocks. He calls it the "Dividend Discount Model." Under Williams' model, you make a forecast of the dividends that you will get if you buy a certain stock. Then you adjust for uncertainty — highly uncertain investments get a bigger adjustment than sure things. Then you make your best bet.

Harry Markowitz, born in 1927, was a graduate student at the University of Chicago in the early 1950s. One afternoon in the library, he was studying Williams' treatise. Markowitz read with great avidity. This cannot be a surprise: Williams' work was and remains both instructive entertaining. But through the fog of inquiry, Markowitz came to see that Williams, for all his brilliance was wrong. Markowitz thereby found himself a dissertation topic. More important, he kicked off a revolution that upended our way of analyzing investment performance.

That afternoon in the library, Markowitz recalls, "I was struck with the notion that you should be interested in risk as well as return."[2] Markowitz thereby invented Modern Portfolio Theory (MPT), perhaps the most widely known idea in modern finance.

MPT is important in telling us how to invest. It is important for lawyers insofar as it sets a standard for governing investment policy. For example, we may have to consider the investment policy of a trustee acting for a beneficiary, or a manager for a shareholder, or any kind of agent for a principal — did the agent invest properly, or did he misbehave and make himself liable for sanction? MPT may offer an answer. So, the question whether a particular investor is behaving properly may depend on the question whether you believe MPT to be true. To explore this point, we begin by examining the rules governing investment behavior before MPT. Then we set forth some basic principles of risk management that underlie MPT.

---

[1] In Pudd'nhead Wilson (1894). The full passage says: "Behold, the fool saith: 'Put not all thine eggs in the one basket' — which is but a way of saying, 'Scatter your money and your attention'; but the wise man saith, 'Put all your eggs in the one basket and WATCH THAT BASKET.' " Twain himself was a failure as an investor and of course it is the message of this chapter that his advice was wrong.

[2] The quotation (along with the rest of the anecdote) comes from Peter Bernstein, Capital Ideas 46-47 (1992).

§ 22.02 The Prudent Investor

One place where lawyers become involved in this process of portfolio selection is in the rules governing *trustees,* people who manage assets for *beneficiaries.* The trustee has a number of obligations, imposed by law. If she fails to meet these obligations, she may be liable to removal, or for a surcharge. Traditional doctrine says the trustee should conduct himself as "prudent man" [sic]. The classic formulation is in *Harvard College v. Amory.*[3] There the court said that the trustee was enjoined to exercise *sound discretion* in managing trust investments, and

> to observe how men of prudence, discretion and intelligence manage their own affairs, not in regard to speculation, but in regard to the permanent disposition of their funds, considering the probable income, as well as the probable safety of the capital to be invested.[4]

For the first half of the last century, the man who did most to shape the meaning of the prudent man rule was Professor Austin Wakeman Scott of Harvard, the reporter for the first two Restatements of Trusts and the author of a hugely influential treatise. As expounded by Scott, the prudent man rule had three important components:

- Preservation of the estate.[5] As Professor Gordon says, "An investment strategy designed to preserve principal will presumably be more cautious than one aimed at permanent disposition . . ."[6]
- Instead of investing as he would invest his own money, the trustee should invest as one "safeguarding the property of others."[7]
- Avoid "speculation."[8]

Professor Gordon adds: "Until the 1940s, most states had required trustees to select investments from a statutory list (called a legal list) of the (supposedly) safer investments, primarily limited to government bonds, mortgages, and occasionally fixed income securities of the most stable companies."[9] Indeed a decision of the New York Court of Appeals had held that common stock investment was imprudent *per se.*[10] But that was in 1869. We chart the later history below.

§ 22.03 Risk

> What if you drop the basket?
>
> —Troublemaker

If Mark Twain said, "Watch the basket," then Harry Markowitz said, "What if you drop the basket?" and taught us to consider not just return, but also risk. In order to understand Markowitz in his full glory, it is useful first to

[3] 26 Mass. (9 Pick.) 446 (1830).

[4] *Id.* at 461.

[5] *See* Restatement (Second) of Trusts § 227(a) (1957).

[6] Jeffrey Gordon, *The Puzzling Persistence of the Constrained Prudent Man Rule*, 62 N.Y.U. L. Rev. 52, 59 (1987).

[7] Austin Wakeman Scott, The Law of Trusts § 227 (3d ed. 1967).

[8] *See Id.* § 117.6.

[9] Gordon, *supra* n.6 at 57.

[10] King v. Talbot, 40 N.Y. 76 (Ct. App. 1869).

explore the idea of risk. In the course of things, we will develop a more general idea of risk management, and of insurance. Indeed, one way to understand Markowitz is to recognize that what he is doing is to apply general principles of insurance to the particular problem of investing. This is no disrespect to Markowitz; a lot of revolutionary ideas are simply the application of familiar principles in unexpected ways.

In any event, if you already know something about insurance, the next part ought to be easy. On the other hand, if you do not already know anything about insurance, then these next sections, by teaching you about MPT, will teach you about insurance as well (at no extra charge).

We begin by defining risk. For our purposes, we can define risk best by example. Consider two investments. One pays a dollar every year forever. The other pays either: (a) \$2 if a success, or (b) nothing if a failure, with a 50-50 chance of each. Think of a coin-flip gain with a fair coin, where the payoffs are \$2 for heads and nothing for tails.

Next, consider the probability of success in either game. Call it "p." This p will be a percentage — 100 percent for the first investment (p = 1), 50 percent for the second (p = 0.5). Note that the sum of all probabilities must be 100 percent, no more, no less. Also, since there are only two possible results in our universe (success or failure), the probability of failure must be 100 percent minus the probability of success or (1 − p). In the first investment, where the probability of success = 100 percent, the probability of failure is 1 − 1 or zero. In the second case, where p = 0.5, then 1 − p also equals 0.5. As we said before, a 50-50 chance.

We are now ready to define the value of the coin-flip investment. Denote success as "S" and failure as "F." We can say that over the long run, the value of this coin-flip investment is

$$p\,S + (1 - p)\,F$$

$$(0.5)(\$2) + (0.5)(0) = \$1$$

Note that this coin-flip investment has the same (probability weighted) value as the (certain) investment — both \$1 a year. The difference is that the probability-weighted investment has more risk.

Does it matter that two investments have the different risk as long as they have the same return? The answer to that question depends on the investor's attitude to risk. If all investors are indifferent to risk, then risk matters not at all — investors will pay the same for a (safe) stream of \$1 payments as they will for a risky stream with a \$1 weighted value.

On the other hand, suppose investors are averse to risk. Then they will pay less for the risky stream, even though it has the same weighted value. For example, suppose the market rate for a safe perpetuity is 5 percent. Then the value of a (safe) \$1 perpetuity is \$1 ÷ 0.08 = \$12.50. If the payment stream is risky (as defined above) then the investor may be induced to take it only with a higher rate of return — say 10 percent. Then the value of the (risky) \$1 stream would be \$1 ÷ 0.1 = \$10 (and of course the rate might be less or more than 10 percent, depending on the taste of the investor and the degree of risk).

Similarly, we can imagine a world in which investors are risk lovers. A risk-loving investor might take the risky investment even if its yield were less than the safe yield of 8 percent. For example, a risk lover might pay $20 for the (risky) $1 perpetuity, implying a return of just 5 percent.

So, just how do investors behave? Are they risk averse, or risk neutral, or do they embrace risk? That is an empirical question. We will know the answer only after we go out and get our fingernails dirty doing some research. The math works the same either way. As a practical matter, we tend to assume that most investors are risk-averse most of the time. The evidence seems to support this result. But the evidence is far less clear as to the degree of risk aversion, or about the distribution of risk aversion among individual investors. Moreover, there is some evidence that seems to make sense only if we infer that at least some investors are risk lovers at least some of the time.

For our purposes in this basic course, we tend to gloss over the problem. Sometimes we postulate risk-neutrality as a simplifying assumption to help us with the analysis. At other times, we make a rough-and-ready assumption of risk aversion, without being too precise about the degree.

§ 22.04 The Market for Risk

Of course, one thing you can do if you do not like risk is to try to reduce it absolutely. If the downside in my coin game is (say) 25 cents rather than zero, then I am better off — I have lower risk and for that matter I also have a higher mean value. But risk reduction is costly and in some cases, you might as well call it impossible. So, what do you do if you face an unavoidable risk? It boils down to two choices. One, you might decide to bear the risk yourself as a price of living in the world. Two, you might transfer the risk to someone else who is more willing to bear it. Indeed, one good reason to suspect that most people are risk averse is that so much energy goes into creating markets for risk transfer.

Consider Hadley, who runs a mill in Gloucestershire. The mill shaft is broken and he needs to ship it back to the factory for repair. He fears that he will lose profits if the shaft is misdelivered. He might choose to bear the risk himself. Or he might make a deal with Baxendale, the shipper, whereby Baxendale agrees to compensate Hadley for loss through misdelivery. Note that the risk does not *go away* if Baxendale agrees to *buy* it. Rather, it moves from one party to the other. Of course, we do not expect Baxendale to provide this service for free. When Hadley learns how much Baxendale will charge for *buying* the risk, he can decide whether to bear the risk himself or to *sell* it to Baxendale.

Why, even for a fee, would Baxendale ever agree to bear the risk of non-delivery? Or to put it differently, why doesn't Baxendale's fee exactly cancel Hadley's advantage, so as to make them indifferent as to who will bear the risk of non-delivery? There are two possible answers to that question — call them the *weak* answer and the *strong* answer. The *weak* answer is the notion that Baxendale may be more risk-tolerant than Hadley — that Baxendale requires less by way of compensation for bearing the risk than Hadley is willing to pay for it. This would hardly be surprising. We know there is no accounting for tastes, and that Baxendale's taste for risk might be greater than Hadley's, just as his taste for sailboats or tomatoes. But there is another and far more interesting possibility, which we turn to in the next section.

§ 22.05 Diversification

My ventures are not in one bottom trusted,
Nor to one place; nor is my whole estate
Upon the fortune of this present year;
Therefore, my merchandise makes me not sad.

—Shakespeare

So far, we have identified two ways of coping with risk. One is the notion of reducing it absolutely. The second is the idea of selling it to a buyer with higher risk tolerance. But there is third way of coping with risk: diversification. If we diversify properly, we may be able to enjoy the best of both worlds — to reduce risk without sacrificing return. This is the central idea of insurance. It is also the insight that underlies Harry's MPT. Here is an account of diversification.

Consider again our coin-flip example. We imagine a *fair* coin that will land heads (H) or tails (T) with equal likelihood. You get \$2 if it comes up heads, nothing if it comes up tails. That is, the possibilities are:

H T

Since the chances are equal, then over the long run you have a one out of two — that is, a 50 percent — chance of each result. We have already seen that the *value* of the of the game as follows:

$$p\ S + (1 - p)\ F$$

$$(0.5)(\$2) + (0.5)(0) = \$1$$

But next, suppose there are two players in this game, and that they decide to pool their resources. That is, they will flip the coins together and split the proceeds. This time, the possibilities are:

H H T T
H T H T

Since there are four possibilities, each with equal likelihood, the chance of each result is now one out of four, or 25 percent. Two heads gives a payoff of (\$2 + \$2), or \$4; one head, a payoff of \$2, and zero heads, a payoff of zero. So the value is:

$$(0.25)(\$4) + (0.25)(\$2) + (0.25)(\$2) + (0.25)(0)$$
$$= (0.25)(\$4) + (0.5)(\$2) + (0.25)(0) = \$2$$

The players divide the proceeds equally so each player gets (0.5)(\$2), or \$1. This is the same as the payoff for the single-player game, but note an important difference. Although the average payoff — the *mean return* — remains the same, the chances of an extreme return are different. In fact, in the single-player game, the player had a 50 percent chance of losing everything. This time, the chance of losing everything has fallen to just 25 percent (the chances of *winning everything* have fallen accordingly).

To press the point home, we add a third player, and a third coin. Once again, the players will *pool their resources* — flipping all coins at once — and split the proceeds equally (in this case, three ways). The possible payoffs are:

H	H	H	T	H	T	T	T
H	H	T	H	T	H	T	T
H	T	H	H	T	T	H	T

This time, the chance of any individual payoff is only one out of eight, or 0.125 = 12.5 percent. Three heads give a payoff of \$6, two give a payoff of \$4, one gives a payoff of \$2, and zero still yields zero. So the value is:

$$(0.125)(\$6) + (0.125)(\$4) + (0.125)(\$4) + (0.125)(\$4)$$
$$+ (0.125)(\$2) + (0.125)(\$2) + (0.125)(\$2) + (0.125)(0)$$
$$= (0.125)(\$6) + (0.375)(\$4) + (0.375)(\$2) + (0.125)(\$0) = \$3$$

Since the players share equally, each gets \$1. So, the mean remains the same. But again, we have reduced the risk by diversifying.

Note there are two important preconditions for this result. One, we assume that the coins are unrelated — that no coin *knows about* any other coin. Suppose, instead that we have two coins (call them "A" and "B") related so that each time A comes up heads, then B comes up heads, and likewise for tails. Then, we gain nothing by way of risk reduction from adding coin B to our game. In terms of investing, suppose you own one share of IBM stock. You do not reduce your risk by adding a second share of IBM stock. Figuring out how two investments may be related is a major enterprise; we return to this topic later.

Two, we assume that all coins have the same risk. In the preceding examples, every coin had a 50-50 chance of coming up heads (or tails). Suppose by contrast that our third coin came up heads only three times out of eight, and tails the remainder. Then our payoff matrix would look like this (the change is boldfaced):

H	H	H	T	H	T	T	T
H	H	T	H	T	H	T	T
H	T	H	**T**	T	T	H	T

The payoffs are:

$$(0.125)(\$6) + (0.125)(\$4) + (0.125)(\$4) + (0.125)(\$2)$$
$$+ (0.125)(\$2) + (0.125)(\$2) + (0.125)(\$2) + (0.125)(0)$$
$$= (0.125)(\$6) + (0.25)(\$4) + (0.5)(\$2) + (0.125)(0) = \$2.75$$

Sharing three ways, each player gets 91.67 cents. So, in this sketch, the move from two coins to three reduces overall risk, but at a cost of nearly 10 percent in mean value. Of course, a risk-averse player might be willing to accept the reduction in value in exchange for the reduction of risk. But we should be clear that he is paying a price. The interesting point is that by diversifying properly, you may be able to reduce risk even if you do not reduce return.

This insight underlies the enterprise of *insurance*. Insurance has a long and honorable history. It was well understood by Antonio in Shakespeare's

Merchant of Venice, above — and indeed, much earlier. For our purposes now, it will be useful to identify only three points about insurance. First, we are now in a position to understand the position of an insurance company as a business that exists for the purpose of aggregating and diversifying risks. The insurance company may have a higher tolerance for risk than the individual insured customer. However, it is far more likely the insurance company is selling is its ability to aggregate and diversify.

Our second point is that it is possible to do insurance without the intervention of an insurance company. Compare Clarence and MegaCo, both operators of taxicabs in BigTown. Clarence operates one taxi; MegaCo operates a thousand. The risk of an accident happening to any individual taxicab is the same for both. But Clarence runs only one cab; MegaCo runs a thousand. If Clarence loses a cab, he is out of business and has no income. The chances are he will buy insurance to pool his risk with others. MegaCo could buy insurance, but MegaCo is a risk pool all by itself and may decide that it is cheaper (as the jargon goes) to *self-insure* and bear the risk on its own.

Finally, there are plenty of deals that appear on the surface to be risk-shifting but which can be understood on closer scrutiny to involve diversification. Consider Farmer Brown, who just planted his elixir crop, for delivery at the elixir grain elevator in four months. Elixir is trading today at $8 a bushel. Just what it will sell for in four months is anybody's guess. Farmer Brown may choose to bear the risk of price fluctuation himself. But it happens that there is also an organized elixir contract market, where customers can buy and sell elixir for future delivery.

Consider your client, Fargo, an elixir farmer, who makes a contract to sell elixir now, for delivery later, at $4.50 a bushel. He foregoes the chance to enjoy the benefit of any advance in prices, but he covers himself against the risk of a price drop. It is common to think of Fargo's deal as a case of risk shifting, as if from a person with a low risk tolerance to one whose risk tolerance is higher. Perhaps it is risk shifting, but very likely on closer scrutiny you will see that the (anonymous) buyer is in fact a kind of *diversifier* able to reduce his risk through pooling, as outlined above. Indeed, it seems likely that most, if not all, risk *shifting* contracts have at least some *pooling* content.

§ 22.06 Harry Again

Harry's insight, in short, was to take the logic of diversification and to apply it to investing. Of course, investors knew about risk before Harry, but no one took it seriously the way Harry did. Indeed, if investment theorists tended to discuss diversification at all, it was to treat it as kind of irresponsibility, an evasion of the manager's true duty to make his choices and stick by them. In his admirable treatise on modern finance, Peter Bernstein gleefully quotes an adviser of an earlier generation declaring that "diversification [is] an admission of not knowing what to do."[11] But Harry showed that this view is exactly wrong. Diversifying is not a declaration of intellectual bankruptcy. It is, rather, a calculated strategy of its own.

---

[11] Peter L. Bernstein, Capital Ideas: The Impossible Origins of Modern Wall Street 49 (1992), quoting Gerald Loeb.

There are a number of implications to be drawn from MPT. The central point, as we have suggested, is that with proper diversification you may be able to *reduce risk without sacrificing return*. Or — what is the same thing — to increase return without increasing risk. This means, for example, that if you take a *safe* stock and mix it with a *risky* stock, the resulting portfolio may be *safer than the safe stock alone!* This is another way of saying that the traditional "prudent man" rule, is exactly wrong.

Another important implication concerns the price of risk. If MPT is correct, then no one can expect to earn a premium return for taking a (diversifiable) risk. The reason is that the holder of a diversified portfolio will not value an investment in terms of its intrinsic risk. Rather, he will value the investment in terms of its contribution to a diversified portfolio — where its risk will be lower than if it were valued alone.

So, for example, consider RiskyCo, which offers a (weighted) average return of a dollar a year in perpetuity, risky enough to justify a return of 10 percent. This implies a market price of $1 ÷ 0.1 = $10. But InvestCo holds a (low-risk) portfolio with an overall return of 8 percent. For a $1 perpetuity, this implies a market price of $1 ÷ 0.08 = $12.50. By adding RiskyCo to its portfolio, InvestCo can reduce the aggregate risk of the portfolio. This means that the portfolio including RiskyCo will have an aggregate risk lower than the present risk, and an aggregate return somewhat higher than the present return. On this analysis, InvestCo, will be paying more than $10 — indeed, more than $12.50 — for an investment worth (standing alone) no more than $10.

So far, of course, we have oversimplified to a fault. We know that investments are not in fact as simple as coin-flips, and that stocks may be "related" in patterns that are obscure or complex. Moreover, evidence abounds that not even the safest investments are entirely risk-free. In order to make use of MPT, we must introduce some refinements. We need to learn how to measure risk, and how to measure the relationship between different risks. We need to find a device for coping with that component of risk that cannot be "diversified away." In order to accomplish these goals, we need to launch ourselves into the lore of statistics. It is to this task that we now turn.

Web sites: Markowitz tells his own story at:

http://www.nobel.se/economics/laureates/1990/markowitz-autobio.html.

For the history of the Markowitz model, see: http://www.ibbotson.com/Research/papers/Markowitz_Approach/.

Chapter 23

Measuring Risk

> I always get the fuzzy end of the lollipop.
>
> —Marilyn Monroe

§ 23.01 Introduction

In the previous chapter, we introduced "Modern Portfolio Theory" (MPT) broadly, the notion that the goal of the rational investor is to assemble an "efficient portfolio," by trying to maximize return while minimizing risk. Now our job is to identify those few key concepts of statistics that we need to define and analyze risk management.

§ 23.02 Random Variable

We start with the idea of a random variable. The core notion may be intuitive. For example, if you flip a coin, your chances vary — heads or tails. Similarly, the chances for particular levels of earnings next year at Microsoft vary — they may vary a little or a lot. For formal purposes, we need only slight refinement of this intuition. Formally, a *random variable* is a *function* for which *each and every possible outcome* can be expressed in a *real number*. Go back to our coin-flip example. Suppose you win $3 for every head and 50¢ for every tail. You now have real-number expressions for each and every possible outcome — this is a random variable. Random variables may be *discrete*, as in my coin example (it is either heads or tails, nothing in between), or they may be *continuous* as the values associated with points on a continuum. Presumably, earnings figures are always discrete, but sometimes it is convenient to treat them as if they are continuous.

§ 23.03 Probability

A *probability function* assigns a real number to each and every possible outcome in a random experiment. This number is called the *probability*. There are two important characteristics for a probability function. One is that the probabilities must be non-negative. The other is that they must sum to one (50 percent heads and 50 percent tails sums to one). Restated in math notation:

$p_n \geq 0$ for all n; and

$$\sum_{n=1}^{N} p_n = 1$$

For continuous functions, the expression would be an integral:

$$\int_a^b f(x)\,dx = 1$$

This is perfectly analogous to the expression for discrete functions; summing a discrete series is the same as integrating a continuous series.

§ 23.04 Expected Return

We talk of "expected returns" in the market, but it does not help a lot, because what you get often varies from what you expect. I may "expect" that International Defenestrators will earn 2 dollars per share next year, but it may earn anywhere from 2 cents to $2 million. You do not even get to play the game again, because the next year harbors different conditions, and therefore cannot be regarded as the same. The best we can do with the concept of "expected" is to say that the "expected" return is the long-run average (mean) return for any function of a random variable. To put if formally let:

n = the number of returns where $n \to \infty$
μ = (the Greek letter "mu") the mean expected return
p_n = probability of outcome n
r_n = a random variable associated with outcome n
N = total possible outcomes

then:

$$\mu = \sum_{n=1}^{N} r_n p(r_n)$$

"μ" is the weighted average of the probable outcomes with p(rn) serving as the weight.

To put this equation to the test, let us add some numbers. Imagine four possible outcomes or conditions, each with a probability and a random variable associated with it. (The outcomes are mutually exclusive; it cannot be both windy and rainy). For instance, assume that if it is windy today, LittleCo will have a return of 9 percent, and the weatherman says that there is a 40 percent chance of a windy day. And so on, such that:

Possible Outcome	Probability	Return
Windy	0.4	9%
Rainy	0.3	10%
Cloudy	0.2	12%
Sunny	0.1	14%

Given these potential outcomes, the average security return will be:

$$\mu = (0.4 \times 9) + (0.3 \times 10) + (0.2 \times 12) + (0.1 \times 14) = 10.4$$

§ 23.05 Variance

"Average" yields of this sort may tell us something, but they do not say a lot about risk, in the sense defined above, when we equated risk with variability. A return of five plus a return of seven gives an average return of six. So do returns of one and 11. But these two situations are very different. It is useful to know not just the mean, but also the dispersion of possible outcomes. We do this by computing the variance, a measure of dispersion. The symbol for the variance is a small sigma squared: σ^2. You compute the variance as follows:

- For each probability-weighted individual return, *subtract* the expected return; then,
- *square the result*; and
- sum the squares.

In notation:

$$\sigma^2 = E[(r - \mu)^2] = \sum_{n=1}^{N} p_n (r_n - \mu)^2$$

Let us recall the simple security example I gave above:

$$\mu = (0.4 \times 9) + (0.3 \times 10) + (0.2 \times 12) + (0.1 \times 14) = 10.4$$

We can work out the variance in steps, starting by squaring the difference between the possible return and the mean value:

$$\begin{aligned}
(9 - 10.4)^2 &= -1.4^2 = 1.96 \\
(10 - 10.4)^2 &= -0.4^2 = 0.16 \\
(12 - 10.4)^2 &= 1.6^2 = 2.56 \\
(14 - 10.4)^2 &= 3.6^2 = 12.96
\end{aligned}$$

and then multiplying each result by its probability:

$$(0.4)(1.96) = 0.784$$
$$(0.3)(.16) = 0.048$$
$$(0.2)(2.56) = 0.512$$
$$(0.1)(12.96) = 1.296$$

and then summing the results:

$$= 0.784 + 0.048 + 0.512 + 1.296 = \sigma^2 = 2.64$$

Be sure to get the sequence right: subtract, then square, then multiply, then sum. Note that (9 − 10.4) gives you *negative* 1.4 (and (10 − 10.4) gives you negative 0.4). But when you square a negative, you get a positive. Of course, when you square a positive, you also get a positive. The consequence is that the variance is *always positive*. Note also that we have passed into what you might call a separate order (or second order) of magnitude here.

A lot of people find "σ^2" highly counterintuitive at this point. It will make more sense later when you see what it can do.

§ 23.06 Standard Deviation

When we figured the variance, we took the deviations from the mean and squared them. At first blush, this appeared counterintuitive, but there are good reasons for doing so. If you were just to sum all the deviations multiplied by their respective probabilities, you would find that the answer each time was zero; all the negative results would exactly cancel all the positive. This is simply a function of the averaging process. Obviously, this would not be a very good measure of dispersion. Still, we would like to find a way to bring our results back to the same order of magnitude as our original components. Is there a way to do so? There is. We take the square *root* of σ^2. The result is the *standard deviation* (σ). That is:

$$\sqrt{\sigma^2} = (\sigma^2)^{1/2} = \sigma$$

In our example, the square root of 2.64 = 1.62, so the σ of our expected return is 1.62. Also, in our example, the expected return is 10.4 percent. So we can say: one σ *below* the mean is (10.4 − 1.62) = 8.78 percent. We could also say that one σ *above* the mean is (10.4 + 1.62) = 12.02 percent. And we can say that *any* return that falls between 8.78 percent and 12.02 percent *falls within one* σ *of* μ.

§ 23.07 Distribution

Do we know anything useful? Not yet. We need one more measure. We need to know how *likely* it is that an individual standard deviation will fall into a given range. In order to know this, we need to get a measure of *distribution*.

Statisticians have invented a number of devices for describing this pattern. Finance types disagree as to which (if any) will best describe the distribution of security prices. For our purposes, we will use the so-called *normal distribution*, the distribution illustrated by the so-called *normal curve*. The definition of the normal distribution is such that:

- 68 percent of all results will lie within *one* standard deviations of the mean;
- 95 percent of all results will fall within *two* σ of μ;
- 99.7 percent of all results will fall within *three* σ of μ.

Let us see how we can use this information to predict security prices. In our example, we know that $\mu = 10.4$ percent and that $\sigma = 1.62$ percent. Suppose that returns are normally distributed. Note that $68 \div 2 = 34$. This means that 34 percent of all returns will fall between 10.4 percent and 8.78 percent (minus one σ). Another 34 percent will fall between 10.4 percent and 12.02 percent (plus one σ). Note that the remaining area (outside of one σ either way) totals only 32 percent, and note that $32 \div 2 = 16$ percent. Suppose your boss is so risk-averse, she wants to know about the worst case scenario. We can tell her and that there is only a 16 percent chance that the return will fall below 8.78 percent.

§ 23.08 Final Note: Comparing σ and σ^2

We saw that σ^2 is made up of deviations from the mean *squared*. This seems to put them in a different order of magnitude from the returns themselves. Meanwhile σ is the square *root* of σ^2, which seems to put us back in the same order of magnitude as the original return. This fact would seem to argue in favor of σ as a better unit of measure. Indeed, often σ will be a better measure, and for just this reason. But σ^2 does have some virtues that make it more convenient in some cases. We saw one such virtue above: without squaring, the terms that make up the variance would sum to zero.

Here is another advantage of σ^2: σ^2s *sum*; σ's do not. Consider our previous example, where we had σ^2 of $(0.784 + 0.048 + 0.512 + 1.296) = \sigma^2 = 2.64$, and a σ of 1.62. Suppose instead we had two separate portfolios: in the first, the components of σ^2 were 0.784 and 0.048, and in the second, 0.512 and 1.296 (in equal proportions). The sum of the first two σ^2 s is 0.83 leading to a σ of 0.91. The sum of the second two terms is 1.81 leading to σ of 1.34. Summing, 0.83 plus 1.81 equals 2.64, which is indeed the σ^2 of the original combined portfolio. But 1.34 plus 0.91 only equals 2.26, which is not the σ of the portfolio.

Another reason why the variance is useful is that it provides a basis for comparison between *different* securities or portfolios, as we shall see in Chapter 25 below.

Chapter 24

Covariance and the Correlation Coefficient

The test of a vocation
is the love of the drudgery it involves.

—LP Smith

§ 24.01 Introduction

In the last chapter, we developed the *variance* (σ^2) and the *standard deviation* (σ) as measures of riskiness. Now we want to measure how the patterns of variation for individual securities relate to those of other securities. We introduce the notions of *covariance* and *correlation coefficient.*

§ 24.02 Covariance

If you want to know how much *risk* there is in a given *security*, you can use variance and σ. If you want to know how much risk there is in a *portfolio*, you will need to know the riskiness of *each* security. But that is not all. If your goal is to reduce risk by diversifying, then you will want to know the *relationship* between the riskiness of two (or more) different securities. To take a trivial example, suppose you own one share of IBM stock. You do *not* reduce riskiness by buying a *second* share of IBM stock. This should be trivially obvious, but the point is important: each share moves up (or down) at the same rate as the other, and in the same decree.

If you are risk-averse (and most of us are), then ideally, you want two securities whose prices move in *opposite* directions, like the carved figures on a Swiss weather-clock, where one is always out when the other is in, and vice versa. Short of that, you want securities that have the least possible relationship, so you can get the most possible diversification. So, we need to develop tools to measure this relationship. To begin, recall our definition of *variance:*

$$\sigma^2 = E[(r - \mu)^2] = \sum_{n=1}^{N} p_n (r_n - \mu)^2$$

That is: variance equals the sum of the squared deviations from the mean. We use variance to measure the return on a single stock. But now suppose we have two stocks, Ben (B) and Jerry (J). We want to know the relationship between the price movements of the two stocks. To find the relationship, we introduce the notion of *covariance*. Here is how you compute covariance:

$$COV_{B,J} = \sigma_{B,J} = \sum_{n=1}^{N} p_n (r_{nB} - \mu_B)(r_{nJ} - \mu_J)$$

What do we have here? You can understand it best if you compare the sigma term in the covariance with the sigma term in the variance. Recall that to compute variance, we computed deviations from the mean *squared*. To compute covariance, we compute the deviations from the mean for B, and then *multiply* by the deviations from the mean for J.

You will see it if we work through an example. Let us start with the data we used in the previous chapter, and use them as data for Ben. Then: μ = 10.4 percent, and σ^2_B = 2.64 and σ_B = 1.62 percent. Recall we computed these numbers using four different possible "states of nature" with probabilities (p) equal to 0.4, 0.3, 0.2, and 0.1. The associated random variables, again representing returns on security y, are 18 percent, 12 percent, 10 percent, and 9 percent:

	Probability	B's Return	J's Return
Windy	0.4	9%	18%
Rainy	0.3	10%	12%
Cloudy	0.2	12%	10%
Sunny	0.1	14%	9%

Using the formulas we used before, we could easily compute a mean, variance and standard deviation for security J. Try it. You should get:

= 13.70

σ^2 = 13.21

σ = 3.63

Now, how do we compute the covariance? First, multiply the differences:

(9 − 10.4)(18 − 13.7)

(10 − 10.4)(12 − 13.7)

(12 − 10.4)(10 − 13.7)

(14 − 10.4)(9 − 13.7)

Weight them by their probabilities:

$$(-6.02)(0.4)$$
$$(0.68)(0.3)$$
$$(-5.92)(0.2)$$
$$(-16.92)(0.1)$$

Then add them up:

$$= -2.408 + 0.204 - 1.184 - 1.692 = -5.08$$

Let us compare and contrast the covariance with the variance. Note first that in each case, we are computing a deviation from the mean. Second, in each case, we multiply two such deviations together. But with the variance, we multiply each deviation *by itself*. With covariance, we multiply each deviation for a particular item by the deviation for the item that matches it. If two sets of observations were *identical* — for example, if two securities moved up and down by the same percentages in every state of nature — then the covariance of the two would be equal to the variance of each individually. Finally, note that covariance can be *negative*. Each individual pairing will produce a negative result whenever the items in the pairing deviate in opposite directions from their respective means — as they do in three out of the four cases here.

Once again, it is important to get the sequence right. First, subtract. Then multiply. Then apply the appropriate probability. Then sum.

§ 24.03 Correlation Coefficient

We are now ready to offer a further, very helpful extension to covariance. We will show you how to derive the *correlation coefficient*, designated as ρ or "rho". It is not that difficult to derive. For two securities, B and J, ρ = covariance divided by the product of the standard deviations. That is:

$$\rho_{BJ} = \frac{\sigma_{BJ}}{\sigma_B \sigma_J}$$

Going back to our earlier computations, we have already done the hard part, having computed the variances and the covariance. Now, we simply plug in the covariance above the line (−5.08) and the σ's below the line (1.62 and 3.63). Multiply the σ's and divide σ by the product. The product of the σ's is 5.91. Negative 5.08 divided by 5.91 is negative.8602, the correlation coefficient.

Note several things about the correlation coefficient:

- The correlation coefficient *can be negative*, because (a): the covariance (above the line) can be negative, but (b) the standard deviations (below the line) are never negative.
- Perhaps more importantly, the correlation coefficient always lies somewhere on a continuum between −1 and + 1. This is an important reason why it is such a popular measure: it puts everything into the same scale.
- You can learn from the sign: positive correlations mean that variables move up and down together; negative correlations mean

they move in opposite directions, like that Swiss weather-clock above. So in this example, the correlation coefficient is negative because high values of Ben are associated with low values of Jerry and vice versa. If high values of Ben had been associated with *high* values of Jerry, then the covariance and σ would have been positive. If there was no relationship, σ would be zero.

- Finally, note that if $\sigma_{BJ} \div \sigma_B\sigma_J = \rho$, then $\rho\sigma_B\sigma_J = \sigma_{BJ}$. This gets important later.

Chapter 25

Portfolio Variance and Standard Deviation

A man sits as many risks as he runs.

—Henry David Thoreau

§ 25.01 Introduction

In the last chapter, we learned how to determine the *covariance* of two securities. Earlier, we learned how to determine the *variance* of a single security. In retrospect, we can recognize variance as a kind of "special case" of covariance — variance measures how a security varies "with itself." We also learned how to compute the *standard deviation* of a security, and the *correlation coefficient* for any two securities.

In this chapter, we apply these tools to compute the variance and standard deviation of a *portfolio* of securities. We develop a formula which will appear, at first glance, unduly cumbersome. In fact, our formula is an application of some basic algebra. The formula is a version of:

$$a^2 + b^2 + 2ab$$

If you think you recognize this formula, or if you are untroubled by some apparent complexity, read on. If you would like a little refresher on the algebra, skip to § 25.08 below.

§ 25.02 Variance — Two Securities

Consider a portfolio that contains two securities, Curly and Moe. Begin with some definitions. Let:

w_x = the proportion of any security x in the portfolio

σ_x = the standard deviation of any security x

ρ_{cm} = correlation coefficient of the combined portfolio

For simplicity, begin with the case where the correlation coefficient is one ($\rho = 1$).[1] Using the notion above, the proportion in Curly must be w_c. The proportion in Moe must be w_m. But since everything in the portfolio that is *not* Curly *must be* Moe, we could just as well say that the proportion in Moe $= (1 - w_c)$.

To define Curly's contribution to the variance of the combined portfolio, we begin by specifying the standard deviation of Curly, multiplied by the weight of Curly in the portfolio:

[1] Setting $\rho = 1$ is convenient because anything multiplied by one is itself. As we shall see, this means that in our computations we can for all practical purposes ignore ρ. We deal with cases where $\rho \neq 1$ later.

$$w_c\sigma_c$$

On the same principles, the contribution of Moe:

$$w_m\sigma_m = (1 - w_c)\sigma_m$$

How do we combine these two? We combine them as we combined the binomial above. Let:

$$a = w_c\sigma_c$$
$$b = (1 - w_c)\sigma_m$$

Then:

$$\sigma^2_{portfolio} = (a + b)(a + b) = (w_c\sigma_c + [1 - w_c]\sigma_m)(w_c\sigma c + [1 - w_c]\sigma_m)$$

Distributing, we get the formula for the covariance of a portfolio, part Curly and part Moe.

$$\begin{aligned}\sigma^2_{portfolio} &= a^2 + b^2 + 2ab \\ &= w_c{}^2\sigma_c{}^2 + (1 - w_c)^2\sigma_m{}^2 + 2(w_c\,[1 - w_c]\sigma_c\sigma_m)\end{aligned}$$

Take a second look at this equation. Note that there are two "plus" signs, dividing the equation into three "segments." Look at the first segment. It contains this term: $\sigma_c{}^2$. We started with σ_c, the standard deviation of Curly. We squared it, but we know that the square of the standard deviation is the *variance*. So, we can recognize this term as a "variance term," expressing the variance of Curly, modified by (squared) weight of Curly. On the same logic, we can recognize the second segment as a variance term, expressing the variance of Moe, modified by the (squared) weight of Moe.

[A] Where $\rho = 1$

What can we make of the third segment? Look at the two terms at the "east" end: $\sigma_c\sigma_m$ – standard deviation of Curly, multiplied by the standard deviation of Moe. Recall that earlier, we defined the correlation coefficient of any two securities as follows:

$$\rho_{xy} = \frac{\sigma_{xy}}{\sigma_x\sigma_y}$$

If this is true, then by rearrangement:

$$\rho_{xy}(\sigma_x\sigma_y) = \sigma_{xy}$$

In words, standard deviations *multiplied* by correlation coefficient equal covariance. But if &rgr$_{xy}$ = 1, then $(\sigma_x\sigma_y) = \sigma_{xy}$ — or, in words, where $\rho_{xy} = 1$, covariance is nothing other than the product of the standard deviations. Or in our case, where $\rho_{cm} = 1$, we can say that $\sigma_c\sigma_m$ = the covariance of Curly and Moe! So, the "third term" can be understood as the (squared) weight of the covariance, times two. Restated, we could describe our equation as:

$$var_c + var_m + covar_{cm}$$

(All with appropriate weights). Or, using the matrix, recall:

a^2	ab
ba	b^2

In our case:

Var_c	$Covar_{cm}$
$Covar_{cm}$	Var_m

That is:

Portfolio Covariance		
Stock	**Curly**	**Moe**
Curly	$w_c^2 \sigma_c^2$	$w_c (1 - w_c) \rho_{cm} \sigma_c \sigma_m$
Moe	$w_c (1 - w_c) \rho_{mc} \sigma_m \sigma_c$	$(1 - w_c)^2 \sigma_m^2$

For example, if Curly has a standard deviation of three and Moe has a σ of five, and if our portfolio consists of 40 percent Curly and 60 percent Moe, we would have:

$$(0.4)^2 (0.3)^2 + (0.6)^2 (0.5)^2 + 2[(0.4)(0.6) (0.3)(0.5)]$$

In matrix form:

$(0.4)^2(0.3)^2$	$(0.4)(0.6)(0.3)(0.5)$
$(0.4)(0.6)\sigma(0.3)(0.5)$	$(0.6)^2(0.5)^2$

So, the variance of the portfolio (where $\rho = 1$) is $(0.0144 + 0.09 + 0.072) = 0.1764$.

[B] Where ρ = *Negative* One

If $\rho =$ *negative* one, then our analysis is similar. Our variance terms would be the same as in the case of $\rho =$ positive one. The only difference would be in the covariance term. Our covariance term would be:

$$2(w_c [1 - w_c](-\rho)\sigma_c\sigma_m) = (- [2(w_c [1 - w_c](\rho)\sigma_c\sigma_m)])$$

So our entire series would be:

$$\sigma^2_{portfolio} = w_c^2\sigma_c^2 + (1 - w_c)^2\sigma_m^2 - 2(w_c [1 - w_c]\sigma_c\sigma_m)$$
$$= (0.4)^2(0.3)^2 + (0.6)^2(0.5)^2 - 2 [(0.4)(0.6) (0.3)(0.5)]$$

That is, $[(0.0144 + 0.09) - (0.072)]$, or 0.0324. Note that this is the same result as in the "positive one" case, except that instead of *adding* the covariance term, we *subtract* it.

If ρ = anything *other than* (positive) one or negative one, the simple analogy to the "algebra binomial" breaks down, but you compute the result as before, using the specified ρ rather than one or minus one. But recall $\rho\ (\sigma_c\sigma_m)$ = covariance. So you can compute portfolio variance if you know: (a) the weights, (b) the standard deviations, and (c) *either*: (1) the correlation coefficient (from which you can compute the covariance), *or* (2) the covariance.

[C] Where The Zero Term

Now, note two special cases involving a "zero term":

If the *correlation coefficient is zero* ($\rho = 0$), the third term will drop out and the variance of the portfolio will be:

$$\sigma^2_{\text{portfolio}} = w_c^{\ 2}\ \sigma_c^{\ 2} + (1 - w_c)^2\sigma_m^{\ 2}$$

In our case (0.0144 + 0.09) = 0.1044.

If the *standard deviation* of either term is zero (e.g., $\sigma_y = 0$), then the second *and* third terms drop out, and the variance of the portfolio is merely the variance of the remaining component, times its (squared) weight. For example, if $\sigma_m = 0$, then the variance of the portfolio will be:

$$\sigma^2_{\text{portfolio}} = w_c^{\ 2}\ \sigma_c^{\ 2}$$

§ 25.03 Standard Deviation

We have defined the standard deviation of any individual security as the square root of the variance. We can use the same definition for the standard deviation of a portfolio:

$$\sigma_{\text{portfolio}} = [w_c^{\ 2}\sigma_c^{\ 2} + (1 - w_c)^2\sigma_m^{\ 2} + 2(w_c\ [1 - w_c]\sigma_c\sigma_m)]^{0.5}$$

Note the exponent, and recall that the square root of any number "*n*" can be expressed as $n^{0.5}$, or $n^{1/2}$.

We can simplify this formula in some cases by recalling our discussion of the algebraic binomial. We saw that if $\rho = 1$, then portfolio variance can be understood as $\sigma^2 = a^2 + b^2 + 2ab$. We know the square root of the binomial formula is just $(a + b)$. So where $\rho = 1$:

$$\sigma_{\text{portfolio}} = w_c\sigma_c + (1 - w_c)\ \sigma_m$$

In our example, (0.4)(0.3) + (0.6)(0.5) = 0.42.

This is just another way of saying that when the correlation coefficient is one, the standard deviation of the portfolio is a weighted sum of the standard deviations of the components. We will use this insight as a point of departure when we start "charting" portfolio risk in the next section.

We can use the same sort of logic to derive the standard deviation where the correlation coefficient is *negative* one. In that case, we know that our portfolio variance equation has the form of $a^2 + b^2 - 2ab$ (note the minus sign). From high school algebra, we remember that the square root of this expression is $(a - b)$. What this amounts to is that:

$$\sigma_{\text{portfolio}} = W_c\sigma_c - (1 - w_c)\ \sigma_m$$

In our example, [(0.4)(0.3) − (0.6)(0.5)], or −0.18. There is one hitch, but it is not fatal. That is: the number 1.8 here is *negative*, and we have said that a standard deviation cannot be negative. But square − 0.18 and you get 0.0324, which is, in fact, the variance. Square *positive* 0.18 and you get the same 0.0324. So, if we treat this "square root" as an *absolute* — which is to say, if we ignore the sign — then we can treat *negative* 0.18 the same as *positive* 0.18 and everything tallies.

§ 25.04 Zero Cases

It remains only to consider the "zero" cases. First, if $\rho = 0$, we know that the portfolio variance is:

$$\sigma^2_{portfolio} = w_c^2\,\sigma_c^2 + (1 - w_c)^2\sigma_m^2$$

So the standard deviation must be:

$$\sigma_{portfolio} = [w_c^2\,\sigma_c^2 + (1 - w_c)^2\sigma_m^2]^{0.5}$$

There is no convenient simplification for this formula.[2]

Finally, suppose the *standard deviation* of either *component* equals zero. We have seen that in that case, the variance of the portfolio is:

$$\sigma^2_{portfolio} = w_c^2\sigma_c^2$$

The standard deviation is:

$$\sigma_{portfolio} = w_c\sigma_c$$

In words, $\sigma_{portfolio}$ is σ_c times the component weight. You can satisfy yourself that this is true by examining the original variance equation and noting which terms drop out when σ of one component is zero.

§ 25.05 More Than Two Securities

We can extend this analysis from a portfolio of two securities to a portfolio of *n* securities. Suppose we are not satisfied with our Curly/Moe portfolio. We decide to add shares in a third stock; call it Larry. Then, the covariance of the portfolio will be:

Portfolio Covariance			
Stock	**Curly**	**Moe**	**Larry**
Curly	$w_c^2\ \sigma_c^2$	$w_c\ w_m\rho_{cm}\ \sigma_c\sigma_m$	$w_c\ w_l\rho_{cl}\ \sigma_c\sigma_l$
Moe	$w_m w_c\rho_{mc}\sigma_m\sigma_c$	$w_m^2\ \sigma_m^2$	$w_m w_l\rho_{ml}\ \sigma_m\sigma_l$
Larry	$w_l w_c\rho_{lc}\ \sigma_l\sigma_c$	$w_l w_m\rho_{lm}\ \sigma_l\sigma_m$	$w_l^2\ \sigma_l^2$

This table is based on our previous table, with the addition of the right-hand column and the bottom row. Reading from northwest to southeast, we have

[2] **CAUTION**: be careful not to confuse the case in which $\rho = 0$ with the case where $\rho = 1$. They look a lot a like. But go back and check to make sure you can distinguish them.

three "covariance terms." The remaining boxes are "covariance terms." A little scrutiny should satisfy you that each of the "covariance terms" comes in *pairs* so we have three sets of two each — a Curly-Moe and a Moe-Curly, and so forth.

Recall our definition of the two-security portfolio. Expanding it for three securities, you could say:

$$var_{portfolio} =$$

$$(w_c^2\sigma_c^2) + (w_m^2\sigma_m^2) + (w_l^2\sigma_l^2) + 2[w_c\, w_m\rho_{cm}\sigma_c\sigma_m] + 2[w_c\, w_l\rho_{cl}\sigma_c\sigma_l] + 2[w_m w_l\rho_{ml}\sigma_m\sigma_l]$$

Now, let us put some numbers in. If our portfolio is 50 percent Curly, 30 percent Moe, and 20 percent Larry, and if $\sigma_c = 20$, $\sigma_m = 30$, $\sigma_l = 40$, $\rho_{cm} = 0.5$, $\rho_{cl} = 0.3$ and $\rho_{ml} = 0.1$ Enter these numbers on a matrix and total them left to right.

Stock	Curly	Moe	Larry	Total
Curly	100	45	24	169
Moe	45	81	7.2	133.2
Larry	24	7.2	64	95.2

The total covariance of the portfolio is (169 + 133.2 + 95.2) = 397.4.[3]

[A] Where $\rho = 0$

If the correlation is zero, then the standard deviation is easy to figure, because any term that gets multiplied by a correlation coefficient drops out. You are left with the three terms on the diagonal: (100 + 81 + 64) = 245. The square root (standard deviation) is 15.56. Note that it is smaller than *any* of the individual deviations.

[B] Where $\rho = 1$

What do you do with $\rho = 1$ for all securities? Following the equation, you must add in the covariance terms, as follows:

[3] Note one manipulation you can perform with this matrix. Suppose you knew the variances and covariances, but did not know the correlation coefficient. Recall the formula: $\sigma_{xy} \div \sigma_x\sigma_y = \rho$. You can use the variance and covariance numbers to derive the correlation coefficient. Thus to determine the correlation between Curly and Moe, we divide the Curly-Moe covariance by the product of the square root of the Curly covariance (20) times the square root of the Moe covariance (30). The quotient is.5, which, as it happens, is what we were told on the chart.

$$2[w_c w_m \rho_{cm} \sigma_c \sigma_m] +$$
$$2[w_l w_m \rho_{lm} \sigma_l \sigma_m] +$$
$$2[w_l w_c \rho_{lc} \sigma_l \sigma_c]$$

But you do not need to worry about the coefficients, because they are all one. So, you just need to multiply the weights and the standard deviations. The numbers are:

$$(2)(0.3)(0.5)(30)(20) = 180$$
$$(2)(0.3)(0.2)(30)(40) = 144$$
$$(2)(0.2)(0.5)(40)(20) = 160$$

Adding to the 245 (see above), we have a total of 729, and a standard deviation of 27. So, what do we know? We know the σ of our partly correlated portfolio was 19.90. The σ of our zero-correlation portfolio was 15.65. The standard deviation of our portfolio with a correlation of 1 was 27 — in fact, just the weighted average of the three correlations.

§ 25.06 Relation of Covariance and Covariance

How far will this go? Can we reduce portfolio variance to zero? Typically, no. To understand this, we need to examine the relative place of variance and covariance in the typical portfolio. We analyze it as follows:

As the number of securities grows larger, the individual variances tend to disappear, and we tend to approach the average covariance. We can figure it this way: there are as many variance boxes as there are variances. Suppose we invest an *equal* portion of our wealth in each of N stocks. The proportion invested in each stock is, therefore, $1/N$. Our grids also have N boxes on the vertical and horizontal axes (observe grids above). So, the total number of boxes must be N^2. There are N boxes on the diagonal, so the number of variance boxes must always be N. Thus, the number of covariance boxes must be $N^2 - N$. Since we have $1/N$ of our investment in each stock, and since each variance box contains the weight of its investment squared, then portfolio variance must be:

$$\sigma^2 = N[1/N]^2 \text{ (avg var)} + (N^2 - N)[1/N]^2 \text{ (avg covar)}$$

Simplifying, we get:

$$\sigma^2 = 1/N \text{ (avg var)} + (1 - 1/N) \text{ (avg covar)}$$

Note that the *larger* N, the more of the fraction that is accounted for by covariance. For example, suppose the average variance is 30 and the average covariance is 12. Then if there are two securities in the portfolio, the portfolio variance is:

$$(0.5)(30) + (0.5)(12) = 21$$

On the other hand, if there are eight securities, the portfolio variance is:

$$(1/8)(30) + (7/8)(12) = 14.25$$

If there are 20 securities, then the portfolio variance is 13.26. Note how the portfolio variance approaches, although never reaches, the covariance.

We can make the same point graphically. If there are two stocks, then the variance-covariance matrix looks like this

Var	Covar
Covar	**Var**

If there are 10 it looks like this:

Var	Covar	Covar	Covar	Covar	Covar	Covar	Covar	Covar	Covar
Covar	**Var**	Covar	Covar	Covar	Covar	Covar	Covar	Covar	Covar
Covar	Covar	**Var**	Covar	Covar	Covar	Covar	Covar	Covar	Covar
Covar	Covar	Covar	**Var**	Covar	Covar	Covar	Covar	Covar	Covar
Covar	Covar	Covar	Covar	**Var**	Covar	Covar	Covar	Covar	Covar
Covar	Covar	Covar	Covar	Covar	**Var**	Covar	Covar	Covar	Covar
Covar	Covar	Covar	Covar	Covar	Covar	**Var**	Covar	Covar	Covar
Covar	Covar	Covar	Covar	Covar	Covar	Covar	**Var**	Covar	Covar
Covar	Covar	Covar	Covar	Covar	Covar	Covar	Covar	**Var**	Covar
Covar	Covar	Covar	Covar	Covar	Covar	Covar	Covar	Covar	**Var**

. . . offering graphic evidence of the proposition that as N gets large, Covariance tends to swamp variance.

§ 25.07 Note: Actual Returns

In our earlier examples, we talked about the measure of *expected* returns. Statisticians make a big distinction between *expected* returns and *actual* returns. For example, if we make predictions as to the likelihood of a particular return, then we are working in the realm of expected returns. If we measure from actual observations, then we are dealing with actual returns. For the most part, the distinction makes no difference to us here — computation in the two categories is just the same. But there are differences in notation, and there is at least one important difference in conceptual structure. We note them here now.

Do you remember how we stated the formula for a probability-weighted expected return? We expressed it as follows:

$$\mu = \sum_{n=1}^{N} r_n p(r_n)$$

For the same data, if we were measuring actual observations, we would have said:

$$\mu = \frac{\sum_{n=1}^{N} r_n}{N}$$

where r-bar = the mean of the actual observations. Or we could just as easily say, if our security had a return of .09 three years ago, .08 two years ago and .04 a year ago, then:

$$\mu = \frac{0.09 + 0.08 + 0.04}{3} = 0.07$$

Do you remember how to state the formula for variance? It is:

$$\sigma^2 = E(r - \mu)^2 = \sum_{n=1}^{N} p_n (r_n - \mu)^2$$

For historical data, using the same numbers, you would think the number would go like this:

$$\sigma^2 = variance = \frac{1}{N} \sum_{n=1}^{N} (r_n - \bar{r})^2$$

But here is where we add our conceptual qualification. When we are dealing with observed returns, as a denominator we will use not N, but N − 1. This is said to account for the *loss of a degree of freedom,* a term whose meaning is buried deep in the morass of the statistical swamp. The correct formulation would be:

$$\sigma^2 = variance = \frac{1}{(N-1)} \sum_{n=1}^{N} (r_n - \bar{r})^2$$

For the covariance, here is the probabilistic formula:

$$cov_{x,y} = \sigma_{x,y} = \sum_{n=1}^{N} p_n (r_{nx} - \mu_x)(r_{ny} - \mu_y)$$

For observed returns, we say:

$$cov_{x,y} = \sigma_{x,y} = \frac{1}{N} \sum_{n=1}^{N} (r_{nx} - \mu_x)(r_{ny} - \mu_y)$$

§ 25.08 A Review of Some Algebra

Here is a familiar bit of basic algebra:

$$(a + b)(a + b)$$

Restated:

$$(a + b)^2$$

What is the product of this pair? The beginner will say:

$$a^2 + b^2$$

But this is incorrect. One of the first things you learn in algebra is that the true product is:

$$a^2 + b^2 + 2ab$$

We might say: to square (a + b) multiply *each* term in the series by *every term* in the series, *including itself*. That is: multiply a by b, *and also* multiply a by a. Then multiply b by a, *and also* multiply b by b.

This formula may seem unintelligible in the abstract. But we can make it intuitive with a simple example. So, let a = 3 and b = 2. Then ask: what is the product of (3 + 2) squared? Of course we know that 3 + 2 = 5, and that five squared = 25. So, the answer must be 25. But analyze it in terms of our equation. First, consider:

$$a^2 + b^2 = 3^2 + 2^2 = 13$$

But 13 does not equal 25. Instead, consider:

$$a^2 + b^2 + 2ab = 3^2 + 2^2 + 2\,[(3)(2)] = 25$$

This seems more satisfying.

For convenience, we might want to lay this sort of data out in a matrix. Here is such a matrix:

a^2	ab
ba	b^2

Total the four boxes and you get $a^2 + b^2 + 2ab$ (recall at ab = ba). This is the same information we presented in our basic equation, but sometimes it may be more useful to present it in this kind of matrix than in a mere equation. To see that both are the same, ask, what is (10 + 4) (10 + 4)? We know that (10 + 4) = 14, and that $14^2 = 196$. We could just as well say:

$$10^2 + 4^2 + 2\ [(10)(4)] = 196$$

Or, we could set the same data forth in a matrix like this:

10^2	(10)(4)
(4)(10)	4^2

Summing, row by row, we get (100 + 40) +(40 + 16) = 196. Or we could just as well sum column, giving us (100 + 40) + (40 + 16) = 196.

And finally, consider this equation:

$$(a - b)^2$$

This is the same as our original equation, except that the sign is *negative,* not positive. A little algebra will show us that the product can be expressed as:

$$a^2 + b^2 - 2ab$$

(Note the minus sign).

Now, go back and reconsider the material on variance and covariance. Note that when the correlation coefficient is one (or minus one), portfolio variance follows the same logic as the process of combination we engage in here.

Chapter 26

The Bullet Curve

Nobody ever says you have a gambling problem
when you're winning.

—Anonymous

§ 26.01 Introduction

This is a critical chapter, climaxing in one of the most important insights of the course — the "bullet curve," which shows graphically how you can reduce risk without sacrificing return, or increase return without increasing risk.

§ 26.02 More on Diversification

To begin, we dig more deeply into the logic of diversification. Let us suppose we are considering investing in two assets, SunnyCo and Free. SunnyCo has a standard deviation of 25. Free has a standard deviation of zero — that is, an investment Free is *risk-free* (for more on risk-free investments, see § 26.06). Free yields 6 percent; SunnyCo yields 14 percent. We can choose various levels of risk and return by adjusting our holdings of these two securities. For example, suppose we want a return of 12 percent. Start with this formula:

$$r_p = w_s r_s + (1 - w_s)r_f$$

Where:

w_s = the share in SunnyCo.

r_p = return on the portfolio

r_s = return on Sunnyco

r_f = return on Free

We already know the returns, so we can plug them in:

$$12 = w_s(14) + (1 - w_s)6$$

Solving, $w_s = .75$, so we can see that to get a 12 percent yield, we should put 75 percent of our money in SunnyCo and 25 percent in Free. To double-check, what should be the proportions if you desire a return of 8 percent?

We can also define portfolio risk, as measured by σ. From our previous discussion, recall that when one of two assets is risk free, σ_p is the weighted standard deviation of the risky asset. So in our case, σ_p is:

$$w_s\sigma_s$$

So in our case, where the w_s will be 75 percent, then σ_p is $(.75)(25) = 18.75$.

We can compute the risk and return for a range of possible portfolios. In the table below, we can see the return and standard deviation for portfolios of five different relative proportions.

SunnyCo (14 %)	0	0.25	0.5	0.75	1
Free (6%)	1	0.75	0.5	0.25	0
Port Return	6	8	10	12	14
Standard Deviation	0	6.25	12.5	18.75	25

We can present this data in a graph, like the one below. We have charted the standard deviations on the horizontal and the returns on the vertical. Note that relationship is "linear," that is, the relationships plot out along a straight line.

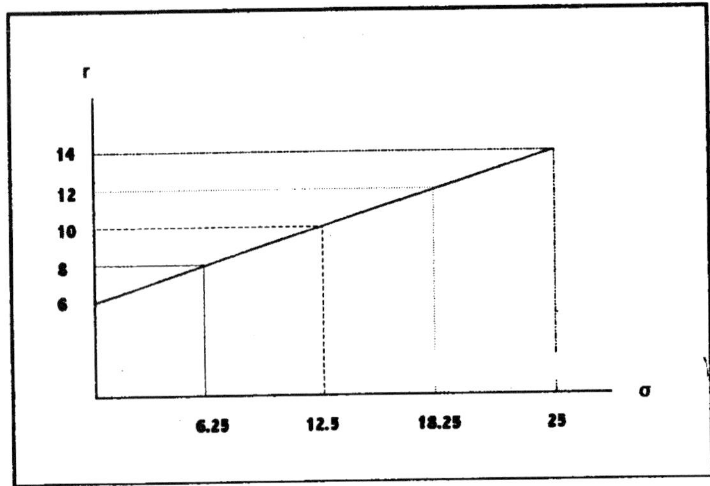

§ 26.03 Diversification and the Dominant Set

We can move on to consider cases where neither security is risk-free. For example, consider the two securities, Thelma and Louise, detailed in the following chart. Thelma has a return of 16 percent and a standard deviation of eight. Louise has a return of 4 percent and a standard deviation of five.

Thelma (16%)	0	0.25	0.385	0.5	0.75	1
Louise (4%)	1	0.75	0.615	0.5	0.25	0
Port Return	4	7	8.615	10	13	16
Cofft	—	1	1	1	1	—
SD	5	5.75	6.15	6.5	7.25	8
Cofft	—	0.2	0.2	0.2	0.2	—
SD	5	4.59	4.77	5.12	6.37	8
Cofft	—	0.1	−0.1	−0.1	−0.1	—
SD	5	4.07	4.13	4.5	6.01	8
Cofft	—	1	−1	−1	−1	—
SD	5	1.75	.00	1.5	4.75	8

We consider six possible portfolios. The six possible weightings are: Thelma zero, 25 percent, 38 percent, 50 percent, 75 percent and 100 percent, with Louise in each case being the remainder of our portfolio (1 -Thelma). We compute return just as we did above. We compute portfolio standard deviation according to the formula from the last assignment. We compute the standard deviation separately for each of four different correlation coefficients: positive 1,[1] positive 0.2, negative 0.1, and negative 1 (note that return is the same for any standard deviation). On the chart, the first two rows are the portfolio weights. The third row is the weighted return of the portfolio. Note that the return is the same for a particular weighting no matter what the correlation coefficient.

For a fuller representation of the data, consider the following graph:

[1] A portfolio with a standard deviation of positive 1 is perfectly possible mathematically, and it is useful as a benchmark. But according to what you have learned about finance, you wouldn't expect to find one in the market. Do you understand why?

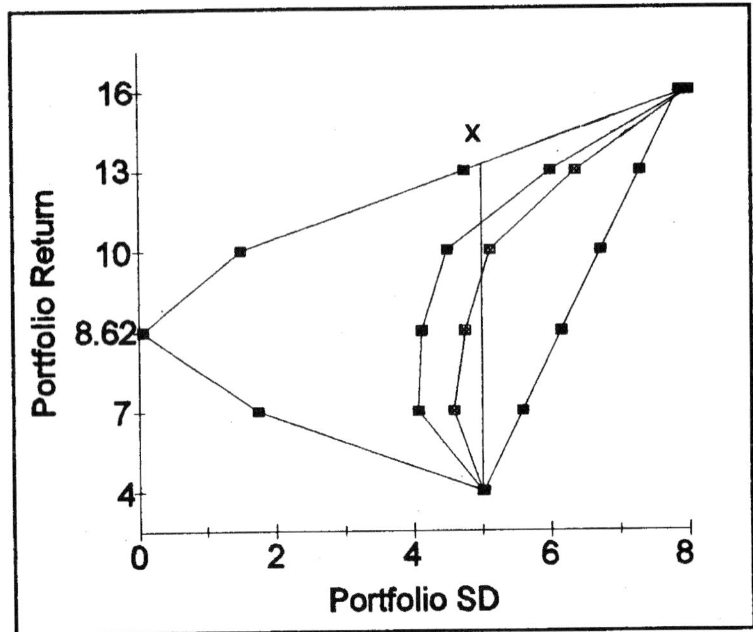

The vertical axis charts the portfolio return. The horizontal axis charts the portfolio standard deviation. Where the points connect at the bottom of the chart represents portfolios of nothing but Louise. They have a return of four and a standard deviation of five. The nexus at the top represents portfolios of nothing but Thelma. They have a return of 16 and a standard deviation of eight. The set of points on the line at far right represents mixed portfolios where the correlation coefficient is one. Note that every increase in the share of Thelma brings a corresponding increase in the portfolio standard deviation. The second set of points show portfolios with a positive correlation of 0.2; the third, −0.1, and the final portfolio, of −1. Note that in any case except where the correlation coefficient is positive one, there is no reason to remain invested entirely in Louise. You can always get a higher return with the same risk by moving to a point on the same curved line straight up from the initial portfolio. Note also the vertical line marked at the top with an "x." If the investor can tolerate a standard deviation of five, she should invest in a portfolio as high on that line as possible — the limit will be a function of the correlation of the two securities in her portfolio. If she wants a lower standard deviation, she can get it by moving to the left of that line, but always staying as high on the graph as possible. She may be perfectly willing to take a greater risk than a standard deviation of five. This will be possible in any case, but once again, she should make sure to stay as high on the graph as the relevant correlation coefficient permits her to go.

Web site: A nifty little risk graph applet is at: http://www.duke.edu/~charvey/applets/Frontier/test.html.

§ 26.04 Finding the Minimum-Risk Portfolio

We have seen a graphic display of how it is possible (and why it is important) to minimize risk. We can get some assistance in minimizing through the use of some basic math. But we are not done yet. For example, recall from our earlier discussion the case where the correlation coefficient is minus 1. Recalling our earlier example, we know that the standard deviation of this portfolio is:

$$\sigma_{portfolio} = w_x\sigma_x - (1 - w_x)\,\sigma_y$$

Rearranging and simplifying:

$$\sigma_{portfolio} = w_x\,(\sigma_x + \sigma_y) - \sigma_y$$

Why is this form interesting? It is interesting because it lets us figure out what *percentage weighting* we should use in our portfolio to produce a standard deviation of *zero.* In the example above, the standard deviation of Thelma was eight; the standard deviation of Louise was five. We set portfolio standard deviation at zero and then solve for weight:

$$\sigma_{portfolio} = w_T\,(\sigma_T + \sigma_L) - \sigma_L = 0$$

$$w_T\,(8 + 5) - 5 = 0$$

In this case, it is easy to see that $w_T = 0.385 = 38.5$ percent. Since $w_L = (1 - w_T)$, it must be that $w_L = 0.615 = 61.5$ percent. In other words, if the correlation coefficient is negative one, and if we put 38.5 percent of our assets in Thelma and the remainder in Louise, we have a portfolio that has no risk at all (to double-check, use these weights and standard deviations in our original "long-form" equation to compute portfolio variance and standard deviation; you should get "zero").

Of course, it is unlikely that we find two assets with so perfect a correlation. What of the more common case where rho is neither plus one nor minus one? In this case, the minimum point of standard deviation can also be found, but it requires some calculus, which is beyond our scope.[2]

These conclusions are tedious, but not impossible, to prove for one pair of securities. But what about the market as a whole, where you can have a near-infinite number of investment opportunities — and a truly infinite number of potential relationships. How do we manage all these data? We will get to that shortly.

§ 26.05 Short Sales/Borrowing

So far, we have considered portfolios where we have 100 percent of our funds in either of two assets, or a combination of the two assets. But there is another possibility. Specifically, we can imagine *augmenting* our initial investment pool by *borrowing*, and investing our own and the borrowed funds. The consequence is that we have *more* than 100 percent invested, offset by a *negative* sum representing the borrowed money. For example, suppose we have

[2] You take the derivative of w_x, and set it equal to zero. Then you take the *second* derivative and note whether it is positive or negative. If the second derivative is positive, you have the correct answer. If it is negative, the value you have specified is not a minimum but a maximum.

a chance to invest at 15 percent, and that we can borrow money at 7 percent. Suppose we decide to borrow a sum equal to half our original holding, and then to invest our own money plus the borrowed money. Over one period, our return will be the return on our investment, *less* what it takes to pay interest on the loan. Recall our original equation:

$$r_p = w_s r_s + (1 - w_s)r_f$$

Plugging in our numbers:

$$r_p = (1.5)(0.15) + (-0.5)(0.07) = 0.225 + -0.035 = 0.19 = 19 \text{ percent}$$

Of course, our portfolio is more risky than it was before. How do we measure the risk? Remarkably, we use the same formulas we used earlier for variance or standard deviation, making sure to adjust for our "negative" position. Perhaps the commonest case will be one in which the "borrowing" is, in effect, a risk-free asset. Recall that in that case, the standard deviation of the portfolio is simply the weighted product of the standard deviation of the risky asset. So, suppose we are 150 percent invested in a project with a standard deviation of 0.6. Then the standard deviation of our portfolio is (1.5)(6) = 0.9.

Perhaps less obviously, the familiar formulas apply when the "negative" asset (the borrowing) has a positive standard deviation. So, for example, suppose we borrow a sum equal to 50 percent of our initial position from a fund with a standard deviation of 30 percent and invest 150 percent of our initial position in an asset with s standard deviation of forty percent. Then the portfolio variance is:

$$\sigma^2 = (1.5^2)(0.4^2) + (-0.5^2)(0.3^2) + 2[(1.5)(-0.5)(-1)(0.4)(0.3)] = 0.5625$$

The standard deviation is, of course, the square root of the variance, or 0.75.

We can summarize the analysis in the following graph:

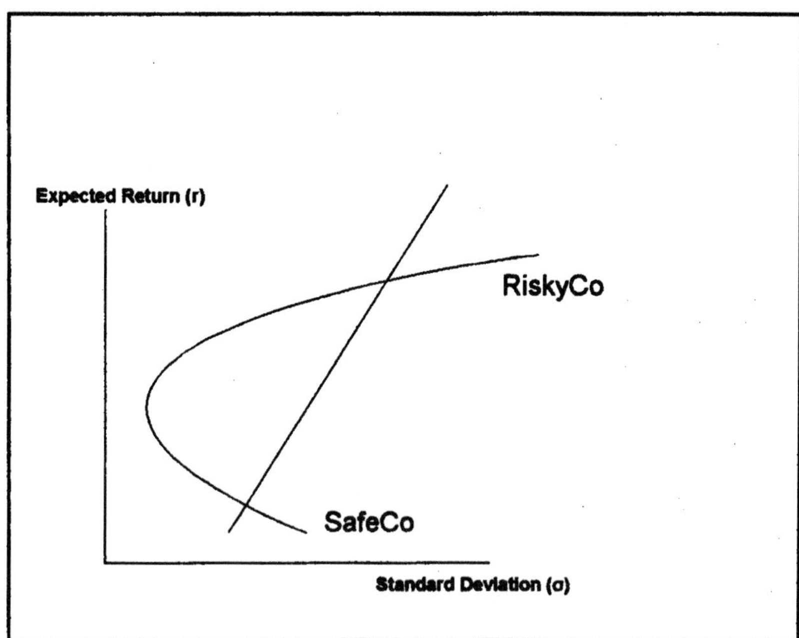

We have two securities: SafeCo and RiskyCo. We imagine two relationships: one, a positive correlation of one (represented by the slanted straight line) and the other, a correlation of less than one (represented by the bullet). The lower crossing-point can be read as identifying a portfolio of all SafeCo. The higher crossing-point can be read as identifying a portfolio of all RiskyCo. Note the points to the north and northeast of the RiskyCo crossing. These represent leveraged portfolios in which the investor holds more than 100 percent of his holdings in RiskyCo, with a corresponding short position in SafeCo. Note that the portfolio with the *lower* initial correlation coefficient yields *higher* risk when leveraged.

Finally, note the portfolios to the south of the SafeCo crossing point. These portfolios represent the worst of all possible worlds: shorting high-risk high-yield RiskyCo to leverage into low-risk low-yield SafeCo. No one does this intentionally, of course. But the arithmetic works, and it is entirely possible to imagine an investor who blunders into this corner by mistake.

§ 26.06 Note on the Risk-Free Rate

From time to time we have referred to "the risk-free rate." Since the term will bulk larger in our later work, we need to scrutinize it briefly now.

We know of an investor who keeps all her stock certificates in a strong box inside the chimney. The reason: she is afraid of fire. Apparently she has noticed that when the house burns down, the chimney is the last thing to go, and so she expects her papers to be secure. We do not know what she plans to do if the fire gets hot. But her foresight is a useful reminder of one basic:

risk-avoidance is a matter of practicality and degree. And nothing ever — ever — is risk-free.

Certainly not common stocks, of course. Nor — less obviously — corporate bonds. They were once the darling of risk-averse investors. But bitter experience has taught us that bonds are vulnerable to the winds of market fluctuation, and that even the grandest of corporations may crumble. Governments? You have got to be kidding. You might as well take your money home and stuff it under a mattress. Right — and lose all its value to inflation (not to mention, of course, the risk of fire).

The "risk-free rate," then, must be a fiction. Is it therefore irrelevant? It is not. It is perfectly useful in theory, at least. After all, physicists postulate a friction-free universe. No one thinks there is such a thing, but no one thinks physicists are fools and should stop. Perhaps of more immediate relevance, even though there is not a "risk-free rate," there are a number of things that come close enough to be useful as rules of thumb.

Different investors will have different choices, but here are some basics. First, the "risk-free investment" ought to be short-term — maybe a year. That leaves one vulnerable to reinvestment risk, of course, but we have seen at least that a short-term instrument is less vulnerable to interest rate fluctuations than a corresponding long-term investment. Second, it ought to be the obligation of a solvent borrower. Practically speaking, this means (no jokes, please) the government. One investment that meets these criteria is the *short-term treasury bill* — an obligation of the U.S. Treasury, payable at the end of three months. Many analysts will use the short-term t-bill as the proxy for the risk-free rate in their calculations.

§ 26.07 The Responsibilities of a Trustee — A Second Look

Now we are ready for a second look at the responsibilities of a trustee. As you might guess, modern portfolio theory worked its way only slowly into law and practice, but its triumph by now is well nigh complete: the "trust list" has pretty much vanished. It is hard to imagine any court today holding that stock investment is imprudent *per se*, or telling the trustee to put all his eggs in one basket. By the 1970s, courts were already recognizing that the trustee may consider not just the individual stock but the portfolio taken as a whole.[3]

More recently the rule has been ratified in the Restatement (Third) of Trusts,[4] and its companion statute, the Uniform Prudent Investor Act (UPIA). The introduction to the UPIA specifies that it was drafted "under the influence of a large and broadly accepted body of empirical and theoretical knowledge about the behavior of capital markets," often described as "modern portfolio theory." It specifies four important objectives (among others):

---

[3] Spitzer v. Bank of New York, 43 A.D.2d 105, 349 N.Y.S.2d 747 (1st Dept. 1973), *aff'd,* 35 N.Y.2d 512, 364 N.Y.S. 2d 164 (1974). Actually, the court's recognition of total portfolio return was somewhat back-handed. What the court said was, "the focus of inquiry . . . is on the individual security as such and factors relating to the entire portfolio are to be weighed only along with others in reviewing the prudence of the particular investment tradition." Oral tradition reports that the judges didn't see themselves as making new law and were if anything somewhat surprised at the attention the case has received.

[4] Restatement (Third) of Trusts § 227 (1992) (Prudent Investor Rule).

- "The standard of prudence is applied to any investment as part of the total portfolio, rather than to individual investments."
- "The tradeoff in all investing between risk and return is identified as the fiduciary's central consideration."
- "All categoric restrictions on types of investments have been abrogated; the trustee can invest in anything that plays an appropriate role in achieving the risk/return objectives of the trust and that meets the other requirements of prudent investing."
- "The long familiar requirement that fiduciaries diversify their investments has been integrated into the definition of prudent investing."

A version of the rule appears also in the Employee Retirement Income Security Act (ERISA). It provides:

> (a)(1) . . . a fiduciary shall discharge his duties with respect to a plan solely in the interest of the participants and beneficiaries and — . . .
>
> (C) by diversifying investments of the plan so as to minimize the risk of large losses, unless under the circumstances it is clearly prudent not to do so.[5]

A most interesting transitional case is *Brock v. Citizens Bank of Clovis.*[6] Citizens Bank maintained an ERISA pension fund for its employees. Some 81.93 percent of fund assets were in first mortgages on commercial real estate in Curry County, New Mexico. The Secretary of Labor, as administrator of ERISA, argued that this heavy concentration ran counter to the diversification provisions of ERISA., The court agreed. The court found support for its view in citations from standard treatises on the law of trusts, and added, "It is also supported by modern finance theory."[7]

§ 26.08 Wholesale Diversification: Mergers and Acquisitions

The investor may diversify on his own account by buying shares in different companies. Or he may "buy diversification" by investing in a diversified mutual fund. But there is another kind of diversification that invites inquiry on its own account. This is the case where the managers of the firm buy other companies and present themselves to the world as a single diversified firm. This kind of "wholesale diversification" through corporate merger and acquisition deserves a word of inquiry on its own account.[8]

A firm can use mergers and acquisitions to dominate its "own" business, as did (say) Rockefeller's Standard Oil in the late Nineteenth Century when

[5] *See* 29 U.S.C. § 1104(a)(1)(C). At the risk of complicating matters, we need to note that the diversification rule in ERISA is not solely the child of modern portfolio theory. Another concern of the drafters was the role of company managers who also manage company pension funds, and who will be impelled to invest pension funds in their own companies. On principles of diversification, his "own company" is about the last place the typical employee would want to have his funds invested: all his human capital is tied up there via his job, so his financial capital ought to be someplace else.

[6] 841 F.2d 344 (10th Cir.1988).

[7] *Id.* at 346-47

[8] A good basic source on mergers and acquisitions is N. Fligstein, the Transformation of Corporate Control (1990).

it sought to buy up most of the oil distribution capacity. Or it can diversify "vertically" as many great oil companies did when they moved "backward" along the product chain from distribution through refining to exploration — and others did as they moved "forward" from exploration through refining to distribution. Or it can diversify "horizontally," as did ITT when it invested in a host of unrelated businesses in the 1960s.

Scholars identify five great merger waves in our history. The first began after the worldwide depression of 1883 left many capital-intensive industries awash in overcapacity. It culminated in the creation of the "trusts" (like Standard Oil) and led, in its turn, to the wave of "trust-busting" under the anti-trust laws around the turn of the Twentieth Century. There was a smaller wave of "consolidating mergers" in the economic boom that followed World War I. A third wave in the 1960s was the heyday of horizontal combinations, and the creation of "conglomerates" like ITT.

A fourth wave of merger activity emerged in the 1980s in an ironic reversal of its predecessor. Many of the great mergers of the 1980s occurred when successful companies or investors took over weaker sisters, often in "hostile takeovers" — and often, to undo the conglomeration that had come to pass in the 1980s.

And a fifth wave subsists today. Many of the recent mergers appear as bids for position in an expanding worldwide market place. Most of these mergers among similar or related businesses, unlike the conglomeration of the 1960s.

Precisely what can a company expect to accomplish by merging? Economists like to identify two important goals:

- Economies of *scale*: A firm achieves economies of scale if it produces a larger number of units at a lower per-unit cost than it would by producing a smaller number of units.
- Economies of *scope*. A firm achieves economies of scope if it can produce different products at a lower total cost than would be paid if the products were produced separately.

For our purposes, perhaps the most interesting topic is the wave of conglomerate mergers of the 1960s: how to justify the consolidation of a variety of businesses that have no obvious relation to each other?

Managers sought to justify the conglomerate mergers in at least two ways. One was the assertion that they possessed a valuable commodity called "management skill and knowledge," which they could apply broadly to a number of businesses. In retrospect, the market's verdict on this "management skill and knowledge" is that it was largely a fantasy. Companies languished; share prices fell and, as we saw above, a new wave of mergers at last undid them.

The other justification was that they were offering diversification as a product to their shareholders — "wholesale diversification," as we called it above. But academic analysts have been largely unsympathetic to this idea of wholesale diversification. The point is that there is little or nothing that the manager can do for the investor (by way of diversification) that the investor cannot do for himself — and do better and more cheaply. After all, it is the investor who knows how and how much he wants to diversify. And there are simply no important barriers to the individual investor who wants to do this kind of diversification on his own.

There is yet one more possible reason for wholesale diversification. Consider the plight of the poor, benighted corporate mogul. He has almost uncountable millions, yes — but his millions are virtually all tied up in his own business. He knows that diversification is a sound strategy for him as an individual investor. Yet how can he diversify if his fate is so tied to the fate of a single corporation? Answer: he can diversify if he can diversify *the corporation.* Seen in this light, conglomerate diversification emerges as a device whereby the manager uses corporate diversification to serve his personal ends — and in glaring breach of his fiduciary duty as a corporate manager.

Chapter 27

What Alice the Bag Lady Knew: The Index Fund

> Men should do with their hopes
> as they do with tame fowl:
> cut their wings that they may not fly over the wall.
>
> —Lord Halifax

§ 27.01 Introduction

You may remember Alice the bag lady in Doonesbury. A while back, Alice inherited a lot of money. Her friend Joanie undertook to get her some investment advice. "No way," said Alice, "I want treasury bills and an index fund." The purpose of this assignment is to show you that Alice was right — and indeed, that the heart of this course segment can be summarized in a four-panel comic strip.

Up to now, we have focused most of our attention on the question of how to find value. In the next two assignments, we shift our attention to the question of how to *measure* value. Specifically, we develop the *Capital Asset Pricing Model* (CAPM).[1] CAPM was developed in the 1960s as analysts drew out the implications of: (a) Markowitz's Modern Portfolio Theory (MPT), and (b) the Efficient Capital Market Hypothesis (ECMH). Beginning students often find CAPM excessively abstract or stylized, and they suspect it cannot have anything to do with the real world.

Their hunch is understandable: CAPM is indeed abstract and stylized. But their conclusion is wrong. In fact, CAPM is widely used. It is used as a device for valuing investments. Perhaps of greater importance, it is also used as a device for judging investors. Specifically, courts use CAPM in evaluating the performance of trustees or managers who invest other people's money. Regulators use it in judging the performance of utilities and other regulated industries in seeking rate increases.

For our purposes, CAPM has two components. One is the *Capital Market Line* (CML), which we study in the next section. The other is *beta*, which we introduce in the next chapter.

In the last chapter, we explored the mechanics of portfolio diversification. In this chapter, we follow the analysis to a surprising conclusion. We will show that there is *only one* stock investment portfolio that any investor will want to hold — call it the "index fund." We will show that this is true *regardless* of her taste for risk. Rather, we will show that the investor will adjust for risk by: (a) starting with the index fund, and then (b) borrowing and lending at the risk-free rate. She will be trading, in short, on the CML.

[1] Also abbreviated as "CAP-M."

Right or wrong, Alice has plenty of company. The largest mutual fund in the world, with assets exceeding $100 billion, is the Vanguard S&P 500 Index Fund.

§ 27.02 The Capital Market Line

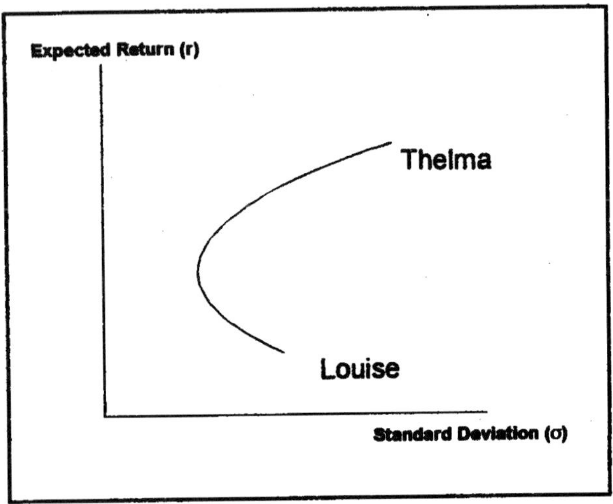

We know how to plot the relationship between risk and return for two securities like Thelma and Louise (see graph above). If their returns are correlated at anything less than $\rho = 1$ (as these two are), then we will end up with a bullet-shaped graph like this one, suggesting that we can increase return and reduce risk by *not* restricting ourselves to the "safe" security. Indeed, we can see there must be a minimum-risk portfolio with a return higher than investing in Louise alone. Of course, the investor need not rest there. Her risk-return tradeoff may place her anywhere on the "top line" — the portion of the curve that lies above the west end of the bullet. She may choose to be anywhere along the top line, according to her taste. But positions on the top line "dominate" positions not on the top line. That is, for every position below the west end of the bullet, there is a position above that yields a higher return with no sacrifice in risk.

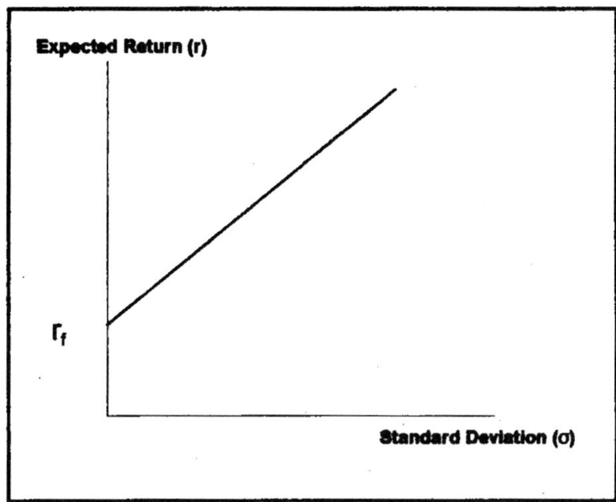

Likewise, we learned how to plot risk and return for a risky security and a risk-free investment. We saw our results plotted out as a straight line (see graph above).

§ 27.03 Combining Risk-Free and Risky Lending

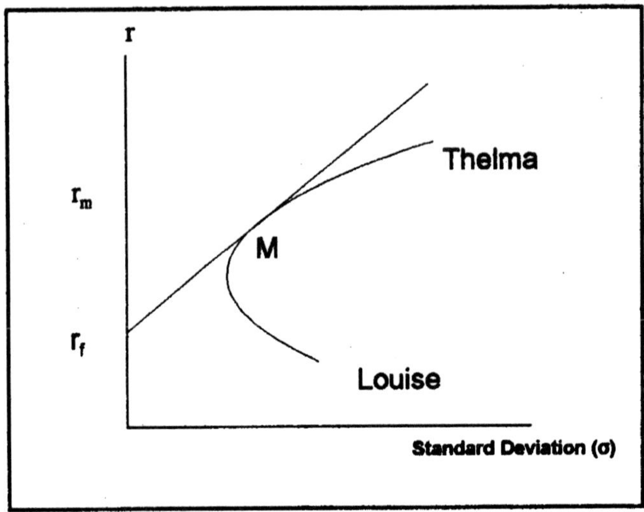

One thing we have not done before is to consider the possibility of combining these two graphss, as suggested in the graph above. Note that if we include only Thelma and Louise, then we can identify a "minimum risk" portfolio at the east end of the curve. Now look at the point labeled "M," where the curved and straight lines touch. From the standpoint of the curved line, M can be read as a portfolio combining Thelma and Louise — slightly riskier than the least risky combined portfolio, with a correspondingly higher return.

But how shall we read the straight line? Read it as a set of portfolios that combine the "risky" portfolio M, *with a risk-free investment.* In other words, a risk-averse investor content to accept the risk-free rate of return could invest in a portfolio with a standard deviation of zero and a return of r_f. An investor who is willing to bear some risk could invest in portfolio M with return r_m.

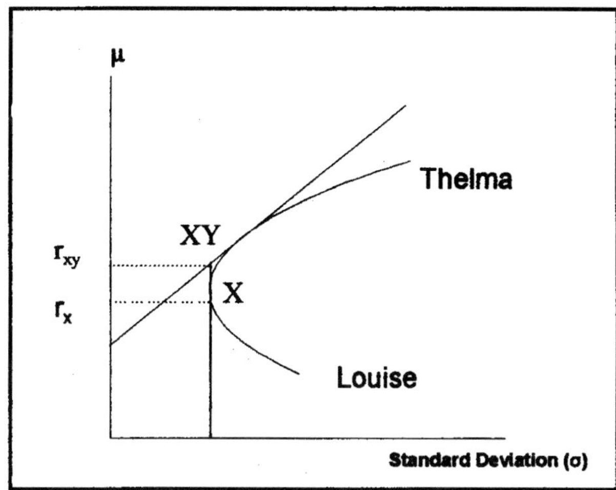

But what about the investor who wants *neither* of these positions? For example, what about an investor who wanted to invest in a "minimum risk" portfolio at the point where the vertical straight line hits the curve (marked by an X)? We can see that an investment in X yields only r_x. But, if the investor invests part in P and part in the risk-free investment, then the investor gets portfolio XY, which has the same *risk* as ordinary X, and the *higher* return, indicated by r_x. Indeed, for *any* portfolio on the curved line — excepting only the "tangent" portfolio M — there is a portfolio on the straight line that offers a higher return with no sacrifice in risk. Note that this investor should *not* invest in Thelma and Louise *alone*, because she can get the *same* standard deviation and a *higher* return by investing in a portfolio that is a combination of the risk-free investment and portfolio M.

This appears correct for any portfolio between the vertical intercept and portfolio M. Over this range, we describe portfolios that contain from zero to 100 percent of portfolio M (with the balance in the risk-free investment). It is *equally* true for portfolios along the diagonal *northeast* of portfolio M. This segment (which in principle may extend to infinity) identifies portfolios with *more than* 100 percent in portfolio M — that is, portfolios in which the investor borrows at the risk-free rate and "leverages up," by investing more than 100 percent of her investment in portfolio M.

We can summarize:

- There is no reason to invest in any Thelma-Louise portfolio except portfolio M.
- For any position except portfolio M, there is a portfolio along the risk-free/risky diagonal that dominates portfolios on the Thelma-Louise curve.

- Hence, the appropriate strategy for *any* investor is to begin with portfolio M and then leverage up or down by borrowing or lending at the risk-free rate.

For example, suppose portfolio M contains 65 percent Thelma, 35 percent Louise. If the investor is satisfied with the market portfolio, that is what she would hold. If she wanted 20 percent less risk (as measured by standard deviation), then she would invest 20 percent of her money at the risk-free rate. Of the remaining 80 percent, she would put 65 percent in Thelma and 35 percent in Louise.

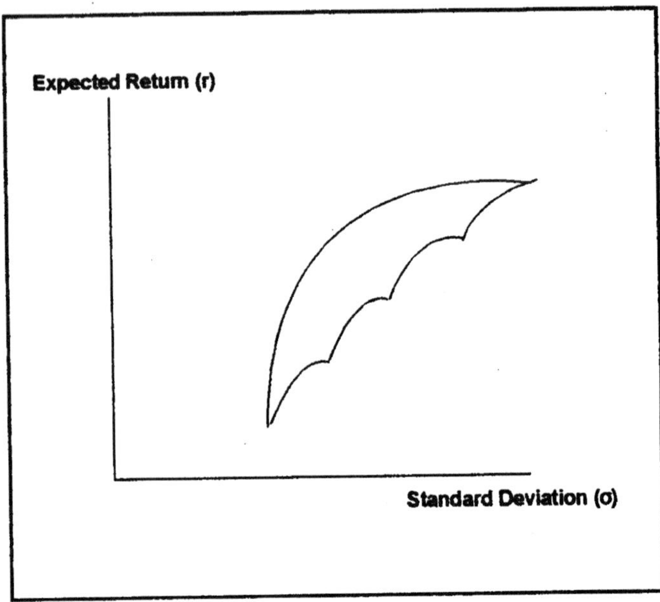

But we need not restrict ourselves to Thelma and Louise. Consider the graph above with the shape like an inverted new moon. Consider this graph as representing the market *as a whole*. That would mean: not just "Thelma and Louise," but *all* the stocks (or indeed, all the investments of any sort) that might go to make up the market as a whole. Remarkably, this multi-investment market works almost exactly like our Thelma/Louise example above. There is one small refinement. With Thelma and Louise, the range of possible portfolios lay along the boundary line. However, when there are many securities, we can imagine a range of plot-points all over the interior of the half-moon-shaped space. But with this qualification, the basic insight remains. Portfolios on the top of the half-moon *dominate* portfolios inside the half-moon. That is: for any possible portfolio inside the half-moon, there is a portfolio on the top surface with a *higher* return and *no lower* standard deviation — and a portfolio with a *lower standard deviation* and *no lower* return, on the surface. As before, we cannot tell you where you want to lie *along* the dominant set — that is a function of your personal risk-return tradeoff. But there is *no* reason to take any portfolio below the dominant set.

Perhaps you have anticipated our next move. That is: we *reintroduce* the diagonal line. What does it represent? It represents exactly what it represented before. That is, it represents a set of portfolios that combine: (a) portfolio M, and (b) borrowing and lending at the risk-free rate.

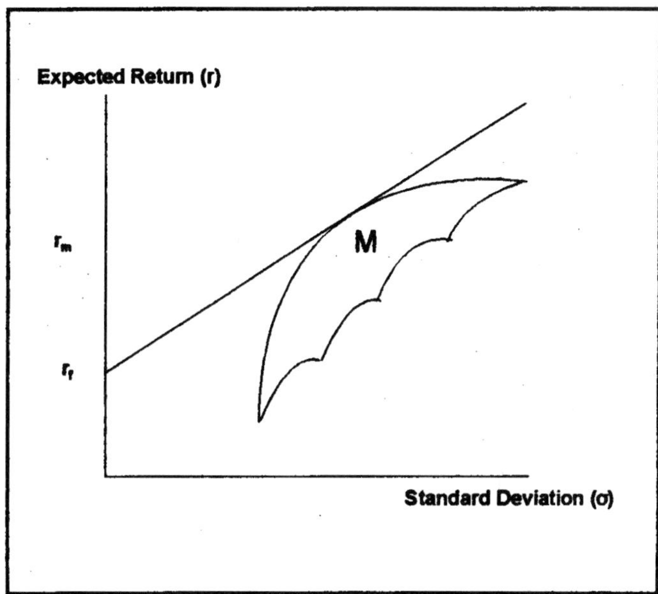

As before, this set of mixed portfolios dominates every portfolio on the curved line except the tangent, portfolio M. And the earlier logic holds: once again, among risky investments, there is no reason to invest in any portfolio except portfolio M. If the investor is not happy with the risk-return tradeoff she achieves in this way, she should leverage up or down the straight line by borrowing or lending at the risk-free rate.

To make the next step, we need only to remove the half-moon, leaving the diagonal line. This is the *Capital Market Line* (CML), which represents the dominant set of all possible investments. The dotted lines mark M, the market portfolio, which offers a return of r_m, with a standard deviation of σ_m. All other points represent portfolios that include (southwest of M) an investment at the risk-free rate or (northeast of M) borrowing at the risk-free rate. Math students will recognize that the *rise* of the portfolio — the horizontal distance between the vertical — and M is ($r_m - r_f$), while the *run* — the horizontal distance — is σ_m.

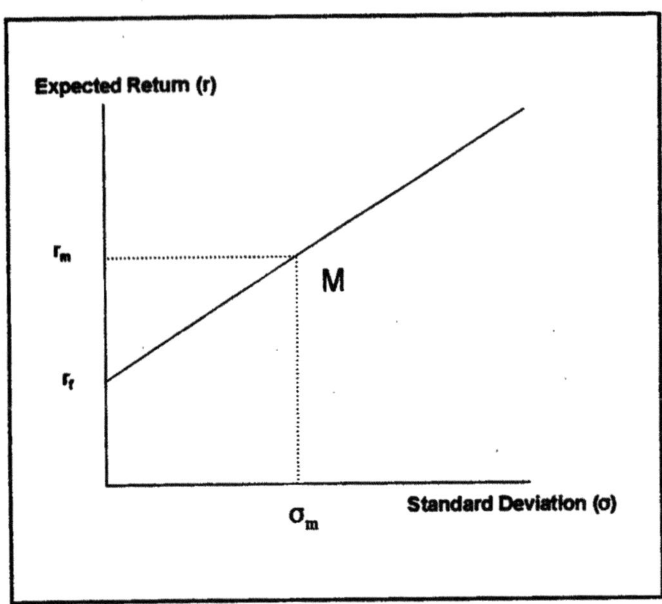

So, the *slope* of the line — the rise over the run — is:

$$Slope\ of\ CML = \left[\frac{E(r_m) - r_f)}{\sigma_m}\right]$$

If the risk-free rate is 4 percent, the market rate is 12 percent, and the standard deviation is 32 percent, then the slope is:

$$Slope\ of\ CML = \left[\frac{0.12 - 0.04}{0.32}\right] = 0.25 = 25\ percent$$

We can put this formula together with our prior learning to estimate the total return on our index portfolio. Recall that we are dealing with a portfolio in which one asset is risky and one is not — which is to say, where one has a positive standard deviation and one has a standard deviation of zero. Adapting a formula from a previous assignment, we can show that the formula for any particular portfolio along the line (σ_p) is:

$$W_m\ \sigma_m = \sigma_p$$

$$E(r) = r_f + \left[\frac{E(r_m) - r_f}{\sigma_M}\right] \sigma_p$$

So, using the same data as is the previous example, assume a portfolio with a standard deviation of 20 percent.

$$E(r) = 0.04 + \left[\frac{0.12 - 0.04}{0.32}\right] 0.20 = 0.09 = 9\ percent$$

Note that where you know data on returns, you can use this formula to estimate the standard deviation. For example, your client Larry just won

$100,000 in the lottery. Instead of spending it all today, he wants to invest it and to try to accumulate a million dollars in 10 years. He will need to get a return of about 26 percent. How much risk must he accept?

$$0.26 = 0.04 + \left[\frac{0.12 - 0.04}{0.32} \right] \sigma$$

The answer is he must be willing to take a standard deviation of 88 percent, which is about 2.75 times the standard deviation of the market portfolio.

§ 27.04 The Risk Premium

The difference between the market return and the risk-free rate is called the *risk premium*. It is a measure of the extra return investors demand to forsake the risk-free investment for the market return. It is a function of the aggregate risk aversion of investors and the volatility of the market. It may change over time as suggested by the following graph.

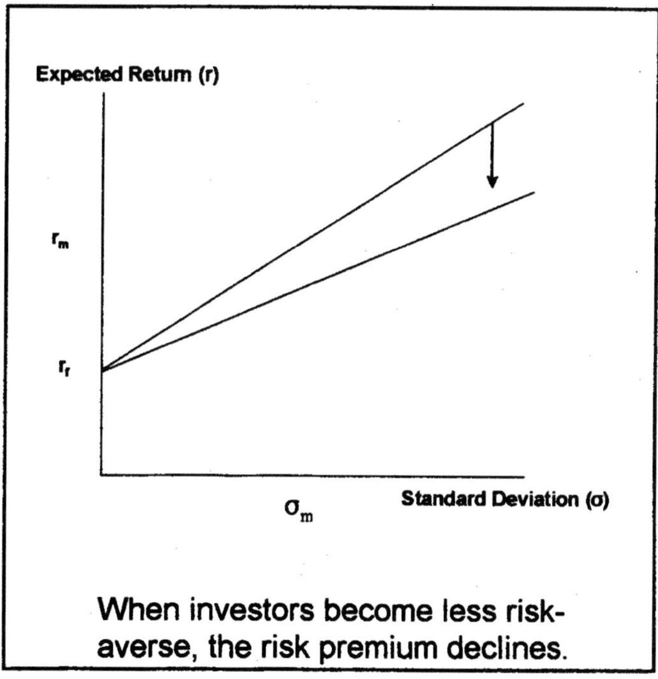

When investors become less risk-averse, the risk premium declines.

Analysts may compute an *index* of risk aversion, for use in studying market behavior. Call it "A." A represents the weighted average of the risk aversion of all investors. We can define A as follows:

$$A = \frac{E(r_M) - r_f}{\sigma_M}$$

So, if the market return is 9 percent, the risk-free rate is 3 percent, and the standard deviation is 30 percent, then:

$$A = \frac{(0.09 - 0.03)}{0.04} = 1.5$$

If A advances to two while the risk-free rate and the standard deviation remains constant, we would expect the market return to advance to 11 percent.

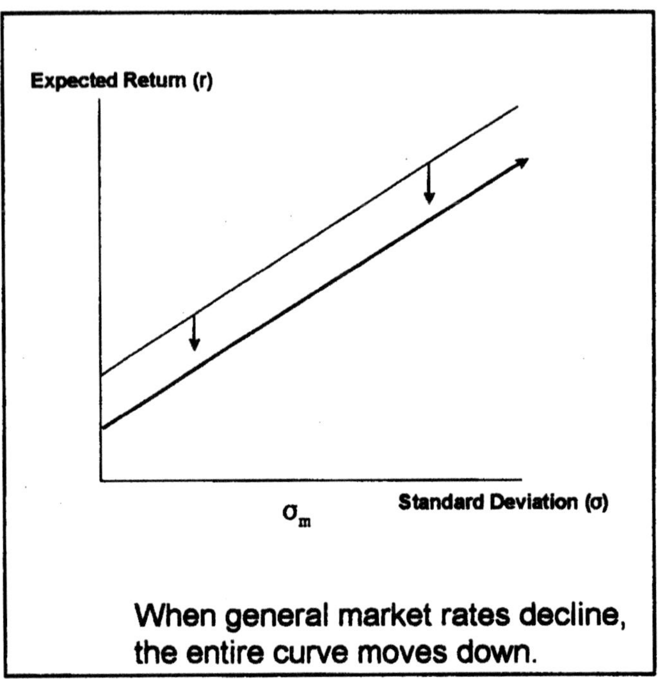
Expected Return (r)
Standard Deviation (σ)
σ_m
When general market rates decline,
the entire curve moves down.

We need to contrast the situation where there is a change in A from those changes where there is a change in the *general* level of interest rates in the market. In that latter case, we can expect all the interest rates on the graph to advance (or decline) together.

§ 27.05 The Index Fund

Does this all sound intolerably abstract? It need not. In fact, billions of dollars are invested every day on principles much like those set forth in this chapter. The principal unit is the so-called "index fund," whereby the fund manager undertakes simply to invest "according to the index," with no pretense at picking individual stocks. Wells Fargo Bank introduced the first major "index fund" in 1971. John C. Bogle, the legendary investment manager at Vanguard, introduced an index fund in 1976. These days they are a staple of money management, not only for individuals, but (perhaps more important) for institutions such as pension funds that manage large sums of money for others.

We have built our model on "the risk-free rate" and "the market." We have already seen that in the real world, there is no such thing as "the risk-free rate," pure and simple. On the same logic, there is no single entity that we can all agree embodies "the market." Hence it is not surprising to find that different index funds compute their indexes the same way. Some might use a broad-gauge measure of a major stock exchange, like the Standard & Poor 500 Stock Index or the Wilshire Large Capitalization Value Index. As if to undercut the very purpose of an index fund, some fund managers will advertise that their "index" outperforms someone else's "index!"

Index funds begin, of course, from the perception that you cannot outguess the market — or, at least, that the costs of trying to outguess the market offset any possible gains. But what really drives index funds is the insight that *you do not need to settle for the market return*. Rather, with an index fund, you can do exactly what we have done here — move up and down the capital market line by borrowing or lending at the risk-free rate.

§ 27.06 Diversification Applied: Mutual Funds, Pension Funds, Securitization

Diversification is probably a good idea from almost any perspective. But it is worthwhile to examine some of the reasons why there is so much diversification in the market. One set of reasons is *institutional* — the economy is structured in a way that makes diversification easy or almost inevitable. The other, you might call *structural*. Imaginative deal-makers — probably including lawyers — have developed a number of market devices that make diversification easy.

Among institutional reasons, the most important is that most money is managed not by individuals in their own behalf, but by professional managers acting as agents for individuals. These professional money managers include those who manage *mutual funds*. Among structural reasons, perhaps the most important is the group of techniques we can lump together under the name of *securitization*.

§ 27.07 Mutual Funds

A mutual fund is a firm that pools investors' money to buy and sell and trade securities — usually, stocks and bonds. Investors who park their money with a mutual fund get the advantage of professional management. But also, and perhaps more important, they get opportunities for diversification they couldn't achieve on their own.

A mutual fund is a corporation. As with any other corporation, the investor delivers his money in exchange for shares. The managers invest the money in the securities of other companies. The investor retains, not a direct interest in those other companies, but a pro-rata share of the mutual fund pool.

Mutual funds come in two flavors, *open-end* and *closed-end*. Open-end funds are far more numerous and manage far more money, so we give them our primary attention here (a word about closed-end funds later).

In an open-end fund, the managers invest the money that comes to them: if they get $100, they invest $100. If $50 more comes in the next day, then they invest $150. But investors can change their mind at any time. So, if the fund has $150 under management and investors with claims totaling $80 demand their money back, then the fund trims its portfolio down to $70 and gives them back the other $80. The value of a share at any time is the value of the portfolio divided by the number of shares.

Taxation: You may anticipate a tax problem here. Corporate investors suffer from *double taxation:* the government taxes corporate profits, and then taxes the money again when it shows up in the hands of the investor in dividends. Corporations may deduct some of the dividends they receive from other corporations, but some double taxation problem remains. Few if any mutual funds could stay in business with double taxation because few if any can offer returns sufficient to cancel the effect of double taxation.

Of course the answer is that mutual fund investors do not pay the double tax. The IRS treats the mutual fund as a *conduit*, and the tax effects go straight through to the investor, who pays the tax as if he invested directly himself.[2] This is one remarkable instance of tax policy affecting public policy: by allowing for pass-through taxation, the IRC makes mutual funds possible.

Funds as Vehicles for Diversification: You can anticipate the possibilities for diversification in the mutual fund. The investor with only a few hundred (or even a few thousand) dollars can't expect to diversify. Her gains will be eaten up in brokerage fees. This cost is not a problem for the fund. Indeed, some funds carry diversification to its logical conclusion by investing only in a "market index," in effect boasting that it offers no special investment wisdom.

On the other hand, many funds purport to specialize: in particular industries, for example, or particular countries, or particular types of securities, or particular kinds of risk. There is nothing sinister about this kind of specialization, and with good management, it may justify itself. But it is important to grasp that the specialized fund by its very nature cedes one of the first virtues of the mutual fund idea. Indeed, investors sometimes choose to buy "portfolios of mutual funds" to get diversification along with specialized management.

How Do They Do It? The Matter of Fees: To see how the fund makes money, we can divide funds into two classes: *load* and *no-load*. A *load* fund charges a front-end fee as a condition of taking your money. Well-managed load funds can justify their fees, but you will have to expect to stick with them for a long time to get the benefit of your load charge. *No-load* funds do not charge a front-end fee, but impose a charge for management. There is some competition among funds on the matter of management fees, but many observers believe that these fees offer an opportunity for abuse because they are small enough, relative to the overall size of most portfolios, to escape the investor's notice.

Closed-end Funds: Closed-end mutual funds are far less common than open-end funds, but they deserve a moment's notice. Recall that the open-end

[2] I.R.C. § 243(a).

fund will take the money of all comers, increasing (or reducing) the number of shares as necessary to meet the demand — this is the "open-end" part. A closed-end fund operates more like an ordinary corporation. It issues a finite number of shares. The fund has no obligation either to retire shares or to issue new ones. If you want to buy into the fund, you will have to find an existing owner who wants to sell. If you want out, you will have to find someone who wants to buy.

Closed-end funds present a puzzle for students of efficient markets, because they often trade at prices that do not seem to be justified by the value of the asset pool. For example, consider CloseCo, a closed-end fund that owns securities with an aggregate market value of $1,000. All the securities it owns trade on recognized exchanges so there is complete information on current prices. CloseCo regularly provides its own shareholders with a detailed account of its holdings. There are 10 shares of CloseCo. They trade at $90 each. The market capitalization of CloseCo is thus $900 ($90 x 10), while the underlying asset value is $1,000. We say that CloseCo "trades at a discount," a discount from its underlying asset value.

Closed-end funds often trade at a discount, but why? One answer is that investors do not trust managers and fear they will siphon off the spread before it reaches the pockets of the investor, through lavish salaries and the like. A problem with this theory is that some closed-end funds will "trade at a premium" — at a capitalization *above* what is justified by the underlying asset values. In the same vein, it is sometimes possible to find two closed-end funds with seemingly *similar* asset pools, one trading at a discount and the other at a premium! As an exercise, you might want to consider what sort of arbitrage strategy you would use to try to take advantage of this disparity.

§ 27.08 Securitization

There was a time when we spent a lot of energy worrying about the social role of the corporation — whether they were "too big," or "too powerful" or "changing the way the world worked." We still worry about corporations, but for most of us in many cases, the corporation is no more than a financing device — a construct of the law, created to get continuity, or transferability, or (perhaps most important) limited liability.

As the corporate form becomes more abstract, we find we can use it in more and more (perhaps unexpected) ways. In the end, we find that its very abstraction has led to the kind of social revolution that caught our attention in the first place.

To see how this can be so, start with the closed-end mutual fund. The fund is a corporation, but it is not a "business" in the sense that widgets are a business. Rather it is a structure for packaging certain (supposed) advantages. Some other "corporations" operate in the same way, even though not structured as closed-end funds. For example, the legendary investor Warren Buffett presides over a corporation called "Berkshire Hathaway." Berkshire Hathaway was once a textile company, but no longer. Now it is nothing but a device that Buffett uses to invest in other companies — and that investors use in the hope of profiting from Buffett's talent (at a price, though — a share of Berkshire Hathaway at this writing costs over $30,000).

Perhaps a more interesting case is the General Electric Company. As it happens, GE came into being a hundred years ago as a creation of the financiers — uniting several smaller electric companies to achieve economies of scale. Some of its business is still "electric," but in fact it has done poorly at some of the great new "electric" business (computers, consumer electronics). Meanwhile it has achieved great success in branching out to other business that have little of "electricity" about them (aerospace and financial services).

From here, the critical leap is to recognize that if it works for Buffett or GE, then it will work for anything. That is: in any case where there is an advantage to the corporate form, create a corporation and seize the advantage.

Possibly no case presents the principle in more dramatic form than the matter of real estate lending. Consider the classic real estate lender: he looks a bit like Jimmy Stewart. He operates at a roll-top desk in a Greek Revival building on a downtown corner across from the drug store. With only mild exaggeration, he says that he can see all his loans from his front window.

This structure has obvious advantages: the lender who meets his customers at the drug store and sees his collateral from the front window can has the best possible information about the economic and the human worth of his loan portfolio. But there is a terrible risk here: our lender is dangerously undiversified. Suppose the local factory closes. Or suppose a tornado touches down It may be a small factory or a small tornado — but to the portfolio of the small lender, it could be devastating.

Here is a way to solve these problems. Create a corporation. Raise money by selling shares. Let the corporation buy all the loans from our local bank — and from all the other local banks all over the country. Now the shareholders own, not any individual loan or loans, but participation in a loan portfolio. You have turned the local loan into an abstract "security" — hence "securitization" of the loan portfolio. The achievements in diversification are dramatic. Since diversification reduces risk, and since safe credit is cheaper than risky credit, the result is to reduce the cost of lending — or, what is the same thing, to increase the amount of money available for lending.

This structure describes the two great real estate conduits, the Federal National Mortgage Association (FNMA or "Fannie Mae") and the Government National Mortgage Association (GNMA or "Ginnie Mae"). Together, they revolutionized the housing market in the United States, making mortgage credit safer and thus cheaper and more widely available than ever it was before. Today, some two-thirds of all real estate loans are securitized.

And in recent years, securitization has moved far beyond home mortgages into every conceivable form or loan packaging. The generic name is "Asset-backed security" (ABS), and the range of asset backed securities is almost infinite. Most student loans are securitized. That is: bundled up into packages and sold off as participations in the package. Current estimates suggest that one seventh of all auto loans and one quarter of all credit card debt have been securitized. Securitization yields numerous advantages over traditional lending methods, primarily diversification of risk.

Securitization does not stop at national borders. In the international market, it has proven effective as a device for coping with third-world debt. The International Finance Corporation (IFC) was created to provide loans to private industry in the developing world. It operates in a similar fashion to the World Bank but it does not lend to governments, just the private sector. The IFC created a pool of 75 loans in 11 different countries in Latin America and Asia. No country represents more than 15 percent of the total value of the pool. The goal of the pool was to avoid concentrations of risk. So, a collapse in (say) Thailand may be buffered if there is continuing good health in (say) Mexico. Of course, no amount of diversification will save the portfolio if the collapse is *global*, and all loans go down together.

Chapter 28

Beta

> I don't know who it was who discovered water,
> but I know it wasn't a fish.
>
> —Historian of Science

§ 28.01 Introduction

In the previous chapter, we introduced the Capital Asset Pricing Model (CAPM) with an account of the Capital Market Line (CML). But there is another, older meaning of CAPM: it is "beta," the subject of this chapter.

Beta occupies a somewhat anomalous position in finance theory. Like the CML, beta offers a shorthand method for valuing investments, or for judging investor performance. The difference is that beta focuses on individual investments, while CML addresses the market as a whole. The anomaly is: if the CML analysis is right, then why do you need beta? After all, CML argues that the only relevant investment unit is the market portfolio, coupled with risk-free borrowing and lending. This approach would seem to argue that individual investment analysis is fruitless and that beta is therefore unnecessary.

Beguiling as this logic may appear, the fact is that many investors do not limit themselves to CML investing. By contrast, many do in fact offer beta data as a method of judging their performance. For this reason at least, beta remains important in practice, although it may have been superseded in theory.

§ 28.02 A Review of Some Math

It may help to begin with a review of some math. Consider the following graph:

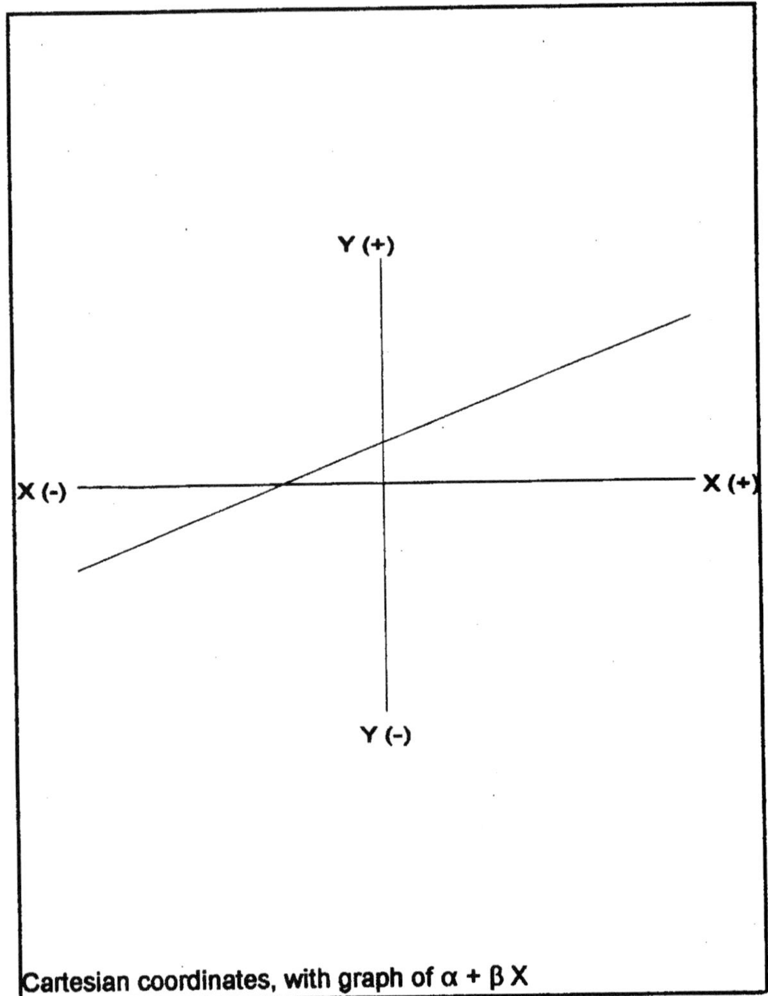

Cartesian coordinates, with graph of $\alpha + \beta X$

What does it show? It shows the *Cartesian coordinates*, together with the *graph of an equation*. The *coordinates* are the two straight lines — the north/south line marked "Y," (plus or minus), and the east/west line marked "X" (plus or minus).

The *sloped* line is the *graph of an equation*. The equation takes the form:

$$\alpha + \beta (X)$$

"Alpha" (α) represents the *intercept* — the point where the sloped line crosses the Y coordinate. Suppose the sloped line crosses the Y coordinate at a point representing four units along the Y coordinate. Then alpha = 4.

"Beta" (β) represents the *slope* of the line, also known as the *rise over the run*. By "rise," we mean the progress up along the Y-axis. By "run" we mean the progress out along the X-axis. Suppose we know that a 10-unit "run" along the X coordinate will yield a six unit "rise" along the Y coordinate. Then we know that rise/run = 6÷10 = 0.6. So, in such a case, beta = 0.6.

We treat the Y variable as *dependent upon* the X variable. That is, we assume the Y variable moves as dictated by the X variable. But once we know the slope and the intercept, then for any particular X variable, we can predict the Y variable. So, if alpha = 4 and beta = 0.6, then:

$$Y = 4 + 0.6(X)$$

So, suppose X = 12. Then:

$$Y = 4 + 0.6\ (12) = 11.2$$

To check your understanding, what if X = *minus* three?

We can understand beta, then, as a measure of *sensitivity*: it shows how sensitive the Y-variable is to the X-variable. If we say that beta is "one," then we are saying that X and Y move in lockstep: a 1 percent increase (or decrease) in X is matched by a 1 percent increase (or decrease) in Y. If beta is *less than one*, then we are saying that a 1 percent increase in X is accompanied by a less than 1 percent increase in Y. If beta is *more than one*, then we are saying that a 1 percent increase in X is accompanied by a more than 1 percent increase in Y. Betas may be *negative*. If beta is negative (say, minus one), then we are saying that an increase in X is accompanied by a *decrease* in Y (but in fact, negative beta is not important for our analysis here).

Statisticians early hit upon beta as a device for evaluating the relationship between an "independent variable" (like X) and a "dependent variable" (like Y). Indeed, one remarkable characteristic of beta is that we can express it in the language of statistics. Specifically, it can be shown that:

$$\beta = \frac{cov_{xy}}{\sigma_x^{\ 2}}$$

In words, beta equals the covariance of X and Y divided by the variance of X. We have seen an equation almost like this one before. It is the equation for correlation coefficient. Recall:

$$\rho = \frac{cov_{xy}}{\sigma_x \sigma_y}$$

Note that the numerator is the same, but the denominator is different. To help you understand the difference, consider the following example.[1] First, specify five X values and five corresponding Y values as follows:

[1] You can do this example with the DATA and STAT functions of the TI BA II Plus.

X	Y
12.5	14
11.25	12
10	10
8.75	8
7.5	6

Now, compute the mean, variance, standard deviation and beta:

	X	Y
μ	10	10
σ^2	3.125	8
σ	1.768	2.828
Covar	5	
ρ	1	
β	1.6	

Note that beta and rho are different. Now scan the data again. You will see that X and Y go up and down "together," which accounts for the correlation coefficient of one. But you will see that Y goes up "faster" and down "faster," which accounts for the higher beta. Note also that the correlation coefficient must lie between negative one and positive one. Beta has no such bound: it can be greater than positive one or less than negative one. Which one is "better?" There is no answer to that question. They each answer different questions, and so they give different answers.

Now, back to the history of finance.

§ 28.03 History

Markowitz showed that by diversification, you could reduce risk without sacrificing return (or increase return without increasing risk). This is Modern Portfolio Theory (MPT). But MPT works only if your different investments are uncorrelated. So, you must measure correlation. We have seen how to measure correlation, and we have seen that measuring correlation, even for just two or three assets, can be a headache. But our problem is only the beginning: in the market, there are hundreds, perhaps thousands of options. Markowitz wrote back in the 1950s, before modern computer power. Everyone could see that, for real portfolios, the task of measuring correlation was just too daunting. Markowitz himself showed that for a portfolio of 50 securities, you would need 1,225 calculations, and for a portfolio of 2,000 securities, you would need two million. Faced with problems like this, analysts began to search for a device to simplify or sidestep the computation problem.

MPT also presented another kind of difficulty regarding diversification. Early on, it became obvious that you could diversify away *some* risk, but not *all* risk. That is: no matter how many securities you add to your portfolio, it seems you are still stuck with a non-trivial component of risk.[2] The curve looks something like this:

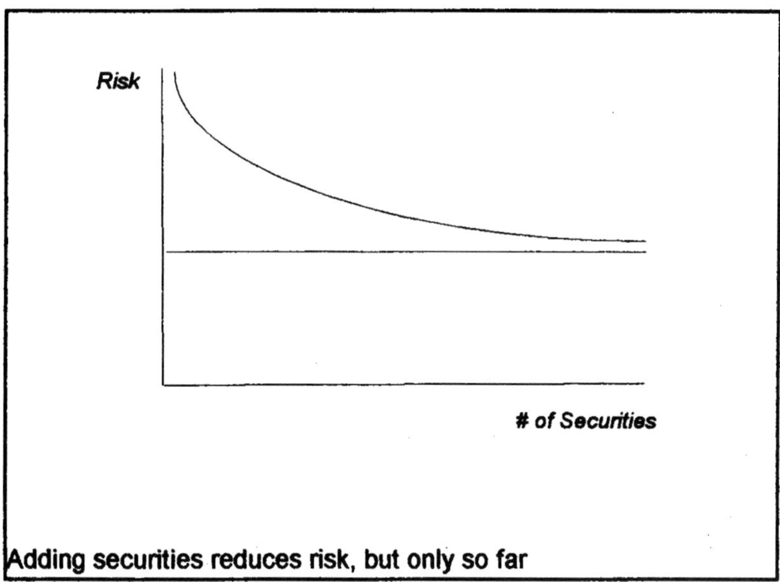

Adding securities reduces risk, but only so far

So one job for MPT was to explain that very large "residual risk" that seemed to persist even after a good deal of diversification. How to explain it? The suggested explanation is that the "residual risk" represents the risk *of the market itself* — the "water" that those "fish" swim in and that they cannot escape. No security can escape "market risk" because no security exists "outside the market." So, now it becomes important to *distinguish* between "unique risk" (also called "diversifiable risk" or, interestingly, "insurable risk") — on the one hand — and "market risk" on the other. "Market risk," then, is that risk that cannot be diversified away.

But this is a remarkable insight. We assume that all risk that *can* be diversified away *is* diversified away. If this is true, then the *only* thing we need to care about is market risk!

---

[2] The point was even sharper. The evidence showed that you did not need very many securities to exhaust all the possibilities for diversification. After you got beyond 15 or 20, the marginal return in extra diversification turned out to be quite small. Note the shape of the curve in the example.

This seems to simplify our job immensely: we measure an individual stock against the market, not against every other stock. The approach is promising, but we do need a further nuance. It may be that stocks have different degrees of sensitivity to the market — that some move up faster than the market, some more slowly. Enter beta.[3] Recall that beta measures the sensitivity of Y to X. Let X be the market, and let Y be the stock. Then beta will measure the sensitivity of any individual stock to the market as a whole.

We can translate this insight into a formula for predicting stock returns. First, as a benchmark, identify an investment as "risk-free," in the sense that it has a variance and standard deviation of zero: call the return on the risk-free investment "r_f". Then identify the weighted average return of the market as a whole: call it "r_m". We can expect the return on the market to be higher than the risk-free rate, because we can assume that the market is risky, and that investors demand a premium for risk. We can specify the difference as "$(r_m - r_f)$," "the risk premium." So, we can say that the return on the market equals the risk-free rate plus the market premium. In notation:

$$r_m = r_f + (r_m - r_f)$$

But we can refine this analysis. We defined beta as the covariance between stock and market, divided by variance of the market. To start with the benchmark case, we can ask, "what is the covariance of the market with itself?" The answer is that it must be the same as the variance "of the market." So, the beta of the market must be "one." As such, we can restate our market return formula as follows:

$$r_m = r_f + \beta\,(r_m - r_f)$$

But if this holds for beta = 1, it should hold equally well for any *other* beta. So we can generalize and define the predicted return for *any* stock as follows:

$$r_s = r_f + b\,(r_m - r_f)$$

Recalling our definition of beta, we could just as well say:

$$r_s = r_r + \frac{\sigma_{sm}}{\sigma^2_m}\,(r_m - r_f)$$

[3] The model outlined here has three, perhaps four, independent discoverers, but the most prominent is William F. Sharpe. *See* Sharpe, *A Simplified Model of Portfolio Analysis,* 9 Management Science 277 (1963).

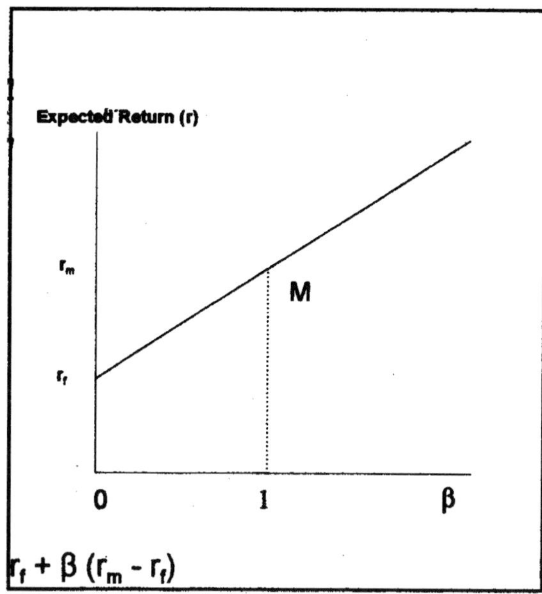

We can represent these data graphically as in the above graph. Here we plot *return* on the vertical axis, and *beta* on the horizontal axis. Note that we have graphed the risk-free investment with a beta of zero. Beta = 1 should equal the market portfolio (or any individual stock that mimics the market portfolio). Its return should be: $r_f + (r_m - r_f)$. We would predict that the return for any other stock would plot along the sloped line.

We need to be careful to avoid confusion here. This sloped line is called the Securities Market Line (SML). It plots the predicted return of securities in a market. It *looks like* the Capital Market Line (CML), which we considered earlier, and indeed it functions in much the same way. But it is different. First, consider the horizontal axis. In CML, the horizontal axis charted the standard deviation of different portfolio's own variance.

For example, returns on the stock market over the long term average around 12 percent a year. Short-term treasuries yield something around 4 percent. Using these numbers, what shall we predict as the return for a security with a beta of 0.75?

$$0.04 + 0.75(0.12 - 0.04) = 0.1 = 10\ \%$$

So, if a security has a return of 14 percent, and a beta of 0.7, we can determine whether it is overpriced or underpriced. The predicted return is:

$$r = 0.04 + 0.7(0.08) = 0.04 + 0.056 = 0.096 = 9.6\ \%$$

This tells us that our security has a percentage yield that is "too high"; that is, it is underpriced.

On these same principles, if we know the risk-free return and the returns on the stock and the market, then we can derive beta:

$$\frac{r_s - r_f}{r_m - r_f} = \beta$$

For example, suppose r_f = 4 percent, r_m = 12 percent, and r_s = 20 percent. Then:

$$\beta = 0.16 \div 0.08 = 2$$

§ 28.04 Testing Beta

Is beta "true?" We must be careful to clarify what we mean by the question. First, the math is "true" by any measure. It is as old as Descartes, and as math goes, it is fairly simple, so there can be no doubt that it is true — as math.

But our question is different. We want to know if beta provides a useful description of the real world. Is it the case that stocks diversify away all insurable risk, *and* that the only remaining risk can be measured in terms of sensitivity to market movement. The answer to that question is, not surprisingly, more muddy. In fact, a great deal of research goes into estimating betas. Researchers sift through past data for patterns, and they almost never find evidence that fits their patterns *exactly*. Instead, they use the tools of statistics to determine whether the data meet the model "well enough."

One device that statisticians use to see whether the data fit the theory "well enough" is the technique of *regression analysis*. Regression analysis undertakes to determine how well particular data fit the model. Regression analysis is too tedious to justify much attention here, but here is an (over) simplified model to give you a sketch of what regression analysis is about.

Consider LittleCo, a component of "the market." We predict four sets of returns for LittleCo and the market, as follows:

Market	LittleCo
−5	−15
−5	−5
+15	+10
+15	+30

To see what we do with these returns, look at the graph below. In this graph, we have plotted the four sets of data points (one for each set of observations). Then we plotted a line between them that represents a kind of "average" of the returns we observed. We can see that our line starts at −10 (on the vertical axis) and "rises" to plus 20 — a rise of 30 points. Meanwhile on the horizontal axis, we can observe a "run" from minus five to plus 15 — a run of 20. So beta = 30 ÷ 20 = 1.5.

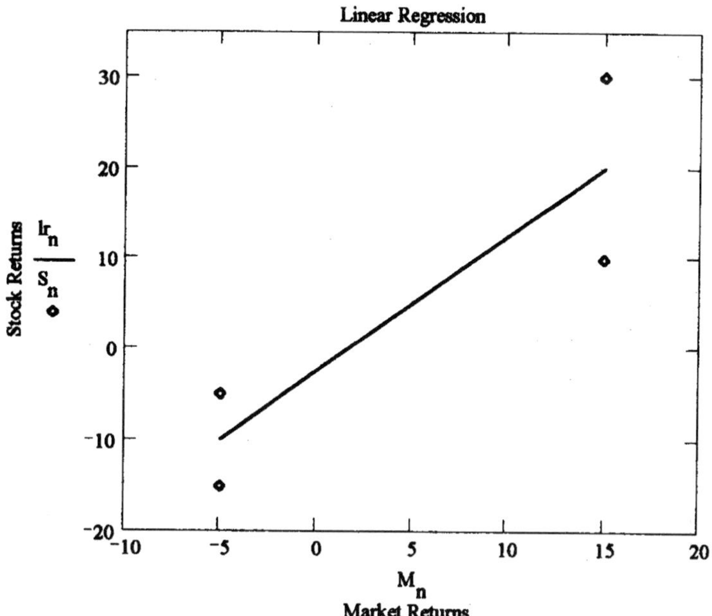

It remains to solve for alpha:

$$\alpha = \beta\ (r_m) - r_s = 1.5\ (0.15) - 0.2 = -0.025 = -2.5 \text{ percent}$$

Obviously, regression analysis is subject to error. The next job a good regression analysis will try to do is to estimate the dimension of error in the regression. To capture the error, we need to restate our original formula for specifying the line. Previously, we specified the line as:

$$Y = \alpha + \beta\ (X)$$

Now we will restate the formula as:

$$Y = \alpha + \beta\ (X) + \varepsilon$$

The Greek letter at the end is "epsilon," but think of it as "the error term," which we use to measure error in a full-scale regression analysis.

Web site: For Sharpe's own view that beta is not dead, see http://www.stanford.edu/~wfsharpe/art/djam/djam.htm.

§ 28.05 Deriving Beta from Portfolio Variance Data

We have defined beta as:

$$\frac{\sigma_{s,m}}{\sigma^2_m}$$

So far we have derived beta "in the abstract" — that is, from unweighted data on risk and return. We can also derive beta from a weighted portfolio, like the weighted portfolio we constructed back in Chapter 25 In order to do so, we must adjust to eliminate the effect of weighting.

For example, earlier, we constructed a three-asset portfolio composed of Curly, Moe, and Larry (you may want to go back and review the full discussion now). We assigned weights, standard deviations, and correlation coefficients as follows:

Weight	W_c = **50%**	W_m = **30%**	W_l = **20%**
σ	$\sigma_c = 20$	$\sigma_m = 30$	$\sigma_l = 40$
ρ	$\rho_{cm} = 0.5$	$\rho_{cl} = 0.3$	$\rho_{ml} = 0.1$

We constructed a table of "component variances that looked like this:

Curly	Moe	Larry	Total
100	45	24	169
45	81	7.2	133.2
24	7.2	64	95.2

The total variance of the portfolio is (169 + 133.2 + 95.2) = 397.4. The standard deviation is the square root of the variance, which is 19.9.

Because we have derived the data directly, we need to adjust so that weights are constant. That means we divide the covariance terms not by the variance per se but by the variance weighted to represent the proportion of the security in the portfolio. With that modification, we proceed as before. Thus, for Curly, which comprises 50 percent of our portfolio:

$$\beta_c = \frac{\sigma_{cp}}{\sigma^2_p} = \frac{169}{(0.5)(397.4)} = 0.85$$

Applying the same principles, we can compute component betas for Larry and Moe.

§ 28.06 CAPM Applied: Valuation

Every game is unique and this one is no different.

—BBC Sports Announcer

Courts occasionally find themselves analyzing evidence on CAPM in valuation cases. A good example is *Steiner Corp. v. Benninghoff*,[4] which we looked at earlier. This is the case where the Steiner family tried to squeeze out the Benninghoffs though a forced merger. In a 13-day trial, the court heard

[4] 5 F. Supp. 2d 1117 (D. Nev. 1998).

testimony on a variety of valuation techniques. To figure the cost of equity, the judge used the CAPM "beta" formula, with the five-year treasury rate as the "risk-free" rate. There was inconsistent testimony on the appropriate market premium. The court said:

> The difference appears to be based on a legitimate split in the valuation profession. The market risk premium is calculated by averaging past differences between the average market rate of return and the risk-free rate. Some analysts recommend using a "time horizon" of only the past twenty years or so, which results in a risk premium of 5%, while others recommend using all available data going back as far as 1926, when the necessary data began to be accumulated and processed. While valid arguments exist on both sides of this issue, we have not attempted to resolve the entire debate. We simply find that the 5% figure is appropriate to use in this case, given that experts from both sides testified to that effect. . . .

As to beta, experts for both sides gave an opinion based on "comparable" companies, but the judge complained that "very little explanation regarding this process was presented in any of the experts' reports." For himself, the judge reasoned:

> Steiner is a very risk-averse company. Given the extremely conservative management style that Steiner was so quick to point out in other contexts, the fact that Steiner has a well-diversified client base, a 100-plus-year history of steady growth, banks willing to lend it money (on a short-term basis) at LIBOR plus ¼%, and would appear to be larger than most of its publicly traded competitors, the beta for Steiner should be near the low end of the range. In other words, Steiner's attempts at trial to portray itself as a risky little private company beset by various financial problems was not very successful.

This is interesting, because it seems to regard beta as function of *firm-specific* risk. Readers of this book will recognize that such an approach is out of tune with standard theory. That is: standard theory treats firm-specific risk as diversifiable and therefore largely irrelevant, leaving beta to measure non-diversifiable systematic risk. It would be fascinating to know whether the judge misunderstood the testimony on the point or whether the experts never presented the classic version in the first place.

In re Radiology Associates, Inc.[5] is another case in which the court chose CAPM to estimate an interest rate. As the risk-free component, the witness used the long-term U.S. government bond rate, which was 8.82 percent. It is interesting to speculate on how, if at all, she justified the use of the long rate instead of some more common shorter rate — or whether, indeed, she was challenged on the point at all. The t-bill rate at the time was about 5.23 percent.

CAPM also emerged as a tool in tariff-based rate regulation, where the courts or the regulator sought to determine a "fair rate of return" on capital.

---

[5] 611 A.2d 485 (1991).

Cases like this are probably fading into history along with rate regulation generally.[6]

On at least one occasion, in the case of a small, closely held company, the U.S. Tax Court has refused to use CAPM:

> We do not believe that CAPM and WACC are the proper analytical tools to value a small, closely held corporation with little possibility of going public. CAPM is a financial model intended to explain the behavior of publicly traded securities that has been subjected to empirical validation using only historical data of the two largest U.S. stock markets. . . . Contrary to the assumptions of CAPM, the market for stock in a closely held corporation like FIC is not efficient, is subject to substantial transaction costs, and does not offer liquidity. . .[7]

The judge may have been influenced by the fact that he did seem to have much confidence in the particular expert witness to begin with.[8]

§ 28.07 Contrast: Hedging

We have defined diversification as a device for reducing risk. There is another way to reduce risk and that is simply to pay someone else to take it. You find someone else with a different risk tolerance from your own, and give him money to induce him to take your risk.

The joy of diversification was that you got to reduce your risk without sacrificing return. Hedging doesn't come so cheap. In a hedge, you get to reduce risk, but only at the price of return. To take a silly example, consider your client, Shorty, who owns a share of IBM stock. He decides he can't bear the uncertainties that come with stock ownership, but he wants to keep the stock. Here is a solution: short the stock. Keep the IBM, but agree to transfer it later in exchange for a sum certain paid now.

Shorty has accomplished his objective: he's traded uncertainty for certainty and he's got rid of all his risk. Of course he has got rid of all his opportunity too. Indeed he could have accomplished the same result — and more cheaply, too — if he had simply sold the stock in the first place. That's why it is silly: sure, it accomplishes the result, but no one would ever do it.

Here is a more familiar hedge. Your client, Soia, raises soybeans. It's a long growing season and she has fixed obligations to the landowner for lease payments, and to the bank for interest on her equipment loan. She can't bear the uncertainty of not knowing what the price of soybeans will be on delivery day. So she makes a contract at a price fixed today to deliver the soybeans when the crop comes in. If the price goes up, she'll watch someone else reap the profits. But if it goes down, at least she gets to keep her sale price.

Commodities trading, like Soia's soybean deal, is a well-established and fairly well-understood form of hedging (though it is mostly beyond the scope

---

[6] *But see* Alabama Gas Corp. v. Alabama Public Service Comm., 425 So. 2d 430 (Ala. 1982).

[7] Furman, Donor T.C. Memo 1998-157.

[8] *See* In re Pullman Construction Industries Inc., 107 B.R. 909, 923 (Bankr. N.D. Ill. 1989); In re Jartran, Inc., 44 B.R. 331, 370 (Bankr. N.D. Ill. 1984); In re The Valuation Proceedings Under Sections 303(c) and 306 of the Regional Rail Reorganization Act of 1973, 531 F. Supp. 1191, 1233 (Regional Rail Reorg. Ct. 1981).

of this book). The number and variety of futures contracts has mushroomed in recent years. Notably, with the growth in international trade, merchants have felt the need to protect themselves against the risk of currency fluctuation. This currency risk led to an explosion in the trading of currency futures. Managers have also learned that they need to manage the *duration* of their portfolios. The need to control duration led to the creation of a market in interest-rate futures. The market for interest rate swaps can be understood as a hedge market also. The trading of options, which we deal with later in Part III below, can be understood as a hedge market, at least in part.

The line between hedging and diversification it not always clear-cut. The person who accepts money to bear a risk may do so because he has a higher risk tolerance. Or he may do so because he can exploit opportunities for diversification. The specific motive may not matter in a particular case, but the difference is still there.

Part III

Leverage and Contingent Claims

Chapter 29

Terminology

You go into a strange poker game
you look around for the sucker.
If you don't see him, get out.
Because you're it.

—Efficient Market Hypothesis (strong form)

§ 29.01 Leverage

Here we begin the final part of our inquiry. The term, "leverage," may be a bit misleading, because we are stretching its common definition. But we need something to unify the material in this part. And at the end of the day, we will see that "leverage" in fact works pretty well.

We begin with a straightforward example. VentureCo is a small company with a promising investment opportunity. But the opportunity will take money and VentureCo doesn't have any cash on hand. To go forward, it has two choices. It can borrow — issue notes or bonds or such. Or it can sell shares — issue new equity.

Which should VentureCo choose? We can't answer that in the abstract: the best we can say is that VentureCo should do whichever is cheapest. But there is an important practical distinction. The difference is that debt gets paid before equity. Equity gets a share if and only if there is anything left after debt is paid. The jargon term here is "leverage": we say that VentureCo is "highly leveraged" if it has a lot of debt, and "unleveraged" if it has no debt at all.

One inescapable fact of leverage is that whenever there is leverage, equity is more risky than when there is none. There is nothing inherently scandalous in this: presumably equity gets a higher return, to compensate it for its higher risk. On the other hand, leverage changes the stakes of the game.

§ 29.02 Contingent Claims

After exploring some of the implications of leverage on the corporate balance sheet, we move on to a more spacious plane. As a point of departure, note that equity is a "contingent claim" — contingent in the sense that its value depends on the value of another claim, and also in that its value depends on the size of the debt claim.

Beginning the day before yesterday (actually 1973) scholars and practitioners have revolutionized our understanding of contingent claims. They have changed the way we think about almost everything in finance. The work is not yet done (which is one reason why we have to stretch the meaning of a word just to get a name for a segment. But it is nonetheless possible to get the flavor of what they are up to.

Chapter 30

Leverage and Beta

I figure I have as much chance
of winning the lottery
if I don't play as if I do.

—Fran Lebowitz

§ 30.01 Introduction

We now want to apply our understanding of the Capital Asset Pricing Model and tie it together with some of our previous learning about capital budgeting. Perhaps more importantly, we want to introduce the distinction between *asset* risk and *financial* risk. That is, for the first time we will pay direct attention to the method by which a project is financed, and to the effect of the choice of financing decisions on the enterprise as a whole.

We consider the application of beta analysis in two special contexts. First, we will see that beta should be applied to analyze *projects* as well as *companies*. Then we make the point that the beta associated with a particular *asset* may not be the same as the beta associated with a *stake* in that asset — because of the structure of the financing package.

§ 30.02 Company Cost v. Project Cost

To begin, we need to distinguish the *company* cost of capital from the *project* cost.

Clara is the CEO of your client, WidgeCo, a maker of widgets. From market data, Clara knows that the risk-free rate is 5 percent and that the market premium is 8 percent. She knows that the beta for widget firms is 1.2. This means that she had better produce a return of 0.05 + 1.2 (0.08) = 0.146 = 14.6 percent.

She locates new investment opportunity in the widget business that offers 15 percent. Should she put WidgeCo into it? It depends. *If the project is in the widget business*, the answer would seem to be "yes." Since the project is in the same business, the beta must be the same, and the required rate of return must be the same. We have, in effect, defined the required rate of return on investments of this sort as 14.6 percent; other things being equal, an investment yielding 15 percent has a positive NPV and will add to shareholder wealth.

But on inquiry we learn that this new opportunity is not in widgets. Rather, what we have here is a chance to open a new mine for the extraction of bathtub grout. In principle, we can analyze the project the same as before, but we have an "unknown." That is: before we can decide whether this project satisfies the required rate of return, we have to know the beta for projects in bathtub grout.

Suppose the beta on bathtub grout is 8 percent. Then the required rate of return is 0.05 + 0.8(0.08) = 0.114 = 11.4 percent. Since the required return is only 11.4 percent and this project offers 15 percent, the project looks like a wonderful opportunity (too good to be true, perhaps, but let it pass). On the other hand, if the beta is 1.3, then the required rate is 0.05 + 1.3(0.08) = 0.154 = 15.4 percent. Since the required rate is lower than the expected rate, we want to stay away from it. The moral of the story is that in weighing a new project, we want to know the beta of the new project. Our company cost of capital is irrelevant.

A corollary of this first point is that it may be perfectly defensible to take projects with a return lower than the company cost of capital, so long as the return corresponds to the risk. Consider BlivetCo, a seller of blivets. The industry beta for blivets is 2; the risk-free rate is 10 percent and the market premium is 10 percent. By definition, the required rate of return 30 percent. BlivetCo has indeed been garnering a 30 percent return from its blivet business. BlivetCo has decided to move half of its assets into risk-free government bonds, yielding 10 percent. Since its aggregate return will be the weighted sum of its component returns, we can expect its overall return to fall from 30 percent to 20 percent.

Has BlivetCo harmed its shareholders? It has not. Even though the aggregate return has fallen, its risk has fallen to match.

§ 30.03 Asset Beta v. Financing Beta

Suppose our company wants to do a new project. If it goes "outside" to raise the money, it has two choices: borrow the money (debt) or issue stock (equity). If the firm is all-equity financed, then the beta of the investor stake is the same as the beta of the company. But if the company is partly financed by debt, then debt and equity bear different risks and consequently entail different betas. Recall that in distribution *debt always comes first*. You can understand this if you recall what happens to someone who buys a house for $300,000, with $30,000 down and the rest borrowed from the bank. If the value goes up to $330,000, the investor has doubled her money. If it goes down to $270,000, she has lost everything. The equity position is thus more risky than the debt position — and the more debt, the more risky the equity.

To describe this point mathematically, start by recalling that if we owned *all* of the debt and *all* of the equity, then we would own the right to *all* of the returns. Our total return would be the weighted sum of our component returns:

$$r_{\mathrm{a}} = w_{\mathrm{d}}\, r_{\mathrm{d}} + w_{\mathrm{e}}\, r_{\mathrm{e}}$$

Restated:

$$r_a = \left(\frac{d}{d+e}\right) r_d + \left(\frac{e}{d+e}\right) r_e$$

Since beta uniquely defines return, our total beta would also be the weighted sum of the component betas:

$$\beta_a = \left(\frac{d}{d+e}\right) \beta_d + \left(\frac{e}{d+e}\right) \beta_e$$

But in the ordinary case, asset beta is the "given," and equity beta will be the "unknown." We can easily rearrange our formula to isolate equity beta:

$$\beta_e = \beta_a + \frac{d}{e} (\beta_a - \beta_d)$$

In a large, conservatively managed company, the debt beta may be zero. So, suppose a company where the asset beta is 1.1 and the equity stake is 70 percent and the debt beta is zero. Then:

$$\beta_e = 1.1 + (3/7)\ (1.1) = 1.57$$

In the typical case, where debt beta is zero and where asset beta is a "given," the only variable defining equity beta will be the size of the equity stake. Note also that in high-leverage cases, where debt beta "goes positive," the result will be actually to *reduce* the riskiness of the equity by moving some of the risk from equity to debt.

§ 30.04 Using Beta

We use beta to determine the required rate of return for a *project* at the company level, and for the *equity* at the investor level. Say we want to invest in widgets. We know the risk-free rate is 12 percent and the market premium is 9 percent. We know that the beta of competing widget companies is 1.32, and that their average debt-to-equity ratio was 20 percent. To determine widget beta, we first need to "deleverage" to get the beta of a pure play without the complications of debt. We know that:

$$\beta_a = \beta_e\left(\frac{e}{e+d}\right) + \beta_d\left(\frac{d}{e+d}\right)$$

Supposing debt beta to be zero, then:

$$\beta_a = (1.32)\left(\frac{1}{1.2}\right) = 1.1$$

The asset return would be:

$$\begin{aligned} r_a &= r_f + \beta_a(r_m - r_f) \\ &= 12 + (1.1)(9) \\ &= 21.9 \text{ percent} \end{aligned}$$

But shareholder beta for a leveraged company will be different from asset beta, because equity behind debt is more risky than equity alone. We know that:

$$\beta_e = \beta_a + \frac{d}{e}\ (\beta_a - \beta_d)$$

So, if the company is 30 percent leveraged, the required return of equity must increase from the all-equity situation because now equity faces greater risk:

$$\beta_e = 1.1 + (3/7 \times 1.1) = 1.57$$

The required rate of return on equity in a leveraged company is:

$$\begin{aligned} r_e &= r_f + \beta_e(r_m - r_f) \\ &= 12 + (1.57)(9) = 26.13\% \end{aligned}$$

Chapter 31

How Skeeter Almost Got It Right: Leverage and Return

I don't have to outrun the bear,
I just have to outrun you.
—Woodland Wisdom

§ 31.01 Introduction

Skeeter, your old college roommate, has just started work in the Investor Relations Office at WidgetCo. Although he cheerfully admits he does not know much of anything about finance, he has a pleasant manner that soothes customers on the telephone. Meanwhile, he figures the new job will give him a chance to play catch-up with some of his classmates and their sparkling new MBAs. So, you are not surprised by his enthusiasm when he comes charging through your door, eager to tell you about his latest insight.

"It's amazing," he says, "I cannot understand how everyone overlooked this so far."

You raise an eyebrow, which is all the encouragement he needs to continue.

"Last year, we had earnings of $100.[1] We are a highly stable company, so we pay it all out to shareholders. We have 10 shares, each selling for $100, which implies a market capitalization of $1,000. Shareholders, then, get $10 a share, which translates into a rate of return of 10 percent."

Skeeter pauses to let you admire these marvels.

"But," he begins again, "we can *borrow* money at eight percent."

He pauses for dramatic effect. The barest flicker on your forehead is enough to set him off again.

"Don't you see?" he continues, "We should *borrow* $500 in perpetuity. Then we will use the $500 to buy back five shares. We will have to pay $40 a year in debt service. That leaves us $60 a year to distribute among our five shares of stock. At 10 percent, that means that we have increased the value of a share from $100 to $120, and the total market capitalization from $500 to $600 — a 20 percent gain. It is like magic! I have asked for an appointment with the CEO so I can tell him all about it first thing in the morning!"

But even has he spoke, Skeeter's expression turned forlorn.

"There is only one puzzle," he said sadly.

Again, an eyebrow is enough.

"I mean," he continued, "if it works for five shares, why shouldn't we go the whole way? Why not retire 10 shares and borrow $1,000? We will pay $80

[1] To ease your comprehension, Skeeter graciously knocks off the trailing zeroes.

a year in interest. That leaves us \$20 a year in return on" — and here he looked genuinely baffled — "well, on no investment at all."

Skeeter sounds like a good kid, and the chances are he will figure out before making a fool of himself in front of the CEO that \$20 ÷ 0 = an infinite return, which is too good to be true even in the widget business. To start with his last, absurd, example: if WidgetCo is financed with *all* debt and *no* equity, then the debt *is the equity*, and will demand a corresponding return — in this case, 10 percent. There can be no triumph of form over substance here; equity is the one who bears the equity risk, no matter what the name.

As to the less extreme case, if Skeeter is in error, he has the excuse of good company. Many investors, older and wiser than he, have believed that you could increase firm value by increasing leverage (at least up to a point). Old-time financial analysts, including the Securities and Exchange Commission, expended valuable resources trying to identify the "optimal" debt-equity ratio — i.e., the mix of debt and equity that would maximize firm value.

Enter the great revolutionaries of modern finance theory, Franco Modigliani and Merton Miller (MM). You may remember MM from our discussion of dividends in Chapter 19 above. MM argued that, under clean-test-tube assumptions, *it should make no difference* whether the firm pays dividends. MM also stood finance theory on its head by making essentially the same argument with regard to leverage.[2] To put it in functional terms, the value of the firm is the value of the assets, and you cannot change the value of the "liability/net-worth" side of the balance sheet by monkeying around with the asset side.

MM understood, of course, that a change in leverage may change the *gross* returns payable to shareholders. Thus, in Skeeter's first example above, Skeeter showed how to increase the payout from \$10 a share to \$12, but what Skeeter overlooked (as MM argue) is that we have also changed the *risk* of the equity investment.

Recall the first rule of leverage: equity comes behind debt. Equity of a leveraged company is always more risky than equity of an unleveraged company, because debt gets paid first, leaving equity to get paid if (and only if) there is enough to trickle down. Equity investors, faced with a higher risk, will demand a higher rate of return, and a higher rate of return translates into a lower share price. For example, suppose the rate on WidgetCo equity rose from 10 percent (unleveraged) to 12 percent (leveraged). Then the value of a (leveraged) WidgetCo share would be \$12 ÷ (0.12) = \$10, just as before.

Another way of putting it is to say that Skeeter's mistake was to treat *equity* return as a constant, letting *asset* return vary. We know that when WidgetCo is all equity financed, then $r_A = r_E = 10$ percent. Skeeter seems to assume that the return on debt and the return on equity are "given," and that the return on assets is derived from these other two. Skeeter is assuming an equation like this:

2 Franco Modigliani & Merton H. Miller, *The Cost of Capital, Corporate Finance and the Theory of Investment,* 38 Amer. Econ. Rev. 261 (1958).

$$r_A = r_E[E \div (D + E)] + r_D[D \div (D + E)]$$

For the firm that is half debt, then:

$$r_A = 0.1[\$500 \div \$1{,}000] + 0.08[\$500 \div \$1{,}000] = 0.09 = 9 \text{ percent}$$

But MM argue that *asset* value remains constant, while *equity* value may fluctuate. The true equation, according to their argument, is as follows:

$$r_E = r_A + \frac{D}{E}(r_A - r_D)$$

Again, using WidgetCo numbers:

$$r_E = 0.1 + \frac{\$500}{\$500}(0.1 - 0.08) = 0.12 = 12 \textit{ percent}$$

Note that this is the same number we used in the illustration above.

§ 31.02 An Arbitrage Proof of MM

There are many ways to demonstrate the MM argument. One is to consider the possibility of *arbitrage*. We have seen that if two identical assets bear different prices, then there is a profit for an instant (no-risk (arbitrage) profit), but that such profit does not exist except in fleeting moments of transition.

We can apply arbitrage analysis to the MM insight. Take the case of Imogen, an investor, who is thinking about a flutter on Skeeter's WidgetCo. As a benchmark, suppose she can buy *the whole company* — which is to say, all of the equity, and (if there is any), all of the debt. In that case, surely, her only concern will be the asset return, and that she will accept an aggregate rate of 10 percent. If WidgetCo earns $100 a year (as above), and if it is all equity financed, she will be willing to pay $1,000 for all the equity.

But suppose WidgetCo is financed with $500 of debt at 8 percent. She can get $40 of the cash flow for $500 by purchasing debt. To get the other $60, she must buy all the equity. But it cannot be that she will be willing to pay more than $500 for the equity; otherwise, she would be paying different prices for the same cash flows, violating the arbitrage rule.

We can elaborate this point by showing what would happen if there were in fact two companies with different values for the same return. Consider these two firms, UnCo and LevCo.

	LevCo	**UnCo**
Assets	$1,000	$1,100
Liabilities	$0	$500
Net Worth	$1,000	$600

Each firm earns $100 per year and the cost of debt is 8 percent. There are ten shares of UnCo worth $1000 ÷ 10 = $100, and five shares of LevCo worth

$600 ÷ 5 = $120 each. Suppose Imogen owns one share of LevCo. This means she has a right to a "coupon" of the following value:

$$(0.2)(\$100) - (0.2)(\$40) = \$20 - \$8 = \$12$$

Or, a 10 percent return, just as we said before.

Is there another strategy that lets her mimic that return? There is. Let her:

- *sell* her share for the market price of $120;
- *borrow* $100 at the 8 percent rate;
- *buy* enough of UnCo to give her the same return she had in LevCo. To get the right cash flow, she will need to buy two shares, at a total cost of $200;
- *pay* $8 in interest on the loan; and
- *retain* the $12 difference between her return on UnCo and her debt service.

Perhaps you have already spotted the arbitrage problem here — the point is that she has the same cash flow that she had before, but her out of pocket cost is only $100 — a saving of $20. So we have identical assets at different prices. The inconsistency cannot last. We can expect either the price of LevCo to fall, or the price of UnCo to fall, until the prices are in equilibrium.

§ 31.03 Another Proof of MM: Homemade Leverage

We can also demonstrate the MM argument by showcasing the potential role for *homemade leverage.* In fact, we used homemade leverage in our arbitrage example above, but we can explore it more completely here.

We have already seen that if the investor could buy *the whole of the company*, then she should not care whether her returns come via equity or via debt: she gets 100 percent either way. If this is true for the aggregate, then it must hold true for the components. So, suppose Imogen wanted *just 20 percent* of the cash flows. If the WidgetCo is an all equity firm, she should be able to get it by buying 20 percent of the securities outstanding. If WidgetCo is financed half with debt, then she should be able to get the same return by buying 20 percent of the equity and 20 percent of the debt.

But this example suggests other possibilities. Suppose WidgetCo is all equity financed and priced as above. Suppose Imogen would be willing to buy at that price, but would like it even better leveraged — i.e., would be willing to buy the residual equity when the equity stands behind $500 of debt. If the company has chosen *not* to leverage, Imogen can still *homemake* her leverage, by *borrowing* $500 on her own account at the 8 percent rate. She then buys *all* the (unleveraged) equity, using $500 of her own money plus the $500 she borrowed. At the end of the year, she gets $100 in earnings. She uses $40 to pay the interest on her 8 percent debt and pockets $60, giving her a return identical to the return she would have received had the company leveraged and she bought the leveraged equity.

Remarkably, the analysis works the same way the other way around. Suppose WidgetCo is indeed 50 percent leveraged, so shareholders get an aggregate $60 return. Suppose Imogen does not want to bear that kind of risk. One way to avoid it is to invest $500 in WidgetCo, and then to invest another $500 at the 8 percent rate. In this case, her returns at the end of a year will be $60 from stock plus $40 from her 8 percent investment, which is what she would have got had the WidgetCo operated debt free and she bought all the securities.

The point is that Imogen has been able to select her own leverage pattern independent of the company. In the former case, she was able to “leverage up” (by risk-free borrowing) and in the latter, to “leverage down” (by running the same process in reverse).

As before, if this sort of homemade leverage is possible in the aggregate, then the possibility will determine the aggregate price of the securities. And since each share of WidgetCo stock is identical to every other share of WidgetCo stock (and bond to bond), the price that holds for the aggregate must dictate the price that holds for any fragment. So, if Imogen can achieve these homemade leveraged results by buying the whole company, then she ought to be able to achieve the same sort of results for borrowing a percentage. For example, suppose she only a 1 percent slice. If the company is all equity financed, she buys one percent of the equity. If the company is leveraged, and she wants an unleveraged investment, then she buys 1 percent of the equity and one percent of the debt. If it is unleveraged and she can tolerate a 50 percent leverage ratio, then she borrows a sum equal to half of 1 percent of the equity. She then matches this sum with her own money and buys the 1 percent.

Web sites: Modigliani gives a cheerful and high-spirited account of how he and Miller revolutionized finance:

http://www.coloradocollege.edu/Publications/Speeches/modigliani.html.

Miller weighs in at:

http://www.dfafunds.com/The_Firm/About_Dimensional/Philosophy/History/Chicago/miller.html.

Chapter 32

Leverage and Taxes

What you lose on the merry-go-round,
you make up on the swings.

—Carnival Wisdom

§ 32.01 Introduction

In the previous chapter, we considered the MM leverage irrelevance thesis. We can summarize it in two propositions:

- The market value of a firm is independent of its capital structure.
- The expected rate of return of an unleveraged firm increases in proportion to its leverage.

MM well understood that their model worked only under the assumption of "clean-test-tubes." Thus, for example, they assumed there were no tax distortions. A tax distortion is introduced any time the government taxes returns to debt at a rate different from the rate it imposes on returns to equity.

In fact, as we shall see, there are tax effects. The purpose of this chapter is to explore the consequences of tax distortions on the original MM hypothesis. The key point was that if the government subsidizes debt, you may get an absolute increase in value by leveraging up.

§ 32.02 Tax Effects

What remains of this discussion is to be more specific about what we mean when we talk about a *tax effect.* Our point of departure is that under present law, the corporation pays taxes on income before paying dividends. But it can deduct interest on debt prior to computing its taxes. Since debt and equity are two alternative devices for raising money, a tax deduction is a kind of subsidy for one capital formation device (debt), but not for the other (equity). This debt subsidy is worth something; you can value it and put it on the balance sheet. Thus, as we will see, by utilizing the debt deduction or the "tax shield," we accomplish exactly what MM have said that we cannot do — we change the asset side of the balance sheet by changing the liability side.

To show this more concretely, hypothesize two firms, completely alike except in capital structure: one is financed all by equity; the other is financed by both equity and debt. Each firm has $100,000 in assets.

Since net worth equals assets minus liabilities, the net worth of the all-equity firm must be ($100,000 − 0), or $100,000. Let us suppose the company has $12,000 in earnings before interest and taxes (EBIT) available for distribution to shareholders, and that it pays corporate taxes at a rate of 34 percent (T_c). What will be the cash flow to the equity owners (CF_E). That is, in the all-equity firm, what is the net payout to equity? The formula is:

$$CF_E = EBIT\ (1 - T_c)$$

Plugging in the numbers:

$$CF_E = \$12{,}000\ (1 - 0.34) = \$7{,}920$$

So, \$7,920 is available for distribution to shareholders. Now let us look at a company which is financed half by equity and half by debt (D) with an annual interest rate of 8 percent (r_D). Recall that the company gets to deduct interest payments from taxable income, so the company gets to pay this money directly to debtholders without a tax. Under these assumptions, the cash flow to the creditors (CF_D) must be:

$$CF_D = r_D\ D$$

In our case:

$$(\$50{,}000)(0.08) = \$4{,}000$$

Now we need to recompute the payout to equity, taking into account the senior debt. Since debt gets paid first, the cash flow to equity of a leveraged company would be:

$$CF_E = [EBIT - (r_D\ D)]\ (1 - T_c)$$

In our case, where the company had \$12,000 available before interest and taxes, the cash flow to equity would be:

$$CF_E = [\$12{,}000 - \$4{,}000](1 - 0.34) = \$5{,}280$$

Adding the payout to equity to the interest that goes to debt we get the total payout to all stakeholders:

$$\text{Total payout} = CF_E + CF_D = \$4{,}000 + \$5{,}280 = \$9{,}280$$

Note that the tax *saving* that arises from using debt can be measured by multiplying the cash flow to debt by the corporate tax rate, yielding the amount of tax that *would have been paid* if the company had paid the money to equity. This is the *tax shield* (TS). We can represent it as:

$$TS = T_c r_D D = (0.34)(0.08)(\$50{,}000) = \$1{,}360$$

If we were to receive this every year in perpetuity, we could value it as a perpetuity. Call it "TSP." Use the 8 percent rate. So:

$$TS_P = \frac{TS}{r} = \frac{\$1{,}360}{(0.08)} = \$17{,}000$$

Note also that the difference between the payout to the stakeholders in this leveraged company (V_L) and the payout to stakeholders in the unleveraged company (V_U) is:

$$V_L - V_U = \$9{,}280 - \$7{,}920 = \$1{,}360$$

In other words, the leveraged company yields to the investors the value that they would have received from an unleveraged company, together with the value of the tax shield:

$$V_L = EBIT(1 - T_c) + T_C r_D D$$

These equations define the cash flows to investors' returns for a single year. Using familiar principles, we can now calculate the value of the firm. For example, for the all-equity firm, if the initial payout is to be repeated indefinitely, and we let r_A equal the "return on assets," (the rate of return on equity for an all-equity firm), then the firm value is:

$$V_U = \frac{EBIT\,(1 - T_C)}{r_A}$$

We know that the incremental value of a debt payment through tax relief is $T_C r_D D$. So, the value of a perpetuity of such payments must be:

$$\frac{T_C r_D D}{r_D}$$

But in this equation, the r_D term would cancel out, so the value of the debt perpetuity must be:

$$T_C D$$

Thus, the value of the leveraged firm must be the value of the unleveraged firm as a perpetuity, plus the value of the tax shield in perpetuity, or:

$$V_L = \frac{EBIT(1 - T_C)}{r_A} + T_C D$$

More simply:

$$V_L = V_U + T_c D$$

Let us flesh out these equations with some numbers. Suppose Lance is considering the formation of a new company to make convex defenestrators. He expects the project to yield $200,000 per year in perpetuity. Since the corporate tax rate is 34 percent, this implies an after-tax cash flow of $132,000 per year. The appropriate discount rate for such a cash flow is 11 percent. This suggests a firm value (in an all-equity setting) of $1.2 million. The corporation can borrow up to $500,000 of senior debt. What will be the value of such a leveraged company? Plugging in to the equations above:

$$\frac{(\$200{,}000)(0.66)}{0.11} + (0.34)\ (\$500{,}000) = \$1{,}370{,}000$$

In other words, the company will enjoy a tax shield of ($1,370,000 – $1,200,000), or $170,000. But there is a curiosity here: we computed the value of the debt shield *without knowing the rate of return on the debt.* The relationship will hold, in any case, unless the rate of return on debt is *higher* than the rate of return on equity — but debt is, by nature, less risky than equity and thus will yield a lower return.

§ 32.03 Rate of Return

Recall that earlier we saw that the rate of return on equity in a leveraged firm will be higher than the rate of return on equity in an unleveraged firm. We now need to adjust this formulation to account for taxes. We won't burden you with the algebra here, but it can be shown that the correct formulation is:

$$r_E = r_A + (1 - T_c)\,\frac{D}{E}\,(r_A - r_D)$$

Note that we *do* need to know the rate of return on debt in order to solve for equity return. For example, using the above numbers and a rate of return on debt of 7 percent, then: r_E:

$$r_E = 0.11 + (0.66) \frac{5}{8.7} (0.11 - 0.07) = 0.12517 = 12.517\%$$

Absent the tax shield, the return on equity would have been 15 percent, so this is a substantial improvement. To check this formula, recall the formula for the value of equity in a leveraged firm. Adjusting for taxes, the formula would be:

$$V_E = \frac{(EBIT - r_D D)(1 - T_C)}{r_E}$$

In our example:

$$\frac{[\$200{,}000 - ([0.07][\$500{,}000])]\ (0.66)}{0.12517}$$

Or $870,000: ($1,370,000 − $500,000), which checks.

§ 32.04 Personal Taxes

Of course, that is not the end of the story. Before the investor gets to put the dividend into his pocket, he must pay personal taxes. So, to show what reaches the pocket of the investor, we begin with our previous formulas and add a factor for personal tax, T_p. We define the factor as $(1 - T_p)$. So for the all equity firm, the cash flow to equity after tax (CF_{EAT}) is:

$$CF_{EAT} = EBIT\ (1 - T_c)\ (1 - T_p)$$

For example, revising our previous example (where earnings were $12,000 and the corporate tax rate was 34 percent), suppose the personal tax rate is 28 percent. Then:

$$CF_{EAT} = (\$12{,}000)\ (0.66)\ (0.72) = \$5{,}702.40$$

For the leveraged firm, recall that we deduct interest before figuring corporate tax. In our earlier example, we set debt at $50,000 at 8 percent. Continuing to use the 28 percent personal tax rate, then the cash flow to debt after tax (CF_{DAT}) is:

$$CF_{DAT} = r_D\ D\ (1 - T_p) = (0.08)(\$50{,}000)\ (1 - 0.28) = \$2{,}880$$

Finally, for the equity of the *leveraged* firm, we must rework our earlier formula:

$$CF_{EAT} = [EBIT - (r_D\ D)]\ [1 - T_c][1 - T_P]$$

$$CF_{EAT} = [\$12{,}000 - (0.08)(\$50{,}000)][1 - 0.34][1 - 0.28] = \$3{,}801.60$$

So, the aggregate cash flow from the leveraged firm to the pockets of all investors is:

$$CF_{DAT} + CF_{EAT} = \$2{,}880 + \$3{,}801.60 = \$6{,}681.60$$

$$V_L - V_U = \$6{,}681.60 - 5{,}702.40 = \$979.20$$

If this were a perpetuity, you could capitalize it just as we did before. Use the rate of return net of *personal* income taxes, $r(1 - T_p)$. Note that this gives us a value of $17,000, which is the same number when we made a perpetuity out of the tax shield ignoring personal taxes.

§ 32.05 Tax-Exempt Bonds

Suppose you are in a 31 percent tax bracket, and you can buy an ordinary corporate bond that pays 12 percent interest. Your effective yield is:

$$0.12(1 - 0.31) = 0.0828 = 8.28\ \%$$

Now, compare this bond with a "municipal bond," i.e., a bond issued by a local government. Interest on municipal bonds is not subject to federal income tax. Not surprisingly, therefore, investors are willing to pay higher prices for otherwise comparable income streams when they come from "munis" than when they come from corporate bonds. Call the return on the corporate bond "r_c". Call the return on the muni "r_m". Since the investor would get r_m tax-free, we would expect:

$$r_c\ (1 - t) = r_m$$

Rearranging, if we know the investor's marginal tax rate, and her required rate of return for a muni, we can infer what she must get from a corporate bond in order to get a comparable return. That is:

$$r_m \div (1 - t) = r_c$$

So, if the municipal bond has an effective yield of 4 percent and the tax rate is 31 percent, then the comparable corporate rate is 0.04?0.69 = 0.058 = 5.8 percent.

§ 32.06 Why?

Surely one of the oddest distinctions we have met in this book is the rule on deductibility of corporate expenses. The enterprise may deduct interest from otherwise taxable income as a business expense. Yet there is no comparable deduction for dividends. To anyone schooled in even the barest rudiments of finance, this makes sense. After all, returns to creditors and returns to shareholders are both returns on capital. You might want to tax both, or neither. But what possible basis can there be for taxing one and not the other? The answer appears to be a muddle of conceptual and error and chance.[1]

At least part of the answer appears to lie in the old-fashioned notion of a corporation. Shareholders were thought of as the "owners" of the corporation, and creditors were thought of as "strangers," with whom the owners dealt only at arm's length. You can see this view still reflected today in the accountant's conception of the income statement; see § 12.03 above.

A second source is the problem of defining "income" for purposes of the income tax. Proponents of the tax recognized that the job was not gross

[1] This section draws heavily on Katherine Pratt, *The Debt-Equity Distinction in a Second-Best World*, 53 Vand. L. Rev. 1055 (2000). Professor Pratt in turn draws on (and acknowledges) the work of Professor William W. Bratton, Jr., notably his *Corporate Debt Relationships: Legal Theory in a Time of Restructuring*, 1989 Duke L.J. 92, and *The New Economic Theory of the Firm: Critical Perspectives from History*, 41 Stan. L. Rev. 1471 (1989).

income, but only income net of expenses. With respect to the individual taxpayer, this appeared to allow a tax on whatever was available for consumption, after deducting costs of acquisition. This would seem to allow the deduction of an interest expense.

Perhaps Congress was applying this "individual" model when it included an interest deduction in the corporate income tax that it adopted in 1909. Yet there are grave difficulties in extending this individual model to the corporation. Most notably, it is far from clear how a corporation can "consume" anything in the sense intended by the model. Only individuals "consume;" the corporation subsists, at best, as the proxy for its stakeholders.

Even in its own time, the congressional decision did not go unchallenged. Edward Seligman, a leading tax commentator, argued against the deductibility of corporate interest, even though he was willing to accept the deduction for individuals. Perhaps for that view Congress, although it did allow the deduction for corporations, nonetheless chose to cap it at the value of the corporation's stock. But Congress lifted the limitation a few years later, leaving the unlimited deduction that remains with us today.

The practical consequences of the distinction are important, but they differ depending on the nature of the corporation. For small, closely-held family firms, the heart of the matter is the problem of double taxation. The corporation pays a tax on income, and the investor-owner pays a second tax when he takes out the income as a "dividend." One way to avoid the double tax is to "lend" money to your own corporation and take out the income as "interest." Not surprisingly, the motivation has led to a ferocious tug-of-war between the taxpayer and the Internal Revenue Service over when the payment is truly interest and when it is just a dividend in disguise.

Although the conflict was bitter, it is now largely over. Congress and the Treasury have created an array of business forms that allow the investor to have the advantage of the corporate form without the penalty of double taxation. So the old disputes are largely history.

Large public companies face the double taxation problem as well, but perhaps surprisingly, until the 1980s, they did not manage debt with tax advantage in view. All this ended with the coming of the restructuring revolution of the late 1980s, when any number of corporations loaded up on "junk bonds" as a way to finance corporate buyouts. Managers found themselves telling shareholders that they were doing them a favor by tanking up on debt, insofar as they were increasing overall corporate wealth by capturing a tax advantage.

The 1980s were also a decade of financial innovation, as bankers and CFOs devised ever more exotic contracts, seeking to capture the tax advantages of debt and the flexibility of equity. As early as 1969, Congress had authorized the Treasury Department to come up with regulations to govern the distinction. After some 10 years of study and analysis, Treasury in fact promulgated a set of regulations in 1980, but events overtook them almost before the ink was dry, and Treasury withdrew them again in 1983.

Chapter 33

More on Leverage

It's the one with the glimmer of humanity.[1]

§ 33.01 Why MM May Be Wrong After All

Recapping, we have seen that the "traditional view" declared that there was an "optimum ratio" of debt to equity, and that you could increase (or reduce) asset value by borrowing below (or above) that point. MM always conceded that their view was a "clean-test-tubes model" — i.e., that it held in only in a "perfect" market and that any market "imperfections" would require correction or adjustment. For example, MM conceded fairly early that the "imperfection" of differential tax rates and argued that the firm should take on debt to capture tax advantages. As a different sort of example, we have suggested that the investor would not *want* the manager to retain the dividends if he will misbehave with the money at hand.

But all this is still abstract. We need to turn now to the empirical question. Is there any evidence that patterns of financing systematically affect patterns of business activity?

It seems there is such evidence. For example, Richard Cantor did a study of 586 highly indebted firms over a 15-year period to see if they behaved differently from others with less debt. He found that they did. The high-debt firms showed greater volatility than low-debt firms, expanding quickly in good times and contracting quickly in bad. Cantor argued that the pattern of volatility may have been the result of "a risk-averse attitude on the part of management." That is (he argued) managers with a lot of debt might be tempted to cut back in good times even though they might (for example) be experiencing offsetting improvements in interest rates and such.[2]

In the same vein, following standard MM reasoning, you might expect a firm's access to credit to be independent of its cash flow. An important study suggests that nothing of the sort is the case. The study suggests that credit is most available to firms that are already cash-rich, giving support to the familiar canard that a banker is a person who lends you an umbrella if you can prove it is not raining.[3]

Both of these studies appear to confirm anecdotal evidence that an "independent" small or medium sized business would go to great lengths to keep from making itself hostage to its banker. It also fits with the evidence that

[1] Customer, to banker, when banker asked customer if he could tell which of the banker's eyes was made of glass.

[2] *See* Richard Cantor, *Effect of Leverage on Corporate Investment and Hiring Decisions*, Fed. Reserve Bank of N.Y. Q. Rev. 1990.

[3] *See* Steven Fazzari et al., *Financing Constraints and Corporate Investment*, Brookings Papers on Econ. Activity 1, 141–66 (1987).

entrepreneurs issue equity when equity prices are high, independent of their need for cash to invest.

There is an analytical principle that may underlie all this evidence. This is the notion of "asymmetric information," lately in vogue among academic finance researchers. To understand asymmetric information, consider the canonical example of the used car. Did you ever buy a new car? Do you remember that subtle "poof" sound that you heard as you drove the car off the lot — like the sound of a falling soufflé. Did you recognize that this was the sound of your car losing maybe 5, maybe 20 percent of its resale value?

At first blush, this "soufflé effect" appears to be one more nail in the coffin of market efficiency. How could investors be so foolish as to mark down the price of a car by 20 percent just because it rolled off the lot? But in an elegant and highly influential paper, Professor Akerlof argued that the behavior is perfectly rational. The problem, argued Akerlof, is not that all cars are 20 percent less valuable the moment they roll off the lot. The difficulty is in the sellers. Only a few buyers offer to resell their new cars — and the prudent prospective buyer is bound to ask: if you are so eager to sell this new car, what can be wrong with it?

The point is that an awful lot of people who offer to resell their new cars are doing so because the car is not as good as they had hoped it would be. Not all, of course. But the trouble is that a prospective buyer is likely to assume the worst — and who can blame him? The prospective seller has to search for some way to convince the buyers that his car is the one (out of all?) that is really not a clunker.[4] If they cannot do it, you wind up with a permanently unsatisfactory market, where buyers consistently refuse to offer the kinds of prices that might in truth be entirely rational. There is an information asymmetry.

If this theory has any merit, then it may be useful to look for the same sort of problem in the matter of firm finance. Smart bankers, of course, will do whatever they can to sort out the good risks from the bad. But what if it turns out that there is a non-trivial subset of firms sound enough to support cheap credit, but unable to distinguish themselves from their unsound brothers and sisters? Then you have another "lemons" problem, and finance (or the lack thereof) turns out to count very much, indeed.

§ 33.02 Application: WACC

> Buy on the cannons,
> sell on the trumpets.
>
> —Lord Rothschild

We are now equipped to add one more tool to our kit of valuation techniques. This one is called "weighted average cost of capital" (WACC). Courts sometimes find themselves called upon to apply WACC as a technique for (say) valuing a small business. The case will turn on the presentation of the expert

[4] *See* Akerlof, *The Market for Lemons*, 84 Q. J. Econ. 488–500 (1970).

witness who will give his opinion of value and then support it by laying out his WACC methodology.

Of course it is not the job of the lawyer herself to prepare the testimony. She will have to understand the process well enough so that she can know whom to hire as an expert, what sort of information to provide him with, and how to help him to frame his testimony — or, as the circumstances may dictate, to prepare a cross-examination.

The protocol for a WACC valuation will go something like this:

- Estimate "free cash flow" — that is, earnings before interest, taxes, depreciation and amortization (EBITDA).
- Specify appropriate rates of return for the components of the firm — in a simple case, the debt and the equity.
- Then specify an appropriate rate for the *entire* firm, weighted to account for the ratio of debt to equity. That is:[5]

$$WACC = r_a = r_e \left[\frac{E}{E + D} \right] + r_d \left[\frac{D}{E + D} \right]$$

- Divide annual EBITDA by WACC.[6]

To get a feel for WACC in action, reconsider *Steiner Corp. v. Benninghoff*,[7] which we looked at earlier. This is the case where the Steiner family tried to squeeze out the Benninghoffs through a forced merger. After analyzing the evidence on the capital asset pricing model (CAPM), the judge concluded that Steiner's cost of equity was 10.65%. Without much further discussion, he estimated the cost of the debt at 8.57 percent. Combining the two rates and making an adjustment for taxes, the court came up with a combined WACC of 9.78 percent. The court discounted the estimated cash flows by this rate and came up with a share value of $1,273.64. But this was not the end of the matter. After approaching the valuation issue from several other perspectives, the court finally concluded that Steiner Corp. was worth $1,407.02 per share. Since the Benninghoffs had received only $840 per share, they got judgment for $2.4 million plus interest.

§ 33.03 Review Note on CAPM: Second Thoughts

Commonsensical readers may have found themselves straining to retain their patience with the increasingly abstract and stylized account of the capital market. If this presentation is accurate, then there is really no job for the investment adviser. You need at most a technician to identify the risk -free rate and the risky portfolio, or perhaps to estimate beta. Can it really be that the choosing of investments is in the end so mindless an enterprise?

It is not easy to answer that question. The question of the validity of CAPM is partly a question of market efficiency, a topic we have explored earlier.[8]

---

[5] Here, r_a = return on assets, r_e = return on equity and r_d = return on debt. E = equity and D = debt, so E + D = the total value of the firm.

[6] There is an excellent discussion of Delaware valuation cases (and valuation issues in general) in Eisenhofer & Reed, *Valuation Litigation*, 22 Del. J. Corp. L. 37 (1997).

[7] 1998 U.S. Dist. LEXIS 8040 (D. Nev. 1998). *See also* In re Radiology Assocs., Inc. Litig., 611 A.2d 485 (Del. Ch. 1991).

[8] *See* § 20.05 above.

But there are other difficulties, more specific to CAPM. For example, consider an essential building block of CAPM, the "risk-free rate." Nothing is ever totally risk-free, so the risk-free rate is necessarily a fiction. Moreover, no one assumes that a stock price fluctuates entirely as a function of the market price. Individual stocks will be more or less sensitive to the market, and you have to get your hands dirty to make an accurate estimate of the degree of dependence in any case.

There are still other, more insidious, flaws in CAPM. This is the idea of "the market." Just what, again, is "the market?" Early investors assumed, more or less explicitly, that "the market" meant "the stocks traded on The New York Stock Exchange," or some close analog. But why limit it to the NYSE? NASDAQ and other domestic markets loom large in generating investor activity. So, surely, do Tokyo, London, Zurich, and heaven knows where else. Moreover, why limit ourselves to stocks? The investor does not. She will consider bonds, or commercial paper — not to mention real estate, gold, pork belly futures, and any of an infinite range of other possible investments. There is, in short, no completely satisfactory model of "the market," and any selection must at best present itself as arbitrary and incomplete.

Furthermore, there are subtle but important flaws in the ways we gather our data for CAPM. Perhaps most important, the truth or falsity of CAPM depends on knowing what investors *expect* as a return on their investment. But we do not know how to measure investor *expectations*. We only know how to measure what they *got*. If we use data on past performance (what they got) to tell us what they expect, then we are making two leaps of faith: one, that they got what they expected, and two, that their expectations will remain the same. Either or both of these may be false. Nor is the point just an academic nicety. One puzzle about investor behavior is that the U. S. stock market seems to have yielded a "risk premium" over time far in excess of what you would think it would need to offer to get investors. How to explain this anomaly? One alluring explanation is that it only *seems* large because in fact investors have been getting more than they expected. In other words, unless we know what they *really* expected, we do not have any idea whether they got it or not.

Finally, CAPM depends on the postulate that markets are efficient — in short, on ECMH. But as we explained before there is large, perhaps growing, doubt, that markets are efficient in anything like the sense the postulate would seem to require.

All this would seem to leave the case for CAPM-style investing in tatters — until you think of the alternative. For in fact, the arguments in favor of more active investing are not very good, either.

For starters, it probably is not appropriate to consider just very recent years. These recent years have been unusually kind to investors by almost any measure (except for the most conservative — shorts have taken a terrible beating). Financial acumen, they say, is a short memory and a rising market.

Second, not even the proof of Warren Buffett or Peter Lynch is enough to prove the case for active investing. After all, *every* random distribution will have outliers. There is no reason in principle to exclude the possibility that these two great success stories are just lucky anomalies.

Third, in appraising the records of these hard-working investors, you need to consider their risks and their costs. One thing we cannot stress too strongly is that you should never evaluate a return in the abstract. A seemingly high return may be no more than compensation for high risk. And if the risk is really high, then the seemingly high return may be subpar. Moreover, consider again those hard-working investors that seem to have modest success. We do not know about you, but in our experience, most of them are people with fairly low opportunity cost. A retiree who spends eight hours a day at the computer screen pricing stocks does not need to beat Warren Buffett. He just needs to beat the night shift food service job at McDonalds. Subtract the effort factor and it might turn out that many of these hard-working investors are earning no more than a day's pay for a day's work.

Of perhaps greater importance is the performance of the great institutional investors — mutual funds, pension funds and the like. There is a mountain of data on this topic, not all of it consistent by almost any measure. The performance record of the big funds is pretty scandalous, Many of these hard-working strugglers do not outperform the indexes — and when you subtract the costs — they end up not even doing as well.

What, then, is the advice here? Probably, as with so many other topics: don't inhale. Do not expect easy returns from the market unless you are very, very lucky or have very, very generous friends. Judge your investment activity by your opportunity cost. Recognize that, as a young lawyer, you probably have a lot better things to do with your human capital than to deploy it in an arduous search for small gains. Recognize that there are ways to protect yourself without a lot of thought. And recall again: it does not matter *where* on the line you are, just as long as you are *on* it, somewhere. Or as the philosopher said, you cannot win if you are not at the table.

Chapter 34

Leverage and Asymmetric Risk

Some seven men form an Association
(If possible all Peers and Baronets)
They start off with a public declaration
To what extent they mean to pay their debts
That's called their Capital . . .

—W. S. Gilbert Utopia Limited, 1893.

§ 34.01 Introduction

We started with MM's assertion that with clean test tubes, leverage should make no difference to firm value. Then we examined one rather large splotch on the test tube: tax policy. The sovereign taxes debt and equity at different rates, so management has a powerful motivation to send revenues down the low-tax chute — in other words, to load up on debt. In this chapter we consider a different form of distortion. This is the problem of decision-making with risk. To be in business is to take risks, and it is the job of the manager to manage risk.

Debt and equity have different stakes in business risk. This is definitional, because debt gets paid first. But it creates a number of problems that the law has never quite learned how to handle. Most of us learned in law school that the managers of the corporation owe fiduciary duties to equity, but not for debt. If we took a course in bankruptcy, we learned that the trustee of an insolvent debtor is a fiduciary for debt. But this is no more than a special case of a general rule: if the debtor is truly insolvent, then the old equity has no stake, and the de facto equity class is the old debt.

The difficulty, as we shall see in detail below, is that these rules distort decisions. To the extent that the rules are as stated, they impel managers to take risks that reduce, rather than enhance, the value of the assets in the business. At other times, they may impel managers *not* to take risks that would increase the size of the pool. The law has done little to solve this problem; indeed, it has barely been articulated.[1]

[1] The topic receives at least passing recognition in the Principles of Corporate Governance, promulgated by the American Law Institute. Section 2.01 of the Principles says: "a business corporation should have as its objective the conduct of business activities with a view to enhancing corporate profit and shareholder gain." A comment says: "possible tensions between corporate profit and shareholder gain" are to be dealt with elsewhere in the Principles. The reader may want to decide for herself whether the drafters do in fact address these "possible tensions."

§ 34.02 Games Debtors Play: How Leverage Affects Investment Decisions

In this section, we survey a variety of ways in which leverage creates asymmetric risk.

[A] OPM

One of the great financial frauds of the 1980s was a company called OPM, Inc. OPM stood for "other people's money," celebrating one of the first principles of modern finance: it is a great life if you gamble with other people's money. In fact, OPM was not really gambling at all; it was more a matter of simple theft.

Lawful business presents more intriguing problems. Consider the affairs of ShoeTip, Inc., the world's foremost maker of tips for shoelaces, which has assets valued at $100. ShoeTip is considering an investment project. To make the investment, ShoeTip must lay out $100. Under the best of circumstances, the $100 invested will yield a gross return with a present value of $900. But it will get that happy result only one time out of 10. The other nine, it will get nothing. So, the expected return is:

$$E[r] = (0.9)(0) + (0.1)(900) = \$90$$

Spend $100 to get $90: it does not seem to make a lot of sense. Suppose instead, that ShoeTip is financed by $90 in debt. ShoeTip's balance sheet looks like this:

ShoeTip, Inc.

Assets		Liabilities	
Assets	$100	Liabilities	$90
		Net Worth	$10
Total assets	$100	Total L & NW	$100

Remember, ShoeTip is a corporation, which means that the shareholders' liability is limited to the amount of their investments. In this example, the shareholders have only $10 at risk — not, as in the first example, $100. If the value of the asset pool falls below $90, the shareholders are out of luck. But all the rest of the loss — i.e., from $90 down to zero — falls on the lenders. On the other hand, if the value increases above $100, every additional dollar accrues to the shareholders — they don't have to share with creditors at all.

Take a look at the summary of probabilities, from the standpoint of the shareholders only:

Payoff	Probability	Value
$0	0.9	$0
($ 900 − $ 90)	0.1	$81
Total	1.0	$81

Keep in mind, this time the shareholders have only $10 at risk. Would you spend $10 to get $81? Sounds like a pretty good deal. Of course, the debtor *still* will not buy this particular lottery ticket if he can make more money some *other* way, but let that be. The point is that from the standpoint of the shareholder, the presence of debt can make a risky investment look far less risky. Indeed, it can turn a sure loser into a profitable opportunity.

We can put another spin on this analysis to show how leverage impels shareholders to favor risky investments over safe ones. Suppose ShoeTip has two, and only two, investment choices. Each one costs $100. Therefore, ShoeTip (with assets of $100) can invest in either one, but not both. One (A) has an expected return of $124, the other (B) has an expected return of $120. Which one will management choose? It would seem that a rational management would choose A. But wait. Recall, as we noted before, that the "return" is no better than a *prediction*, which is to say a weighted average of *all* the possibilities. Take a look at the probability tables for investment A:

Payoff	Probability	Value
$ 50	0.2	$10
$120	0.5	$60
$180	0.3	$54
Total	1.0	$124

Now, compare investment B:

Payoff	Probability	Value
$ 0	0.2	$0
$120	0.5	$60
$200	0.3	$60
Total	1.0	$120

The decision is clear: choose A over B. But suppose ShoeTip is financed half by equity, half by debt, with a balance sheet like this:

ShoeTip, Inc.

Assets		Liabilities	
Assets	$100	Liabilities	$50
		Net Worth	$50
Total assets	$100	Total L & NW	$100

Remember, shareholders of the debt-laden firm *do not care* about the full range of possibilities. They only care about possibilities *that yield a return of greater than $50*. That is because ShoeTip is a corporation, which means that the shareholders have limited liability. The shareholders do not get the entire expected return; they only get the return *less the $50 debt*.

If the return falls below $50, then shareholders just take a hike, and the lender is stuck with the problem. Look at the shareholders' table of probabilities, first for A:

Payoff	Probability	Value
$50	0.2	$0
($ 120 − $ 50)	0.5	$35
($ 180 − $ 50)	0.3	$39
Total	1.0	$74

And then for B:

Payoff	Probability	Value
$ 0	0.2	$0
($ 120 − $ 50)	0.5	$35
($ 200 − $ 50)	0.3	$45
Total	1.0	$80

So, B is "best," from the standpoint of the shareholders, even though it is suboptimal in terms of the firm as a whole — that is what we meant when we talked about gambling with "other people's money."

Note that we have smuggled in some assumptions that are critically important to the dynamics of this scenario. Specifically, we assumed that *management*, in choosing the investment strategy, was free to serve the interest of *shareholders* at the expense of creditors or (what may not be the same thing) that creditors were powerless to prevent management from so abusing their trust in this way. If you are offended by this state of things, then, from the viewpoint of public policy, how do you attack it? One approach might be to change the rules governing management behavior: to require, for example, that management act as fiduciary for *all* interests — shareholders and creditors alike — in making corporate decisions.

There is another school of thought that counsels against this kind of rule change. Under this approach, you do not need to require management to act as a fiduciary for creditors, because creditors have already anticipated the inducements on management of a debt-laden firm and have taken account of the problem as part of their original debt contract — e.g., through bond covenants, or property security interests, or simply through higher interest rates. If you believe this scenario, then it would be wrong to impose any additional constraints on management, because you would be giving the creditors something more than they had bargained for.

[B] Take It and Run

In any event, there are other strategies available to debtors in trouble. Remember ShoeTip's previous balance sheet: assets of $100, liabilities of $50. Suppose the company runs into misfortune and the pool of assets declines to, say $30. What does the right-hand column look like now? You might say that it should show liabilities of $30 and net worth of zero — meaning that the "old" owners are out of the picture, and that the debtholders are the "new" owners, chalking up the $20 shortfall as a deadweight loss. But it might be that the debt is not yet due. In that case, the creditor may have to stand by and watch while the debtor spends "his" assets. A careful creditor may be able to protect against this eventuality. For example, it is possible to write a contract term providing that the debtor shall be in default if he lets the ratio of assets to liabilities fall below a certain point. But not every creditor is able to get such a term.

Combine OPM with a debtor who has nothing to lose and you add insult to the creditor's injury. Any combat soldier knows that the one who takes the greatest risk is the one who has nothing to go home to.

[C] Do Not Feed the Debt

But the train runs both ways on this track. Just as the debtor in distress may make crazy investments (where he can dump the risk on creditors), so also will he avoid good investments when the primary benefits accrue to creditors. Suppose ShoeTip has assets of $100 and liabilities of only $50. Suppose a really dandy opportunity comes along — an almost sure winner — calculated to add $20 (net) to ShoeTip's balance sheet. To keep the game interesting, assume that ShoeTip is the only one who can exploit the opportunity. The catch is that the investment requires an initial outlay of $65. This would mean using the entire $50 existing asset pool, plus $15 of "new money" — a total $65 now, for a potential $85 return later. It will not happen, of course

— and how could it? No one is going to put $15 of new money into this corporation, where all it does is "feed the debt."

[D] The Bankruptcy Puzzle

One final subversive thought: this analysis is based on ways in which the debtor may gamble with the creditor's money. But are there any circumstances in which the logic works the other way around? That is to say, is there any circumstance in which the creditor will be able to enjoy any possible gain, while dumping any possible loss on the debtor?[2]

Consider a hard case. SkyHigh, Inc., is having trouble paying its debts. Creditors at first deferred exercising their right to levy, hoping that SkyHigh's finances would improve and fearing that if creditors pressed too hard, SkyHigh's finances would get worse. At last, however, SkyHigh, fearing that creditors would not defer much longer, filed for relief under Chapter 11 of the Bankruptcy Code, thus invoking the statutory automatic stay against collection activity. Pursuant to the Bankruptcy Code, the pre-bankruptcy managers of SkyHigh remained in control with the powers and obligations of a trustee.

SkyHigh's books show that they owe $100. Appraisers advise that the existing business is worth $80, being the sum of two probabilities: a 50 percent chance that the business will turn out to be worth $70, and a 50 percent chance it will be worth $90. The managers have an opportunity to withdraw all the assets and put them into a new venture with a probability-weighted value of $95, representing a 50 percent chance of a return of $10 and a 50 percent chance of a return of $180. In the discharge of their fiduciary responsibilities, what should the managers do?

§ 34.03 Managing Risk

The problem of skewed incentives through leverage may arise in a variety of contexts. In many, the government seeks to control the problem through regulation. There are three types of regulation. One is to limit the *amount of leverage* an investor may assume. These include *margin requirements* in the stock market and *capital adequacy requirements* in banking. A second limitation is to control the *kinds of investments* equity owners may choose. For example, government rules often limit the investments of banks. Third, the government may provide *insurance* or similar *guarantees* to protect against the consequences of excessive risk. Thus, the government typically provides *deposit insurance* to protect bank depositors against bank failure.

§ 34.04 Margin

You decide to buy a share of Consolidated Tomorrow, Inc., (ConTom), which currently trades at $200. You have only $80. Your broker graciously agrees to loan you the additional $120, retaining the share as security for the loan.

[2] This account draws very heavily on the examples in F.H. Buckley, *The Bankruptcy Priority Puzzle*, 72 Va. L. Rev. 1393, 1427–33 (1986).

You take his deal; you pay him the $80, he buys the share and retains it in your name. You leave for vacation. When you come back, you are pleased to see that ConTom is trading at $280. Considering that you had only $80 at risk, that means you have doubled your money.

But on inquiry, you are chagrined to find that before its current runup, ConTom sank from $200 to $140. You learn for the first time that the exchange rules require that there be at least 25 percent equity in your account. You hit the 25 percent limit when the stock fell to $160 because at that point you had debt of $120 (75 percent of your portfolio) and $40 equity (25 percent). Since you had bought *on the margin*, as the jargon says, then at that point your broker made a *margin call*: he told you that either (a) you must come up with more money or, (b) he would sell your stock. Since you were not in town, you never got the message and he sold you out.

We have seen that the higher the leverage, the greater the volatility of the underlying equity. Leveraged investing (margin buying) thus offers the prospect of great risk and great reward. By the conventional wisdom, such margin buying is believed to have contributed to the speculative frenzy of the 1920s and the resulting 1929 stock market crash. Ever since, by congressional mandate, the Federal Reserve Board has set margin requirements to limit the speculative potential.[3] The Fed's margin requirement has varied from as low as 25 percent cash in the 1920s to as high of 100 percent in the 1940s. Fed requirements limit only the *initial purchase*. But stock exchange rules provide *maintenance margin* limitations for accounts in being. Comparable rules limit *short selling*, for comparable reasons.

§ 34.05 Banks and Leverage

We have seen that high leverage motivates equity to take risks, including bad risks. So if you want to discourage risk-taking, you make owners hold a fairly high component of equity, relative to debt, in the bank. Proposals for such *capital adequacy* rules began to appear among bank reformers in the Depression of the 1930s. Support grew in the early 1980s, after a string of near-disasters (and disasters) in lending to borrowers in Latin America. Congress in response passed the International Lending Supervision Act (ILSA).[4] The statute required bank regulators to establish minimum capital ratios for the banks under their control.

One defect of ILSA was that it applied only to American banks, who feared it would leave them at a competitive disadvantage. But concern over capital adequacy did not stop at the United States border. In 1987 an international group, the Basle Committee on Banking Regulations and Supervisory Practices, laid down a set of minimum capital ratios for international banks. The United States incorporated them into federal banking regulations in 1989.[5] Congress adopted elements of the Basle proposals in the Comprehensive Deposit Insurance Reform and Taxpayer Protection Act (Comprehensive Reform Act), a banking regulation measure.[6] Under the Comprehensive

[3] Securities Exchange Act § 7 (15 U.S.C. § 78g).

[4] 12 U.S.C. § 3901 *et seq.*

[5] 12 C.F.R. §§ 208.1.127 & app. A-B (1991); 12 C.F.R. 160–88 app. A-B (1991).

[6] Pub. L. No. 102–242 (1991).

Reform Act, inadequacy of capital will become a sufficient criterion for government intervention in a troubled institution.

§ 34.06 Junque: The Grandeur and Decadence of Michael Milken

Oh, I'd never sit down by a tumbledown drunk
If it wasn't, my dears, for the high cost of junk.

X.J. Kennedy[7]

"What is risk?" the teacher asked his students in Management 298D: Corporate Finance, at UCLA one fall morning in 1993. "There's risk in everything — when there's no risk there's no future."

And risk includes, as a newspaper columnist added, the possibility of incurring criminal charges on 98 securities counts, pleading guilty to six and serving 22 months in a California prison camp. The speaker ought to know: he was Michael Milken, who has come to personify the financial revolution of the 1980s, the man, as they say, who invented the junk bond. He'd done the crime (or so he conceded in open court) and as they like to say in prison, he'd done the time. The press likes to describe him as the "disgraced" Michael Milken, but the reality is far more complex. On the one hand, there are plenty of people who think the sentence was the real disgrace, that 22 months was fair punishment for the toupee alone. For these people, even if you throw in the billion dollars in fines and civil damage settlements, still for the havoc he inflicted, he got off on chump change.

But Milken has his staunch — even fierce — defenders. These include many of his clients — investors and entrepreneurs whose careers weren't going any place in particular until Milken gave them an opening. The defenders also include many who point to the ways Milken changed the face of the American business, midwifing whole industries, the sovereign remedy for a sluggish economy. What would the world look like today without (for example) MCI's fiber optics network? Or CNN? Joseph Schumpeter, the Austrian economist, says capitalism grows by "creative destruction."[8] Schumpeter never met Milken, but he would have understood.

Equally unapologetic is Milken himself. On TV, he told Barbara Walters that he'd never earned a dishonest penny, and that his guilty pleas acknowledged mere technical violations — as it were, fines for overtime parking.

To understand Milken's contribution (if it is that) to modern finance, imagine a public company with assets of $100, and no debt. Suppose the company goes into the bond market and seeks to borrow $40. Will the bankers lend the money? Of course. Any way you slice it, the loan looks collectible. Okay, maybe the company isn't worth $100. Maybe it's only worth $80. Or $60. Or even $40 — yes, that's right. At any value down to $40, the debt is fully protected and correspondingly gilt-edged. Here we have the old fashioned triple-A corporate bond, safe for widows and orphans, beloved of the trust department at your grandfather's bank.

---

[7] From "In a Prominent Bar in Secaucus One Day," in Crossties (1985).

[8] Joseph Schumpter, Capitalism, Socialism and Democracy 84 (London 1954).

Once in a great while, of course, the worst may come to pass: a triple-A blue chip may fall upon evil days, and the estimated worth of the firm tumble below the aggregate value of the debt: in our case, imagine $30, or 75 percent of the debt. Disaster? Of sorts, yes, but maybe not for everybody. If the bonds are not yet due, they may continue to trade. Their trading price will simply reflect the then-current expected payoff. The original holder may be hurt, but suppose a secondary market buyer who buys at $30. Suppose thereafter corporate fortunes improve and the bond price, reflecting the improvement, rises to $80. The buyer who buys at $30 and resells at $80 may have done very well, indeed.

Such, in shorthand, were the terms of engagement in the bond market in the early 1970s when Milken left the Wharton school at Penn, the ink still wet on his M.B.A., to begin his career across town at "the Drexel firm," the old-line Philadelphia investment banking firm, eventually rechristened Drexel Burnham. As a young bond salesmen, Milken built his market niche on the proposition that junk was underpriced: that junk was no less risky than other investments with lower returns — a market imperfection, or, as we would say today, an opportunity for arbitrage. If Milken was right, then the prudent investor ought to buy his bonds.

Milken's pitch met with deafening indifference in the ears of old-fashioned safe-arid-sane bond investors To find his real action, Milken had to go shopping back west, more precisely California, more precisely Beverly Hills. There Milken (who grew up in Encino) found people who talked his language. Slowly he began to build up a market of customers for fallen angels. He was so successful, in fact, that as the decade drew on, he found himself piling up personal earnings in the millions — and running low on product.[9]

Which brings us to Chapter II of the Milken saga. Suppose this time you have a company with assets of $100, liabilities of $40, net worth of ($1 00 – $40 =) $60. Suppose the senior debt is secured by all corporate assets. From the standpoint of the senior, the package looks plenty conservative: almost inconceivable that assets could ever fall below the $40 plimsole line. But suppose you lay on a second tier of debt, second behind the senior secured. This second tier isn't nearly so secure as the senior debt. Indeed with the right kind of numbers, from the moment of issue, this debt will bear the risks and (some of) the rewards of common stock funk from day one.

There is no reason in principle why a company should not issue this kind of subinvestment-grade debt.[10] Anything is a bargain at the right price, and

[9] Talk of the Beverly Hills bond plungers raises a related issue. This is the question of the connection between Milken's junk bond revolution and the celebrated multi-billion dollar collapse of the savings and loan industry. The fact is that a number of Milken's conspicuous early allies were also prominent figures in the S&L debacle. But the real root of the S&L problem lay in a government policy decision for which Milken was not remotely responsible. *See* § 38.04 below.

[10] Indeed, once you start thinking this way, you can see that there is no reason in principle not to invent a virtually *infinite* variety of securities packages, all slicing and dicing the liability side of the balance sheet in different ways. This insight introduces yet another component of the revolution of the 1980s. At the fancy Wall Street firms in those days, they used to say there were two ways to make partner. One was to invent a new security. And no one remembered the other.

if the buyer gets the right return, she might well wish to run the risk. But as a matter of history, not much of anybody had offered this sort of product.[11] Milken was the first to do so in a big way. Buoyed by early successes with "fallen angels," Milken decided to cut out the middleman and issue original junk on his own account. And this is the point where the Milken story moves out of the musty back rooms of the banking house and into the arena of high drama. For to build his network of new-issue junk, Milken developed his network of new financiers — high rollers with big ambitions and even bigger egos who welcomed the kinds of risks that Milken's deals invited them to run — but who might not have had a chance at any such exhilarating opportunities without Milken's money machine.

These were the point men for the great wave of corporate acquisitions that dominated the 1980s: the leveraged buyouts (LBOs), where investors induced companies to pile on more debt (= leverage) to permit a merger or an acquisition, always hoping the future would provide earnings enough to service the obligations. For dating purposes, perhaps you could say that the tide hit full spate in April, 1985. That was the date of the great junk bond convention, so memorably characterized by Connie Bruck in her book, *The Predator's Ball (1988)*, which probably did more than anything else to inscribe the picture of Milken in the public mind. That 1985 convention was perhaps the occasion when "junk" became "junque," a central tool and weapon in mainstream finance.

This is hardly the place to try to tell the LBO story — as if anyone could sum it up in just a page. Milken and his allies certainly had a lot of fun in the process, and made money in sums that are well-nigh inconceivable: Milken himself is said to have made $550 *million* in 1987.[12] If you were an entrepreneur who got caught in the updraft, you may remember Michael Milken as the man who made you rich when no one else would give you the time of day. If you were a detached observer of the economy, you might say that the leveraged buyout — perhaps we should call it a "leveraged shakeout" — gave corporate America the kind of jolt it needed to make it competitive.

But if you lost your job, or found yourself faced with a wage cut and loss of benefits in a corporate strip-down, your attitude was likely far less sympathetic. Susan Faludi won a Pulitzer Prize for a remarkable Wall Street Journal story on the human costs of the restructuring at Safeway Stores. And if you were part of an "ordinary" family — working harder and perhaps earning less — you perhaps saw little except the stark fact that lots of people weren't doing so well while some people were getting spectacularly rich.

---

[11] And strictly speaking, Milken was not the first modern investor to create this "original-issue junk." That distinction belongs to the old-line investment firm of Lehman Brothers. In 1977, Lehman issued some low grade debt for some troubled corporate debtors, including Pan American Airways and LTV Corporation. Another of Lehman's early customers was Zapata Oil, the firm founded by the young Texas oil speculator (and later President of the U.S.) George Bush. Milken got into the game by buying Lehman product for resale to his growing network of junk customers.

[12] To put Milken's salary in perspective, someone pointed out that the great J. P. Morgan had once said that no one in a company should make more than 25 times the earnings of the lowest paid employee. Had that rule held at Drexel in 1987, the janitor would have made $22 million.

And heaven knows the riches were in evidence. Remarkably, it wasn't so much Milken himself: even at the height of his power, he continued to live in a (somewhat) ordinary house out in the Valley, and to show up at his Beverly Hills office at the crack of dawn But there was another story among the wash of Milken beneficiaries, the cocky kids in the firehouse suspenders, sweeping the yuppie toys off the shelves at Sharper Image when they should have been home pounding beefsteak or pulling up dandelions. Somehow, it just didn't sit right.

There was, in short a profound sense of "us versus them": working stiffs on the unemployment line watching some infant roll by in an $80,000 sports car. In a way, this is ironic, because in the structure of corporate finance, it is Milken himself who is "them" as against the clubby, exclusive "us" of the old money. To the folks on the unemployment line, Milken might have looked like some kind of marauding crocodile. To the folks in the old-fashioned boardrooms, he looked like — well, like some kind of marauding crocodile.

In a sense, both were right. Banking has always been a "relationships" business. You lend not on collateral, but on trust. Anyone who attaches great value to his purely legal rights is a fool. Old-time bankers always knew this. Milken's only real novelty was to create his own circle of friends. Almost invariably, when Milken had to float a new deal, he cut in his old friends. There were diverse motives: sometimes it was a reward, sometimes a punishment, but in any event it helped to prop up the market and to spread the risk.

And in the end, it was insiderism that brought him down. Just as Milken was riding the wave of his greatest success, someone — apparently a disgruntled girlfriend — tipped the brokerage firm of Merrill Lynch that a couple of its employees in Caracas, Venezuela, seemed to be making a bundle off illegal insider trading. The employees, on inquiry, said they weren't profiting from any special information at all: they were just piggybacking on orders that came through an account in the Bahamas that seemed to have uncanny success. The trail wound its way from the Bahamas back through a Swiss Bank and thence to New York and one Dennis B. Levine, an unprepossessing kid who could have passed as an extra on "Seinfeld." Levine confessed that he was in fact trading on inside information, and in turn he fingered a much bigger fish — Ivan Boesky, the celebrity stock plunger. Boesky was arrested and also confessed to insider trading. He agreed to a fine of $100 million and a jail sentence of three years. Then Boesky gave the prosecutors Michael Milken. On March 29, 1989, the government indicted Milken on its 98 felony counts of financial wrongdoing.

Milken, as explained above, eventually did plead guilty to a half dozen charges (they did seem rather technical). He paid fines and penalties of storybook proportions. And he served his time — in a prison *camp,* as the press liked to specify, equipped with a swimming pool and a tennis court, as his critics liked to say.

But in less than two years he was out, trying hard to refurbish his reputation. That was what led him to the UCLA classroom. But his term as an instructor proved short-lived: the deal met a fire storm of criticism and UCLA, with Milken's consent, backed out.

But time, if it does not heal, may at least have some knack for anesthesia He let himself be seen teaching poor kids arithmetic (part of the community service component of his criminal sentence). He reported that he had prostate cancer. He published his autobiography (it wasn't a hit). Someone named a high school after him. And then in the autumn of 1995 an old friend offered him a sort of gratuity for his assistance in a merger deal. Not for securities work per se — Milken is banned from the securities business for life. More for "advice." Or maybe just for gratitude. The "tip" was said to be $50 million. The donor: Ted Turner, the man who created CNN. Without Milken, Turner might still be plastering up billboards in Atlanta.

Bibliography: Connie Bruck's book, cited above, tells us what we have come to believe about Michael Milken, quite independent of the question whether it is true. James Stewart, *Den of Thieves* (1991) is overheated but full of anecdote. Jesse Kornbluth *Highly Confident* (1992) often reads like it was drafted by Milken's personal PR consultant. A somewhat subtler picture emerges from Roy C. Smith, *The Money Wars* (1990). Unfortunately, nobody yet has done a convincing job of totting up the larger economic costs and benefits.

Chapter 35

Valuing Contingent Claims

I don't have to outrun the bear.
I just have to outrun you.

—Woodsman's Creed

§ 35.01 Introduction

In this chapter, we begin a study of the valuation of contingent claims. The topic is more important than it sounds, and it is easier to define by example than by abstraction, which we will do in a moment. But begin with this: a contingent claim is any claim whose value is dependent on the value of another claim. Perhaps the most important contingent claim is the share of stock in a leveraged company. Another contingent claim is the stock *option* — the right to buy (or sell) stock at a defined price.

But contingent claims analysis goes far beyond stocks and options. Do you own a car? Do you carry insurance on the car to cover against loss by fire or theft? We will see that property insurance of this sort can be understood as a contingent claim. Do you recall our discussion of "exit strategy" and salvage value? It turns out that even an exit strategy can be valued as a contingent claim. Indeed, we will develop two general points about contingent claims. One is that they are everywhere — as evidenced by the catalog above. Two, as we shall see, even if they are not there, we can call them into being. That is: once you know how to analyze contingent claims, you realize you can fashion a "synthetic" contingent claim for — shall we say, for any contingency.

§ 35.02 Stock as a Contingent Claim

We begin by studying a familiar contingent claim — the share of stock in a leveraged company. Here is an example:

Your client, Stella, owns all the stock of StellCo, Inc. Here is the balance sheet of StellCo:

Assets	Liabilities & Net Worth	
?	$100 ?	(L) (NW)
?	?	

So, StellCo has debt whose value (V_D) is $100. The value of its assets (V_A) is unknown. Since value of the equity (V_E — also known as "net worth") = $V_A - V_D$, it follows that V_E is also unknown. So, if V_A = $120:

Assets	Liabilities & Net Worth	
$120	$100	(L)
	$ 20	(NW)
$120	$120	

We have said that Stella is the stockholder. We have said that stock in a leveraged company is a contingent claim. What we mean is: as the stockholder, Stella owns *the assets* (V_A), of StellCo, *contingent upon* her paying *the debt* (V_D). Call the debt "the exercise price" (sometimes "the strike price") for the assets. Stella can have the assets by paying the strike price. Less obvious, but no less important, recall that StellCo is a *corporation*, which implies *limited liability*. So, if V_A is "too low," Stella can end her relationship simply by walking away. Refining our earlier statement, we could say that Stella has an *option* on the assets, subject to the exercise price of the debt. We can formalize this description:

$$V_E = \max(V_A - V_D, 0)$$

For a closer look, suppose VA is not $120, but only $75. Then:

Assets	Liabilities & Net Worth	
$ 75	$100	(L)
	$ (25)	(NW)
$ 75	$ 75	

That is to say, StellCo has a *negative* net worth of $25. In this case, it would appear that the equity is worthless. Stella might as well throw the keys on the table and walk away.

We are now in a position to set forth a pair of principles of contingent claims:

- The greater the value of the asset, the greater the value of the contingent claim.
- The higher (or lower) the exercise price, the lower (or higher) the value of the contingent claim.

All this is helpful as a first approximation, but a little reflection on what we have learned so far will convince us that it is too simple. For starters, take a second look at $V_A = \$120$. We can surmise that this is the discounted present value of the future cash inflows that we can generate from the assets. But very few things in life are certain. The chances are that V_A does not represent a certainty, but represents rather the sum of an array of probabilities. For example, it may be that V_A represents a 50 percent chance of each of two possible outcomes, as follows:

$$\begin{aligned} 0.5\ (\$110) &= \$55 \\ 0.5\ (\$130) &= \underline{\$65} \\ \text{Total } V_A &= \$120 \end{aligned}$$

On the same principles, we can compute the value of the equity:

$$\begin{aligned} 0.5\ (\$110 - \$100) &= \$\ 5 \\ 0.5\ (\$130 - \$100) &= \$\ 15 \\ \text{Total } V_E &= \$\ 20 \end{aligned}$$

Pay careful attention to the way in which we computed the return to equity. Note that in each case, we started with the *total* return ($110 or $130). Then we *subtracted* the amount that must go to pay debt. To complete the bookkeeping, we should compute the probability-weighted value of the *debt:*

$$\begin{aligned} 0.5\ (\$100) &= \$50 \\ 0.5\ (\$100) &= \underline{\$50} \\ \text{Total } V_D &= \$100 \end{aligned}$$

Definitionally, holders of debt never get *more* than the value of the debt claim. The result may seem trivially obvious in this case but it will be useful as a benchmark later.

So much for total return. But we can do more. Using techniques you learned earlier, you ought to be able to confirm that the *standard deviation* of the assets (σ_A) = 10:

$$\begin{aligned} (0.5)(110 - 120)^2 &= 50 \\ (0.5)(130 - 120)^2 &= 50 \\ \sigma_A^2 &= 100 \\ \sigma_A &= 10 \end{aligned}$$

It is worth our while separately to compute the standard deviation of the *equity* (σ_E):

$$\begin{aligned} (0.5)([110 - 100] - 20)^2 &= 50 \\ (0.5)([130 - 100] - 20)^2 &= 50 \\ \sigma_E^2 &= 100 \\ \sigma_E &= 10 \end{aligned}$$

Make sure you understand what we did here. We took the mean value of the equity claim ($20, computed earlier). Then we subtracted that mean from the payout *to equity* in each of our two cases ($10 in one case, $30 in the other). Then we squared and weighted, as always. On this analysis, we found that $\sigma_E = 10$. So in absolute terms, $\sigma_E = \sigma_A$. But for comparison, we should recast them as a *percentage* of the *mean* return. On this basis, $\sigma_A = 10 \div 120$, or 8.33 percent of total (asset) return, while σ_E equals $10 \div 20$, or a whopping 50 percent of total (equity) return.

Note also that in this example debt bears *no risk* (check the payout numbers above). From this fact you can infer by intuition that the standard deviation of the debt is *zero.*

Of course, there is no necessity that the variation between $110–$130, as above. It could just as well be $100 and $140, as we can see from this computation:

$$
\begin{aligned}
0.5\ (\$100) &= \$\ 50 \\
0.5\ (\$140) &= \underline{\$\ 70} \\
\text{Total } V_A &= \$\ 120
\end{aligned}
$$

On the same principles, we can compute the value of the equity:

$$
\begin{aligned}
0.5\ (\$100 - \$100) &= \$0 \\
0.5\ (\$140 - \$100) &= \underline{\$20} \\
\text{Total } V_E &= \$20
\end{aligned}
$$

Note that the mean values are the same as before, even though the range is different. Recomputing measures of variation, we find that the standard deviation of both assets and equity has risen to 20. This is double in absolute terms. But as a percentage of the mean, $\sigma_A = 20 \div 120 = 16.67$ percent, while $\sigma_E = 20 \div 20 = 100$ percent. All this suggests another principle of contingent claims:

- If the underlying asset is risky, the contingent claim is more risky.

Now, compute a third example. Suppose the range = \$80 to \$160, so that VA equals:

$$
\begin{aligned}
0.5\ (\$80) &= \$40 \\
0.5\ (\$160) &= \underline{\$80} \\
\text{Total } V_A &= \$120
\end{aligned}
$$

Standard deviation on the assets has risen from 20 to 40. As a percentage of the mean, it is 33.33 percent. On the same principles, we can compute the V_E:

$$
\begin{aligned}
0.5\ (\max\ [\$80 - \$100],\ 0) &= \$\ 0 \\
0.5\ (\$160 - \$100) &= \underline{\$30} \\
\text{Total } V_E &= \$30
\end{aligned}
$$

The standard deviation is now 30, but as a percentage of equity, the standard deviation remains at 100 percent, i.e., just where it was before. This is a puzzle. How can it be that *asset* σ (as a percentage of assets) has *risen* while *equity* (as a percentage of equity) is no worse than it was before? Note that the value of the equity has *risen* from \$20 to \$30, although the asset value is unchanged. This means that equity *did not absorb* all the loss associated with the greater risk. This suggests another principle of contingent claims:

- Greater risk in the underlying asset may *increase* the value of the contingent claim.

Read that last principle again to make sure that you understand it. It is counterintuitive, in that it appears just the *opposite* of what you have been taught up to now. That is: you have been taught that risk is bad and reduces value. Now you are being told that risk is good and increases value. In fact, both statements are right. Ordinarily, risk is bad and reduces claim value. But in the case of the contingent claim, the claim holder holds an "upside" — a chance to profit — without bearing the corresponding "downside" — the risk of loss. So the contingent claim depends on the asymmetric risk package and risk behaves just the opposite of what you have been led to expect.

To bring this point home, it may be useful to consider what happens in this scenario to debt. We have established that V_A = \$ 120 and V_E = \$30. What is V_D? Recall that V_D in any case is the lower of (a) the value of the assets or (b) the face amount of the debt. Then:

$$
\begin{aligned}
0.5\ (\min\ \{\$80,\ \$100\}) &= \$40 \\
0.5\ (\min\ \{\$160,\ \$100\}) &= \underline{\$50} \\
\text{Total } V_D &= \$90
\end{aligned}
$$

So in this case (unlike either of the two previous cases), some of the risk "spills over" onto debt. A "revised" balance sheet, adjusted for market realities, would look like this:

Assets	Liabilities & Net Worth	
$ 120	$ 90	(L)
	$ 30	(NW)
$ 120	$ 120	

Finally, just to remove all doubt, reconsider this balance sheet:

Assets	Liabilities & Net Worth	
$ 75	$ 100	(L)
	$ (25)	(NW)
$ 75	$ 75	

On the face of things, StellCo is insolvent. Indeed, if the creditor liquidates his claim now, then Stella will lose everything. But if Stella remains in control of StellCo, then maybe she can find a gamble with a payoff like this:

$$
\begin{aligned}
0.5\ (0) &= \$0 \\
0.5\ (\$150) &= \underline{\$75} \\
\text{Total } V_E &= \$75
\end{aligned}
$$

This looks like a bad deal, does it not? We get much greater risk for no more return. But consider the return from the standpoint of Stella as the holder of the equity (meaning the holder of the contingent claim):

$$
\begin{aligned}
(0.5)(\max\ [\$0 - \$100,\ 0]) &= \$\ 0 \\
(0.5)(\max\ [\$150 - \$100,\ 0]) &= \underline{\$\ 25} \\
\text{Total } V_E &= \$\ 25
\end{aligned}
$$

You should be able to confirm that the value of the debt = $50. This suggests a revised balance sheet as follows:

Assets	Liabilities & Net Worth	
$ 75	$ 50	(L)
	$ 25	(NW)
$ 75	$ 75	

The common theme in this last series of cases is that the contingent claimholder profits from increased risk. But we know that risk is a function of time — the more time, the more risk, and in our context, the more chance of an upside for the holder of the contingent claim.

- The more time to the end of the claim period, the more valuable the contingent claim.

One final point will complete our set. Go back to the "simple" case where assets equal $120 and liabilities equal $100, and the range of risk is $110 to $130. On these numbers, debt is essentially risk-free. But even risk-free debt bears an interest cost: we have called it "the risk-free rate of return." So it is reasonable to assume that StellCo's debt bears interest at a "contract" rate equal to the risk-free rate of return.

We know other things about debt, as well. For example, we know that market rates may fluctuate during the life of the debt. And we know that the market value of debt is an inverse function of the market rate of return — that is, as the market rate goes up, the present value of the debt goes down. For example, suppose our "risk-free" debt was a 10-year bond with a coupon of $10 a year and a face value of $100. If the risk-free rate is 10 percent, then these numbers imply a present value of $100.

But now suppose the risk-free market rate advances to 12 percent. The value of such debt falls to $88.70 (you can check this on your calculator), but the underlying assets are not risk-free; for purposes of analysis, we can assume their value remains at $120, as before. These numbers imply an "adjusted" balance sheet as follows:

Assets	Liabilities & Net Worth	
$120	$ 88.70	(L)
	$ 31.30	(NW)
$120	$ 120.00	

This suggests a final principle of contingent claims:

- An increase (or decrease) in the risk-free rate will increase (or decrease) the value of the contingent claim.

These are the principles of contingent claims (we will repeat them by way of summary in § 35.03). We have examined them in the context of a corporation — a "limited-liability" entity — with debt and equity. We saw that the shareholder held, in effect, a contingent claim on the assets, which she might exercise by paying the debt.

This is good basic corporate finance. But it is important to understand that it applies to *any* contingent claim. For example, we may consider the case where the debtor holds Blackacre subject to a "non-recourse" mortgage. By "non-recourse," we mean that the mortgagee may look to the property only to satisfy his claim, and may not seek a deficiency from the debtor. It would be easy to show that the debtor's right in Blackacre has the same characteristics as Stella's right against StellCo.

Or, for another example, we might consider the organized option market, where investors (and speculators?) buy and sell contingent claims. We will explore the option market in the next several assignments.

A Final Note on the "Binary Model": Throughout this assignment (and in some later assignments), we work with what the jargon calls a "binary model" — a model in which there are two possible outcomes, one "good" and one "bad." Does this strike you as unacceptably unrealistic? It need not. Of course it is *simplified*, and there may be no case in the real world where an asset will entail only two possible outcomes, no more. Far more common is the sort of situation where there is a *range* of possible outcomes — possibly an infinite number along a more or less continuous line.

We could model an infinite range of possibilities. Indeed later on, we study the so-called "Black-Scholes pricing model," which presupposes just such a range. The math underlying the Black-Scholes model is formidable, but we do not need to understand it. The attractive point is that the *intuition* that underlies the Black-Scholes model is only an advanced case of the intuition that underlies these binary models. So for our purposes, you can learn everything you need to know about the functioning of options from the simplified model. Thank your lucky stars for simplicity, and quit worrying about abstraction.

§ 35.03 Summary: The Principles of Contingent Claims

- The greater the value of the asset, the greater the value of the contingent claim.
- The higher the exercise price, the lower the value of the contingent claim.
- If the underlying asset is risky, the contingent claim is more risky.
- Greater risk in the underlying asset may *increase* the value of the contingent claim.
- The more time to the end of the claim period, the more valuable the contingent claim.
- An increase (or decrease) in the risk-free rate will increase (or decrease) the value of the contingent claim.

Chapter 36

Graphing Contingent Claims

Create a concept, and reality leaves the room.

—Ortega y Gasset

§ 36.01 Introduction

To recap, a contingent claim is any claim whose value is *contingent upon* the value of some *other* asset. For example, in several earlier assignments, we saw that a share of stock in a leveraged company was a claim against the assets of the company, contingent upon paying the debt. We noted that there are many other contingent claims. For example, there is a vigorous market for *options* on shares of stock. You can buy the *right* to buy a share of stock at a defined price (a *call option*), or you can buy the right to *compel* someone *else* to buy a share of stock at a defined price (a *put* option). And, there are boundless other varieties of contingent claims.

In this chapter, we take a closer look at the value of contingent claims. Our strategy is to examine a number of *graphs* that display the value of the contingent claim in relation to the underlying claims. This will help to clarify our understanding of contingent claims valuation.

For convenience, we will use the language of stock options puts and calls and the like. At the end, we offer some further info on the options market. We cannot stress too strongly that the use of options language is only a convenience: the analysis ought to apply to contingent claims of any kind.

§ 36.02 Graphing Claims

In this section, we offer a number of graphs to help us in understanding the nature of options. Each of these graphs has two "axes" one vertical (north-south) and one horizontal (east-west). On the horizontal axis, we chart the value of the underlying *asset* (called "stock"). The further east we travel on the horizontal axis, the higher the value of the underlying asset. On the vertical axis, we will chart the value *available to the investor* (called "investor"). That is, the further north we go on the vertical axis, the higher the value to the investor. On each graph, there is also a 45 degree diagonal line dividing the space between the vertical and the horizontal axes. The diagonal shows the relationship between asset value and investor value. In one case, the value of the asset will be the *same* as the value to the investor, and the line will cut a simple 45-degree angle from the inside corner heading northeast. In other cases, the value of the asset will be different from the value to the investor, and the diagonal will reflect difference. All of this will become clearer in the context of some examples.

Stock as a Gift: Let us start with a simple case where the investor got the stock as a gift and now owns it outright. Every increase in stock price yields a corresponding increase in investment value. The line is a perfect 45-degree angle going northeast from west end of the horizontal axis (where Price and Value both = 0). You could (if you insisted) call it an option with a "zero exercise price," because the stockholder gets all the value of the stock.

Stock as a Gift Graph

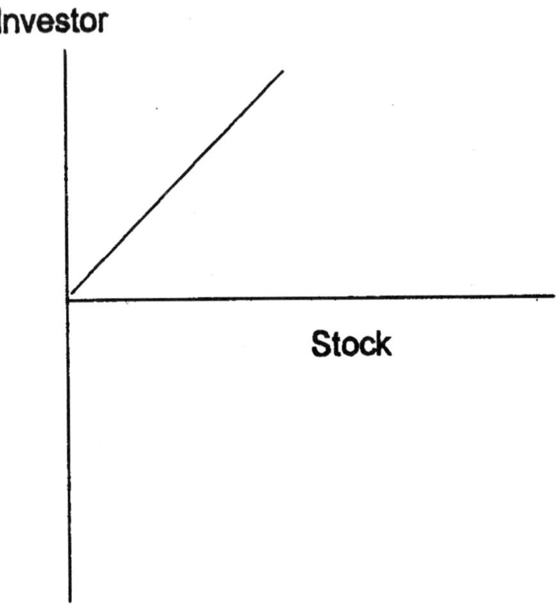

Stock Ownership: For contrast, here is the price-value relationship to the investor who bought the stock at the point where the diagonal crosses the horizontal. If the stock price rises above the purchase price, then the investor enjoys a net gain, but if it falls below, he has a loss.

Stock Ownership Graph

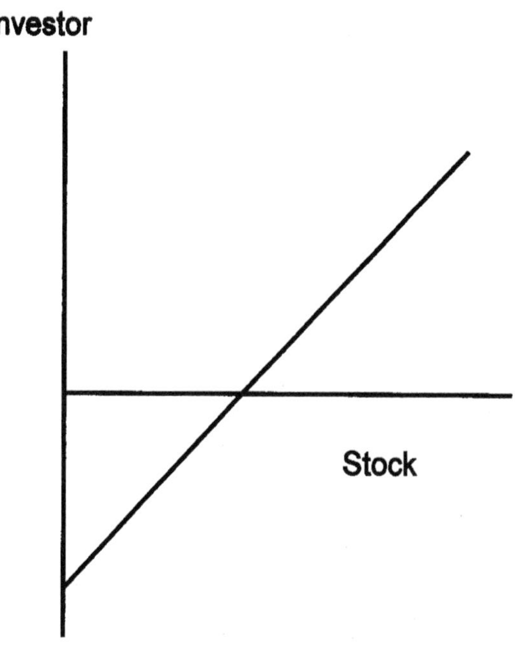

Call Option: Now, compare stock ownership with the rights under a "call option." The call option gives the option holder the right to buy (to "call") the stock from the "option writer" at a defined price. Note that the diagonal line proceeds on a 45-degree angle just like the stock graphs, but this time the line begins midway along the stock price line. This reflects the fact that the option holder does not get the stock until he pays the call price. So, the option has no value to him until the stock price exceeds the exercise price. This means that it has no intrinsic value until it reaches the exercise price. From the exercise price up, it gains in value dollar for dollar with the stock price.

Call Option Graph

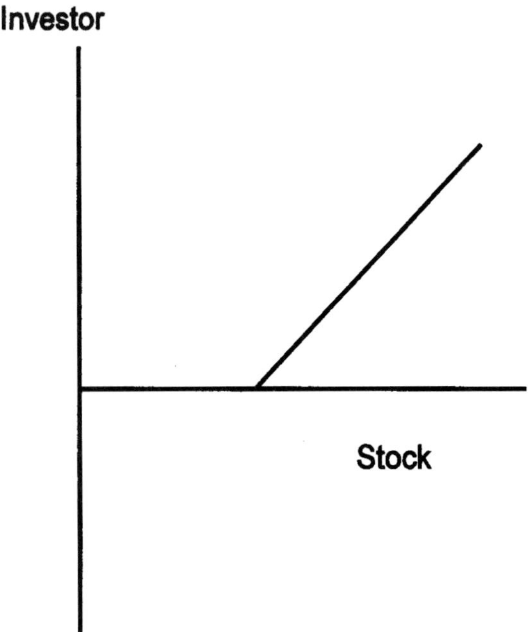

But note that there is nothing on this graph below the horizontal. That means that the option holder has neither rights nor liabilities below the option price. In summary:

$$V_C = \max [(V_S - Ex), 0]$$

That is, the value of the call (V_C) is the *greater* of the value of the stock minus the exercise price ($V_S - Ex$) or zero.

Put Option: On this graph we plot a different relationship — a "put option," which gives the investor the right to *sell* the stock at a given exercise price. You can see that it is the symmetric opposite of a call option. The option takes on value for the holder only when the stock price falls *below* the exercise price. From that point down, the option holder gains value dollar for dollar, as the stock price *falls*.

Put Option Graph

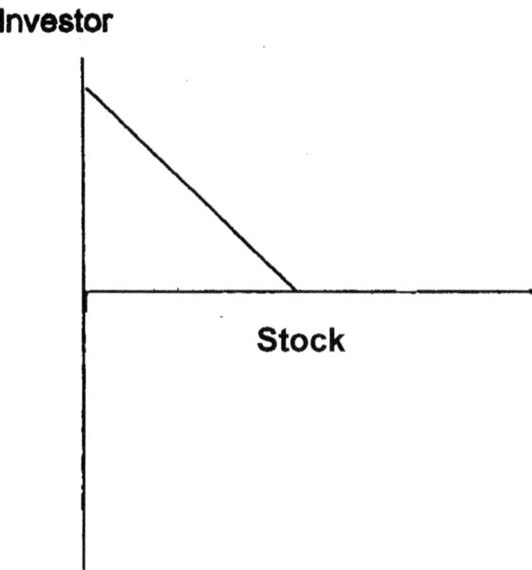

For example, suppose the exercise price is $60. If the stock price is $70, the put option is worthless to the holder. If the price falls to $45, the holder will exercise the option and collect $60 for a share of stock worth $45.

In summary:

$$V_P = \max [(Ex - V_S), 0]$$

In words: the value of the put (V_P) is the *greater* of the exercise price minus the value of the stock ($Ex - V_S$) or zero. Put options are less familiar than call options, and students often have trouble figuring out why anyone would ever write a put option. But they are more common than you might at first suppose. Indeed, there is a good chance you own a put option right now. Do you own a car? Do you insure the car against fire, theft and casualty? If so, you have a kind of put option: you have the right to "put" the car on the insurer (= the "option writer") under defined circumstances, in exchange for a defined sum. The insurer is willing to write the option because he is willing to "bet" you that the defined circumstances will not come to pass. He may lose the bet, but if he wins enough bets overall, he will make money.

Stock Plus Put: This graph shows a combination of interests. It shows a *stock* (the diagonal from the west end of the stock price line), *together with a put*. The put is overlaid on the stock. This is because, taking the stock together, the effect of the put is to "flatten" the loss on the stock. That is, from the exercise price down, for every dollar lost on the stock, the holder *gains a dollar on the put*. Taken together, the values plot as a horizontal line.

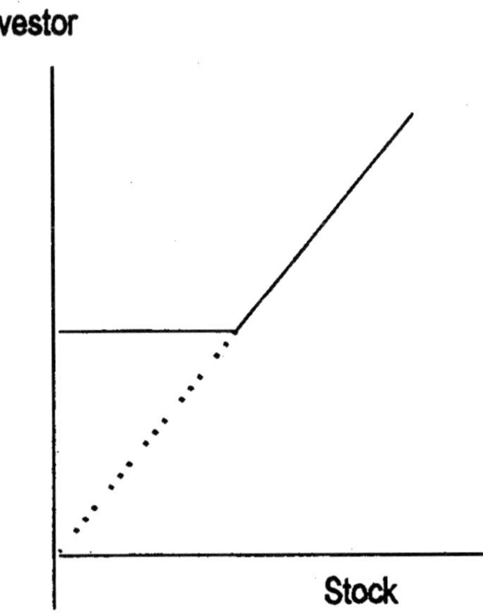

Stock and Short Call: This graph plots another combined position. Again, we have a stock, expressed as a diagonal from the west end of the stock price line. But this time, the investor is also *short a call*. That is, he has *written* a call at the designated exercise price. The practical consequence is that once the stock passes the exercise price, the stock will be *called away*. So, beyond the exercise price, every potential gain on the stock is canceled by the loss on the call.

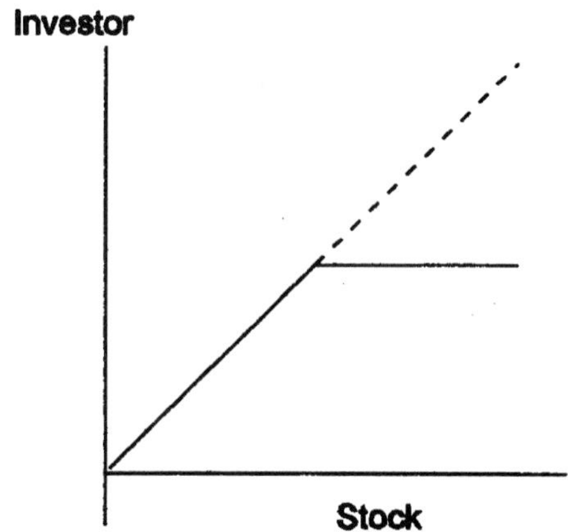

Web site: for some cool graphics, see:
http://www.intrepid.com/~robertl/strategies1.html.

Stock Plus Put, Minus Call—This is the Big One

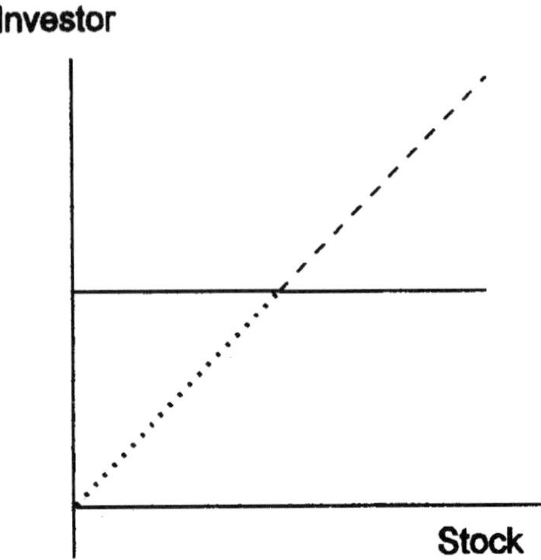

This graph draws together our previous examples to make an important and perhaps unexpected point. This graph combines the previous two graphs. It represents the payoffs from:

- BUY STOCK
- BUY PUT
- WRITE CALL

The payoff line is the dark horizontal line at the exercise price. The dotted line below the exercise price is the price-value relation of the stock alone. The dashed line above the exercise price is the price-value relation of the stock alone. To the left of the stock line, we see the payoff of a put with the stock. To the right, we see the payoff of a stock minus the call.

§ 36.03 The Basic Equation: Put-Call Parity

This last example brings us to a critically important result. It is this: the sum of our combined positions is represented by a *horizontal line*, parallel to our value line, but an inch above it on the graph. The line says that the value *to the investor* is the *same* no matter what happens. Translated, this means that the *combination is* a risk-free investment. So, the cost of this combination must be the present value of the exercise price, discounted at the risk-free rate. We have the following surprising and important result:

$$S + P - C = \frac{Ex}{(1 + r_f)}$$

In words: the aggregate value of a share of stock, plus a put and minus a call at the same exercise price, should equal the present value of that same exercise price. This is an important result for several reasons. Perhaps most important, it helps us to identify arbitrage opportunities. For example, rearrange the equation to isolate the value of the call:

$$C = S + P - \frac{Ex}{(1 + r_f)}$$

This means we can imitate the call by buying a share of stock and a put and borrowing the present value of the exercise price. For example, suppose the exercise price of a call is $106, the risk-free rate is 6 percent, and that there is a put priced at $12. The stock sells for $95. In an efficient market, we would expect a call to be priced at $7. But we should be able to get the same result by borrowing $100 ($106 ÷ 1.06) and paying $95 for a share of stock and $12 for a put.

This may be important if, for example, call is selling (for example) for $9. In that case, we would imitate the call as above, giving ourselves a package of payoffs that should sell for $7. Since they sell for $9, we next *sell* a call for $9, and pocket the $2 difference as an arbitrage profit. On the other hand, note that we can turn the equation around like this:

$$P = C + \frac{Ex}{(1 + r_f)} - S$$

Using data from our earlier example, suppose a call sells for $7 and the stock for $95, while the present value of the exercise price is $100. We can imitate a put by *shorting the stock* selling it for $95 now, with the obligation to deliver on the exercise day. Then we buy a call for $7, and invest $100 at the risk-free rate. We have imitated the payoffs of a put.

Then the predicted price of a put is, of course, $12. But what if a put sells for $9?

§ 36.04 Options and the Option Market

[A] Call Option

Now it is convenient to say a bit more about the market for options. Consider the affairs of the Circular Files, Inc. (CF), a large public company with shares traded on the New York Stock Exchange. CF is selling for $62 a share. Suppose you think CF has good prospects and that at $62, it is underpriced. You could vote your convictions by buying CF at $62 a share. But you have another choice. It turns out that there is a six-month option available on CF with a purchase price of $4 a share and an *exercise price*, also called a *striking price*, or just a *strike price* of $65 a share, to be exercised, if at all, only at the end of the option period. What kind of deal is this?

What you have here is a *call option* — the right to call on the seller to deliver the shares under specified conditions. It is a *European* call because it is exercisable at only one point in time, unlike an *American* call, which may be exercised at any time during the six-month period. European calls are conceptually easier to work with and we will focus most of our attention on them here, but in fact, the differences are less than you might expect, and an awful lot of what you learn about European calls will transfer over to American calls.[1]

What are my rights upon purchasing a call option? That all depends on the market price of the share at the time I have an opportunity to exercise my rights. If the price of a share is below \$65 — say, \$47 — there is no right to exercise in any event and I have lost my \$4. If the price is anywhere above \$69 — say, \$80 — I can make a profit by buying the share for the *exercise or striking price* of \$65. I have made an immediate \$15 profit on the deal, in the sense that I can turn around and resell the stock that I just bought for \$65 at \$80, if I like. Of course, I paid \$4 for the option, so my *net-profit* is only (\$15 – \$4), or \$11. Formalizing, we can say:

$$V_{Call} = MAX\ (S - Ex, 0) - P_{Call}$$

That is: the *value* of the call equals the *maximum* of (stock price less exercise price; or zero) minus whatever we paid for the call. In our examples, we paid \$4 for the call, and the exercise price was \$65. In the first example, the share price was \$47, so share price minus exercise price equals –\$18. Zero is larger than –\$18, so the call value is zero minus the \$4 we paid for it, and we are net negative \$4. In the second example, the share price was \$80. Share price minus exercise price is \$15. But we must subtract our original call investment, so our net gain is \$11. To test your understanding, what will be our net if the share price is \$66?

$$V_{Call} = MAX\ (\$66 - \$65; 0) - \$4$$

Since (\$66 – \$65) = \$1, and since \$1 is larger than zero, we take the \$1. Then we subtract the \$4 cost. This leaves us with a net loss of \$3 — but note that our net loss of \$3 is smaller than the \$4 loss we would have sustained had we not exercised the call at all.

If the call is valued at minus \$4 until the strike price is reached at \$65. Then the call starts to increase in value and takes on a positive value four dollars later at a share price of \$69. Notice also how, from the sellers perspective, it is the mirror image. The seller is in the black dollars until the strike price is reached. Beyond \$69, the seller starts to lose money; he is selling his stock for less now than he could get on the open market.

[B] Put Option

So much for the call option. Now, let us look at the *put option*, whereby the owner of the stock buys the right to *put* the stock on someone else when it falls below a prescribed price. The *seller* (or *writer*) of the put must take it and pay that price, which we can call, on analogy to the call option, the *exercise* or *striking* price. For example, suppose I buy a put for \$4 with a striking price of \$32. On exercise day, the price of the share is \$12. My value is:

$$V_{Put} = MAX\ (Ex - S, 0) - P_{Put} = MAX\ (\$32 - \$12, 0) - \$4$$

Since (\$32 – \$12) = \$20, and \$20 is greater than zero, we take the \$20. To establish our net gain, we subtract the \$4 cost of the put, pocketing \$16.

[1] The appellations are misleading, by the way: American calls trade in Europe and European in America.

Note that in our previous formula, we subtracted *exercise* price from *share* price. Here, we subtract *share* price from *exercise* price.

If you are having trouble getting your mind around the idea of a put option, think of a casualty insurance policy, like the policy you may carry on your car. You pay a premium to the insurance company. If the value of the car declines below a certain point (say, after a head-on collision), the insurer "buys the car" by paying the policy proceeds. The insurer does not guarantee against *all* misfortunes, of course — only those specified in the policy. But that is just a detail, the principle remains. And this is no mere metaphor, either: as we shall see, "insurance" and options are in fact aspects of the same analytical framework, each one informed by what we know about the other.

Here is a graphical representation of a put. Notice that at a share price of zero, the put is worth its exercise price minus its cost: ($32 − $4) = $28. Also, once the share price rises above the exercise price, the put itself becomes worthless and the investor is stuck with a $4 loss. Notice finally that the mirror image relationship between buying and selling holds for puts as well as calls.

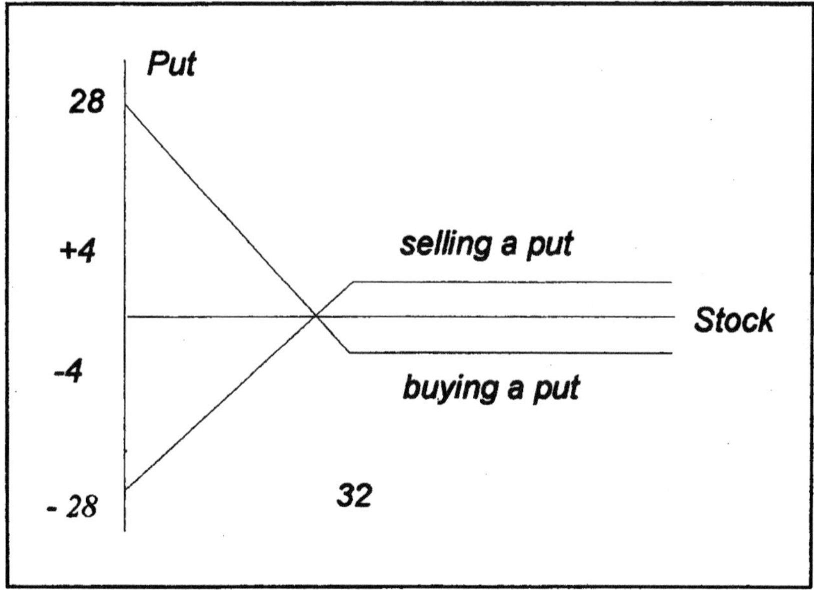

What would happen if we went ahead and just bought the stock but wanted to cover our downside? Is there a way to do this? Yes, we buy a put option which is exercisable at the price below which you do not want the stock to fall. The 45 degree line represents ownership of the stock, that is, the line on which the value of the share has a one-to-one relationship with share price. The second line is the same as stock ownership when the share price is above the value of the put, but equals the value of the put for any lower share prices.

Notice two important results. First, the investor's down side is protected. She will never fall below the $28 net that she will receive upon exercising the put option. Second, in this scenario, the "buy-stock/buy-put" charts out at the same angle as buying a call. If the investor had just put money equal to the exercise price into the bank and then went out and bought a call with the same exercise price he would be in exactly the same boat as buying the share and covering his downside with a put. Essentially, in this second scenario, the investor is covering her downside by *not* buying the stock and reaping the benefits of the upside not through stock ownership but through a call option. This is the olive press example where you get a call option on the use of olive presses, put your "olive-press" money in the equivalent of a savings account, and then watch the weather reports. We can formalize these insights in the following equation:

Value of Put + Share Ownership = Value of Call + Present Value of Exercise Price

As we saw in § 36.03, this equality is called *put-call parity*, and it plays a critical role in our attempt to value options.

Now, what do you make of the last graph? Do you recognize the pattern? Well, yes, it does look like a butterfly, but, as Gertrude Stein once said, "There is no there there." It also looks like the buyer's and seller's perspective of an option package involving a put and a call. The buyer gets the upside and the downside both. His put covers a falling stock. His call covers a rising stock. Why would there even be a seller, here? What is in it for him?

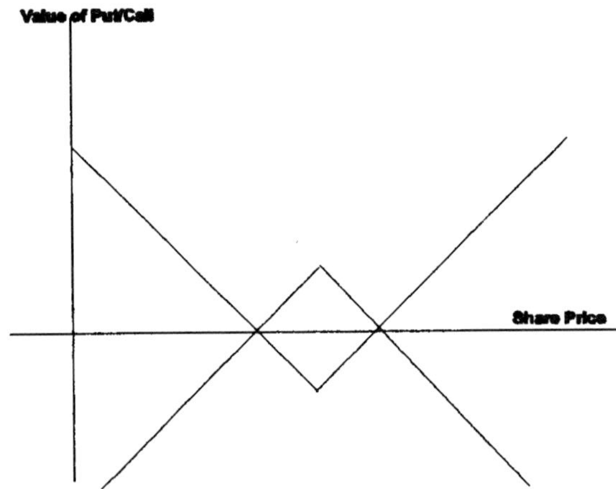

Notice that the seller does have one opportunity to make some money, that little triangle just above the horizontal axis. When would we be in the triangle? When the exercise price and the share price are very close, or, in other words, when the stock is not very volatile. In that case, the seller's gain from the price of the put and the call outweighs the buyer's gain from the stock's movements. The seller is betting on stability. The buyer is expecting volatility. This point highlights a theme that we will see again and again in our study of options: options are essentially a tool for risk management and are fundamentally related to the underlying stock's volatility.

§ 36.05 Note: Another Look at What You are Paying For

Many students have trouble with the basic intuition — the issue of what you were "paying for" when you exercise the option. Let's give it another try.

Consider an American call option with an exercise price of $50, where the stock is selling for $35. What will you pay for such an option? If the option will expire *today*, precious little. The option is out of the money — it does not pay to exercise now — and with an imminent expiration date, there is little chance it will wind up in the money. But next, suppose that the option will expire *a year from today*. The extra time increases the chance that the option will wind up in the money, and correspondingly increases the chance that the option will be worth something. You could tell a similar story about volatility: the more volatile the underlying stock, the greater the chance that the option will wind up in the money, making it correspondingly more valuable. So what you are being offered is a *chance* — okay, if you insist, a lottery ticket. Your appraisal of that chance is the price you will be willing to pay.

Now, suppose that the underlying stock price is $60 a share. Conceptually, pricing is a bit more complicated here because you have *two* opportunities: one, the "lottery ticket," as above, and the other, the opportunity for immediate exercise. Note that the premium for immediate exercise is ($60 − $50) = $10. Suppose the option sold for $9. You would buy the option ($9), pay the exercise price ($50) and enjoy an instant $1 arbitrage profit [$60 − ($50 + $9)]. Therefore, the *net price* of the stock (stock price minus exercise price) *always* sets the *lower bound* on the price of an in-the-money American call: the price *must* be no less than $10.

No less, but how much more? Suppose you have high hopes for the underlying stock: you expect it to go up another $100, to $160. Suppose you pay $55 today for the option alone. If the stock does go to $160, you exercise your call and make a profit of [$160 − ($55 + $50)], or $55.

You might get the sense that there is no limit to how high an option price might go, but in fact, there is a limit. Take the previous case. Suppose your hopes for the underlying stock are even higher than the hopes of the previous bidder. You would be willing to bid all the way up to $62. Will you in fact? Not if you know what you are doing: instead, you will just *buy the underlying stock* that is now selling for $60. In other words, the *stock price* sets an *upper bound* on the option price.

Summarizing, the option price impounds both the "lottery ticket" value and the value of immediate exercise (in the case of an out-of-the-money option, zero), with the net price serving as a lower bound, and the stock price, as the upper bound.

§ 36.06 A Numerical Demonstration

Either this man is dead
or my watch has stopped.

—Groucho Marx

Earlier, we asserted the basic rule of put-call parity. We demonstrated the rule graphically: we showed that a combination of stock plus put minus call turned into a straight line, denoting a risk-free investment. We can also demonstrate the point numerically.

To see that this is so, consider the case of ChanceCo, which sells for $81 a share. One year from today, ChanceCo will sell for either of two prices: $115 or $68. The market offers both puts and calls against ChanceCo stock. Both are European options that expire a year from today. In each case, the strike price is $110. The risk-free interest rate is 10 percent. There are any number of possible option strategies with ChanceCo, but consider this one. Buy the stock, buy a put, and sell a call. What will be the payoff from this strategy? It will look like this:

Payoffs from ChanceCo		
Initial Transaction	Price = $115	Price = $68
Buy Stock	$115	$68
Buy Put	$0	$42
Sell Call	$(5)	$0
Total	$110	$110

Note that this strategy entails *zero risk*. The underlying stock may be very risky, but we have eliminated the risk by the way we constructed our option package. If the stock price goes up, we throw away the put. The stock gets called away from us, but we get $110. If the price goes down, the call expires unused, and we collect $110 on the put.

§ 36.07 Designer Cash Flows and the Collapse of Title

Earlier we considered a number of devices that helped the investor to manage. He might look for opportunities to reduce his risk by *diversification*. Even if he couldn't diversify, he might find ways to transfer some or all of his risk through the use of *futures*, or *short sales*, or *swaps* and suchlike. With the introduction of options, the tool kit is complete: now the investor can get substantially any combination of cash flows he may want. An "asset" emerges as no more than the center of a force positive and negative signs, with an infinite range of possible variations. This revolution in asset management poses a challenge to at least one concept hallowed in law: the idea of "ownership," also known as "title."

In truth, your professors have always told you to be suspicious of the concept of ownership. Your property teacher told you that property is "a bundle of sticks" meaning, apparently, that the term subsumed a variety of concepts, not inevitably linked together. The great Karl Llewellyn was so ill of "title," tried to banish it from his Uniform Commercial Code.

Of course you know enough not to take your professors too seriously, and in fact, for every day purposes, the concept of ownership works pretty well. Consider your client, Otto, who carries a widget in his pocket. If the value of the widget goes up, Otto gets to enjoy the gain; and if it goes down, he bears the loss. Since he enjoys the "upside" and the "downside," we are habituated, almost without thinking about it, to recognize that Otto is the owner of the widget. Even Karl Llewellyn gives this reading a kind of backhanded endorsement: in Article 2 of the Code, without relying on explicitly on title, we speak of the transfer of the "risk of loss," which comes pretty close to the same thing.

You get further confirmation of this view if you consider the law of secured credit real estate mortgages, for example, or personal property security interests under UCC Article 9. Suppose Otto borrows $100 from Leander and gives Leander an interest in the widget to secure repayment of the loan. If Otto does not repay the loan, then Leander may be able to sell the widget. But his rights remain a function of the loan. So, if the widget yields more than $100 at sale, then Leander may have to pay over the surplus to Otto. And if yields less, then he may have a right to sue Otto for the deficiency.[2] The effect of these rules is that Otto continues to enjoy the risk of loss and the opportunity for gain: in ordinary parlance, despite the security interest, he remains the "owner."

Indeed, this was the point of so many of the "form over substance" cases that we discussed in the note on usury (see § 4.02). In the typical "sale plus resale," the seller (borrower) remains liable to repay the entire purchase *price*, whether or not the asset is worth that much. Courts pretty generally recognize this as a giveaway of the fact that "ownership" remained with the "seller."

The same applies although the analysis gets a little trickier to a case where Leander owns the widget and transfers it to Otto by lease. As long as Leander retains the *residual* risk of loss (and opportunity for gain) we are comfortable treating him as the "owner."

But now things begin to get dodgy. Consider, for example, the fact that many lenders will not be able to get a claim for any deficiency in value. The loan may be "non-recourse" by contract, meaning that the lender has recourse to the property given as security only and not the transferor. Or it may be defined as non-recourse by statute. If the loan is non-recourse (for whatever reason), it is the lender who bears the risk of decline in value, while the borrower retains the opportunity for gain.

There has been a subtle but important shift here. No longer do risk of loss and opportunity for gain lie in the same hands. You could say the fundamental

[2] UCC § 9-504. The Code allows for a kind of "strict foreclosure" in some cases, but that point doesn't destroy the main line of the argument. UCC § 9-505.

principle of ownership has been broken. Of course we don't say that: we continue to treat the borrower as the "owner," even though he has only one of the two characteristics that we used to define ownership.

But compare this with the situation where Otto takes widget from Leander under a contract that gives him the right but not the obligation to become the full owner on payment of the purchase price i.e., an option contract. We don't think owner of the call option as the owner of the item upon which he holds an option yet in terms of risk and benefit, he is no different than one who gives security for a non-recourse loan.

If you buy this argument, then the definition of "title" has broken down altogether we treat "like" items as "unlike," with no basis for making a distinction. Of course in practice, it doesn't work that way: in practice we continue to distinguish owner from non-owner, sale from lease, security interest from transfer of title. Yet in a world of option pricing, where there is no limit to the way you disaggregate cash flows, it is interesting to wonder whether and how long the old ways can hold on.

Chapter 37

The Binomial Option Pricing Model (BOPM): Calls

I can call spirits from the Vasty Deep!
Why so you can, and so can any man;
but will they answer you?

—Shakespeare

§ 37.01 Introduction

In the last chapter, we tried to understand options. We started out with the traditional model of property as "a bundle of sticks" — rights that can be divided up. One way to divide the bundle that represents security ownership is to separate the upside from the downside. Focusing on the upside, we discussed the *call option*, where you pay a *call premium* for the right to buy a share at an *exercise price* in the future. If the share price *exceeds* the exercise price, then you make money. If not, you lose the price of the option. Moving to the downside, we discussed a classic *put option*, where you pay a *put premium* for the right to *sell* your share at an *exercise price* in the future. If the share price is *lower* than the exercise price, you make money. If not, you do not.

We pointed out that the world of options has exploded over the past 20 years — exploded in two different ways. First, there has been an explosion in the *creation* of option products that trade on organized exchanges — designer options, if you will. You can buy options on the movement of interest rates, options on foreign currency, even options that are based on the price of an entire stock market. Companies sometimes issue *warrants* on their own stock; a warrant is nothing but a call option issued by the issuer itself, rather than a secondary market option.

Second, we said that new ways of understanding and valuing options has led to the realization that there are option-like transactions everywhere. We argued that a casualty insurance policy is for all practical purposes a put option: the right to put the commodity on the insurer under defined conditions. Another instance is the hierarchy of ownership within a corporation. The equity position in a leveraged company is for all practical purposes a call option: it is the right to purchase the company at a certain exercise price, namely, the total value of outstanding debt. Debt, in this instance, is essentially a put option, the right to sell the company for the level of the debt if it drops below the exercise price (i.e., if the total assets fall below total outstanding debt).

It is time now to show you how option pricing works. To do so, we will work through the *binomial option pricing model* (BOPM). Not only will the model provide us with a device for pricing an option, it will also introduce us to a strategy for solving our general valuation problem. And finally, it will give us a hint as to how it comes about that we "invent" so many options in practice.

§ 37.02 The Model

To examine the binomial model, consider the stock of OptCo. There is a one-year European call outstanding against OptCo with an exercise price of $105. We do not know the price (or the value) of the option. But we do know that OptCo stock sells for $100 and that one year from today it will sell for either of two prices — either $125 or $80. Assume the risk-free rate of interest is 10 percent.

How can we price the call option? Here is a strategy. Suppose we can construct a portfolio from "known" securities — OptCo stock and risk-free borrowing — that exactly mimics the payoff of the OptCo call option. Since we know the prices of the components, we will know the price of this *"replicating" portfolio*. Can we contend that the price of a call option must equal this replicating portfolio? Yes, because if it did not, there would be a money machine: investors would rush to take advantage of the disparity between the value of the call option and its current price, thus bidding the price up (or down) to equilibrium, but taking advantage of the arbitrage windfall in the adjustment period.

We do it as follows. Let "s" = a fractional investment in one share of OptCo stock. Let "f" = risk-free borrowing and lending. Since the risk-free rate is 10 percent, we know that at the end of one year, the value of the risk-free investment will be 1.1f. Now we want to construct a portfolio that mimics the payoff of the call option in our two future states. The portfolio must satisfy these two equations:

$$\$\ 125s + 1.1f = \$\ 20$$

$$\$\ 80s + 1.1f = \$\ 0$$

This series contains two unknowns (s and f), but there are two equations so we can solve them by using a little algebra. In fact, if we subtract the second equation from the first, then:

$$(\$125 - \$80)s = \$20$$

$$s = 20 \div 45 = 0.4444$$

Substituting 0.4444 for s, we can see that:

$$(\$80)(0.4444) + 1.1f = 0$$

$$f = -\$32.32$$

To check, derive f from $125s + 1.1f = $20. You should get the same number.

Note that f is *negative*, while s is *positive*. This means that s is an *inflow* and f is an *outflow*. We can infer from this fact that the investor *owns* her stock, but must *repay* a risk-free loan equal to ($32.32)(1.1). How did she achieve this position? She achieved it by *buying* 44.44 percent of a share at t=0, and *borrowing* $32.32 at the risk-free rate. Since the share price was $100, the stock purchase must have cost $44.44. So her out-of pocket cost was $44.44 – $32.32 or $12.12. What do we get for $12.12? We get the following payoff matrix:

	High		Low	
Stock Valued at:	($125)(0.44)	= $55.56	($80)(0.44)	= $35.56
Loan Debt of:	($32.32)(1.1)	= $35.56	($32.32)(1.1)	= $35.56
		$20.00		$00.00

But this is precisely the payoff we would get from owning a call. Under the principle of one price, an investment package that offers the same payoff as a call must trade at the same price as a call. So, the price of a call must also be $12.12.

§ 37.03 Testing the Model: Arbitrage

The reason why the price of the call must be $12.12 is that if the price were anything other than $12.12, then on the rule of one price, there is an opportunity for arbitrage.

Call Overpriced: To see that this is so, first consider the case where the call is $15. According to your model, this call appears overpriced with respect to the stock. Since the call appears overpriced with respect to the stock, the strategy is: buy stock, write call.

In terms of our model, buy 44.44 percent of a share (for $44.44), and write a call for $15. To pay for the stock, borrow $32.32 at the risk-free rate, and use $12.12 from the proceeds of the call. No need to worry about repaying the loan: the stock will be worth $35.56 in the worst case, so you will have enough to cover it. The strategy leaves you $15 − $12.12 or $2.88 left over, which you can put in your pocket. At t = 1, your payoffs will be:

If the price goes	**Up**		**Down**
Your stock is worth. . .	($125)(0.44) = $55.56	Your stock is worth. . .	($80) (0.44) = $35.56
But on the call, you lose. . .	−($125 − $105) = $20	The call expires unexercised. . .	
And you must repay the debt. . .	($32.32)(1.1) = $35.56	But you can cover your debt. . .	($32.32)(1.1) = $35.56
So your net payoff is. . .	$0	So your net payoff is. . .	$0

In words, you are certain to break even on this deal. But you pocketed $2.88 with no risk.

Call Underpriced: Can you make money if the call is *under*priced? You can. For example, suppose the call is selling at $9. According to your model, the call is underpriced with respect to the stock. Your strategy is:

Short stock, buy call

In words, short 44.44 percent of a share at t = 0, for delivery at t = 1. This gets you $44.44. Buy a call at $9. To cover your downside, invest $32.32 at the risk-free rate. You now hold ($44.44 − $9 − $32.32) = $3.12, which you can put in your pocket. At t=1, the payoffs will be:

If the price goes	Up		Down
You close the risk-free account	($32.32)(1.1) = $35.56	You close the risk-free account	($32.32)(1.1) = $35.56
And exercise the call. . .	($125 − $105) = $20	The call expires unexercised	
And cover your short. . .	−($125 − 0.44) = $55.56	But you can cover your short . . .	− $35.56
So your net payoff is. . .	$0	So your net payoff is. . .	$0

Once again, you have a guaranteed zero payoff. But you pocketed an arbitrage profit (here, $3.12) with no risk.

§ 37.04 Option Delta and the Hedge Ratio

Here's a general statement of the binomial model: buy a fraction of a share of stock and finance in part with risk-free borrowing. Call the appropriate fraction the "*option delta*," or Δ and we can restate the formula for call value as:

$$C = \Delta S - F$$

Rearranging, we get a surprising (but important) result:

$$F = \Delta S - C$$

Translated: if you want a risk-free investment, you can get it as follows:

Buy stock, write call

This gives you equivalent of investing at the risk-free rate. In other words, by investing the option delta and selling a call, you can effectively *hedge* the risk of the original share. Because it allows you to construct a perfect hedge, the option delta is also known as the "hedge ratio." Note that the strategy in this example is the same strategy we followed to capture an arbitrage profit when the call was overpriced.

Recall our previous example, where the potential payoffs were $125 and $80, and where the hedge ratio was 0.44. The share price was $100; the equilibrium price of a call was $12.12. Suppose we buy 0.44 of a share for $44.44 and sell a call for $12.12. Our net out of pocket investment is ($44.44 − $12.12) = $32.32. What are our payoffs? They are as follows:

If the Stock Price Goes	Up		Down
You have stock worth . . .	(\$125)(0.44) = \$55.56	You have stock worth . . .	(\$80)(0.44) = \$35.56
But you honor the call . . .	(\$125 – \$105) = \$20	The call expires unused. . .	
So you end up with . . .	\$35.56	So you end up with. . .	\$35.56

But a payoff of \$35.56 one year from now is only worth \$35.56 ÷ 1.1 = \$32.32 today. This is identical to our original investment, so we could just as well have invested the \$32.32 at the risk-free rate.

The hedge ratio is a function of other variables in the option equation, so the ratio will change from moment to moment as the other variables change. Other things being equal, the further out of the money the call is, the lower the hedge ratio, and vice-versa. When the exercise price is high and the asset value is negligible, the hedge ratio will be near zero. When the call is deep in the money, the hedge ratio will approach one. The *rate* at which the hedge ratio *changes* will also vary: in fact, the rate of change is highest when the call is "at the money." Students of options call this rate of change *gamma*.

Web site: for a more extensive view of binomial option pricing, see:

http://wwwsel.iit.nrc.ca/~erdogmus/SIA/Binomial/BinomialOPM.html#Note.

Chapter 38

Binomials Again: Puts

Lovely to look at,
Delightful to hold,
But if you break it,
We mark it sold.

—Gift Shop Sign

§ 38.01 Introduction

In this chapter, we extend the logic of the call option to the task of valuing a put. The extension is important, and if you followed what has gone before, surprisingly easy.

§ 38.02 Valuing a Put

Can we use the binomial theorem to value a put? We can. Recall OptCo from the previous chapter. A share of OptCo costs \$100. The possible payoffs at t = 1 are \$125 and \$80. Risk-free borrowing and lending is available at 10 percent. Last time, we studied a *call* option with an exercise price of \$105. Here, we study a *put* option with the same exercise price of \$105. To value the put, we will apply the same strategy we applied before: we will construct a "synthetic put" out of stock and risk-free borrowing and lending. Our replicating portfolio must have the same payoffs as the put. We can summarize the results in these two equations:

$$\$125s + 1.1f = \$\ 0$$

$$\$\ 80s + 1.1f = \$\ 25$$

Subtracting the second equation from the first, then:

$$(\$125 - \$80)s = -\$25$$

Note the negative sign. So, s must equal −25 ÷ 45 or −0.5556. Having solved for s, now we can solve for f: the solution is \$63.13. But notice that this time the signs are reversed: Our s is *negative* while f is *positive.* What can this mean? It means that at t = 1 we must *pay out* a sum equal to the value of 55.56 percent of a share of stock, while we *receive* a sum equal to 1.1 *times* risk-free borrowing. What could have led to this result? It must mean that at t = 0 we *sold the stock short* — received the price of the stock on a promise of future delivery and *invested* at the risk-free rate. Our original risk-free investment must have been \$63.13. Our short sale would have been (\$100)(0.5556) = \$55.56. Our out of pocket investment is thus:

$$\$63.13 - \$55.56 = \$7.58$$

Since this portfolio duplicates the result of a put, the equilibrium price of the put must be the same as the cost of the portfolio, or \$7.58.

To double check, recall the principle of put-call parity: S plus P must equal C plus PV(E). In a previous assignment, we determined that the equilibrium value of a call is $12.12. The exercise price is $105, so PV(E) must equal $95.46. Therefore:

$$\$100 + \$\ 7.58 = \$107.58$$

$$\$12.12 + \$95.46 = \$107.58$$

So, everything checks. Note also that the hedge ratio on the put equals the hedge ratio of the call minus one. The hedge ratio on the call was 0.44. On the put, it is −0.56.

§ 38.03 The Risk-Neutral Method

So far, we have learned how to value *call* options and *put* options (contingent assets) by creating *synthetic assets.* To construct our synthetic portfolios we used: (a) the underlying stock, and (b) risk-free borrowing and lending. We *know* the market value of the stock, and the cost of risk-free borrowing and lending. Our strategy was to use these assets whose prices are *known* to construct a synthetic asset with the same payoffs as the (*unknown*) contingent asset. Since the synthetic asset was constructed out of assets whose market values were known, we could derive the market value of the synthetic asset. Then, under the law of one price, it must be that the contingent asset has the same market value as the synthetic asset; otherwise, there would be an opportunity for arbitrage.

We can check our results by another strategy. It is called the *risk-neutral method.* The logic of the risk-neutral method is as follows. In our previous analysis, we priced our contingent asset by factoring out all risk: we made the call (or the put) into a kind of risk-free investment. In the risk-neutral method, we treat it explicitly as a risk-free investment and try to price it as such.

To carry out the risk-neutral analysis, we need to know: (a) the risk-free rate, and (b) the potential outcomes at $t = 1$. In our OptCo example, we have these data at hand. We assume a risk-free rate of 10 percent. We predict that the $t = 1$ value of OptCo will be either: (a) $125, or (b) $80. We note that the present market value of an OptCo share is $100. Translating these numbers into percentages, we can see that the value of OptCo will either: (a) increase by 25 percent [($125 − $100) ÷ $100], or (b) decrease by 20 percent [($80 − $100) ÷ $100].

We proceed as follows. First, we determine the *probability* that the value of OptCo will increase or decrease. Let p = the probability of a price rise, and note that (1 − p) must represent the probability of a price drop. If (as we have assumed) OptCo is a risk-free investment, it must be that:

$$0.10 = p(0.25) + (1-p)(-0.20)$$

Solving for p, we can see that the probability of an "uptick" is 66.7 percent (and of a "downtick" 33.3 percent). Next, take these probabilities and the *call* payoffs to figure the $t = 1$ value of a call:

$$\text{Call}_{(t=1)} = (0.667)(\$20) + (0.333)(0) = \$13.33$$

At 10 percent, the PV of $13.33 is $12.12. So the risk-neutral method shows us that the present value of a call is $12.12, which is exactly the same number that we got by the binomial method.

We can also use the risk-neutral method to value a *put*. We use the same equation we used to price a call, but we substitute the t=1 payoffs on a put.

$$\text{Put}_{(t=1)} = (0.667)(0) + (0.333)(\$25) = \$8.33.$$

The t=0 value of $8.33 = $7.58, so everything checks.

§ 38.04 Managing Risk

It is 1982. We will make our fortune in the business of running savings and loan associations (S&Ls), those bank-like institutions created to lend money for home building in the neighborhood. We will proceed as follows: we will buy *two* S&Ls. We will invest the portfolio of one on the assumption that interest rates will rise. We will invest the portfolio of the other on the assumption that rates will fall. One will succeed and one will fail. The success, we will keep. The failure, we will hand over to the government.

The beauty part is that our depositors won't mind because they are protected either way. If we succeed, we honor their contract claims and return their deposits with interest. If we fail, they are protected by the program of deposit insurance.

Such, in only mild exaggeration, is a summary of the result of one of the dumbest public policy decisions since — well, there have been a lot of dumb decisions, but you'd have to go a long way to find anyone today who would defend the way we let the S&L crisis boil up in the 1980s.

The S&L crisis had its roots in the wave of inflation that drove interest rates to record levels in the late 1970s and early 1980s. Recall that the traditional S&L made its money by "borrowing short" (from demand depositors) and "lending long" (to home buyers). Since long-term rates generally exceed short term, this is a pretty good recipe for slow, dull, easy money in good times. Old-time S&L insiders used to talk about the 3-6-3 regime — borrow at 3 percent, lend at 6 percent, hit the golf course by 3 on Friday afternoon.

In a regime like this you hardly need insurance, and indeed, the S&Ls went almost failure-free until the inflation jolted short-term rates and left S&Ls scrambling to find depositors willing to cover their fixed portfolio of loans.

Congress responded by lifting the constraints on S&L loans. Previously, the S&Ls had been more or less restricted to residential real estate. By lifting the limit, Congress allowed the S&Ls to look for investments with higher returns, and also to diversify into risky investments — which, as we have seen, may actually make the whole portfolio safer.

In itself, the decision to lift the limit on S&L lending seems defensible. But while it lifted the limits on lending, Congress did nothing to disturb the hallowed pattern of deposit insurance. The combined result was almost a recipe for failure. Indeed, hundreds of S&Ls went broke in the later 1980s.

Nobody can tell you a plausible number for the total cost of the resultant bail-out, but a guess in the range of five to 15 billion is not out of line.

Inevitably, there was a lot of finger-pointing as the debacle crested, and a good many assertions of theft or fraud against the managers of the failed S&Ls. Clearly there was some fraud. A few S&L executives went to jail and others probably should have. Yet it is wonderful to consider how much of the debacle was the result, not of grand theft, but of a purpose to exploit so misguided a public policy.[1]

[1] For good background on the S&L crisis, see Azar, *Note, FIRREA: Controlling Savings and Loan Association Credit Risk Through Capital Standards and Asset Restrictions,* 100 Yale L.J. 149 (1990).

Chapter 39

Option Theory Applied: The Option to Abandon

> Simpkin . . . I am undone
> and worn to a threadpaper,
> for I have NO MORE TWIST.
>
> —The Tailor of Gloucester

§ 39.01 Introduction

We have noted that option pricing theory applies not just to "market options," but to any kind of contingent claim. And we have observed that once you understand how options function, you can create "designer options," to give you the benefits that options may yield.

Indeed if we pressed the point, we could probably find a good many option transactions in topics we studied earlier in this book. Some of them are fairly obvious. For example, a "callable bond" gives the borrower the "option" to "call" his bond under defined circumstances. A callable bond will cost the borrower more than an otherwise similar noncallable bond. We could easily analyze the price disparity as a premium for the option to call. Similarly, a lease with the option to purchase will cost the lessee a bit more than a lease with no such right. Again, we could analyze that the disparity as the premium for the right to call.

In this chapter, we take a more extended look at option analysis. We consider the case of the put option. We examine, first the case of the "option to abandon" in an ordinary investment opportunity — a case where put option analysis helps us to improve our valuation. We move on to the case of an *artificial* put option — where the parties agree to create a kind of put option to give the investor a tailor-made investment package. Then we consider a famous public policy disaster, best understood in put option terms. Finally, we consider these "options to abandon" from the standpoint of the person who bears the brunt of exercise.

§ 39.02 Option to Abandon

Just as we can find call options everywhere once we start to look for them, so also it is with puts. We have already seen that casualty insurance is a kind of put option. For another example, we return to a topic we have considered earlier — the matter of salvage value, and the importance of defining an exit strategy (see Chapter 16 above).

Consider LemCo, which wants to buy a new compressor to make lemons out of lemonade. The device will cost $19,000. Revenue estimates differ, depending on whether business goes well or badly. LemCo believes there is a 60 percent chance that business will go well, and a 40 percent chance that it will go badly. LemCo cannot know at $t = 0$ which it will be. But whichever scenario emerges in the first year can be expected to continue through the second. The device will last for two years and then be scrapped at t=2. The cash flows are as follows:

Business Goes	0	1	2	Scrap (at t=2)
Well (60%)	($19,000)	$11,000	$15,000	$1,000
Badly (40%)	($19,000)	$5,500	$7,500	$500

LemCo estimates its cost of capital at 13 percent. Discounting and weighting for probability, this translates into a project value as follows:

Business Goes	0	1	2	Total	Weighted
Well (60%)	($19,000)	$ 9,735	$12,530	$3,265	$1,959
Badly (40%)	($19,000)	$ 4,867	$6,265	($7,868)	($3,147)
				NPV	($1,188)

The NPV is negative. The project should be rejected.

But now, suppose in addition that LemCo believes it can sell the device at t=1, if it chooses, for $12,000. How should LemCo evaluate the opportunity to sell?

To answer this question, note first that the opportunity has no effect on the operating revenues to be credited at t=1. All these are earned during the first year of operation before the opportunity to sell arises. Rather, the task is to evaluate the project as a "keep or sell" choice *at the margin* from t=1. Here are the cash flows that arise from keeping the device (including the opportunity cost of foregoing the t=1 sale), as seen from t=1, but discounted back to t=0.

Business Goes	1	2	Total
Well	($10,619)	$12,530	$1,911
Badly	($10,619)	$6,265	($4,354)

Note that the column for t=2 is identical to the t=2 column on the previous chart. Note also that probability weighting is no longer an issue. As of t=1 we will know whether the business is going well or badly, and by definition we expect the existing pattern to continue into the future. We can see also that if business goes well and we forego the t = 1 sale, we enjoy a positive NPV of $1,911. If business goes badly and we forego the sale, our NPV is negative $4,354. The conclusion is inescapable: sell if things are going badly, keep if they are going well.

We can integrate this decision into a revised statement of cash flows:

Business Goes	**0**		**1**	**2**	**Total**	**Weighted**
Well (60%)	($19,000)		$9,735	$12,530	$3,265	$1,959
Badly (40%)		From Operations	$ 4,867			
		Abandon	+ $10.619			4,554
	($19,000)		= $15,487		(3,513)	($1,405)
					NPV	$ 554

So taking account of the opportunity to abandon, the NPV is positive and the project can be accepted. Put another way, since the NPV is negative $1,188 with a purchase price of $19,000, the gross PV must be ($19,000 − $1,188) = $17,812. Since the NPV with the possibility of sale is $554, the gross PV must be $19,000 + $554) = $19,554. The difference is $1,742, which can be regarded as the contribution of the opportunity for resale.

A critical reader will object that the opportunity for resale was there all along, and only narrowness of vision precluded us from valuing it in the first place. That may be, but the fact is that many investors and project planners will in fact neglect to price the opportunity for resale in computing project value.

Moreover, to focus on this "exit strategy" is helpful for our purposes because it points to an important insight. That is: from the standpoint of LemCo, the opportunity to resell at t = 1 functions exactly like a "put option," with an exercise price of $12,000: it sets a floor on the investor's return, and it increases the aggregate weighted return.

Once you start to think in terms of put options, you find them all around you. Perhaps more important, once you understand them, you realize that you may be able to construct them at will to customize the returns on particular projects. For a particularly noteworthy example, see the next section.

§ 39.03 Portfolio Insurance

Suppose an investor wants to participate in the gains of the stock market but does not want to take the losses. What are her choices? She might purchase an *insurance policy*, whereby the insurer agrees to compensate her for any shortfall, just as the insurer guarantees the value of an auto against fire, theft or collision. Unfortunately, no conventional insurer writes such a policy. She might purchase a *protective put*, permitting her to "put" the portfolio on the put-writer at a defined exercise price. In fact, protective puts may be available for at least some markets and some terms. But even in the absence of a protective put, she may be able to achieve the same result by constructing a *synthetic put*.

How do you create a synthetic put? Remember how we constructed replicating portfolios. Suppose you are considering a portfolio with a present value of \$100,000. The t = 1 payoffs are \$125,000 and \$80,000. The risk-free rate is 5 percent. You are interested in the portfolio, but you cannot tolerate the downside risk. How can you participate in the upside but not in the downside? Follow the strategy we used to price options. First, note that to protect our "downside" we would need to receive the equivalent of investing our portfolio at the risk-free rate: \$105,000. Then set up simultaneous equations to represent the future payoffs. We will want to meet the following conditions:

$$\begin{array}{ll} \text{Upside:} & \$125{,}000s + 1.05f = \$125{,}000 \\ \text{Downside:} & \$\ 80{,}000s + 1.05f = \$105{,}000 \end{array}$$

Once again, we have two equations with two unknowns. We subtract the second from the first:

$$\begin{aligned} (\$125{,}000 - \$80{,}000)s &= \$\ 20{,}000 \\ 45{,}000s &= \$\ 20{,}000 \\ s &= 0.44 \end{aligned}$$

This is the stock component of our initial investment. Now, use the "downside" equation to compute the value of f:

$$\begin{aligned} (\$80{,}000)(0.44) + 1.05f &= \$\ 105{,}000 \\ \$35{,}556 + 1.05f &= \$\ 105{,}000 \\ 1.05f &= \$\ 69{,}444 \\ f &= \$\ 66{,}138 \end{aligned}$$

To double-check, compute the value of the bond component in the "upside" scenario. Note that both signs are *positive* in this case. This means that at t = 1, you receive a cash *inflow* on both stock and risk-free components of your portfolio. This means that you *invested* both in stock and in risk-free securities at t = 0. Your total investment must have been \$66,138 (for bonds) plus \$44,444 (stocks) or \$110,582. Since the cost of the original portfolio was \$100,000, it is fair to regard (\$110,582 – \$100,000), or \$10,582 as the price of a put with an exercise price of \$105,000.

Note that you will have to change the mix as the stock price changes. As stock prices go up, will the stock component increase? Or decrease?

§ 39.04 Note on the Dumbest Public Policy Decision Since the Embargo Act of 1807

The problem of skewed incentives through leverage may arise in a variety of contexts. In many, the government seeks to control the problem through regulation. There are three types of regulation. One is to limit the *amount of leverage* an investor may assume. These include *margin requirements* in the stock market and *capital adequacy requirements* in banking. A second limitation is to control the *kinds of investments* equity owners may choose. For example, government rules often limit the investments of banks. Third, the government may provide *insurance* or similar *guarantees* to protect against the consequences of excessive risk. Thus, the government typically provides *deposit insurance* to protect bank depositors against bank failure. In this section, we say a word about two major cases of leverage limitation. In the next section, we explore a particular episode in which the government tried — and failed — to cope with risk.

Margin: You decide to buy a share of Consolidated Tomorrow, Inc., (ConTom), which currently trades at $200. You have only $80. Your broker graciously agrees to loan you the additional $120, retaining the share as security for the loan. You take his deal; you pay him the $80, he buys the share and retains it in your name. You leave for vacation. When you come back, you are pleased to see that ConTom is trading at $280. Considering that you had only $80 at risk, that means you have doubled your money.

But on inquiry, you are chagrined to find that before its current runup, ConTom sank from $200 to $140. You learn for the first time that the exchange rules require that there be at least 25 percent equity in your account. You hit the 25 percent limit when the stock fell to $160 because at that point you had debt of $120 (75 percent of your portfolio) and $40 equity (25 percent). Since you had bought *on the margin*, as the jargon says, then at that point your broker made a *margin call*: he told you that either: (a) you must come up with more money or, (b) he would sell your stock. Since you were not in town, you never got the message and he sold you out.

We have seen that the higher the leverage, the greater the volatility of the underlying equity. Leveraged investing (margin buying) thus offers the prospect of great risk and great reward. By the conventional wisdom, such margin buying is believed to have contributed to the speculative frenzy of the 1920s and the resulting 1929 stock market crash. Ever since, by congressional mandate, the Federal Reserve Board has set margin requirements to limit the speculative potential.[1] The Fed's margin requirement has varied from as low as 25 percent cash in the 1920s to as high of 100 percent in the 1940s. Fed requirements limit only the *initial purchase*. But stock exchange rules provide *maintenance margin* limitations for accounts in being. Comparable rules limit *short selling*, for comparable reasons.

Banks: we have seen that high leverage motivates equity to take risks, including bad risks. So if you want to discourage risk-taking, you make owners hold a fairly high component of equity, relative to debt, in the bank. Proposals for such *capital adequacy* rules began to appear among bank reformers in the Depression of the 1930s. Support grew in the early 1980s, after a string of near-disasters (and disasters) in lending to borrowers in Latin America. Congress in response passed the International Lending Supervision Act (ILSA).[2] The statute required bank regulators to establish minimum capital ratios for the banks under their control.

[1] Securities Exchange Act § 7 (15 U.S.C. § 78g).

[2] 12 U.S.C. § 3901 *et seq.*

One defect of ILSA was that it applied only to American banks, who feared it would leave them at a competitive disadvantage. But concern over capital adequacy did not stop at the United States border. In 1987 an international group, the Basle Committee on Banking Regulations and Supervisory Practices laid down a set of minimum capital ratios for international banks. The United States incorporated them into federal banking regulations in 1989.[3] Congress adopted elements of the Basle proposals in the Comprehensive Deposit Insurance Reform and Taxpayer Protection Act (Comprehensive Reform Act), a banking regulation measure.[4] Under the Comprehensive Reform Act, inadequacy of capital will become a sufficient criterion for government intervention in a troubled institution.

Note that while there is a margin requirement for stock investing, and a *de facto* margin requirement for bank stocks, there is no margin requirement for corporate leverage. In other words, as the manager of BigCo, a publicly traded company, you can tank up on as much debt as the traffic will bear without violating any general law.

§ 39.05 Pricing Distressed Debt

In previous sections, we saw that the option to abandon might have value for the option holder. In this section, we turn the matter upside down. We go back to the balance sheet of a leveraged company. We note that the option to abandon adds value to the equity. But by corollary, the value of the option to abandon must impair the value of the debt. In this section, we consider how to price distressed debt.

Assets	Liabilities & NW
$100	$ 80 (L) $ 20 (NW)
$100	$100

The asset value (V) represents a realistic estimate of the market value of the assets if sold *in total* as a going concern. The debt (L) is the *face* (payoff) of a zero coupon bond due at $t = 1$. Risk-free borrowing and lending is available at 8 percent.

On the face of things, SadCo appears to be solvent, if highly leveraged. So what is the problem? The problem is that the assets are invested in a risky endeavor. You have struggled and strained to foresee the future of SadCo. You summarize your research by specifying two possible values for SadCo at $t = 1$. The prospective values are: good news, $125 million; bad news, $60 million (note that we do *not* assign weights to these two possibilities, although the weights will emerge in our analysis).

[3] 12 C.F.R. §§ 208.1.127 & app. A-B (1991); 12 C.F.R. 160–88 app. A-B (1991).

[4] Pub. L. No. 102–242 (1991).

So under the bad news scenario, debt bears some of the asset risk. Because debt bears some of the asset risk it follows that the market value of the debt is less than the $80 million balance sheet face value. For the same reason, it follows that the market value of the stock is greater than the $20 million balance sheet face value. What is the true market (as distinct from balance sheet) value of the stock and the debt?

To answer this question, we begin by noting that the stock is a contingent claim. We go on to follow a strategy like the strategy we used to value another contingent claim — i.e., a call option against a share of stock. That is, we construct a synthetic claim that mimics the stock of SadCo, in the sense that its t=1 payoffs are the same as the t=1 payoffs of SadCo stock. Under the principle of one price, we recognize that in a no-arbitrage world, the stock must command the same value as the synthetic claim, so the value of the synthetic claim must denote the value of the stock. To determine the value of the bonds, we subtract the value of the stock from the value of the assets.

We will construct the claim by figuring what it would cost to acquire: (a) a portion of the company as a whole (V), and (b) risk-free borrowing or lending (call it "f") that will mimic returns on the stock. We specify the required outcomes in a pair of equations:

$$\begin{aligned} \$125V + 1.08f &= \$\ 45 \\ \$\ 60V + 1.08f &= 0 \end{aligned}$$

The solutions to these equations are: V = 0.69 and f = $-38.46. This means: at t=1, we *own* 69 percent of the value of the firm, and must *repay* a risk-free loan equal to 1.08 × $38.46 million. How do we achieve this result? We achieve it by *buying* 69 percent of V at t=0 and *borrowing* f. Our cost is the difference between the cost of 0.69 (V) and the sum we borrow. More precisely, at t=0, V = $69.23 million. Our risk-free loan must be $38.46 million. The difference is ($69.23 million − $38.46 million), or $30.77 million. So, $30.77 million = the cost of our synthetic package. Under the principle of one price, since the synthetic package has the same payoffs as the stock, it must have the same market value as the stock. As such, the market value of SadCo stock must be $30.77 million.

Can we continue the analysis to determine the market value of SadCo's debt? We can. We know the value of SadCo's assets (V) = $100 million. We know that the value of the stock is $30.77 million. So the value of the debt must be $100 million − $30.77 million or $69.23 million. Pressing the analysis still further, we can determine the YTM on the debt. That is, we know the t=1 payoff on the debt is $100 million and the t=0 value is $69.23. The YTM must be the ($80 ÷ $69.23) − 1 or 15.56 percent.

Assets	Liabilities & NW
$100	$69.23 $30.77
$100	$100

§ 39.06 Appendix: The Option to Wait and See

This chapter has focused mostly on versions of the "put option." But call options present just as many and varied a range of opportunities for inquiry. To take just one example, consider the "option to wait and see" in the hands of FridgeCo, a maker of refrigerator magnets. FridgeCo may buy a new magnet mine, with a cost of $1,700. The expected return is a perpetuity. The value is a function of the success of the mine. If it is a good mine, then the perpetuity will pay $400 per period and if a bad one, then only $50.

FridgeCo cannot know in advance which version will come to pass, and the chances are 50-50. But at the end of the first year, FridgeCo will know whether the mine is a good one or a bad one, and the associated return will continue forever. These data imply a probability-weighted perpetuity payment of $225 per period. FridgeCo's cost of capital is 8 percent, so we have perpetuity value of $225 ÷ 0.08 = $2,813 and an NPV of $2,813 − $1,700 = $1,113.

But consider what happens if FridgeCo can wait until t = 1 before deciding whether to buy the mine. At t = 1, FridgeCo will know whether the mine is a good one or a bad one. If it is a good one, the expected return (looking forward from t = 1) is $400 ÷ 0.08 = $5,000, and the NPV is $5,000 − $1,700 = $3,300. If the mine is a bad one, then the expected return is just $50 ÷ 0.08 = $625. This implies a negative NPV (of $1,075) and FridgeCo will not buy. So, what FridgeCo can anticipate is a 50 percent chance of a $3,300 NPV:

$$0.5[-\$1,700 + (\$400 \div 0.08)] = \$1,650$$

This is a t = 1 value. Discount it to t = 0 and we have an NPV for the project of $1,528. Comparing the revised project with the original project, we can see that the revised project is more valuable to the tune of $1,528 − $1,113 = $415. This $415 represents the value of waiting as distinct from investing now.

So far, we have acted as if waiting was free and that FridgeCo could enjoy the extra value without any extra expense. It probably isn't free. For example, a real-world FridgeCo may have to dig the mine before it knows whether the mine is a good one or not. In such a case, the costs may cancel any gains.

But suppose FridgeCo can make an "exploratory dig" during the first year at a cost of $100 that will tell it what kind of mine it has. You can analyze the cost of the exploratory dig as the price of a call option on the underlying (literally!) asset; the $1,700 is the exercise price. Just as with any call option, FridgeCo will either take or walk away as the facts may ultimately justify, but having the right to choose may be valuable in itself.

Once you start looking for them, you can see that "real" call options abound in the investing world. Many investors will take on a modest project that looks like a loser because it gives them a foothold in a market, or a chance to make follow-on investments if the facts justify — or to walk away if things go badly.

Chapter 40

The Black-Scholes Option Pricing Model (BSOPM)

Myron once told me they are sucking
up nickels from all over the world,
but because they are so highly leveraged,
that amounts to a lot of money.

—Merton Miller[1]

§ 40.01 Introduction

Earlier we examined the valuation of contingent claims under the so-called binomial option pricing model (BOPM). The binomial is in fact a simplification of a more ambitious model, named after its discoverers, Fischer Black and Myron Scholes,[2] the *Black-Scholes Option Pricing Model* (BSOPM). BSOPM is far more ambitious. That is, up to now we have worked in a world where there are only two future states, "up" and "down." BSOPM assumes an *infinite* range of possible future states. Happily for us, we do not need to understand the underlying math in detail. And remarkably, while the background of BSOPM is more sophisticated, the core intuition is the same. That is: in BSOPM, as in the binomial, we parcel out the "risky" and the "risk-free" portions of the possible future. Then we use stocks and risk-free investments to mimic-option returns. Then we infer option prices from our synthetic portfolios.

§ 40.02 Value of a Call

First, some terms:

S = price of the stock now
Ex = exercise price of the option
r_f = risk-free rate
t = time to exercise date
σ = standard deviation of the rate of return on the stock

Here is the BSOPM formula for a call:

[1] Miller, co-creator of the Miller-Modigliani hypotheses, commenting on his fellow Nobelist Myron Scholes. Scholes is the co-inventor of the Black-Scholes theorem and also the co-author of one of the greatest investment fund disasters of recent history, the near-collapse of Long-Term Capital Management LP.

[2] Fischer Black & Myron Scholes, *The Pricing of Options and Corporate Liabilities,* 81 J. Pol. Econ. 637 (1973). By general agreement, Robert Merton shares equal credit with Black and Scholes, but his name was not on the first published article, so it has not passed into the folklore.

$$C = S[N(d_1)] - \frac{Ex}{e^{r_f t}}[N(d_2)]$$

Next, we need to define d_1 and d_2. Remember that *ln* = the natural log. First, d_1:

$$d_1 = \frac{\ln\left(\frac{S}{Ex}\right) + r_f t}{\sigma\sqrt{t}} + \frac{\sigma\sqrt{t}}{2}$$

And now, d_2:

$$d_2 = d_1 - \sigma\sqrt{t}$$

To understand d_1 and d_2, imagine a statistician's *standard normal distribution* — a distribution with a mean of zero and a standard deviation of one. We define d_1 and d_2 as points along that distribution. $N(d_x)$ identifies a statistical measure associated with d_x. Specifically, $N(d_x)$ is a *cumulative distribution function.* $N(d_x)$ expresses the probability that a particular result will come in below the number d_x.

For example, locate the probability density function charts at the end of Chapter 41.[3] Suppose we know that $d_x = 0.31$. Go to the first chart (Probability Density Function — I). Trace down the column to 0.3. Trace across the row to .01. Identify the intercept. It is 0.6217. You have learned that where $d_x = 0.31$, then there is a 62.17 percent chance that a random variable will lie at or below 0.31 if we are dealing with a normal distribution. Now, suppose that $d_x = -1.34$. Go to the second chart (Probability Density Function — II). Go down the column to −1.3. Go across the row to 0.04. Read off the intercept. It is 0.0901. This means (assuming normal distribution) that there is a 9.01 percent chance that a particular item will fall at or below −1.34.

Now, take a second look at our call formula:

---

[3] The charts were generated from an ordinary spreadsheet package, using the function normsdist(x). If you have a spreadsheet, you can generate the responses yourself without looking them up in the charts. Note that the answers in this chapter were prepared using the charts, where the terms are rounded to just two decimal places. If you use a spreadsheet, your answers will be a bit different, and more precise.

$$C = S[N(d_1)] - \frac{Ex}{e^{r_f t}}[N(d_2)]$$

Note that it breaks down into two parts, separated by a minus sign. Recall how we did the binomial pricing model. There, too, we defined our formula in two components, separated by a minus sign. The formula provided, in effect:

$$C = \Delta S - B$$

where ΔS = the stock times the hedge ratio, and B = the risk-free borrowing. In fact, this present formula has the same character. $N(d_2)$ identifies the size of the borrowing component. Ex is the exercise price. We divide by

$$e^{r_f t}$$

to reduce Ex to present value. $N(d_1)$ is the stock's delta. In other words, BSOPM, just like the binomial model, tells us that *the call is worth the stock times its delta, less the risk-free borrowing.*

An Example: All that remains to do is to plug in the numbers. Imagine a call option on a stock, S, with the following parameters:

- a current price of $58 (S = $58)
- a nine-month option (t = 0.75)
- with an exercise price of $60 (Ex = $60)
- in a market with a risk-free return of 6 percent ($r_f = 0.06$)
- a standard deviation of 30 percent ($\Sigma = 0.3$)

We start with d_1. For convenience, let us break it up into components:

$$d_1 = \frac{\ln\left(\frac{S}{Ex}\right)}{\sigma\sqrt{t}} + \frac{r_f t}{\sigma\sqrt{t}} + \frac{\sigma\sqrt{t}}{2}$$

Now we can paste our terms:

$$\frac{\ln(\$58 \div \$60)}{0.259808} + \frac{(0.06)0.75}{0.259808} + \frac{0.259808}{2}$$

$$= -0.1304871 + 0.173205 + 0.129904$$
$$= 0.1726217$$
$$= 0.17$$

For d_2, we take d_1 and subtract the standard deviation times the square root of the time (which we have already computed). We get:

$$0.037555 - 0.259808$$
$$= -0.08719$$
$$= -0.09$$

To get $N(d_x)$, we go to the charts. We get:

$$N(d_1) = N(.04) = 0.5675$$
$$N(d_2) = N(-.22) = 0.4641$$

All that remains is to reinstall these numbers into our original equation:

$$\$58\ (0.5675) - \frac{\$60}{e^{0.045}}(0.4641) = \$6.29$$

So, $6.29 is the equilibrium value of a call option.

To test your understanding, suppose a call option is identical to the one described above, except that this stock is selling for $56 a share. First, ask yourself whether the option price should be *higher* or *lower* than the price we just computed. Then ask yourself whether you think it will move (higher)/(lower) by (a little)/(a lot)/(just the same) relative to the underlying stock. Then compute the value of the call option and compare it with your guesses.

§ 40.03 Value of a Put

We have seen how to use BSOPM to value a call option. Can we use the model to value a put? We can. Remember put-call parity:

$$P = C + Ex(e^{-rt}) - S$$

We already know the values of the call and the stock, and the present value of the exercise price. So:

$$Put = \$6.29 + \frac{\$60}{e^{0.045}} - 58 = \$5.65$$

Finally, recall the case where the share price is $56. Do you think the value of the put will be higher or lower than it was when the share price was at $58? Relative to the underlying share, do you think the change in the put value will be greater, less or just the same? Now compute the value of the put and compare it with your guesses.

§ 40.04 A Few Observations

Let us see if we can draw together the major threads of this inquiry so far:

- *First,* perhaps the key idea driving the revolution in modern finance is the notion that a "firm" is not an entity that makes widgets or repairs fountain pens or whatever, but that it is an *abstraction* — the center of a force field, as it were, unifying all sorts of positive and negative cash flows. An old fashioned investor would say, "the best fertilizer a farm can get is the footprints of the owner, walking over it every day." A new-style (post-Markowitz) investor would say, "diversify your portfolio — reduce your risk while stabilizing (or even increasing) your return."

- *Second*, the BSOPM contribution is to recognize that you can take the cash flows (positive and negative) in this force field, and slice them and dice them a thousand different ways. A *call option* gives you the upside but not the downside; a *put option* does just the reverse. The opportunity for *risk-free borrowing and lending* offers you a chance to doctor risk and return to choose your own point on the *risk frontier*. *Borrowing* is just the negative of *lending*, and *short-selling* is just a special kind of borrowing. All this comes into focus through the lens of *arbitrage*, where you try to identify and exploit gaps in informational efficiency. However small they may be, if you can find enough of them, you may make it up on volume.

It remains a question, of course, whether this is any way to run a universe. There is much uneasiness among folks who fear we have let loose forces that we do not understand (genetic engineering metaphors apply here), sacrificing whatever well-being we may have enjoyed for the aesthetic integrity of a bunch of blips on a computer screen, while quaint notions such as loyalty, craftsmanship, etc., seem to disappear into a blaze of Greek letters. But there is no shortage of rebuttal witnesses who say that these fussbudgets are just a bunch of romantic reactionaries, afraid of the future and the opportunities it may bring.

Chapter 41

BSOPM Applied: Equity

> One may love a place even
> if one has suffered there.
>
> —Jane Austen
>
> Maybe this is as good as it gets.
>
> —Jack Nicholson

§ 41.01 Introduction

One of the most important insights of the option revolution is the recognition that the value of a leveraged company can be analyzed through option theory. In fact, we can identify several de facto options in the structure of a leveraged firm. For the moment, we concentrate on just one. We consider equity as a call option, with the debt as the exercise price.

We face a tricky problem of nomenclature here. What used to be "the underlying asset" (the stock) now becomes "the call option." For purposes of exposition, we must embrace one of two bad choices. Either we change the meaning of words, or we change notation in the equation. To keep the equation consistent, we choose to change the meaning of words. But the underlying pattern remains the same.

	Call option on stock	**Stock in a leveraged company**
The contingent claim	Call option	Stock
The underlying asset	Stock	Corporate Assets
The condition	The exercise price	Corporate Debt

§ 41.02 Applying the Model

To see how options analysis helps us understand a company, consider the case of NewCo. NewCo has an asset value of \$100 per share, but there is \$80 of senior debt for every \$100 in asset value. The debt is a 10-year zero. The risk-free rate is 10 percent. This would seem to imply a present value of $\$80(1.1)^{10}$ = \$30.84 per share for the zero, leaving \$69.16 for the equity. The standard deviation of returns is 40 percent. Now let us analyze equity as a call and see if we can confirm this result.

We already have most of the variables we need:

S = the unencumbered asset value, $100
Ex = the face amount of the senior debt, $80
t = the term, 10 years
r_f = the risk-free rate
σ = the standard deviation 40 percent

Start with the basic call formula:

$$C = S[N(d_1)] - \frac{Ex}{e^{r_f t}}[N(d_2)]$$

Recall how we described d_1:

$$d_1 = \frac{\ln\left(\frac{S}{Ex}\right)}{\sigma\sqrt{t}} + \frac{r_f t}{\sigma\sqrt{t}} + \frac{\sigma\sqrt{t}}{2}$$

We can add some numbers:

$$\frac{ln(\$50 \div \$80)}{1.264911} + \frac{(0.1)10}{1.264911} + \frac{1.264911}{2}$$

$$0.17641 + 0.790569 + 0.632456$$
$$= 1.599435$$
$$\sim 1.6$$

For d_2, we take d_1 and subtract the standard deviation times the square root of the time (which we have already computed). We get:

$$1.599435 - 1.264911$$
$$= 0.334524$$
$$\sim 0.33$$

To get $N(d_x)$, we go to the probability density function charts at the end of this chapter. We get:

$$N(d_1) = N(1.6) = 0.9452$$
$$N(d_2) = N(0.33) = 0.6293$$

It remains only to reinstall these numbers into our original equation:

$$\$100\ (0.9452) - \frac{\$80}{e^{(0.1)(10)}}\ (0.6293) = \$76$$

So, $76 is the value of the call option, the equity. But see what we have done: earlier, we defined the equity as being worth only $69.16, with debt at $30.84. The new higher equity number suggests that debt is $100 − $76 or only \$24. What can have happened to reduce the value of the debt by more than \$5, transferring value to the equity?

The answer, of course, is that earlier we did not account for risk. The option model measures for risk (recall we defined the standard deviation as 40 percent). And the teaching of the option model is that we have transferred some of the risk from equity to debt, reducing the value of the debt and conferring a corresponding increase in the value of the equity.

Note also how this affects the imputed interest rate on the zero bond. Previously we discounted the bond at the risk-free rate, 10 percent. We should be able to derive a corrected rate from the data at hand. Recall that:

$$r = (FV \div PV)^{1/n} - 1$$

In this case:

$$r = (\$80 \div \$24)^{0.1} - 1 = 0.1279 = 12.79\%.$$

§ 41.03 The Underwater Firm

The same approach shows us how an "underwater" firm — where liabilities appear to exceed assets — may nevertheless hold some value for the residual equity. As before, consider a firm with a ten-year zero bearing a face of \$80 and with a standard deviation of 40 percent. This time, however, assume the asset pool equals only \$50 per share. Remember our formula for d_1:

$$d_1 = \frac{\ln\left(\frac{S}{Ex}\right)}{\sigma\sqrt{t}} + \frac{r_f t}{\sigma\sqrt{t}} + \frac{\sigma\sqrt{t}}{2}$$

Recall that standard deviation (0.4), risk-free rate (0.1), and time (10 years), remain the same. So, only the first term of our equation differs; the second and third terms remain the same. This time we have:

$$\frac{\ln(\$100 \div \$80)}{1.264911} = -0.37157$$

$$= {}^{-}0.37157 + 0.790569 + 0.632456$$
$$= 1.051454$$
$$\sim 1.05$$

Computing d_2:

$$1.051454 - 1.264911 = {}^{-}0.21346$$
$$\sim {}^{-}0.21$$

The functions are:

$$N(d_1) = 0.8531$$
$$N(d_2) = 0.4168$$

So the equation is:

$$\$50\ (0.8531) - \frac{\$80}{e^{(0.1)(10)}}\ (0.4168) = \$30.39$$

This means that the value of the debt is only $19.61 and the implied rate of interest is 15.1 percent. Note that at the risk-free rate, the present value of the debt ($30.84) is the same as it was for the $100 company. In each case, the imputed value of the debt is lower than the risk-free present value, but it is lower in the case of the $50 company than in the case of the $100 company.

§ 41.04 Changing the Risk Mix

Option theory can show us how leverage can lead management to perverse incentives. Consider our original example, where the asset value was $100 per share. Suppose management is considering a new project with a negative NPV equal to $2 per share, but with a standard deviation of 50 percent. The effect of this project is to reduce the asset pool from $100 to $98 per share. Let us keep the debt the same — a 10-year $80 zero with a risk-free rate of 10 percent — and see how the new risk calculus rearranges value:

$$\frac{\ln(\$98 \div \$80)}{1.581139} + \frac{(0.1)10}{1.581139} + \frac{1.581139}{2}$$
$$= 0.128351 + 0.632456 + 0.790569$$
$$= 1.551376$$
$$= 1.55$$

For d_2, we take d_1 and subtract the standard deviation times the square root of the time (which we have already computed). We get:

$$1.551376 - 1.581139 = -0.02976 \sim {}^{-}0.03$$

From the charts we get the density functions:

$$N(d_1) = N(1.55) = 0.9394$$
$$N(d_2) = N({}^{-}0.03) = 0.488$$

And finally we recompute the formula:

$$\$98\ (0.9394) - \frac{\$80}{e^{(0.1)(10)}}\ (0.488) = \$77.70$$

The value of equity actually *rose* by a little under $2 (from $76 to $77.70), while the value of the assets *declined* by $2. The value of the debt fell more sharply, from $24 to $20.30, for an implied rate of return of 14.7 percent. Management has increased the value of the equity even though the NPV of the project was negative. But this gain was at the expense of debt. Does management have the same obligations to debt that it does to equity? Will debt just sit by and watch as management increases its risk?

§ 41.05 Mergers

A merger very likely will *reduce* the variance of the combined company, to the disadvantage of equity and to the advantage of debt. If the companies have a correlation coefficient of less than one, then the combined company will have a standard deviation lower than the weighted sum of the component standard deviations, and perhaps, lower than either one. Here is a demonstration:

NewCo has a balance sheet just like the first company in this section: $100 per share, subject to a 10-year zero with a face of $80, and a risk-free rate of 10 percent. Using a standard deviation of 40 percent, we saw that the risk-adjusted value of the debt of such a company was $24., with an implied yield to maturity of 12.79 percent. The value of the equity was $76.

Suppose NewCo merges with OldCo, a firm with an asset value of $150 per share and a 10-year zero bearing a face of $50. The risk-free rate for OldCo is of course the same as for NewCo — 10 percent. The standard deviation of OldCo is 50 percent. Using these numbers, it is possible to show that the value of the stock in OldCo is $134.47 per share, and of the debt, $15.53 per share, with a debt return of 12.41 percent.

But, supposing NewCo and OldCo have a correlation coefficient of 0.25, how will we figure the standard deviation of the combined company? Recall our general formula:

$$(w_1^2\,\sigma_1^2 + w_2^2\,\sigma_2^2 + 2[w_1 w_2 \rho \sigma_1 \sigma_2])^{1/2}$$

Since total assets in the combined company will be 250, we can see that NewCo will make up 40% of the assets (100 ÷ 250) and OldCo will make up 60% (150 ÷ 250). Applying our numbers:

$$((0.4)^2(0.4)^2 = (0.6)^2(0.5)^2 + 2[(0.4)(0.6)(0.4)(0.4)(0.5)])^{1/2}$$

So, our combined portfolio has a standard deviation of 39.24 percent — lower than either of the components.

To value the equity of combined firm, we start with d_1:

$$\frac{\ln(\$250 \div \$130)}{1.181524} + \frac{(0.1)10}{1.181524} + \frac{1.181524}{2}$$

$$= 0.55346 + 0.8486364 \times 0.590762$$

$$= 1.990586$$

$$= 1.99$$

Now compute d_2:

$$1.990586 - 1.181524 = 0.809062 \sim 0.81$$

From the charts we get the density functions:

$$N(d_1) = N(1.95) = 0.9767$$

$$N(d_2) = N(0.71) = 0.791$$

And finally we recompute the formula:

$$\$250\,(0.9767) - \frac{\$130}{e^{(0.1)(10)}}\,(0.791) = \$206.35$$

Note that pre-merger a NewCo share was worth $76 and an OldCo share was worth $134.47. If you had owned one share each in the two old companies, you would have had a total wealth of $210.47. If you then get one share in the surviving company, your wealth has declined by $4.19, a decline of about four percent. Where has the wealth gone? The answer is that has gone to enrich debt, in the form of lower asset risk.

§ 41.06 Note: Option Pricing in Court

In *Snyder v. C.I.R.*,[1] counsel tried to persuade the court to use the BSOPM model to value common stock. The court rejected the analysis. It found, among other things," that the Black-Scholes method is designed to value call options, not common stock" — an flat error and a complete misunderstanding of BSOPM. But it would be wrong to blame the court. BSOPM is hardly common knowledge today, saying nothing of 12 years ago. If the court fell into error, it is because counsel let it fall: failed to provide the briefing or testimony necessary to explain it.

If BSOPM or its kin ever do become part of the analytical tool box, the most likely venue will be the Delaware Chancery Court, unchallenged as the principal forum for valuation issues in our judicial system. Indeed a number have tried to present BSOPM arguments to the court, so far with just limited success. In *Lewis v. Vogelstein*,[2] Chancellor Allen held that it was not necessary to include a BSOPM valuation in public disclosure documents. In *Rovner v. Health-Chem Corp.*,[3] the court refused to apply BSOPM analysis in setting attorneys' fees in a class action settlement. Deciding *In re the Coleman Co. Inc.*,[4] the court accepted a BSOPM objection that had come in without objection. The court remarked that Black and Scholes had won the Nobel Prize for their work, though in fact only Scholes did (Black had died), Of greater importance, the vice-chancellor added:

> The existence of variables (the risk free rate, volatility of the underlying stock, expiration date of the option, etc.) may cause the model to have less reliability in certain circumstances."[5]

But this seems to be a misunderstanding. It is the "variables" (in the mathematical sense) that make the model work

Web site: For a good classroom intro to Black Scholes, see:

http://www.bradley.bradley.edu/~arr/bsm/model.html.

---

[1] 93 T.C. 529, 1989 U.S. Tax Ct. LEXIS 138; 93 T.C. No. 43 (1989).

[2] 699 A.2d 327, 311 (Del. Ch.1997).

[3] 1998 Del. Ch. Lexis 65, *17 (Del. Ch. 1998) ("this Court has always accepted such valuations with a healthy dose of skepticism.").

[4] 1999 Del. Ch. Lexis 234 (Del. Ch. 1999).

[5] *Id.* at *15.

§ 41.07 Probability Density Function Charts

Probability Density Function — I

	0	**0.01**	**0.02**	**0.03**	**0.04**	**0.05**	**0.06**	**0.07**	**0.08**	**0.09**
0	0.5000	0.5040	0.5080	0.5120	0.5160	0.5199	0.5239	0.5279	0.5319	0.5359
0.1	0.5398	0.5438	0.5478	0.5517	0.5557	0.5596	0.5636	0.5675	0.5714	0.5753
0.2	0.5793	0.5832	0.5871	0.5910	0.5948	0.5987	0.6026	0.6064	0.6103	0.6141
0.3	0.6179	0.6217	0.6255	0.6293	0.6331	0.6368	0.6406	0.6443	0.6480	0.6517
0.4	0.6554	0.6591	0.6628	0.6664	0.6700	0.6736	0.6772	0.6808	0.6844	0.6879
0.5	0.6915	0.6950	0.6985	0.7019	0.7054	0.7088	0.7123	0.7157	0.7190	0.7224
0.6	0.7257	0.7291	0.7324	0.7357	0.7389	0.7422	0.7454	0.7486	0.7517	0.7549
0.7	0.7580	0.7611	0.7642	0.7673	0.7704	0.7734	0.7764	0.7794	0.7823	0.7852
0.8	0.7881	0.7910	0.7939	0.7967	0.7995	0.8023	0.8051	0.8079	0.8106	0.8133
0.9	0.8159	0.8186	0.8212	0.8238	0.8264	0.8289	0.8315	0.8340	0.8365	0.8389
1	0.8413	0.8438	0.8461	0.8485	0.8508	0.8531	0.8554	0.8577	0.8599	0.8621
1.1	0.8643	0.8665	0.8686	0.8708	0.8729	0.8749	0.8770	0.8790	0.8810	0.8830
1.2	0.8849	0.8869	0.8888	0.8907	0.8925	0.8944	0.8962	0.8980	0.8997	0.9015
1.3	0.9032	0.9049	0.9066	0.9082	0.9099	0.9115	0.9131	0.9147	0.9162	0.9177
1.4	0.9192	0.9207	0.9222	0.9236	0.9251	0.9265	0.9279	0.9292	0.9306	0.9319
1.5	0.9332	0.9345	0.9357	0.9370	0.9382	0.9394	0.9406	0.9418	0.9429	0.9441
1.6	0.9452	0.9463	0.9474	0.9484	0.9495	0.9505	0.9515	0.9525	0.9535	0.9545
1.7	0.9554	0.9564	0.9573	0.9582	0.9591	0.9599	0.9608	0.9616	0.9625	0.9633
1.8	0.9641	0.9649	0.9656	0.9664	0.9671	0.9678	0.9686	0.9693	0.9699	0.9706
1.9	0.9713	0.9719	0.9726	0.9732	0.9738	0.9744	0.9750	0.9756	0.9761	0.9767
2	0.9773	0.9778	0.9783	0.9788	0.9793	0.9798	0.9803	0.9808	0.9812	0.9817
2.1	0.9821	0.9826	0.9830	0.9834	0.9838	0.9842	0.9846	0.9850	0.9854	0.9857
2.2	0.9861	0.9864	0.9868	0.9871	0.9875	0.9878	0.9881	0.9884	0.9887	0.9890
2.3	0.9893	0.9896	0.9898	0.9901	0.9904	0.9906	0.9909	0.9911	0.9913	0.9916
2.4	0.9918	0.9920	0.9922	0.9925	0.9927	0.9929	0.9931	0.9932	0.9934	0.9936
2.5	0.9938	0.9940	0.9941	0.9943	0.9945	0.9946	0.9948	0.9949	0.9951	0.9952
2.6	0.9953	0.9955	0.9956	0.9957	0.9959	0.9960	0.9961	0.9962	0.9963	0.9964
2.7	0.9965	0.9966	0.9967	0.9968	0.9969	0.9970	0.9971	0.9972	0.9973	0.9974
2.8	0.9974	0.9975	0.9976	0.9977	0.9977	0.9978	0.9979	0.9979	0.9980	0.9981
2.9	0.9981	0.9982	0.9983	0.9983	0.9984	0.9984	0.9985	0.9985	0.9986	0.9986
3	0.9987	0.9987	0.9987	0.9988	0.9988	0.9989	0.9989	0.9989	0.9990	0.9990

Probability Density Function — II

	0	**−0.01**	**−0.02**	**−0.03**	**−0.04**	**−0.05**	**−0.06**	**−0.07**	**−0.08**	**−0.09**
0	0.5000	0.4960	0.4920	0.4880	0.4840	0.4801	0.4761	0.4721	0.4681	0.4641
−0.1	0.4602	0.4562	0.4522	0.4483	0.4443	0.4404	0.4364	0.4325	0.4286	0.4247
−0.2	0.4207	0.4168	0.4129	0.4090	0.4052	0.4013	0.3974	0.3936	0.3897	0.3859
−0.3	0.3821	0.3783	0.3745	0.3707	0.3669	0.3632	0.3594	0.3557	0.3520	0.3483
−0.4	0.3446	0.3409	0.3372	0.3336	0.3300	0.3264	0.3228	0.3192	0.3156	0.3121
−0.5	0.3085	0.3050	0.3015	0.2981	0.2946	0.2912	0.2877	0.2843	0.2810	0.2776
−0.6	0.2743	0.2709	0.2676	0.2643	0.2611	0.2578	0.2546	0.2514	0.2483	0.2451
−0.7	0.2420	0.2389	0.2358	0.2327	0.2297	0.2266	0.2236	0.2207	0.2177	0.2148
−0.8	0.2119	0.2090	0.2061	0.2033	0.2005	0.1977	0.1949	0.1922	0.1894	0.1867
−0.9	0.1841	0.1814	0.1788	0.1762	0.1736	0.1711	0.1685	0.1660	0.1635	0.1611
−1	0.1587	0.1562	0.1539	0.1515	0.1492	0.1469	0.1446	0.1423	0.1401	0.1379
−1.1	0.1357	0.1335	0.1314	0.1292	0.1271	0.1251	0.1230	0.1210	0.1190	0.1170
−1.2	0.1151	0.1131	0.1112	0.1093	0.1075	0.1057	0.1038	0.1020	0.1003	0.0985
−1.3	0.0968	0.0951	0.0934	0.0918	0.0901	0.0885	0.0869	0.0853	0.0838	0.0823
−1.4	0.0808	0.0793	0.0778	0.0764	0.0749	0.0735	0.0721	0.0708	0.0694	0.0681
−1.5	0.0668	0.0655	0.0643	0.0630	0.0618	0.0606	0.0594	0.0582	0.0571	0.0559
−1.6	0.0548	0.0537	0.0526	0.0516	0.0505	0.0495	0.0485	0.0475	0.0465	0.0455
−1.7	0.0446	0.0436	0.0427	0.0418	0.0409	0.0401	0.0392	0.0384	0.0375	0.0367
−1.8	0.0359	0.0351	0.0344	0.0336	0.0329	0.0322	0.0314	0.0307	0.0301	0.0294
−1.9	0.0287	0.0281	0.0274	0.0268	0.0262	0.0256	0.0250	0.0244	0.0239	0.0233
−2	0.0228	0.0222	0.0217	0.0212	0.0207	0.0202	0.0197	0.0192	0.0188	0.0183
−2.1	0.0179	0.0174	0.0170	0.0166	0.0162	0.0158	0.0154	0.0150	0.0146	0.0143
−2.2	0.0139	0.0136	0.0132	0.0129	0.0125	0.0122	0.0119	0.0116	0.0113	0.0110
−2.3	0.0107	0.0104	0.0102	0.0099	0.0096	0.0094	0.0091	0.0089	0.0087	0.0084
−2.4	0.0082	0.0080	0.0078	0.0075	0.0073	0.0071	0.0069	0.0068	0.0066	0.0064
−2.5	0.0062	0.0060	0.0059	0.0057	0.0055	0.0054	0.0052	0.0051	0.0049	0.0048
−2.6	0.0047	0.0045	0.0044	0.0043	0.0041	0.0040	0.0039	0.0038	0.0037	0.0036
−2.7	0.0035	0.0034	0.0033	0.0032	0.0031	0.0030	0.0029	0.0028	0.0027	0.0026
−2.8	0.0026	0.0025	0.0024	0.0023	0.0023	0.0022	0.0021	0.0021	0.0020	0.0019
−2.9	0.0019	0.0018	0.0018	0.0017	0.0016	0.0016	0.0015	0.0015	0.0014	0.0014
−3	0.0014	0.0013	0.0013	0.0012	0.0012	0.0011	0.0011	0.0011	0.0010	0.0010

INDEX

[References are to sections.]

A

B

[References are to sections.]

C

[References are to sections.]

[References are to sections.]

[References are to sections.]

[References are to sections.]

[References are to sections.]

[References are to sections.]

[References are to sections.]